To Jeanie Ribeiro
Best Wishes

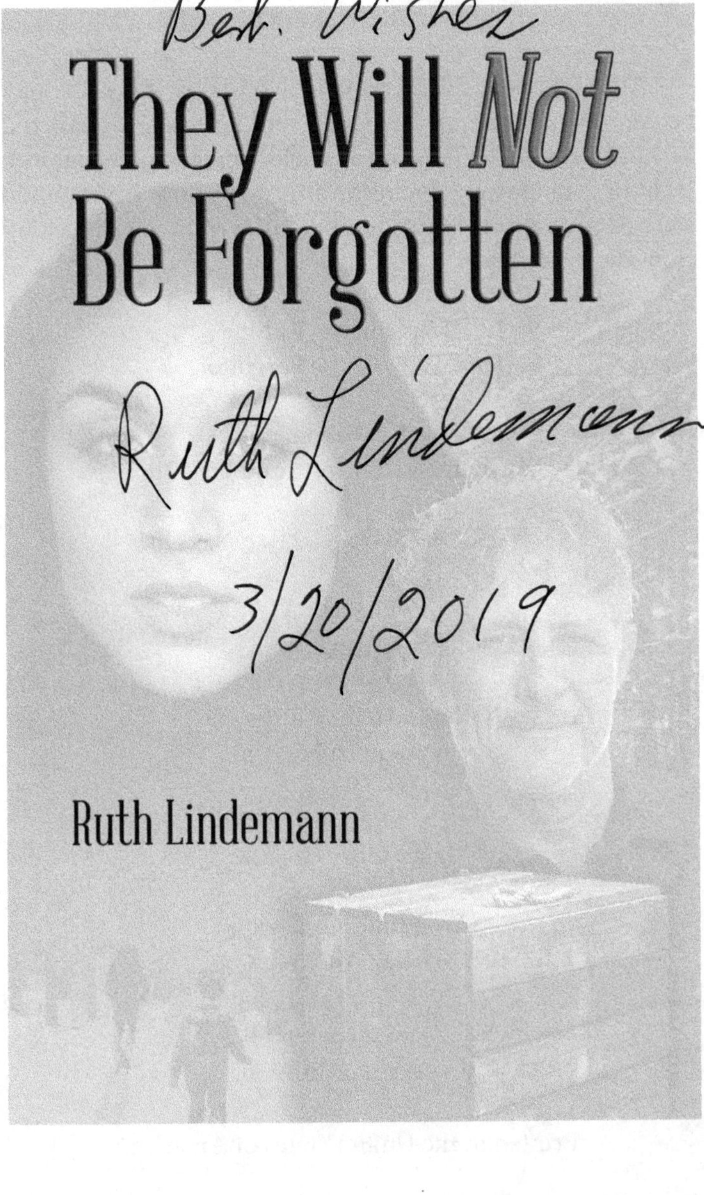

Lindemann, Ruth
They Will Not Be Forgotten

1st edition
Library of Congress Control Number: 2018947963

ISBN 978-1-7324567-0-9 (paperback)

Published by
AquaZebra™
Book Publishing
Cathedral City, California
www.aquazebra.com

Editor
Lynn Jones Green

Cover/interior design
Mark E. Anderson
AquaZebra™
Web, Book & Print Design
www.aquazebra.com

Printed in the United States of America

Dedication

This book is dedicated, with everlasting gratitude, to the Righteous Gentiles who had the courage to resist the tidal wave of evil that engulfed their world.

And to my husband, Romano Lanno, whose support and love made this book possible.

They will not be forgotten.

It was as if someone had lifted up a big stone. All the vermin came scurrying out. At last they had found a lot of big words to make their meanness and vulgarity look like something else.

—quote from Erich Maria Remarque
author of *All Quiet on the Western Front*
describing Germany's Third Reich

Prologue

Poland, 1940

When the door closed behind twelve-year-old Hedy and the three men who were taking her away, Konstanza sank to the floor, her face in her hands. She was consumed by rage, despair and utter helplessness. She fought to stifle her agonized screams as the tears ran down through her fingers, drenching her blouse. She had no idea how long she sat there. When she finally looked up, her legs were asleep and she struggled to stand up. She began to pace the length of the apartment, much as her employer, Hedy's father, had done after his wife had disappeared while visiting her mother in Vienna.

Eventually Paul Mandel had left his daughter with Konstanza and traveled to Berlin to look up old contacts who might help him. He had hoped his acquaintances would have some influence with Nazi officials and help him find his wife and her recently widowed mother.

For several weeks they waited for a call or a letter. Then the new Nazi regime in Poland began to enforce the anti-Jewish laws. Little by little they drew the noose tighter, confiscating radios, bicycles, bank accounts. Then their pets were confiscated; dogs, cats, canaries, and even goldfish were taken away—their fate was "unknown." All mail coming into and going out of the post office was censored. If a letter was addressed to a Jewish household it was returned to the sender, marked "Address Unknown." Jews were under a strict curfew and allowed outside only during a few daylight hours.

Although she was horrified, Konstanza was not surprised at this brutality. She had attended school in Germany and witnessed the callous actions of her fellow classmates and the cruel punishments meted out by their authoritarian parents. The members of the staff at the schools she attended were no less harsh at enforcing discipline with mindless cruelty.

Although girls in her school had not been whipped, the long, slim rods that teachers used for pointing to the blackboard doubled as instruments of inflicting severe pain. A rod could come down on the hands, back, or even across the face, when a girl least expected it. Certain girls were hit more often and much harder than others. Konstanza had come to the conclusion that many teachers were sadistic and did not need an excuse to give themselves the pleasure of causing pain. Only once had she tried to defend a girl who was repeatedly struck on the hands for writing with her left hand. Following that incident, Konstanza's arms and back had been covered with red welts that she carefully hid from her mother.

It wasn't until the moment when Hedy was led away by the Germans, followed by the grinning Polish neighbor, that Konstanza realized how deeply she loved the girl she had cared for from birth.

She stopped pacing for a moment, pushed aside a bit of the blackout curtain. She saw movement in the darkness below. A small group of people were slowly moving toward the central square of the town. The light from a half moon reflected off rifle barrels and she could hear the clang of heavy boots on the cobblestones.

Getting dressed without a thought to what she was wearing, Konstanza pulled on her coat and knitted hat and ran down the stairs to the street. People were standing along the sidewalk watching the retreating figures.

When she had walked to the corner, Konstanza could see that the small crowd being guarded by the soldiers was heading to the train station. From the slight elevation of the street on which she stood, Konstanza could see them go inside. For a moment she stood watching, and then she started to run.

door. Clutching her coat tightly around her, she began to sob uncontrollably. For a few minutes Andre stood watching her. Then he put his hand on her shoulder. Simultaneously they became aware that they were alone in the reception room of the police station. He stepped back a few paces, arms stiffly at his sides.

"The other two officers and the captain are out helping the Germans round up Jews," he explained after seeing Konstanza's eyes flit around the room.

"Andre, they took Hedy away," she whispered. He nodded his head. His blue eyes darkened and his mouth twitched as if to say something, but he remained silent, while Konstanza went on talking. "My beautiful Hedy is gone. Why would those fiends bother with a twelve-year-old girl? What harm could one innocent child do to the powerful Third Reich?" Konstanza's voice rose near to hysteria.

This was only the beginning of the many questions that would haunt her days, along with the recriminations that soon tortured her sleepless nights.

"I'll try to find out where she is," Andre told Konstanza, as he eased her out the door and quickly shut it behind her.

Not for the first time, Konstanza wondered what had made her mother leave the warmth of Greece to come to Germany, where she endured the harsh climate as well as the even harsher attitude of the arrogant, rude Germans toward foreigners.

Something about Andre reminded Konstanza of her father. She was not certain what that was, exactly. Walking home through the dark street and then up the stairs to the apartment, she tried to remember one of the few Germans whom she had learned to love. He was the man she had called "Uncle Konrad" who was a kind, polite presence in her life. Only after his death had she learned that he was actually her father.

She had no idea what she would do if she caught up to the group, but she was determined to get Hedy back. When she neared the huge doors of the train station, Konstanza heard the train pulling out of the station. She stopped just outside the doors, a figure as still as the statue of the local saint beside the entrance. Slowly she turned around and started walking back to the apartment.

A sliver of forbidden light glowed from under the police station door. Without thinking of what she expected to happen, Konstanza went to the door and rang the night bell. It was four o'clock in the morning and a wind was blowing from the North. Konstanza started to shiver as the door began to open. Sergeant Andre Woslovisc stood in the light from the bare bulb hanging from the ceiling.

"Konstanza?" he asked. His round, boyish face was pulled into a frown; his clear blue eyes looked puzzled. He drew her into the high ceilinged room and quickly closed the door.

They had met over ten years ago while he was patrolling the park and she was wheeling Hedy in her pram. Andre had just become a father and had developed a newfound interest in children. Konstanza and Hedy were the only people in the park that morning and the young officer had stopped to admire the pretty two-year-old. After that day they saw each other almost daily and a friendship had developed.

Konstanza had patiently answered his questions about babies and childcare while he told her stories relating to his work—how he apprehended an occasional apple thief or arrested an unruly drunk.

They had not met for over a year now, since Hedy was no longer allowed into the park and Andre had been promoted to a desk job.

"Hello, Andre," Konstanza breathed through her chattering teeth.

"Are you in trouble?" Andre asked, looking concerned. He was the same age but looked years younger than Konstanza, who sat down on the nearest wooden bench, just inside the

Part One

Chapter 1

Athens, Greece, 1910

A hush came over the classroom as the German ambassador and his Consul General for Athens entered through the door at the rear of the room. The two men, dressed in formal dark suits, approached the two chairs reserved for them toward the front of the room. The portly, gray-haired ambassador winced as the chair creaked under his weight. The younger man stood for a moment to be sure the elder man was comfortable. Konrad von Stahlenberg endured the appreciative glances of the twenty young women in the room. He was not vain, but he knew he was handsome with the regular features of the German aristocracy, light brown hair, and well-trimmed handlebar mustache. His green eyes flashed around the room as he sat down on the gilded chair next to the ambassador. The men had an unobstructed view of the small podium where the winners of the translation contest sat stiffly on their chairs. The four young women who were in their last year of school had translated classic German poetry into Greek and then written a short synopsis in German to demonstrate their knowledge of the language.

The first contestant rose to her feet. She seemed perfectly composed even though the class and their nervous instructor, an excitable woman of indiscernible age, had been waiting for twenty minutes for the ambassador to arrive. The instructor had hesitated a moment before starting the proceedings to allow time for a possible apology for his tardy arrival, but the honored guest waved an imperious hand to indicate that he was ready to listen.

Coming to visit this prestigious school for girls, considered the best in Greece, was an act of diplomacy, suggested by the king of Greece and ordered by Kaiser Wilhelm himself. Greek relations with Germany had been a bit rocky lately; although the king and his queen (the sister of the German Kaiser) were pro-German, many members of parliament and the population at large were inclined to be pro-British. The Greeks had always prided themselves on their sea going prowess and felt an affinity with the powerful British navy. The rivalry and growing hostility between these two powerful nations in Europe was evident and in case of war (which seemed imminent, despite words to the contrary) each of these factions wanted Greece on their side.

The visit to the Arsakeio girls' school was only the latest effort to spread good will for Germany among the Greek aristocracy and upper middle class. The Consul General had been sent on visits to factories, farms, Greek cultural events, and school graduations. This was one of the few times that the ambassador himself deemed it necessary to attend. The young women in this school came from important and wealthy families whose support was imperative for allying Greece into the German sphere of influence.

The third contestant had finished her presentation and was sitting down to muted applause from her classmates, when Konrad von Stahlenberg brought his mind back to the present. He had been making mental notes of his engagements for the next few days, remembering names and places and preparing greetings. The voices coming from the podium were background noise to him.

The fourth contestant, a tall, imposing young woman, rose slowly and walked to the edge of the podium. She began to read the Greek translation of "The Song of the Bell" by Schiller. Konrad knew the poem by heart and hearing the words in Greek was strange.

He had to concentrate, as his knowledge of Greek was mostly from his university days, twenty years ago. He unclenched his teeth and crossed his legs in a leisurely manner, hoping this gesture would show nonchalance. Clutching his hat in sweaty hands, he stared at the lovely girl in front of him. Her face was the color of the pale coffee he drank each morning, the contour of her breasts and rounded hips were discernible, even under the shapeless school jumper. An uncomfortable warmth suffused Konrad's groin and his thoughts strayed back thirty years.

~

A few days after Konrad's fourteenth birthday his father, who was a high-ranking foreign service officer, took Konrad to a banquet in honor of a visiting maharaja at the British embassy in Berlin. The opulence of the décor, the exotic food and the royal guests dazzled the young Konrad. It was a feast for all the senses.

After the meal the twenty guests left the huge western-style room with its red, silk-lined walls and gas-lit, crystal chandeliers and entered a smaller room, where they sat on cushions in a semi-circle around a raised platform. The room was dimly lit with candles on low tables in the back, but two bright lanterns shone onto the stage.

Music started to play from an area behind a curtain, and three young women appeared and began to dance. They waved white, diaphanous veils in front of their nude bodies, giving the audience a glimpse of large, brown nipples and flashes of pubic hair. Red ribbons held back their long black hair, while silver bands encircled their hips, emphasizing the erotic movements. They moved in perfect rhythm and coordination and looked almost exactly alike, but Konrad thought the middle one was more graceful and moved with more self-awareness than the others. She was the one who caught Konrad's eye and she did not look away when their eyes met. Then Konrad noticed her nipples puckering up into hard, black balls. Her movements indicated that she knew what was happening to Konrad's body as well. After that evening, he imagined her warm, brown body in his bed almost every night throughout his school years.

Now, the girl on the stage was speaking in German, explaining how the poem told of the labor involved in creating a church bell, and how it would ring to herald each life-changing event experienced by humans, from birth until the final tolling of the funeral dirge. Her voice was soft, yet carried into the back of the classroom.

Konrad was mesmerized by her concise telling of the story that he had memorized during his third year of grade school. It had taken nearly an hour to recite and he could still do it. Sometimes he recited the lengthy poem while trying to go to sleep. If he was able to finish, he knew he would not sleep that night.

The ambassador whispered to Konrad, "She speaks German with hardly an accent." Konrad nodded in agreement without taking his eyes off the girl as she walked back to her seat.

The German ambassador and his consul general for Athens had been invited specifically to help the judges choose the winner and runner-up. The criterion for winning the contest was accuracy of the translation and understanding the meaning of the lengthy poetry

The four finalists, their parents and their instructors were invited to an adjoining salon to await the final decision of the judges who would be meeting in another room. Everyone stood up and the girls in the audience filed out to return to their classrooms. The contestants and their entourages entered the ornate salon, where they relaxed on cushioned sofas. A round table near the tall window was covered with a white, starched cloth and laid with a variety of sweets—baklava, candied nuts, figs and dates. Several bottles of wine and a large bottle of ouzo were lined up on a counter against the wall opposite the door. Glasses of various shapes and sizes were placed on a square table beside the counter.

The four girls stood nervously by the window, while their parents settled into the couches and the two teachers sat on the straight chairs facing them.

In the dean's office next door, the four men and one woman, the dean's secretary, briefly conversed about the choices they must make. The ambassador took Konrad aside and told him he had to leave for another engagement and that Konrad should make an apology and excuse for him. Without further notice, he left the building.

The dean and his assistant stood side by side in front of the desk that filled the room. They faced the secretary and Konrad with ingratiating smiles. "The winner of this contest is obviously the young woman who presented 'The Bride of Messina.'" The dean spoke first. Konrad started to say something when the assistant broke in.

"Miss Arthenis gave a clear interpretation of the play. She showed how the evils of paganism can cause great tragedy."

"You do agree, don't you?" The dean addressed Konrad, but it was not really a question.

Konrad and the dean's secretary looked at each other and remained silent.

"You may choose the runner-up," the dean said, waving his hand in their direction.

Konrad wanted to consult with the stout woman standing beside him, but after what he had just heard he did not trust her to agree with him, so he blurted out, "I believe the fourth contestant did an admirable presentation and deserves the second place." He looked at the secretary and she quickly nodded her head in agreement.

As they walked across the hall to the reception room, the secretary pulled Konrad back a few paces and whispered quickly, "Miss Arthenis is the daughter of a very wealthy family. The school needs their money and Germany needs their support to win over the Greeks." Konrad nodded. He understood. Diplomacy and politics was his life, but for the first time he regretted the deceit and underhanded schemes that his work entailed.

When the four judges came into the room where the contestants and their parents were waiting, everyone stood up and then waited for one of the officials to speak. The four finalists looked up expectantly and three of the girls moved toward the couches to stand next to their parents. The tall girl who had spoken last remained by the window. No one from her family had come to hear her presentation.

The dean of the school, an imposing figure with a mop of black hair and full beard of the same color, walked toward the window side of the room and faced the anxious parents and their daughters.

"These four young women are a credit to their school and to Greece," he started out. "They have displayed the best of what we teach here at Arsakeio academy. It was a struggle to choose one above the others but a choice had to be made."

He cleared his throat, and looked around as a maid came in pushing a small cart laden with plates, napkins, silverware and a samovar of tea. She left the cart next to the table with the glasses and made a hasty retreat under the stern look of the dean.

"The first-prize winner," he continued after a dramatic pause, "will be awarded an all-expense-paid trip to Berlin. Her family will need to provide a suitable chaperon, of course. She will visit the world famous cultural institutions of Germany and be presented to Empress Augusta Victoria herself."

Everyone in the room gasped with surprise and pleasure.

The dean went on. "The runner-up will have a guided tour of the German embassy and be a guest of the ambassador for an informal dinner. The other two young ladies will receive a signed portrait of the king and queen of Greece with a letter of congratulations."

Konrad did not hear the names of the two runners up, but when at last the dean mentioned the winner of the contest he saw the girl by the window step forward and hear her name for the first time.

"Estanza Nikiolopolis." The dean's voice was raised a pitch as he said her name. "We award you second prize for your wonderful translation and interpretation of Schiller's epic poem." He must have been smiling, but it was not evident behind his bushy beard.

Estanza stepped forward to accept the envelope with the invitation to the German Embassy and a small wall plaque to commemorate her status in the "contest." Konrad stepped in front of her, held out his hand and introduced himself. She looked at him and he could see astonishment as well as pleasure in her large black eyes. They both knew that this behavior was unacceptable in polite society. A man did not introduce himself to a lady. He waited until someone he knew who was already acquainted with the woman introduced them to each other.

Estanza's smile dazzled Konrad as she repeated his name. "Herr von Stahlenberg, I am very pleased to make your acquaintance," she said in almost unaccented German.

Konrad gently put a hand on her elbow and guided her away from the refreshment table where the other guests were beginning to gather. His mind was working feverishly on how to prolong his time with her.

He noticed the dean's secretary starting toward the door. Quickly he stepped in front of her. "Let me introduce you to Miss Nikiolopolis," he said with a smile. "You did like her presentation and you should tell her so. May I ask your name?" he added, formally.

"Armena," she said, and he cut her short as she was about to tell him her last name.

Konrad said quietly, "Have you met Estanza?" The two women nodded to each other as he continued speaking. "Perhaps you would like a drink or a snack, Armena? If so, could you also bring us a small glass of wine?"

Armena looked at one and then the other of the two people in front of her, then breathed, "Of course, sir," and went to the wine bar without looking back.

Konrad turned his attention to Estanza. "Your German is excellent," he complimented her. She smiled that dazzling smile again and he forced himself to keep talking. "Your parents did not come today." Her face clouded and he reprimanded himself. He could see immediately that this was not a diplomatic thing to point out. How could he be so clumsy?

"My parents live very far away and could not take time from work to come to Athens," she replied and then went on. "They did send me a telegram of congratulations." She pulled a folded piece of paper out of her skirt pocket to show him.

He gave it a cursory glance and looked back into her eyes.

Armena came back with a glass of wine for Konrad and a cup of tea for Estanza. "I must return to the office. Please excuse me," she said, as she backed away and went out the door.

Several of the other occupants were leaving the room and Konrad hoped he could keep Estanza there for a few more minutes.

He decided to start a conversation about her upcoming visit to the embassy. "When the ambassador chooses a date for your visit, it will be my pleasure to personally deliver the invitation." He said these words with the fervent hope that they were true. "Congratulations, Estanza." He almost whispered her name. He knew he should use her last name, but he wanted to say her name out loud. To him, it felt as if he had caressed her.

She had put down the tea cup on the table nearby and folded her hands at her waist. Konrad took one of her light brown hands into his own. He bent over as if to kiss her hand.

His lips did not touch her skin, but a tingle went up her spine when she felt his breath. She was disappointed when he dropped her hand and straightened back up.

After leaving the school Konrad decided to walk to the German embassy. It was a warm day for April and he needed time to think. A vision of Estanza danced around in his head. Konrad had also felt the tingle of excitement and arousal as he breathed in the scent of the cologne under her sleeve. He could almost feel the smooth, black braids that curled around each of her ears. The hairdo exposed her long, curving neck and he imagined running his fingers along that curve and down her back.

His thoughts were mixed. He knew it would be best to not see this girl again, but part of his mind was devising a plan of how he could arrange another meeting as soon as possible.

Chapter 2

When Konrad got to his office he found a pile of paper work that needed his immediate attention. The rest of the afternoon went by quickly; it wasn't until he was being driven back to his apartment in the German sector of Athens that he had time to think about a scheme that would allow him see Estanza again. Nothing came to his mind that would be effective. He dismissed one plan after another. However, that evening it was his wife who gave him the idea he needed.

Elisabet von Stahlenberg, nee Groestiger, had been married to Konrad for ten years. They had an amicable relationship, but there had never, even at the beginning, been passionate feelings between them. She was a tall, slim, light-skinned blonde with faded, blue eyes that rarely showed emotion. The fact that she was five years older than Konrad had never been an issue, and she looked younger than her forty-three years.

It had been a marriage of convenience. She was considered an "old maid" at thirty-three, Konrad was an eligible bachelor of twenty-eight, and their fathers (one an aristocrat in the diplomatic service of the Kaiser, the other an owner of munitions factories) agreed that a merger between their two wealthy and powerful families would increase the prestige and influence of each and be beneficial for everyone.

Over dinner that evening, Konrad's wife mentioned that she was having problems with her Greek dressmaker because of the language barrier.

"I wish I knew a Greek woman who speaks German," she

sighed, after a long diatribe of how frustrating it was to make herself understood by all the Greek servants and vendors with whom she had dealings every day.

Konrad looked up from the dessert that he hardly knew was there. A plan began to form in his mind and the excitement was hard to suppress, but his voice was calm and steady as he spoke. "My dear Eli"—the nickname the family used for Elisabet—"I think I have a solution to your problem."

She looked at him with interest. If he said something about resolving a situation, he usually did just that.

"What do you have in mind?" she asked, with a hint of curiosity.

"I need to do some research, but I may have found just the person who would be a help to you and possibly to me also." He smiled and moved to leave the table.

Over coffee in the sitting room, they spoke of the weather and the garden, and soon Eli excused herself and went to her own rooms at the other end of the hallway. Konrad and Eli had separate bedrooms in the Victorian style and had not slept together for many years. They had always been good friends, even as children, and their platonic relationship had developed quite naturally. From the very outset of the marriage, she had made it clear that she did not enjoy sexual contact. However, it was expected that she produce an heir for the von Stahlenberg name and so endured the process of copulation and did her best to hide her distaste. After the second miscarriage, seven years ago they resumed their platonic relationship.

Konrad got up from the chair as his wife left the room and strolled into the library next door. He picked up the book he had been reading the night before and sat down in the armchair near the window that overlooked the park below. The book remained in his lap as his mind went to the process of getting Estanza into his household.

The next day he began to investigate the Nikiolopolis family. According to the records kept at the school, they owned a hotel in Distomo, a mountain town near Delphi. The family had run the business for many generations. Further inquiries revealed that, sometime in the past, a German ancestor had built the hotel to cater to German tourists and archeologists who stopped there on their way to the ancient ruins of Delphi. The family was not wealthy, but they had a reasonable income from the hotel and the sale of olive oil from a press they owned and operated. They had undoubtedly made financial sacrifices to send Estanza to the prestigious school, but they had thought it worth the investment.

The next step for Konrad was to expedite the plans for Estanza's visit to the Embassy. He called the ambassador that very afternoon to ask about a date for the dinner party to which the poetry contestant was to be invited. He then offered himself as the guide for her tour of the embassy.

Konrad managed to get one of his secretaries to be appointed to hand-deliver the invitation for the embassy dinner to Estanza. At the last minute, just as the young man was putting on his coat to go out the door, Konrad called him back. "I am going on an errand in that neighborhood," he told the departing secretary. "I will take the invitation to the young lady myself."

The surprised young man gave the envelope to Konrad and congratulated himself on his good luck. So now he didn't need to miss the lunch date with his fiancé after all.

On his way to the school, Konrad worked out his plan on how to see Estanza more often, possibly on a daily basis. His approach had to be diplomatic with both his wife and Estanza, possibly including her family. But he was a diplomat, after all, and he knew how to make people feel that what they were agreeing to do was in their best interest. Also, in this case, he wanted to convince himself that his intentions were honorable.

He talked with Estanza about her plans. Her family expected her to come back and help run the hotel. Her skill with languages (she had learned German, French and a smattering of English) would be very useful with the international guests that came each summer.

They were standing in the parlor where they had stood the last time he saw her. Konrad handed Estanza the invitation while his eyes caressed the long sheaf of hair that hung down her back. A white ribbon held back the curls from her face. It was a much more becoming look than the braided buns over each ear that she had worn for the contest.

Estanza took the envelope and smiled up at him, admiring his green eyes. She opened the flap and read the invitation with wide, eager eyes.

"This is in two weeks," she said. "That is so soon. I don't have anything suitable to wear." Then she continued in a hushed tone, "I won't know how to act."

"Perhaps we can find someone to guide you in these matters." Konrad replied. He was going to bring up the subject himself, but it was almost as if Estanza had read his mind.

Konrad was pleasantly surprised at the maturity and wisdom of this young woman. He stayed with her all afternoon and they had tea with Armena as chaperon. Their conversation drifted from one subject to another and covered world affairs, the vicissitudes of running a family hotel, and the joy of growing the perfect rose—a subject that also interested Armena.

The next morning at breakfast, Konrad and Eli discussed the upcoming dinner at the embassy to honor the winner of the German poetry contest.

"It would be a good idea to groom this girl and give her some lessons in protocol at embassy affairs," Konrad said to Eli.

"I suppose the school has a tutor who could give her some guidance," she said helpfully.

"It is a type of trade school, not a finishing school," Konrad responded. "The students are taught languages, bookkeeping skills, and even typing. They are being trained to be translators and secretaries; they do not have expectations of dining at an embassy.

"I see," Eli murmured. "I was sent to a special seminary to learn how to be a good wife for a diplomat. Does the embassy have personnel that can help this girl?"

Konrad didn't answer for a few moments then said thoughtfully, "The embassy doesn't have that type of service. Eli, perhaps you could discuss some of these matters with the girl?" He went on quickly. "Her name is Estanza and she is very intelligent and speaks perfect German."

"What are you suggesting?" Eli asked, already knowing what the answer would be.

"I was hoping you might deign to talk with her when you have a free afternoon. She might be helpful to you, as well as getting your ideas across to your dressmaker."

Eli agreed to invite Estanza to the apartment that next Saturday afternoon for tea. She had an appointment with her dressmaker later that day, and she would ask Estanza to stay and translate her wishes.

That next Saturday Eli sent an embassy car to bring Estanza to her apartment. The head mistress had been informed of the plan and sent her maid along as a chaperon.

Eli received the two young women in her sitting room without getting up from the sofa. The tea tray was laid out in front of her; she nodded to Estanza and dismissed her maid who took the chaperon into the nearby pantry for a snack.

Thanks to her training as the wife of a diplomat and her breeding, Eli gave no indication of her shock at Estanza's dark complexion. At first she had thought that Estanza was the maid that had been sent as a chaperon. After a few more minutes Eli thought that this girl had the look of an Arabian princess. (Eli had met one during a visit to Cairo.)

After a polite greeting and some words about the lovely spring weather, Eli served the tea and offered Estanza a piece of baklava from the silver tray. She watched the girl carefully to see how she held her cup and dealt with the cake and napkin. There was upper class training in her movements and her German was excellent, just as Konrad had said.

After the tea they went to Eli's private sitting room where the dressmaker was waiting with bolts of fabric spread out over a table and sketches in her hand. The afternoon went well. Estanza gave the dressmaker instructions that she had translated from the German and the sketches met with Eli's approval. When it was time for Estanza to leave, Eli asked her to return in a few days so she could tell the girl more about the protocols required at embassy dinners.

"The details are endless," she told Estanza, who stood at the door with her chaperon. "There are rules for which cutlery to use with which course, when to start eating the food that is placed in front of one by the server, how to place the knife and fork on the plate when one is done with a dish and, most importantly, how to address the various guests." Eli paused for effect. Estanza nodded as Eli insisted she stay longer on her next visit and offered to have a dress made for the embassy visit.

Estanza was delighted with Eli's kindness and generosity. She offered to pay for the dress, but Eli would not hear of it. "Let me do this for you as a reward for your patience in helping sort out my instructions to the dressmaker," Eli told her. "You will tell her that your gown is to take priority over mine."

When the day came, Estanza waited for Konrad just inside the school's front doorway. As he stepped out of the embassy car, he almost didn't recognize her in the sophisticated gown and upswept hair. The maroon of the dress set off her dark skin, and her hair sparkled with two rhinestone combs. The silk pumps on her feet matched the dress, and her black cape was lined with the same fabric.

Konrad had brought her a white gardenia to pin to her dress, and it was the perfect ornament. They rode in silence for the half hour trip to the embassy as the headmistress of the school sat stiffly next to the chauffeur. Upon their arrival at the embassy, the headmistress was told by the butler that she could wait in the servants' dining area until Estanza was ready to return to the school.

The dinner was a great success. Although the ambassador was unable to attend, his wife made everyone feel welcome.

She briefly conversed in German with Eli and Estanza. Then the wife of the French attaché began a conversation in French and was delighted to find that Estanza understood every word she said.

After the dinner Eli and Konrad took Estanza on a tour of the public area of the embassy. There was a wide stairway that led from the spacious reception area to a long hallway. Electricity had been installed in most of the public buildings in Athens, and the hall was alight with dozens of sconces along both walls. Between them were paintings of dark and dreary landscapes, portraits of former ambassadors and a few statues from Greek antiquity. Half way down the hall, Eli asked to be excused for a few moments as she needed to attend to the ladies who had gathered after dinner in the ladies' reception room. Konrad nodded and Estanza murmured, "Of course." Then they turned back to viewing the remainder of the artwork.

Konrad made what he hoped were amusing comments about the men in the portraits—how the wigs didn't fit well, or the mustaches were overpowering, and how sitting on a horse made the short stature of an ancient king seem more majestic. Estanza chuckled and added a few disrespectful words of her own. Konrad was delighted at her wit and intelligence. He felt his heart beat faster as the hallway and the artwork all disappeared, and all he saw was this lovely, young girl. He never ever wanted her out of his sight.

"I do hope you enjoyed the evening." Konrad said to Estanza in German. Estanza gave him one of her dazzling smiles and he caught his breath.

"This has been a most memorable adventure for me," she said in her soft lilting voice. There was a bit of an accent when she spoke German, but Konrad found it charming.

He took her hand in his, looked into her dark eyes and hoped the meaning of his next words would be understood. "This has been a memorable occasion for me also, Estanza. I sincerely hope to see you again soon." He slowly released her hand as Eli came back down the hall and all three of them descended to the street level. Konrad helped Estanza with her cape as the headmistress came bustling up the stairs from the servants' quarters.

Konrad helped the headmistress into the car, and she sat stiffly next to the chauffeur; Estanza climbed into the backseat. Konrad sat down beside her and addressed a few words in German to the headmistress. It was obvious that she did not understand him. Then he asked her in French if she had eaten a good meal.

"The food was quite delectable," she answered in French. "But I did not expect to be treated like a servant."

Konrad expressed surprise at this answer. Then he remembered that he had not told the butler, who did the receiving for the party, that it was not the maid, but the headmistress herself who was chaperoning Estanza.

"Now I have the honor of sitting next to the driver of this contraption as if I were a footman," she added. The sarcastic tone was not lost on Konrad.

He spent a few moments composing a suitable answer and thought of how auspicious it was that the he could use French to explain the situation. It was, after all, the language of diplomacy, and placating irate people was a large part of his job. He told her that, since she had sent her maid on the other occasions when Estanza had visited with his wife, no one had expected the presence of the headmistress. He went on to say, "We are honored that you came and deeply regret how you have been treated."

The headmistress turned her head slightly to acknowledge his apology and Konrad quickly dropped Estanza's hand. After a few minutes he picked it up again; it was warm and dry. He spoke in a conversational tone, but in German. "I would very much like to see you again. Would Saturday afternoon be convenient?" He applied a little pressure to her hand and she responded with hers.

At eighteen, Estanza was not an innocent girl from a

protective family. She had reached her full physical maturity when she was thirteen and men had begun to notice her as she worked with her mother and sister doing housekeeping in the hotel. She was repelled by the advances of most of their hotel guests, but one of the village boys had caught her eye and they had met for clandestine hugs and kisses in the attic of the hotel. He had promised to love her forever, but when she left for school, he had soon found another girl. She had almost forgotten him. But the feelings that he had aroused in her had lain dormant until she had met Konrad. When she looked into his green eyes she felt that almost-forgotten warmth and a pleasure that was totally new to her. She agreed to meet him the coming Saturday.

"I will arrange things," he assured her. "Perhaps we can take a stroll in the park that surrounds the school." Suddenly the seven days until Saturday seemed a long way off. Konrad's brain began to churn with plans that might allow him to be alone with Estanza.

The next morning at breakfast Eli remarked that the dinner party at the embassy was a success as far as she was concerned. "Do you agree that Estanza behaved well?" she asked Konrad. "I do take some credit for her excellent deportment."

"Yes, she was a real credit to your careful tutoring," Konrad replied.

"I overheard her discussing Greek culture with the French attaché's wife. She knows so much about the art and architecture of ancient Greece, but mentioned that she has not been to the Acropolis or the Royal Gardens," Eli continued. "One would think that her school would make an effort to show the students these important sights."

"They really should," Konrad agreed, and began to form a plan for the Saturday outing.

Chapter 3

Twelve girls were selected to participate in a field trip to the Acropolis. The selection was based on their grades, language skills and the good graces of the headmistress. Since the transportation and trained tour guides were being supplied by the German Embassy, it was expected that some of the staff of that establishment would accompany the expedition. After making certain that Estanza was included in the group, Konrad volunteered to go along as one of the chaperons.

He had convinced the school administration that, with their language skills, the graduates of the Arsakeio seminar would make excellent translators to accompany tour guides. "After all," Konrad had argued, "your graduates are being trained to work in the business world, and one of the main businesses of Greece is tourism."

That Saturday, in the middle of May, the Acropolis was crowded with visitors from every country in the world. However, the majority were British and German, and Konrad pointed this out to the school official who had come along to supervise. This well-educated gentleman and the official guide vied for the attention of the young women in their charge who soon lost interest in the lengthy explanations, provided first by the guide and then by the professor.

The school group began to scatter among the ruins. Konrad found Estanza inside the elegant little temple of Nike. The huge pillars filled the interior with dark shadows and offered a cool sanctuary from the relentless sun. They stood side by side for a few minutes, looking out over the city of

Athens far below them. When they turned to face each other there was no hesitation. Konrad put an arm around Estanza's waist and pulled her to his chest. She dropped her parasol and flung her arms around his neck. When their lips met, for Estanza it was like the final crescendo of a symphony. She felt the music pounding throughout her whole body. There would never be a moment like this again and she wanted to prolong it no matter the consequences.

Konrad waited for the sexual arousal that he was expecting when he finally had this girl in his arms, but instead her warm lips gave him a feeling of comfort and peace; of having arrived, at last, where he belonged.

Slowly the world re-entered into their consciousness. They took a step back from each other. He couldn't see her eyes in the dim light, but she saw joy in his green pupils.

He picked up the parasol, handed it to her and held out his arm for her to take. They walked out into the bright sun, stopped to look at each other, seeing nothing and no one but each other. Their thoughts were identical: *When and where can we kiss again? It must be soon.*

The next two weeks were filled with final exams, packing up for departure from the school, and graduation ceremonies. Estanza had no time to think of Konrad during the day, but at night, lying in her narrow bed in the small room she shared with three other girls, she imagined herself in his arms.

Konrad was caught up in negotiations with the Greek government. The king was for a German alliance, but the parliament leaned toward the British because of their powerful fleet. Kaiser Wilhelm of Germany felt slighted that there was even a question of which side to choose for beneficial trade agreements. He sent orders to close the embassy and recalled his ambassador and all his staff, immediately.

There was no question in either Estanza's or Konrad's mind that they must find a way to be together. He wrote her a short, cryptic note: "I have a plan." She had to wait and trust him.

Estanza's father came to Athens for the graduation and

to escort Estanza back to Distomo. She sent a note to Konrad addressed to him at the Embassy. She hoped he would understand her meaning: "9 is fine."

At nine o'clock that evening Konrad walked into the dining room of the Olympia hotel. He made his way between the tables until he found Estanza and surmised the man with her was her father. When Konrad stopped at the table the older man stood up. Konrad introduced himself as the Consul General at the German embassy in Athens. He nodded to Estanza, who was clutching her hands in her lap to keep them from shaking. Konrad invited Mr. Nikiolopolis to visit him at his office the next day, before returning to Distomo.

He went on to explain, "The ambassador has just been informed that the Kaiser is recalling all personnel and temporarily closing the German embassy in Athens. A person who spoke fluent Greek and German could be helpful in avoiding misunderstandings and expedite the procedure." Seeing the blank look on Mr. Nikiolopolis's face, he realized that he had been speaking German. He continued in his broken Greek, feeling awkward in front of Estanza.

"The administrator of her school has recommended Estanza because of her excellent German," he told Estanza's father. "She will be paid quite handsomely and will be well-chaperoned. Can we talk about the details at my office tomorrow?"

To his credit, Mr. Nikiolopolis turned to Estanza and asked her if she wanted to consider such a position. She whispered, "Just for a short time—if you can spare me."

Her father did not reply at once. He thought about what the expectations had been when he and his wife had decided to send Estanza to school. It had not been an easy decision because running a hotel was a family project and every pair of hands was needed.

Each of their children had attended school until they reached the age of eleven, then each had started to learn the hotel trade. Estanza had started out badly. When she helped in the kitchen the food burned or was undercooked; serving drinks meant broken glass and spilled liquid. It was decided to keep her away from the food service. Even her nine-year-old sister was quicker and neater when it came to making beds and cleaning rooms. Estanza was quick with numbers and had a talent for making sense of the endless government regulations regarding tourist hotels.

Although it was totally against all his instincts he had agreed to send Estanza to school. It had been clear to him that Estanza was not going to make her living working with her hands as women should. So in spite of her gender he would allow her to manage the hotel. He hoped he was not making a mistake, allowing her to stay in Athens for another two weeks.

The next day an agreement was reached after consulting with Estanza's mother. Estanza would act as interpreter during the moving arrangements for the embassy, and Elisabet von Stahlenberg would act as her chaperon.

Kaiser Wilhelm the II sent the smaller of his oceangoing yachts to transport the wives and children of the embassy staff, including their personal servants, back to Germany. The men who made up the embassy staff and their personal secretaries and valets were to travel to Berlin on the fastest route possible, taking minimum luggage so as to expedite the trip.

By 1910 most of Europe was crossed by railroad tracks. Where there were no tracks, roadways were conducive to horse or automobile travel. However, this form of transportation was both uncomfortable and possibly dangerous. Besides the outlaws who lurked along the roads, the despots who ruled the countries that must be crossed allowed, and even encouraged, their minions to charge arbitrary fees for fictional permits and take bribes for providing safe passage to travelers.

Two days before the scheduled departure of the SMY *Hohenzollern*, Konrad came to Estanza's room at the embassy. She had been staying in the servants' quarters, sharing a room with the embassy housekeeper who spoke only German and two of the kitchen maids who spoke only Greek. It took all her language skills to keep order and a shaky truce between the three women. On this morning it was fairly quiet as each of the room's occupants was busy packing their metal trunks for the upcoming departure. They were going in three different directions. The housekeeper was going back to Germany on the ship, the Greek girls were returning to their village, and Estanza was taking the train back to Distomo.

Estanza opened the door to Konrad's knock and immediately her heart skipped a few beats. There was a strange look in his green eyes that puzzled her. He drew her out into the hall without a word. She glanced over her shoulder to see if the other women were watching, but they didn't even look up from their packing.

Konrad drew Estanza into his arms and they re-lived the scene from the Nike Temple. This time he cupped her left breast with his right hand and she could feel him tremble. His lips were more demanding than that Saturday afternoon when they had their first kiss. Estanza felt her knees buckle and her heart was pounding in her ears.

Against all her true desire she began to push him away. She was conscious of being in a hallway where people would be walking by any minute. For him to be seen embracing a young girl would be more than an embarrassment for a girl in her position—it would be disaster.

Konrad loosened his grip around her waist and allowed her to step back. He took his hand away from her breast and dropped it to his side. For a moment they stood looking at each other. Their eyes met and Estanza knew he was saying good-bye.

"I have important news for you." Konrad said quietly. When she just kept looking at him, he continued. "Elisabet has asked if you could travel to Germany with her. She will need a secretary that can write in Greek." He looked questioningly at Estanza, who looked startled and was turning pale.

"When we all get back to Germany, Elisabet will need to write letters thanking the people who hosted parties for us and generally showed us a warm and generous hospitality during our stay in Greece. This is part of her job as a consul's wife," he went on to explain.

It was not that Estanza was reluctant to go to Germany, in fact she was eager to see the country of Goethe and Schiller, but she was totally unprepared for such a voyage without more notice.

"Please say you will go with Elisabet. She really wants you to accompany her on the ship. She is planning to come speak to you about it this morning, but I wanted to tell you first and urge you to say you will come for my sake—for *our* sake."

"I don't know," Estanza began to stammer. "My family needs me at the hotel." Her brain was whirling. "Konrad," she whispered. She was still getting accustomed to calling him by his first name. "This is too sudden. I can't just leave. My family is expecting me. They need me."

Then Konrad said the words that determined her fate. "Estanza, I love you. I need you to be where I can see you every day." His eyes were blazing as he reached for her again. All at once she couldn't visualize life without him. She had to go.

Chapter 4

Getting ready for an ocean voyage and an indefinite stay in a strange, new country is usually a lengthy and involved process, but Estanza had few possessions and her small metal trunks were almost all packed. So when Elisabet sent for her later that same day and asked Estanza to accompany her to Germany, Estanza agreed to Elisabet's request without hesitation.

When Elisabet, who was called "Gracious Lady" by the household servants, asked Estanza to call her Mrs. Eli, Estanza was reluctant. Elisabet explained that, in Germany, employees who were not household servants used different forms of address, depending on what they did for their employer.

"According to Konrad, you are to be a secretary at the embassy, so I am not even directly your employer," Eli explained. "However, I am the wife of an embassy staff member, so our relationship is sort of in-between employer and friend."

Estanza waited for further information about the journey to Germany, but Eli didn't add anything beyond, "I'll see you at the gangplank," which was clearly a dismissal.

The next day Estanza wrote a note to her parents. She tried to explain her decision even though she could not explain it, even to herself. She mailed the letter, still feeling the tiny corner of indecision in her mind. Forcefully, she thought of Konrad, and all doubt vanished. She had no idea of what might occur between them, but for the moment she wanted only the thrill of his embrace, their passionate kiss. To see him every day would be sweet torture.

She went to bed early that night, but it was nearly dawn before she fell asleep. Two hours later the housekeeper shook her awake. Her function as interpreter would be needed at the dock in Piraeus. Estanza had laid out her clothes the night before. For boarding the ship, she had chosen the dark blue skirt and matching jacket with the cream-colored blouse, a graduation gift from her parents. The skirt was cut straight down to her knees, then flared out and barely grazed her ankles. It was the latest style from Paris. She rechecked the contents of the little trunk. The gray school uniform would do for office work. The black Sunday dress was out of style; skirts no longer swept along the floor, but it could be altered. The two sets of long, black stockings and two sets of underwear which were also out of fashion, but would do for now, and two white cotton nightgowns. The maroon evening gown and cape were at the bottom of the trunk. Would she ever wear it again? She had decided not to pack the corset; it was too cumbersome for a woman who had to dress alone. Her high button shoes were also out of style, but too new to discard as yet. On top was the heavy shawl of black sheep wool, scented with cedar oil.

Estanza closed and locked her trunk, put on her new straw hat, slung the bulging carpet bag—containing all her personal papers, German and French dictionaries, and some of her money—over her shoulder. The man from the embassy staff, who had come to fetch her, carried her trunk to the waiting car. Estanza paused in the broad, marble hallway that led to the portico where the car was parked. She looked around at the myriad trunks and chests waiting to be taken to the ship, and then turned to the young man who waited for her to proceed to the car.

"Who is going with me to the ship?" she asked, fully expecting a female employee to accompany her. Nineteen-year-old women did not go out without a chaperon in 1910.

"You do not have a lady's maid?" the young man asked impertinently. Then he added, "I was told to bring you to the ship. There is a problem with the loading of some cargo. The ship crew is German and the stevedores are Greek and do not understand the German directions."

Estanza had spent the last ten days translating between two factions of household workers with reasonable success, but doing the same with a crew of sailors and stevedores was intimidating. Also, was she expected to leave the house without another woman to accompany her?

"Please, Miss Nikiolopolis, come along," he pleaded. "I was told to hurry. The Crown Prince Constantine and Princess Sophia are coming to the ship to see it off this afternoon, and all work must be done before they arrive. I think your presence will greatly expedite the loading."

The name of the royal couple made an impression on Estanza. This was no ordinary situation, and she would have to go along. Sophia was Kaiser Wilhelm's sister, a friend of Elisabet von Stahlenberg, and a staunch supporter of a Greek/German alliance. She was also the future queen of Greece.

An hour later Estanza arrived at the port. A German officer from the ship greeted her as she stepped out of the embassy car. He ordered the chauffeur to take her little trunk to the gangplank. Then he escorted Estanza to a shady spot near the loading platform. While she waited for him to direct her further, her gaze traveled to the sea beyond the port. Many ships were anchored offshore, but the Kaiser's yacht was the only ship tied up to the new pier. A few men were milling around the port area. Estanza felt self-conscious as she became aware of being the only woman in sight; some of the men were staring at her. Much of the male attention was directed to her hemline, which was above her ankles, a style not yet fashionable in Greece. The German officer also let his eyes drift down and then up again as he inspected her figure. Estanza pulled the veil over her face, hoping he would not see her blush. She thought about how there were advantages to having dark skin, blushes were not as visible.

For the next three hours German crew members of the

ship kept coming over to talk to Estanza. Greek stevedores in tow, they explained to her what they wanted done and she in turn told the Greek workers.

The cargo hold that made up the center of the lowest deck was almost full. The line of trucks and horse-drawn wagons was nearing an end. Huge crates marked "preserved food" were being rolled into the hold when one of the biggest crates toppled over at the edge of the ramp and split open. Estanza saw the contents. It was not preserves. A statue lay exposed in the morning sun for all to see.

Taking antiquities out of Greece would eventually be strictly forbidden. But it would be twenty years before such a law was passed and long after the British archeologists had plundered most of the ancient sites of anything that could be moved. Much of Greek antiquity was already in the British Museum in London. Now it seemed the Germans wanted their share. Estanza and the German officer exchanged glances. He had heard her gasp and looked worried. This early in the morning the air was still cool, but Estanza saw the young German had moisture on his face. Upon further examination she noticed the armpits of his white uniform were getting dark. As the men gathered up the contents of the broken crate and managed to get it on board, Estanza tried to keep her face expressionless.

By eleven o'clock the loading was done and Estanza went aboard the docked ship.

Chapter 5

The SMY *Hohenzollern* was one of the most luxurious vessels in the world. On the upper deck were five stateroom suites, each with a sitting room, bedroom, dressing rooms, maid's room and expansive bathroom. Four salons for various entertainment were on the promenade deck and down another broad stairway were two dining rooms and a state-of-the-art galley. In true Victorian style, ornate furniture, sculptures and Tiffany lamps occupied every inch of the public rooms. Costly tapestries and gold framed painting covered the walls. On the voyage from Athens to Bremerhaven, which would take about two weeks, given good weather, the aristocratic passengers were to be treated like the royal owner.

The lowest part of the ship was like another world. Right beside the heat and grime of the engine room were the hammocks of the twenty crew members. A thin partition separated them from the six men of the kitchen crew. The middle of the lowest deck was taken up by the huge cargo hold. The heaviest items were stored there and provided ballast.

The ship's doctor, a man of uncertain age and ability, had a bunk in the infirmary near the bow. Next door to the infirmary, tucked into the last few feet of the bow, was a cubicle, six feet wide by eight feet long, with a tiny porthole near the low ceiling. This was a place for crew members who might need to be quarantined or incarcerated.

After boarding the ship, Estanza was led to one of the smaller salons on the promenade deck and told to wait until further orders. She sat down gratefully on one of the overstuffed chairs. Tucking her hat into the ample carpet bag, she brushed her hand over her thick coil of black hair and looked around with interest. Every inch of the wall space and much of the center of the room was filled with furniture and decorative articles. In one corner, near a window, was a small writing table complete with royal crested stationary, pens, ink, and even a small box of stamps.

Estanza had been thinking about the antiquities that were being loaded aboard the yacht. She did not believe that anyone in the Greek government could be involved, or why would the crates be disguised as food? She was not aware of a law preventing antiquities to be taken out of Greece, but it was her firm belief that there should be. If she wrote a letter to the Department of Antiquities alerting them to the pilfering of Greek treasures, maybe they would make a law.

She sat down at the desk and began to write. She fervently wished there had been a typewriter, since her hand writing might be traced. *I will have to take that chance*, she told herself. She tried to disguise her writing as she proceeded to tell the administrator about the antiquities on the German yacht being "smuggled out of Greece, right under the nose of the crown Prince himself." She signed it, "a concerned and loyal Greek citizen."

The envelope was addressed and marked personal, with the hope it would be opened by the intended party. After applying the postage, Estanza went back to the gangplank. She saw that the rest of the passengers were beginning to arrive. A long line of cars was wending its way to the pier. A chauffeur had just helped a family out of his limousine and finished stacking their luggage near the gangplank. Estanza approached him, held out the letter and a few Drachmas.

"Please, could you do me a great favor?" she asked, giving him her most dazzling smile.

"If possible, miss," he said, lifting his cap. To his credit he did not look at the money being held out to him, but gazed steadily at Estanza, returning her smile.

"I forgot to mail this letter earlier today, and it needs to go out immediately. Please drop it off at the nearest post office. Here is a little something for your trouble," she said as she handed him the envelope and the money. She patted his hand to show her gratitude as he took them. Then breathing another, "Thank you," she turned and followed the embarking passengers up the gangplank and made her way back to the small salon.

Her carpet bag was where she had left it, and there was still no other person around. She sat down in the same over-stuffed chair, just a little worried about what she had just done. There had been many conversations with her father about the removal of antiquities, ever since the British archeologists first started staying at their hotel. Estanza and her father had agreed that the removal of so many artifacts was bad for Greece, while other members of the family were not so sure or just didn't care, as long as these foreigners paid their hotel bill.

Just as the little waves from the wake of a passing ship join with bigger waves to have an impact far beyond their origin, Estanza's letter was passed hand to hand until it arrived on the desk of the man who was influenced to make a historic decision. Trying not to think about what might result from her letter, Estanza closed her eyes and leaned back in her chair. It had been a long and stressful morning and soon she was dozing off.

She woke to the sound of a bell ringing, and when she opened her eyes a young sailor was standing in front of her.

"Lunch is ready in the lower dining room," he said, bowing slightly from the waist. "Please to follow me." It was not an invitation or a question, but definitely an order.

Estanza picked up her carpet bag and followed him down a wide stairway. The sound of rattling dishes and clinking glasses came drifting up to her, followed by the aroma of something cooking. Before she reached the bottom of the stairs a woman came up to Estanza, whom she recognized as Elisabet von Stahlenberg's lady's maid.

"My Gracious Lady wants to see you right away," she said in a tone that left no doubt that it, too, was an order.

Estanza turned and followed the woman up the stairs. The stairway to the staterooms was wider with more ornate carving on the banister. The hallway was carpeted with a red and gold design that matched the drapery. They passed the gold trimmed door that marked the royal suite, where the ambassador's wife and daughters were ensconced. The next doorway led to the Von suite. Elisabet was standing by the fireplace, dressed in a pink dressing gown, her pale hair loosely falling past her shoulders. She smiled as Estanza came into the sitting room, waved a hand of welcome and moved toward the girl.

Elisabet addressed the maid with an imperious tone: "Hilde, find the steward and ask what is being served for the midday meal. I may want it served here."

When the maid had closed the door behind her, Elisabet stepped closer to Estanza, who stood waiting beside the elegant sofa for further direction. Elisabet raised her arm and put a hand on Estanza's shoulder and with a sudden movement slid her hand around to the middle of her back. The tight embrace pinned Estanza's left arm against her side. Elisabet raised her left arm and cupped Estanza's right breast, simultaneously bringing her lips down on Estanza's mouth in a passionate kiss that forced Estanza's lips apart. With an automatic reflex Estanza swung the carpet bag toward Elisabet in a hapless gesture to protect herself.

Elisabet released her grip. Estanza gasped a barely audible, "No."

Stepping backward, Elisabet raised her arm to slap Estanza but when she saw the shock and fear on Estanza's face she dropped her arm and abruptly turned way. Stumbling toward the open door of the bedroom she turned and hissed, "Get out!" then slammed the door behind her.

Estanza stood very still for the next few minutes. She was confused, afraid, and at a total loss about what to do next. When the maid came back in Estanza took advantage of the open door and slipped out into the hallway.

Estanza stood just outside the closed door recovering her equilibrium. Her stomach was churning and there was a haze in front of her eyes. A man, carrying a small trunk on his shoulders came walking toward her through the haze. He stopped in front of her, touched his sailor cap and made to knock on the door behind Estanza. It was at that moment that she recognized her green trunk.

"That's my trunk," she said pointing at the trunk that now stood on the floor between them.

"I have orders to bring it to this cabin, madam." The young sailor explained.

"I am not staying in this cabin." Estanza said. "Please take it to the cabin assigned to me, Estanza Nikiolopolis."

The man looked at her uncomprehendingly, although she had spoken in fluent German.

Estanza repeated her words, with more emphasis on the fact that it was her trunk.

"But I have orders to take it to this cabin," he said. "Those were my orders," he repeated.

Just then one of the officers happened to pass by and heard the discussion. He ordered the sailor back to his regular duties, and to drop the trunk off at the purser's office where the matter would be sorted out.

The officer introduced himself to Estanza as Ensign Schmidt. He started to apologize for his rudeness, but the circumstances were unusual, he added.

Estanza was feeling faint and nauseous. She had not had any food or drink since the night before and the shock of Elisabet's attack had left her mind reeling. In reply to the polite words of the officer, she said the first words that came into her mind.

"I want to get off the ship, sir. At once." She fought to keep her voice level, but it rose slightly as she repeated her plea.

"That is not possible," he replied. "We are leaving the port as we speak."

Estanza was stunned by this revelation. "The royal couple was to wave us off." She almost pleaded, in the hope that the officer's words were not true.

"There was a message, Fräulein," he explained. "They were delayed and we had to take advantage of the tide. They sent their regrets to all of you."

Estanza stood rooted to the floor for a few more seconds, then rushed past the officer and down the stairs to the promenade deck, where she found a door to the outside. She was standing near the place where the gangplank had been. Looking out she saw the pier receding, as the expanse of water between the ship and the land was widening. Clutching the railing, she stood mesmerized as the ship passed the seawall and started along the coast line near Piraeus. Ensign Schmidt had followed her down and stood behind her. He touched her shoulder lightly and spoke to her rigid back.

"Please excuse me, Fräulein, but I must return to my post. Please go see the purser for further directions." With a slight bow and a touch to his cap, he was gone.

Estanza remained at the rail and watched the little fishing villages pass by. She recognized the dome of the church in her father's village. It brought back sweet memories of visits to his family who had fished these waters for centuries. The first time she had come here, her father had rowed her and her brother in a tiny, rented boat, all the way from Piraeus. Estanza had been impressed by how skillfully he handled the oars.

"I love the sea," her father had told them. "But I loved your mother more."

When they had pulled up alongside the narrow pier they were greeted by the sight of naked boys jumping into the sea. To the twelve-year-old Estanza it looked like the greatest pleasure in the world to be able to strip and dive into those clear, blue waves. She had trailed her hand in the cool moisture and imagined how it would feel to strip off her clothes and bathe in the silky water. Later that week, when she had returned to Distomo, her mother had overheard her tell her younger sister about the boys swimming in the ocean. "It must be wonderful to have such freedom," she had exclaimed. "Sometimes I wish I were a boy."

"Estanza, you should be ashamed to have such thoughts." Her mother had scolded. But Estanza could find no shame in wishing for freedom. Now she remembered that day when she had stripped off her clothes and plunged into the clear waters of the Aegean Sea.

During a late summer visit to her paternal grandparents, Estanza had decided to take a stroll along the beach. As soon as she was out of sight of the house, she took off her shoes and stockings, rolled up her skirt and multiple petticoats around her waist, and waded into the surf. The beach turned sharply to the left making a small inlet beside some willow bushes. With only a moment's hesitation, Estanza slipped out of her clothes, hung them carefully on the branches of the thick bushes, and waded into the water.

Thanks to the progressive thinking of the headmistress, and in spite of violent objections of some of the parents, the trustees of the Arsakeio Girls' School had been persuaded to build a swimming pool and provide swimming lessons for the students. Bathing facilities for women were becoming prevalent throughout Europe. If the ladies were learning to swim in such landlocked cities like Vienna and Budapest, wasn't it about time that the women of Greece, a maritime nation, learned how to swim? The bathing suits for females were not conducive to staying afloat, but it made strong swimmers out of the ones who dared to fight the bulky pantaloons and long sleeved, high necked bodices. Estanza was at home in the water.

That summer evening two years ago was one of the most memorable and joyful times of her life. She swam out to the end of the spit, where the trees ended. The water felt like warm silk on her skin. For a few minutes she floated on her back, her hair spread out like seaweed, she watched her ample breasts bob like balloons in front of her. She would never forget the sheer bliss of total freedom and the wonderful sensation of weightlessness.

With a deep sigh, she turned from the railing and went to find the purser's office.

Chapter 6

The next few hours were a blur in Estanza's mind. She had found the purser's office, tucked under the stairwell on the promenade deck. The portholes faced the starboard side of the ship and light flooded in from the setting sun. In the glare she saw the purser behind his desk. He stood up as she came in. Seeing her sway, he took a step toward her and caught her just as she started to faint. The purser, a large man who sometimes doubled as a body guard for the Kaiser, carried Estanza to the couch that sat against one wall of his office. He called in his cabin boy and told him to fetch the ship's doctor.

While he waited for the doctor, the purser looked into the carpet bag that Estanza had dropped at his feet. He found her passport and identification papers, as well as the letters from the German Department of Foreign Affairs, designating Estanza Nikiolopolis as an official interpreter/translator to be stationed in the Berlin Foreign Affairs office. There was an address of an apartment in Berlin where she was to reside, ostensibly under the protection of Vice Consul and Mrs. Konrad von Stahlenberg

The doctor came in less than five minutes. He took a look at the girl on the couch and started to take her pulse. He sent the purser to bring a cold towel from the adjoining bathroom while he unbuttoned her blouse.

Sitting on the edge of the couch, the doctor listened to Estanza's erratic heartbeat with his stethoscope. Then he heard her stomach growl loudly while her heartbeat became more regular.

The purser brought the wet towel and, looming over the couch, he gently laid it on the girl's forehead. At six feet and three inches, he was the tallest man on the ship, and as the doctor stood up beside him they made an incongruous pair.

"It is my opinion that she fainted from hunger, Johann," the doctor told the purser, whose gray eyes showed a puzzled concern. "Sometimes women faint from tight corsets, but she isn't wearing one."

"With a figure like that she doesn't need a corset," the purser murmured under his breath, with an appreciative glance at Estanza's prone figure. "She is a real beauty," the purser continued, "but a bit dark for my taste. According to her papers she is Greek, but she looks Turkish to me."

The doctor was looking in his bag for smelling salts, which were the usual remedy for reviving unconscious ladies, when he realized he had never needed them before this voyage. He looked up at the purser with a rueful little smile.

"Johann," he addressed his friend in a fatherly tone, "the Mediterranean Sea is like a huge stew pot and the countries surrounding it have been trading and raiding for centuries. There is no pure race like in northern Europe. They are all a bunch of mongrels, but they do produce beautiful women."

Estanza was regaining consciousness. She opened her eyes and saw the doctor's mustached face glaring down at her. He smiled and patted her hand. Sitting on the edge of the sofa he waited for her to speak, but she just looked up at him anxiously.

"You fainted, Fräulein," the doctor explained. "I believe you need some food and drink."

Estanza looked into the kind brown eyes behind the thick glasses and tried to smile.

"I am so terribly hungry," she admitted.

"Johann," the doctor ordered his friend, the purser, "send the boy to the galley for some bread and butter and a glass of milk." Then he added, "A glass of wine might be better and some of that delicious goat cheese we picked up in Athens."

The doctor helped Estanza to the little washroom next to the purser's cabin. Then he left her to freshen up.

While Estanza ate the bread and cheese and gratefully drank the dry red wine, the men discussed where she would sleep on the ship. The doctor suggested the little "spare room" next to the infirmary.

"I will try to find the key," the doctor said. They agreed that it would be the best place for now, since the two bunks in the infirmary were occupied by sailors who had sustained serious injuries while on shore leave.

The purser's cabin boy brought Estanza's trunk, while the doctor guided her to the little cabin near the bow of the ship. They walked past the galley, the sailor's mess hall, the cargo hold, and the infirmary. A narrow door led to the closet like area that would be Estanza's quarters for the next two weeks.

There was space for her trunk under the bed. A narrow table with a kerosene lamp stood against one wall and a small sink with a spigot against the opposite wall. Having running water in the room was a luxury of which Estanza was very appreciative. She noticed two hooks on the wall beside the washstand and realized that would be the place to hang her clothes since there was no other facility available.

The doctor placed her carpet bag on the bed and turned to leave the room. "'The head,' which is what we call the water closet, is out in the hall," he said, as he prepared to leave. "There is a chamber pot under the bed for your convenience," he added. Then he was gone. She heard his footsteps next door in the infirmary.

The purser stood out in the hallway; clearly, he was eager to be on his way. "Dinner is served at eight o'clock," he said, and called over his shoulder, "You will hear the bell!"

Estanza closed the door and sat down on the narrow bed which was covered with fresh linen and a woolen blanket, bearing the royal navy crest. The room was clean. There was no sign of dust on the table; the lamp was freshly polished and the floor showed signs of recent scrubbing. It would pass the strict inspection her mother gave each hotel room before showing it to a guest.

The light was fading from the little porthole and Estanza found the matches and lit the lamp. The room looked friendlier, more cozy in the glow of the lamplight. Estanza began to think about what to wear to dinner that night and subsequently who would be her dinner companions.

The purser, on his way back to his quarters, began to think about the very same subject. Because of the strict class distinction between employers and employees, seating the present passengers of the Kaiser's yacht was somewhat of a dilemma for the purser, who, among his other duties, was in charge of seating everyone on board at the proper table for each meal. The young woman, who was now left to her own devices, as she was no longer under the protection of the von Stahlenbergs, was not an employee of a passenger, but a member of the state department. If she had been a man, he would seat her with the officers. But as she was a young woman, he wondered if it would be suitable to seat her at a table with six men without a chaperon. After about an hour of deliberation, the purser decided to consult with the captain. After all, he was in charge of the happenings on the ship and he had the final say on all matters.

Captain Gerhardt Holtzer was not happy with his present assignment. He had never sailed with female passengers; the Kaiser did not allow women aboard his yacht. Already there had been complications with Frau von Stahlenberg requesting separate quarters for the young Greek woman who was to be under her protection. He presumed it was due to some silly feminine spat and they would soon reconcile. (He had experience with these snits among his three sisters).

When the purser came to consult him about where to seat the young woman for her meals he was not in the mood to discuss the matter.

"Johann," the captain barked at the purser's question,

"*you* will need to make the assignments for the meals! I have vital matters of navigation to consider. These waters are new to me. The ports are full of hostile people who do not speak German and want exorbitant bribes for everything we need. Do *not* bother me with trivial matters!"

The purser was taken aback at the captain's angry reply, but he totally understood his frustration. All their previous voyages had been into the North Sea, the tranquil fjords of Norway, and villages along the Swedish coast. The men in the ports had resembled the German crew and most spoke a few words of German as well. When the *Hohenzollern* had entered the Mediterranean Sea the crew had become less disciplined—especially after going ashore in Greece. The beer-drinking Germans had been introduced to the local drink and underestimated its potency.

"You have no idea what I must contend with," the captain continued, his voice rising to a whine. "After only two shots of ouzo most men lose control of their motor skills. Two of the crew are already severely injured; one with a broken leg, the other might lose his eye. They will be totally useless for the rest of this misbegotten voyage."

The purser retreated out of the captain's cabin. He began to develop an idea for the seating arrangement.

The evening meal was an informal buffet since the main meal of the day was around noon. At eight o'clock, the head dining room waiter rang the bell, and the ladies began to troop into the various dining areas. The main dining room was for the aristocratic ladies, the lower dining room (a few steps down and divided from the main room by an ornate railing) was for their maids; on that same level, separated by a row of ferns, was the table for the officers. The purser guided Estanza, dressed in her black Sunday dress, to a seat next to the doctor. Then he stepped to the side of the stern woman in gray, the governess for the ambassador's two teenage daughters.

"The captain has decided that it is more suitable for you

two educated ladies to sit with the officers rather than at the working class table," he told her in a confidential whisper. Then he went on to introduce Estanza to Madame Volant, who acknowledged the girl with a nod and a slight frown on her pale face. It was obvious that she was displeased. Estanza wondered if she was reluctant to share the table with a dark skinned, foreign woman, because she made sure that the doctor was placed between them.

The men at the officers' table chatted amiably about the food and the weather. The women picked at their food and ate in silence. No one at that table glanced toward the upper level. The maids, sitting at a table nearer the kitchen, exchanged bits of gossip in hushed giggles. As soon as she had eaten her fill, and emptied a mug of beer, Estanza picked up an apple from the side board, nodded to the doctor and made her way to her cabin.

Chapter 7

Sitting on the narrow bed, Estanza looked around at the little room. Her practiced eye noticed the lack of items that were routinely furnished in the rooms at her family hotel. There was no glass on the washstand, nowhere to hang the folded towel beside the basin, no mirror anywhere in the room and—a most grievous oversight—no chair. It was then that she remembered the doctor's offer to furnish a key. The empty keyhole stared back at Estanza. She had not heard the doctor come back from dinner. Should she wait for him, go find him, or wait until tomorrow for the doctor to give her the key?

Her fatigue made the decision. All these needed items could wait until tomorrow. Estanza hung her dress on one of the hangers. (Her traveling outfit hung on the other one.) Removing her chemise and petticoats, she folded them into the trunk, took out her long-sleeved nightgown, and slipped it over her head. She decided to wear her pantaloons to bed as the room was getting chilly. The last thing she remembered to do was to unpin her hair. There would be no brushing her hair or her teeth. After sliding under the sheet with thoughts of Konrad trailing through her mind, Estanza fell into a deep sleep.

At first Estanza thought she was having a nightmare, but the hand over her mouth was real. It pressed down hard, jamming her lips against her teeth and stifling a scream in her throat. A man was straddling her prone body, his knees holding down her arms by her side. One hand was over her mouth and the other showed her a lethal-looking knife.

"If you make any sound, I will slit your brown throat," he

hissed into her face. Taking his hand away from her mouth, he released her arms from under his knees and jerked her nightshirt up over her head then used the sleeves to tie each of her wrists to the bed frame.

Still sitting on her, he began to rub and pinch her nipples. "Stop squirming," he ordered. Then he bent close to her ear, whispering, "We'll be gentle." His breath and his hair smelled from cooking grease and fried onions and another familiar odor Estanza couldn't place.

In the next moment she heard the sound of cloth being ripped and felt cool air on her groin. Someone was holding her legs apart. Something was being thrust into her.

"She getting wet enough yet?" the man sitting on her chest asked his partner.

"Oh, yeh!" gasped the man from between her legs. "I think she was a virgin."

After the sharp, but momentary pain, Estanza felt mostly fear, but it was mixed with outrage. In the next moment she went totally limp, as she realized that these men had total control of her and that her body was betraying her.

The men changed places. The man now sitting across her waist bent down and began to bite on her nipples. Then he sucked on the hard flesh, kneading her breasts. An unknown thrill began to mix with the pain coursing through her body, culminating in her groin.

The moonbeams came directly into the porthole now, and Estanza could see the faces of the men as they stood over her, while adjusting their trousers. She hoped she would recognize them when she saw them again. She knew where to look for them. There was no mistaking the stench of the German kitchen with its ubiquitous sauerkraut.

The men stood looking at her for another moment. The taller one bent down and whispered, "You are a good lay, little brown whore. We'll be back." Then he reached up and untied one of her wrists, picked up the knife from the table, and they were gone.

After a few minutes Estanza untied her other wrist and sat on the edge of bed. She began to cry, mourning the loss of her virginity, but her rage soon overcame her sorrow. That these men had treated her like an object to be used for their pleasure was beyond endurance. Her rage was palpable. She wanted to kill them, or have them killed.

Her next thought was to wake the doctor and tell him what had happened to her, but before she even stood up she came to the full realization of her position. She knew very well that a girl who was violated was usually ostracized, as if she had done something dishonorable. Few girls revealed a rape. The consequences were dire. They were sent away to the city (which meant to a brothel), to a convent, or were forced to marry the rapist. Even when the men in her family killed the rapist, the girl's fate was still sealed.

Sitting on the narrow bed with the shaft of light from the moon coming in through the porthole, Estanza remembered a speech the Headmistress had made at the memorial service for a fellow student. The girl had "fallen" from a cliff near her home after being dismissed in the middle of a school term. No reason was given for the dismissal, but everyone knew she was pregnant, after being raped by someone connected to the school. There had been no acknowledgement of who the rapist might have been. The administration was only concerned with the reputation of the school. But the words of the Headmistress had rung true.

> Alexia died of shame, a shame she did not need to feel. It was the man who should be punished, who should feel deep shame for brutalizing that child. Yet, in our society it is the girl who is wronged, and often the resulting bastard, who is shunned and shamed.
>
> Ladies, your honor is not between your legs. It is not what men do to you that can make you an object of shame. You are the only one who can besmirch your honor by how you deport yourself throughout your life.

When you try not to harm others, honor your parents, and deal honestly in all your relationships, you are an honorable person. Being attacked by a criminal cannot take that away from you.

The words resonated in her very soul as she recalled the hushed room, a few gasps from shocked parents who did not expect such graphic language from a school official in charge of deportment. Over the years Estanza had occasion to appreciate the wisdom and progressive insight of the headmistress.

The moonlight faded from the porthole and Estanza got up to light the lamp. Her pantaloons were on the floor, torn to shreds. She started to kick them under the bed, but then thought better of it. She began to run water into the washbasin and used the rags to wash herself. The water stung on the broken skin and she had to clench her teeth hard to keep from wincing out loud. She dried herself with the nightgown, slipped it over her head and went to put out the lamp. In the lamplight she noticed the blood stains on the sheet, pulled the blanket over them and got into bed. She reminded herself to get that key from the doctor first thing in the morning, and that she had two weeks left on the ship to get her revenge.

The fiends who raped her must be hurt and degraded as she was. When that was done she might feel clean again, able to go on with her life and put the matter behind her. She needed a plan.

With a rueful smile, Estanza thought of how she should have paid closer attention to the brave instructor who tried to teach the restless teenage girls the fundamentals of Logic and Critical Thinking. It had been a brief experiment, introduced by the Headmistress, denigrated by the school board and many parents. Although Aristotle and all the other ancient philosophers who were mostly Greek were part of a classic education worldwide, it was considered a waste of time and energy to teach logical thinking to females. They would not need such skills since they were not going to be lawyers or run governments (or anything else, for that matter). The men could always be relied on to resolve any problems. Women only needed to concentrate on running their households and raising healthy children. Once again, Estanza gave a brief tribute of thanks to the wisdom of the Headmistress who had prevailed in getting at least one term of Philosophy taught at her school. Now Estanza racked her brain and came up with a sequence of events that needed to be organized into a plan.

As usual, just before falling asleep, her thoughts went to Konrad. She resolved that by the time she saw him again, she must have completely closed this chapter of her life as if it had never happened.

Chapter 8

Estanza woke out of a deep sleep. *I had a terrible nightmare,* she told herself as her brain began to register her surroundings. When she began to move she realized that every bone in her body ached. She lay still, waiting for the pain in her bruised arms and legs to subside. Sitting up she became aware of the burning sensation between her legs. Trying to move was painful, but she knew it was the best thing to do for her bruises.

There was some kind of a commotion in the hall—men calling to each other, and then the sound of heavy objects on the deck above her. A sharp knock on the door startled her.

"Fräulein, are you awake?" the doctor's voice was heard above the din. "Breakfast is being served." After a moment's hesitation, "Please be so kind as to join us." Followed by another set of short, hard raps on the door.

"Thank you, Herr Doktor," Estanza managed to call out. Her throat was very dry and she knew she sounded strange. Cupping her hands under the faucet she managed to get a swallow of water. "Please go on without me. I need a few minutes to dress."

Ten minutes later Estanza—stiff and sore, but very erect—made her way to the lower dining room. She sat down next to the doctor, who was just finishing his open sandwich of Blutwurst and cheese. He washed it down with a half mug of warm beer, and then got up to leave.

"Good morning, Fräulein Estanza," he said amiably, bowing slightly from the waist. "We are anchored in the bay of Messina, off the coast of Sicily. The Captain is sending some life boats to bring fresh supplies from shore." He told her by way of explaining all the noise. Then he went up the stairs and he was gone. She had wanted to ask about the key, but in her condition she could not move fast enough to stop him.

Brilliant blue sky covered the windows of the dining room, then ocean and land came into view as the ship rocked back the other way. The waiter brought the usual basket of fresh rolls. Estanza breathed in the aroma and reached for the butter. The young man poured her half a cup of coffee (full cups were dangerous on a rocking ship). Then he poured a little hot milk into her cup. As she reached for the sugar cubes, leaning over the rolls to reach the bowl, a faint memory tiptoed around the edge of her mind.

Hungry though she was and as much as she liked these crusty rolls, something about them bothered her this morning.

"Are these the same type of rolls you served last night?" she asked the waiter.

"Yes, madam," was the young man's quick answer. "These are called Kaiserstollen; they are the Kaiser's favorite. They are baked fresh every morning in special ovens."

The waiter went to serve the two maids at the other table, then came back to pour more coffee for the two officers sitting across from Estanza. He then asked if she wanted more coffee.

"I need a glass to take to my room," she told the waiter. "May I take this one from the table?" she continued.

"Yes, madam," he answered. He smiled and began to clear the table.

Estanza took the large water tumbler from the table. She hesitated a moment before taking a roll out of the basket and putting it into the pocket of the apron she wore over the shapeless, school frock that morning.

While passing an open door to the deck she decided to step outside for some air. She was feeling a little queasy from watching the sky and water change places out the dining room window.

The yacht was at anchor in a narrow bay. Estanza saw brown hills flanking a curved beach. As the ship kept spinning around the anchor, a small city came into view and just as suddenly disappeared and only blue ocean was visible. The movement made her dizzy and she decided to return to her cabin.

It was only after Estanza took the glass and the Kaiserrolle out of her pocket that a faint spark of memory flared up and just as quickly died down. She had intended to write her parents a letter and mail it from the next port. As she sat down on the bed, and started to look for writing material in her bag, she remembered about getting a key for her door.

No one answered Estanza's loud knocks on the Infirmary door. She pushed down the handle and opened the door.

"Herr Doktor," she called softly, and then again a little louder. A groan came from a curtained area and Estanza stood still, looking around the room. She was hoping to find a board with a rack of keys, like at her parent's hotel. Since there were no keys in sight, she tried to look into the drawers but found they were all locked. She decided to go back to her little room and wait for the doctor to come back.

Upon entering the room she saw the Kaiserrolle and the ember of memory sparked. It was the odor of freshly baked rolls that had lingered in the room after the men left. She had smelled it on their hair, mixed with other foods odors, but the yeast dough was unmistakable.

The SMY *Hohenzollern* was leaving the bay of Messina and Estanza decided to go on deck to watch the departure. A cool breeze brushed her hair back from her face and she took deep breaths of the soft and salty air. She walked carefully around the coils of rope on the deck, avoiding the puddles in her way. Strolling all around the promenade deck took about ten minutes and Estanza made several turns enjoying the opportunity to stretch her legs, although there were still sore spots along the inside of her thighs.

A soft bell tone announced the noon meal and Estanza made her way to the lower dining room. Even with the portholes open, the warm Italian sun was heating up the room. The huge jugs of cold beer on each table were a welcome accompaniment to the ample platters of food.

Estanza noticed that there were two new men at the table where the sailors sat. Then her attention went to the table where the lady's maids were making more noise than usual. It was evident that the younger girls had drunk too much beer. As their voices got louder, their laughter filled the room. One of the new men at the next table got up and shouted, "Shut your big mouths, you rowdy bitches."

The girls looked embarrassed and began to eat between stifled giggles. The man who had shouted addressed his tablemates in a raised voice, "The Kaiser often said that women should remain at home and tend to the children."

"What if they do not have children?" one of the more daring girls called out.

"Then the men must provide them with some," he laughed.

At the mention of the Kaiser the men at Estanza's table looked up. The governess, who was French, had little use for the crowned heads that ruled so much of Europe, and kept eating. Estanza had looked up to see who had spoken, curious about the accent. Where had she heard it before? Their eyes met for a split second before Estanza looked back down at her plate. She did not look up again during the meal and hastily left the dining room, deciding to go back out to the promenade deck and take a few more turns around the ship. The man who had yelled at the girls sounded like one of the men who had attacked her. He also had a similar mustache. The tall man beside him had the reddish hair that she remembered from the man who had tied her wrists. Forcefully she pushed down the anger rising in her mind. She must keep a clear head if she was going to successfully avenge herself.

After the first lap around the deck she met Ensign Schmidt coming toward her. He greeted her amicably and started to walk along beside her. When she stumbled over one of the coiled ropes on the deck he placed a hand under her elbow. Estanza jerked away as if he had struck her. Ensign Schmidt sensed her discomfort and dropped his hand to his side, but kept walking.

"Fräulein Nikiolopolis," he said, carefully pronouncing the foreign name, "the crew members of this ship are all honorable Germans in the service of the Kaiser. We would do nothing to offend a lady."

Estanza thought about an answer to this protestation. She had surmised that Ensign Schmidt had grown up in a respectable home. He always stood when ladies came into the room or rose to leave the table. She stopped walking and faced the young man.

"Not all the men on this ship seem to be honorable Germans. That ruffian at lunch spoke with a strange accent," she said, in what she hoped sounded like a conversational tone.

Ensign Schmidt cleared his throat as his deep blue eyes looked directly into Estanza's flashing dark brown ones. "That was an unfortunate outburst at the noon meal," he said and continued, as he could see she expected him to say more. "Those two men are not German, as you noticed. They are actually Austrian, and a bit rough around the edges. But they are the Kaiser's special bakers. They make those delicious rolls we all enjoy so much." He smiled apologetically. "I do hope they did not offend you too much. You may not see them again during our voyage, as they rarely come to eat in the dining room."

I will see them again very soon, Estanza was thinking. She excused herself and went to her cabin. She needed time to think, to make a plan and a back-up plan. One of the first things she decided to do was explore the place where the bakers worked.

By now it was near the time when the cooks would be preparing the meal to be served in the evening. Estanza went to the galley, ambled in nonchalantly. If anyone stopped her or asked what she wanted she had a few ready replies. (Getting a glass for her mistress, returning a plate, needing smelling salts, or just being lost.)

The galley was a busy place with six work stations, one for each cook. There was a curtained archway at the end of the long, narrow room. Since no one paid any attention to her, Estanza moved along slowly. The men were all facing away from her—preparing plates, cutting, washing, mixing, and so forth. When she reached the dusty, gray curtains, she parted them slightly and saw what she surmised to be the special area designated for baking the Kaiser rolls. On one wall was a floor to ceiling oven with three segments on top of each other and each with its own door. A table took up the rest of the space in the square room. Baking pans lined one side and a floured area took up the other half of the table. A huge rolling pin lay near one edge and a long, pointed knife lay beside it. The bakers were gone for the day.

Quickly Estanza made her way back out through the galley and into the corridor. She needed more information about the baking process and the bakers. She made a decision about what she wanted to do. She would have only one chance to do it.

Deep in thought, she entered the lower dining room where most of the tables were already being served. She took her place beside the doctor, nodded a greeting and took a roll out of the silver basket near her place.

"These rolls are the best type of bread I have ever eaten," she said to no one in particular.

The doctor gave her an appreciative look and nodded his reply. "Do they bake them fresh every morning?" she asked the doctor.

"Of course," was his quick reply. "The bakers are specially selected by the Kaiser himself. They are the best in Europe." He smiled at Estanza as he broke a roll in half.

"I noticed that they are available for breakfast by seven o'clock. They must work all night to get them ready by that hour." Estanza hoped she sounded casual.

"Those dedicated and talented men start work at four in the morning every day they are aboard. At the end of each voyage we send up a special cheer to show our appreciation." The doctor continued.

At this point their meals were being served and they ate in silence. Twice Estanza wanted to ask the doctor for the key to her room, but he was busy talking to the governess and then turned his attention to Ensign Schmidt, who happened to sit across from them.

Later that evening, she asked the cabin boy who served the doctor if he knew of an extra chair she could use in her cabin. It would need to be a narrow, ladder-back, wooden chair. He said he would try to find one for her. In less than an hour he brought her exactly the type of chair that would fit under the narrow table by her bed.

That night and every night after that she braced the back of the chair under the door handle with two legs on the floor and her trunk braced against them. As far as she knew, no one tried to open the door during the rest of the time on the ship. This seemed a better alternative than the elusive key.

With her door secured, Estanza sat in her room that evening after dinner trying to visualize her revenge upon her attackers. She fingered her sewing scissors, speculating about the sharpness of the pointed end. Gingerly she pushed a fingertip against the point and winced as the dagger-like edge pricked her skin. She slipped them into her apron pocket. Next she wound her lapel watch, as she did each evening. The daylight was beginning to fade and she lit the lamp. She took out her French language book. She enjoyed studying French. Unlike German and Greek, languages in which each letter was always fully pronounced and in the same way, French required memorization. One could never tell how a word would be pronounced, and many letters, especially at the end of a word, were silent or barely audible down in the throat.

Near midnight, Estanza had to fight to stay awake. She

ran water from the tap and splashed it over her face. She decided to comb and braid her hair, roll it around her head, and fasten it with combs. That exercise took about an hour. Finally she took to pacing the small space beside her bed. She walked to the head and back down to the foot and tried to visualize what she had in mind to do to the two bakers. Every few minutes she took the scissors out of her pocket. They were barely six inches from end to end, but they fit into her hand just at the exact angle she would need. If she succeeded, those men would never molest another female.

At last, the little watch showed that it was 4:30 a.m. Moving the chest and chair, Estanza slipped out of her room and walked to the galley. She heard faint noises from behind the dusty curtains at the archway. In what was the special roll baking area, she saw the two men. The tall one had his back to her preparing long rolls of dough. The short one stood at the left side of the table cutting the dough into pieces, putting them on a large sheet. There was already a batch of rolls in the ovens. The aroma filled the room.

The short man turned toward the oven to his right. For a moment Estanza thought he was looking right at her, but his attention was on the heavy oven door of the top oven. He stood on his tip toes, reached up with gloved hands and started to pull out the heavy baking sheet with the baked rolls.

Estanza crouched down and tiptoed out from behind the curtain. She swung her right arm out, tightening her grip on the scissors as she brought them around into the crotch of the baker. She drew them out in one motion and, still in a crouch, moved behind the tall man. He had turned slightly to his left, keeping his right hip against the table. He was staring at his partner, who was slowly sinking to his knees beside the oven, rolls tumbling around his bowed head. He didn't see Estanza as she crouched behind him. From this position there was no chance to reach her target, but the man's hand was spread out on the table almost at her eye level. Without hesitation, Estanza drove the scissors into the back of his right hand.

They lodged deep into the table. Small drops of blood fell on Estanza's hand as she tried, in vain, to pull out the scissors. Before the tall man could turn in her direction she slipped behind the curtains and ran out of the galley.

Walking down the hall she heard footsteps and voices behind her. Some of the cooks were coming to work. Back inside her room, with a pounding heart, Estanza braced the chair against her door and sat down on the bed. By the light of the lamp she saw that there was blood on her hand and a few spots on her apron. With shaking hands she washed off the blood and rinsed out the fabric.

The next sound she heard was someone knocking on the infirmary door, calling for the doctor. A half hour later there was scuffling and men's voices coming from the infirmary. She tried to make out what was being said, but the voices were muffled and very low. Estanza suddenly felt exhausted. She undressed, washed her hands again, checked to see if she had washed all the blood from the apron, and got into bed. In less than five minutes she was asleep.

Chapter 9

It was almost noon before Estanza woke up. She heard the sound of the bell announcing the mid-day meal and hurriedly got ready to leave the cabin. Her hair was still tightly wound in the braid around her head. She gave it a quick pat and, pushing the chair aside, stepped into the corridor outside her door. The ship was moving rapidly through the water, bouncing over waves, making the walk to the dining room a contest with the walls on either side.

The people at her table were already busy eating. The doctor was not at his usual place. Ensign Schmidt was also missing. Two of the officers were there along with the governess. Estanza sat down and reached for the usual silver basket of rolls. There was one slightly burned roll and another that looked very pale. She decided to forego the rolls. One of the waiters brought her a plate of potatoes and sauerkraut covered with caraway seeds and sliced onions. A mug of beer appeared at her place and she drank it down gratefully.

One of the officers was talking to the governess, who had obviously asked him a question. "We are going to be making an unexpected stop in Palermo," he was explaining. "The captain has sent a message to the harbor master. We will be allowed to anchor just outside the harbor as we have not reserved a berth."

"Is there a problem with the ship?" the governess asked.

"No, of course not," the officer replied. "There has been a regrettable accident in the galley. Two of our bakers have been badly hurt. The infirmary is not equipped to handle such serious cases."

The governess seemed to have lost interest in the subject, and the officers soon left the table. Estanza ate a few bites of the unappetizing food on her plate, drank the rest of her beer, nodded to the Governess, who ignored her as usual, and went out onto the deck. It was very warm, even with the breeze produced by the fast moving ship. She stopped to look over the side at the blue/green water swishing by. She tried to imagine what it would feel like to be immersed in its cool embrace.

She went below decks, quickening her pace as she passed the infirmary. In her cabin she took off her shoes and lay down again on her unmade bed. After an hour, Estanza decided to distract herself by studying her French. The time went by quickly and she was surprised to hear the bell for the evening meal. Reluctantly she put on her shoes and debated whether she should go to the dining room at all. Although she felt a bit seasick she was curious about what was being said about the bakers; also she knew the best thing for the nausea was a few bites of food. The ship had slowed down considerably and getting to the dining room was much easier than her earlier trip.

Ensign Schmidt was present this evening and he stood, as usual, when Estanza approached the table. She tried to smile but she knew it looked like a painful grimace, because he looked concerned and asked her if she was well.

"I'm not well at all," Estanza told him, trying not to sound too plaintive.

"You will be better in a short time," he assured her. "We will be dropping anchor in a few hours. Two of the men need to go to a hospital in Palermo."

The governess who had previously barely spoken to Estanza chimed in. "The First Mate told me that the two bakers must have had a drunken brawl and stabbed each other. I am not surprised. They were those two Austrian ruffians who made those insulting remarks yesterday."

Estanza nodded to the governess to show she had heard

her and took a few bites of the hard-boiled egg on her plate. The sailors at their table were subdued as were the maids at theirs. It was a quiet meal and no one said anything about the absence of the usually ubiquitous rolls.

That night, long after dark, Estanza heard the anchor chain rattle past her window. Soon there were noises coming from the infirmary and she could hear the splash of a boat being lowered into the water. Later she heard the sound of another boat being lowered, she became curious and went out into the corridor and toward the hold, where she heard the sound of crates being moved. The cargo doors were open and a big crate was being lowered into a waiting row boat. From where she stood, Estanza could see two rowboats heading toward the twinkling lights of Palermo Harbor. Then the cargo door slammed shut, being pulled up from inside the hold and all was quiet.

Opening the porthole, Estanza saw that it was a warm, windless night. Shafts of light from the quarter moon reflected on the calm water. She decided to go up to the promenade deck for some fresh air. Carefully she stepped around the ropes on the deck and then noticed the rope ladder fastened with metal hooks to the railing. With a sudden longing, Estanza looked down at the glassy surface below her. She pulled off her shoes, then drew her dress and chemise up over her head in one swift motion, kicked off her pantaloons and carefully folded her clothes, placing her shoes on top of the pile. Quickly she climbed down the rope ladder and into the silky, cool water. She saw the anchor chain and decided the safest plan was to swim around it and back to the ladder. The sheer pleasure of feeling weightless and free was briefly interrupted by the pain of the salt water on the broken skin between her legs. She welcomed the pain. It had a purifying effect on her body and her mind. She began to feel clean again. *This is like going through a baptismal cleansing,* she told herself. She swam around the anchor chain, and then came back to the side of the ship and floated on her back, letting the water wash over her. For a few more minutes she enjoyed the soothing lap of the water on her base skin, until the stinging sensation in her crotch became too uncomfortable.

With a few strokes she was next to the rope ladder, and when she came level with the deck railing a hand reached out to her. Without thinking, she allowed herself to be helped over the side of the ship. A short gasp escaped her lips as she stood stark naked in front of the man who had helped her aboard.

Ensign Schmidt, without a word, released her arm, turned his back on her, and continued walking the rounds of his watch. Estanza studied his retreating back for a moment, then used her apron to dry off, and slipped on her dress, picked up her shoes and undergarments, and ran to her cabin. Once inside she fastened the chair under the door handle, removed her dress, and washed off the sticky salt water with pitchers of water from the faucet.

When she was satisfied that she was really clean, she slipped on her nightdress (she had washed it out thoroughly earlier that day). Then she unbraided the coils of hair around her head. The long strands were still damp and sticky and needed washing. It was impossible to get a comb through the tangled curls. She was too tired to do the washing now; it would need to wait till morning. Lying on her back in the narrow bed, Estanza resolved to put the frightful occurrences of the past two days out of her mind forever. She would concentrate on Konrad.

In a few minutes she was asleep with his name on her lips.

Chapter 10

The banging of a hard object against the side of the ship woke Estanza from a lovely dream of being in Konrad's arms. She stretched luxuriously, and sat up. Through the high porthole she saw a clear, blue sky—even a ray of sunshine. That meant it was late morning and she had surely missed breakfast. From the noises that were coming from above her, she surmised that the men had come back with the lifeboat.

She got up slowly, expecting pain in her groin and other bruised parts of her body, but this morning she was almost pain-free. The ocean's water had done its job. She felt for her hair and realized that she had unbraided it the night before. It stuck to her head in a sticky, salty mess of snarls that would take hours to untangle. Running water into the basin and into the pitcher, she dunked her head into the cold liquid and emptied the pitcher over her head. Much of the salt washed out, and after a few more dunkings she could run a comb through most of it, but the ends were snarled beyond recourse. Automatically she reached for her sewing basket, and then realized the scissors were not there. The scene in the bakery swam before her closed eyes and she quickly opened them. The tangles would yield to the water. She would continue to soak the ends. After another hour her hair was smooth and ready for the brush.

The bell rang for the noon meal while Estanza was still brushing her hair. She tied it back with a piece of string she had found in the sewing basket and finished dressing. The school dress was much too heavy and she wished she had another garment that was more suitable for summer.

Estanza was the last person into the lower dining room and everyone looked up as she came in, but it was Ensign Schmidt who met her eyes as he stood until she was seated.

The dish the waiter set in front of her looked like schnitzel, but upon cutting into it she was surprised to see it was not meat. Ensign Schmidt must have noticed her surprise, because he seemed to be addressing her when he said, "This dish is the national food of Sicily. It's called eggplant." He pointed to a shiny, purple, pear-like object lying in the middle of the table.

"Isn't it a lovely fruit?" The doctor said, pointing to the object with his fork. "Take a taste," he urged Estanza, who had her fork almost to her mouth, but seemed to hesitate.

"I love the color," Ensign Schmidt murmured and then with a quick glance at Estanza, added, "It reminds me of the beauty one can see in the Sicilian nights."

She understood his meaning and hoped she wasn't blushing. To his everlasting credit, Ensign Schmidt never again alluded to their midnight meeting.

The eggplant was delicious and Estanza enjoyed every bite. It was one of the best meals she had aboard the *Hohenzollern* during their two-week voyage. She noticed there were no rolls on the table, but a few slices of Italian-style white bread were left in the basket. She began to realize that it would be a long time, perhaps never, that the events of her ordeal would fade from her memory.

The purser came into the dining room and asked everyone to remain while he made an important announcement. The room went quiet as the diners stopped eating.

"Tomorrow is Sunday and the Captain will lead a prayer service after breakfast in the grand salon," he announced in a louder than necessary voice. "Everyone on the ship is expected to attend and the service will not start until everyone is present." He cleared his throat and asked, "Do you understand?" This was greeted by silent nods from all present.

Then he continued: "The ship will be at dock later tonight in the Spanish port of Malaga. It is necessary to stop because we will need to take on water." Here his voice became an octave lower and he added: "Having so many ladies aboard means we are using much more water than is usual for this amount of time at sea." He took a quick glance around the dining room, looking at each female in turn. Then he clicked his heels and went out.

The conversation in the dining room continued and everyone at the officer's table wanted to know about the doctor's adventure ashore.

The doctor began: "We took the two wounded men to the hospital nearest the dock. When the two nuns who opened the gate heard we were German, they slammed the heavy doors shut in our faces. You can believe we were very surprised at this behavior from sisters of mercy. Our purser knows a few words of Italian and he began to shout that we had wounded men here and desperately needed help. After a few minutes a priest came to the gate. He spoke German with a strange accent, but we understood that he was apologizing for the nuns. He opened the gates and showed us the way to a treatment room, then went into the hall to telephone for a doctor. They do have telephones, but no electricity.

While we waited for the doctor the tall man regained consciousness. We thought he might tell us what had happened but instead he babbled about bad luck allowing women on board a ship, how they turn into cats and kill men. Then he fainted again. He had lost a lot of blood, as had the short one. The short one must have stabbed the tall one's hand after he was attacked. His wounds were horrible—I can't say anymore in front of the ladies. But he died before the doctor could get to him."

A gasp arose from most of the people listening to this story. The governess, sitting next to the doctor, looked down at her empty plate suppressing a chuckle.

Estanza wanted desperately to leave, but she hesitated to

call attention to herself. So she sat quietly like all of the other people in the dining room.

The doctor looked around to see if he still had an audience and continued his story: "Presently, the Sicilian doctor came. He looked suspiciously at the three of us. First at the purser and especially at me, after I told him I was a doctor. He sneered at us, said he was writing a note to the captain. I don't know what it said exactly, but two men set out from the dock with a motorized little boat. Only after the boat had been dispatched to the *Hohenzollern*, did that Sicilian doctor look at the patients. He declared the short man as dead and told the nun that was cowering in a corner to call the burial squad.

After a cursory glance at the tall man's hand, he told us that it had been ripped by something sharp. (Probably the knife we found on the floor next to him.) He doubted he could save the hand, or even the man. Then two nuns came and took the patient away on a stretcher. We were told to wait in another room for further direction."

The doctor took a drink and drew a deep breath before continuing his story. After drawing himself upright, he continued: "While the three of us waited for the men to come back from the ship, the priest asked us to sit down on the benches that lined the wall. He wanted to explain the behavior of the two nuns who had been at the gate. He told us that these nuns had just come back from a mission to a German colony in West Africa."

He leaned in and said, "They were traumatized by the brutality they witnessed. They are staying here for a few weeks and then will return to their mother house in Milan. In fact, the head of the mission has sent a report to Kaiser Wilhelm II about the cruel treatment of the natives by his administrator. We were startled to hear such things and wanted to ask questions, but just then the motor boat arrived back from our ship. We watched the men unload a large crate, like the ones in our hold. Obviously, the Sicilians appreciate

Greek art."

Again there were gasps from some of the listeners. The doctor left off his story while he looked meaningfully around the room. Estanza and the officers understood what his glance meant to convey. They knew what was in the hold.

Shifting his mood, the doctor continued, "As we started back to the ship we had to pass through a farmer's market that was just getting organized. It was barely daylight. Those Sicilian bandits like to sell their wares in the dark. The purser suggested we buy some supplies while we were there. He had been in these waters before and knew about the eggplant. He even showed the chef how to prepare it."

"So the trip to shore wasn't a total waste," quipped one of the sailors at the next table.

The doctor drank one more mug of beer and got up from the table. Everyone else in the dining room followed him out.

On her way to her cabin, Estanza tried to get the bakers and their fate out of her mind. She had to force herself to think of something else—something trivial, something enjoyable. She couldn't strip and jump into the sea; the ship was traveling at full speed and it was broad daylight. She went up on deck. A warm wind made the heat bearable, but after one turn around the deck, Estanza's bodice was moist with perspiration.

It was then that she began to think seriously about reworking her black dress into a more suitable garment. She remembered how some of her schoolmates from affluent families went to Paris every summer to buy the latest fashions. *Those French women know how to dress,* she thought, as she rounded the bow of the ship. A wisp of blue smoke blew across her face and she felt a pang of nostalgia. In the next moment, she saw Madame Volant sitting on a huge coil of rope, in the shadow of a lifeboat.

Madame Volant quickly lowered the cigarette she had been smoking and frowned at Estanza, who totally understood that look. Some of her friends in school had taken up the forbidden habit and knew expulsion would follow discovery. Nevertheless, they smoked in various hiding places. Estanza had stumbled upon some of them in corners of the library and the stairwells, and they had the same look as she now saw on Madame Volant's face, who made no move to put out the cigarette. The cornered look had left her face and she gazed up at Estanza expectantly.

In her best French, Estanza addressed Madame Volant, hoping to sound casual. "The smoke from your cigarette reminded me of my father. He smoked the same brand." She was rewarded with a quick smile and another blue puff of smoke.

Madame Volant stood up and offered Estanza a cigarette from a silver case, which she drew out of her skirt pocket. Estanza thanked her, explained she didn't yet smoke and started to continue her walk, when Madame Volant asked would Estanza mind if she walked along.

"Not at all," was her quick reply. "It would be my pleasure."

The two women began to walk toward the stern. After a few minutes Estanza had an idea. She would ask Madame Volant about what to do with the black dress to make it more fashionable and suitable for summer wear.

"Madame Volant, I would like your advice." Estanza began,

"Yes," interjected the older woman thoughtfully.

Estanza had to think a few moments on how to phrase her question in French. With an effort to sound deferential, she described her old-fashioned, black dress and how she hoped it could be altered.

Madame Volant stopped walking and turned to Estanza. "What fabric is this dress?" she asked, clearly showing an interest in the project.

"It is organdy. A diaphanous fabric, but lined with black muslin." Estanza's knowledgeable reply impressed Madame Volant.

"Perhaps I can help you. Can you bring it to my stateroom?" she asked with a pleased look, which softened her usually stern face.

"Whenever you would like," was Estanza's breathless reply.

"I have Saturday afternoons free and my hobby is sewing. So go get it now. You will find me in cabin 5," Madame Volant said, and started to move toward the nearest door.

Chapter 11

While dashing down the stairs to her little cabin, Estanza tried to picture what the black dress would look like after an alteration. Although she had folded it carefully, it was a wrinkled mess as she pulled it out from the small trunk.

Cabin 5 was the last one on the stateroom deck. The rooms became smaller as the number went up. Madame Volant had only a sitting room and a bedroom, and shared the washroom in the corridor. Estanza couldn't help but compare these quarters with her own little space.

Madame Volant had taken out her well-equipped sewing box and was threading a needle with strands of black thread when Estanza came into the sitting room.

"Put on the dress," Madame Volant directed.

Estanza obeyed and struggled out of her uniform garment and into the black gown.

Madame Volant walked slowly around Estanza then took a pair of huge scissors out of the sewing box.

"Please tell me what you plan to do," Estanza said tentatively in her primitive French.

"All right," said Madame Volant. "Come over to the table." She took a sheet of paper from her writing desk and began to draw. A dress appeared on the paper. It had puffy sleeves that came to just above the elbow, a square neckline, a wide band around the waist and another around the skirt, just below the knees. The hemline would be just above the ankles.

"This is the latest summer style from Paris." She explained. "It is suitable for girls your age. By the way, how old are you?"

"I am nineteen, Madam." Estanza replied while looking at the drawing with wonder.

"It is called a 'Hobble' skirt," Madame Volant went on. "It does restrict the stride and forces young women to take smaller steps. That is considered more lady-like, but like so many ideas that hinder women, it was designed by a man. I believe that your dress would lend itself to an alteration to this style. Shall we proceed?"

Estanza smiled and whispered a grateful, "Yes, please."

With a few quick slashes of the scissors, the dress was transformed.

"Do you know how to sew?" Madame Volant asked Estanza.

"Not professionally, Madame," Estanza sounded apologetic.

"Well, then you will stitch up the hemline and I will work on the sleeves and the neckline." Madame Volant sounded like a person used to giving orders and getting things done.

She laid out the fabric that had been cut from the hemline, making two wide bands to be attached during the fitting. Estanza put on the dress and pranced around the room, admiring herself in the mirror.

"You must hold still now while I pin the bands." Madame Volant was smiling, but she sounded firm. "I will ask one of the chambermaids to press out the wrinkles." Then she left the room through an adjoining door which led to the spacious bedroom of her two wards.

Estanza took off the dress and, putting her school smock back on, sat down to wait for Madame to come back. She took the opportunity to look around the room. It was sparsely furnished with a desk, a table and two chairs. A cabinet with two shelves and a drawer stood under the porthole. There was an assortment of books on the shelf. The titles were hard to read because they were lying down in stacks. She surmised that it was safer to lay them down rather than have them upright because of the movement of the ship. She took a peek into the next room, where she saw a narrow bed, a wardrobe against the wall by the door, and a small dressing table under another porthole. A framed picture on the dressing table caught her eye, and she went a little closer to see it more clearly. It was the picture of a teenage girl. Estanza guessed it was probably one of Madame's recent wards.

After a few minutes Madame Volant returned with one of the chambermaids who was carrying a small coal burner and two flatirons. She made space on the table and brought in two towels from the bathroom, laid them out on the table and smoothed out the dress on top of them.

In the meantime Madame Volant had placed the burner with its ceramic base on the desk, skillfully lit the coals with matches she carried in her pocket (next to the cigarettes), and put one of the irons on the grill. To Estanza, she looked very skilled and efficient. For a half an hour the maid ironed the hems, seams and the long bands, preparing them for the sewing process.

Madame Volant ordered tea from the steward who hovered outside her cabin. In a few minutes he brought a tea cart with the tea service and several biscotti. Madame Volant prepared the tea, and the two women sat at the desk, sipping and munching while they waited for the maid to finish the ironing. Then they helped the maid, an elderly lady with gnarled hands and a face to match, pack up the irons and burner. Estanza held the door for her as she left and caught a glimpse into the next room, with its large windows, white satin-covered beds and several upholstered chairs. The contrast between the two rooms was startling.

The two women spread the dress on the bed with the bodice toward the head and the hem toward the foot. Madame Volant drew a spool from her sewing basket, deftly threaded four needles with long black threads, pinned two of the threaded needles to her own bodice and handed the other two to Estanza.

"Start on the hem near a seam," she instructed, "while I work on gathering the sleeves. The neckline will require cross-stitching to make it look decorative."

They worked in silence for a few minutes. Madame Volant made rapid, professional stitches while Estanza made slow, but even progress on the hemline. With their heads down, concentrating on their work Estanza began to think about how they met. She remembered how her friendly greeting was met with a frown. Madame Volant had looked at her as if she had tasted something very disagreeable. This afternoon she had been pleasant, even warm, and certainly accommodating, about altering the dress for her. Estanza hated to break the friendly mood, but her curiosity won out.

"Madame Volant," she began, "I need to ask you something."

The older woman looked up and their eyes met. Estanza quickly lowered her head and kept stitching as rapidly as she was able. She continued talking before she lost her nerve. "When we met at that first dinner aboard the ship, you frowned at me as if you had just tasted something very unpleasant. Did I do something to displease you?"

"Please, call me Renée," Madame Volant said, without looking up from her sewing. "What I am about to tell you is very confidential and requires that we be trusted friends from now on."

There was a moment of silence as the women looked up at each other. Their eyes met and they realized that a decision was about to be made concerning their future. (In Europe of that era, only childhood friends called each other by their first names. Friendships formed in adulthood required a more formal address. Even married couples who were not acquainted during their childhood addressed each other by their last names. But, as with all customs and traditions, there were exceptions when a strong bond developed between two adults.)

"May I call you Estanza?" Madame Volant then queried.

"Yes, of course." Estanza replied and waited for further words from her new friend.

Renée continued speaking in a low, monotone voice and Estanza had to concentrate to hear the words.

"I heard from my employer, the Ambassador's wife, that you had displeased Frau von Stahlenberg, and she was withdrawing her offer to give you her protection. In fact, she asked if one of the other two ladies would volunteer to be your chaperon. They all declined and the purser was told to find you a cabin and suitable dining companions. After meeting you and hearing you talk with the other diners at our table, I began to wonder what exactly you had done to arouse the ire of Frau von Stahlenberg. I asked the maids about you, and they assured me that it was not an unusual occurrence for their employer to have a falling out with a female friend. When I asked about your honesty the lady's maid assured me that you were not a thief. The girl said that her employer often had clashes of personality with other women."

Renée continued: "On the third night at sea Frau von Stahlenberg came to dinner and was very pleasant. After the meal we played cards with my two wards. Their mother had departed for the larger salon for after dinner drinks and musical entertainment with the officers. Erna is fourteen and Else is twelve and they play a wicked game of Skat. Erna excused herself after a couple of hours, said she wanted to write letters and read a book, but Else stayed on and played a two handed set with Frau von Stahlenberg. I was very tired by then and I dozed off on the plush sofa. Finally Frau von Stahlenberg told me to go to bed, saying that she would get Else back to the cabin in a little while. So I went to bed."

Estanza had listened so far with her head bent over her work, but now she looked up with interest. Afraid of what she might hear next, Renée had also looked up and once again their eyes met as an understanding grew between them.

"I was sound asleep, when near midnight I was awakened by a softly sobbing Else. I sat up, put an arm around her and asked her if she was ill. She shook her head. I then asked if her sister had done something to hurt her. She only kept on crying and eventually fell asleep next to me. It is a very narrow bed, as you can see, and I thought it best to take

Else back to her room. She was still dressed in the clothes she wore to dinner, but her shoes and socks were gone. Later, I noticed some of her undergarments were missing."

Again there was a long pause in the narration, as Renée finished off one sleeve and started on the other. She resumed speaking, and her voice was even lower. "I insisted that Else brush her teeth and wash her hands and face. Then, while I was brushing her hair out in the dressing room, I asked her again what was making her cry. This time, the story came tumbling out. I could imagine how frightened this innocent child must have been when a grown woman tried to fondle her private parts, while holding her down with passionate kisses. After that night, I suspected that whatever unpleasantness had occurred was not due to your behavior."

Estanza had the feeling she was blushing, but Renée did not look up from her sewing. They sewed in silence while each of them finished her area of the dress and kept her thoughts to herself.

Finally, as she stitched the last corner of the neckline Renée spoke again. "Were my suspicions correct, Estanza?"

Estanza only nodded and continued sewing. Tears were running down her cheeks, but she was unaware that she was weeping.

"There are bad people in this world, my dear girl." Renée had come to stand over Estanza, and she put a hand on her shoulder. She handed her a handkerchief and sat down on a chair to wait for Estanza to finish the hem. When it was done, Estanza took off her school smock for another fitting of the dress. Renée saw the bruises on her arms and shoulders and gave a slight gasp. Estanza became aware of what she was looking at and hurriedly put on the dress.

Renée pinned the band on the skirt where it would cause the least restriction and adjusted the sash around Estanza's slim waist, pinning the place it would be hooked. Then she helped Estanza out of the dress trying not to look at the bruises that had startled her before.

The two women were startled when they heard the dinner bell ring.

"We can finish the bands after dinner." Renée said as they left the room.

Dinner was a short affair. Most of the crew was on deck to prepare for the docking in Malaga, which occurred during the dinner. The usual sounds could be heard as the ship was tied up and the cargo door lowered. It would be a noisy night.

Renée and Estanza returned to Renée's room to finish the dress. They found that the work went much faster when the ship was not rocking. It was easier to talk without needing to concentrate on each stitch.

"Tell me about yourself," Renée said in her schoolteacher manner.

Estanza looked up, but Renée had her head down, awaiting her reply.

"I had an unremarkable childhood in the small town of Distomo, Greece," Estanza began her narrative. When she said, "Distomo," a cold chill passed through her body. It was only momentary, but many years later she had cause to remember that feeling. She went on to tell about her experiences at Arsakeio Girls' School and how she fell in love with German literature, but omitted the fact that she also fell in love with a German.

"Besides typing and other office and accounting skills, the school offered language courses. The graduates were required to be proficient in at least three languages."

Renée looked up from the sash she was working on and smiled at Estanza. "You speak French well; perhaps English also?" she asked expectantly.

"Yes, but German is my best language," was Estanza's quick reply, first in English and then in French.

"French is difficult to pronounce for foreigners, but you do quite well," Renée said.

"This dress has become a lovely and fashionable garment, and I am very grateful to you for helping me," Estanza said in flawless French.

"Bravo!" Renée cheered. "You speak German with hardly an accent also. How is your English?"

"I have had problems with English," Estanza admitted. "It is not precise and there are so many words that have multiple meanings." With a deep sigh she went on to explain that English was very important because it was mostly English archeologists who stayed at her parents' hotel.

"While you are in Germany you will need mostly German, but knowing French can be helpful in the diplomatic world. I studied Greek in the university, but could use a refresher course," Renée said.

At these last words Estanza looked up from the band she was stitching and smiled. "I would be happy to help with the Greek as a way for me to repay you for your kindness."

The women looked at each other. Without a conscious effort they were forming a bond of friendship that would become stronger despite long separations and the very different lives they led.

Chapter 12

The first thing Estanza saw when she opened her eyes on Sunday morning was the black, hobble-skirt dress hanging from a hook by her narrow bed. She lay in bed for a few more minutes admiring the garment that had developed from the dowdy, old-fashioned dress it had been. With a quick look at her watch and at the full daylight streaming in from the porthole, she washed, brushed her hair, and slipped into the black dress. Piling her hair on top of her head in what she hoped was a fashionable style, she sighed with frustration at not having a mirror. There were many mirrors in the grand salon where the prayer meeting would be held; however, she wanted to see herself before she entered that room. It was not to be.

The looks the officers gave her when she came to breakfast made Estanza feel uneasy. Renée and the doctor just smiled at her and continued eating. She wished she could see herself in a mirror. When she finally entered the grand salon for the Sunday prayer service, she was pleased with her reflection in the many mirrors.

Chairs were available for all the ladies. Plush, upholstered ones for the aristocrats and canvas, folding chairs for their employees. Wooden benches had been set up in the salon for the crew members, including Estanza, who was the only female to sit in that area. The officers stood stiffly behind the captain, who began the service with several prayers that were unfamiliar to Estanza. Her family rarely attended the Greek Orthodox Church in their village, but she had enjoyed the pageantry when they went to weddings, and once she had been to a funeral.

Captain Holtzer was a spiritual man, who in his early youth had studied to be a minister. However, his stay at the Lutheran seminary was short-lived when he fell in love with a sailor and subsequently with life at sea. His year at the seminary was not wasted. He did know his scriptures, and this morning he chose some lines from Proverbs 31 for his sermon, to acknowledge the rare presence of ladies on his ship.

Estanza began to listen as he spoke about the woman of valor, and how she is honored for the works of her hands. The crux of his speech was that women are valued for the physical work they do to take care of their families. The words reminded her of her mother, a woman who was always busy. The work of her hands had surely sustained the family, kept the hotel running smoothly. Even when she sat down, her hands were always busy, mending, shelling peas or doing needlepoint. She was definitely a woman of valor.

Yet she was judgmental and critical. According to her mother, Estanza was a miserable failure at making beds, ironing clothes, dusting rooms, or any of the myriad chores that women were required to do by civilized society. Her mother berated her as lazy when she sat down to study, and after she went away to school, there was no praise for good grades. As if he were reading her mind, the Captain went on to admonish his audience that it was incumbent upon them to honor their parents. Estanza was relieved to hear these words, because she did honor her mother, but it was her father whom she loved and missed. She had felt guilty about how eager she had been to leave her home.

After the prayer service, Renée took her charges out on the deck for their daily stroll. She started to ask Estanza to join them when Ensign Schmidt came up to Estanza and offered his arm.

"You look absolutely ravishing," he said, and lifted his hat in a respectful salutation.

Estanza smiled and breathed a barely audible, "Thank

you, Ensign Schmidt."

The young couple followed, sedately, behind Renée and the two girls, who were kept busy holding down their skirts and keeping their hats on in the stiff breeze coming off the ocean.

Estanza experienced the utility of the hobble skirt. It shortened her stride, but it kept the hem of the dress sedately around her ankles. She had forgotten to wear her hat, which would have elicited a scolding from her mother (ladies did not go outdoors without their heads covered and their faces shaded from the sun), but there was such a feeling of freedom as the long, black curls streamed out behind her. When they rounded the stern, the wind shifted and kept Estanza busy holding her hair back from her face.

Renée and the girls gave up walking the deck and went inside at the next doorway. Estanza began to follow them, telling Ensign Schmidt that she needed to go in and get her hat. He offered to escort her down, but she just laughed. "I'll find my way back, I promise," and she disappeared into the next doorway.

With her hat firmly tied down on her wayward hair, Estanza climbed the stairs to the promenade deck and headed for the doorway that she had used before. A sailor she didn't recognize and Ensign Schmidt were standing in an alcove near the door. She saw them embrace and quickly step apart. The sailor passed her as she reached the door. Ensign Schmidt tipped his hat to her and they resumed their walk around the deck. Ensign Schmidt made no reference to the sailor but Estanza had found the incident disturbing, yet couldn't say why.

"Eight complete turns around the deck are a mile," Ensign Schmidt informed her. "I try to do at least that many every day while I am on this ship."

"So let's do it," Estanza joined in. He put his hand protectively on her elbow and they began their walk. When they rounded the bow, Ensign Schmidt pointed out a nearing shoreline. "That is the coast of Africa," he said and continued to explain that the warm wind was coming all the way from the Sahara Desert. "I believe it is called a Sirocco. It causes severe sandstorms that are worse than blizzards in the Alps." Then Ensign Schmidt changed the subject and asked Estanza if she was aware that Germany was one of the great colonial powers on the vast continent of Africa.

She told him she had no idea, and he continued to explain how it was the destiny of European countries to colonize and civilize the African people. "France and England already monopolize North Africa in areas that are not part of the Ottoman Empire," he went on. "I have an uncle who is in the Schutztruppe, the German police force, which is working on civilizing the black natives of our colonies. His brigade of black troops and German officers make certain that the lazy workers report to work every day. The Africans have no work ethic. They never had to work before we came. They hunted and fished and gathered wild fruits so they had enough to eat. They also had some outrageous religious practices."

"It must be dangerous for your uncle to be in such a hostile place," Estanza commented.

"Yes, it is dangerous, but necessary work," Ensign Schmidt admitted. "Have you heard of the experiments conducted by Dr. Eugene Fischer, the famous German scientist?"

Ensign Schmidt took her silence for ignorance on the subject, and paused for a few moments to gather his thoughts. Waving his arm in the general direction of Africa, he continued: "Dr. Fischer proved that there are superior and inferior races. He advocated that, in the interest of advancing civilization, it is the duty of the superior races to subordinate or exterminate the inferior races."

Since Estanza looked startled at this statement, Ensign Schmidt went on to explain that the German government had brought education, medical facilities and the civilizing influence of Christianity to these primitive people. (He neglected to mention that the education was of the most elementary and only for the handful of Africans who could be useful in helping to discipline their fellow tribesmen. As far as medical facilities were concerned, thousands of natives were used in experiments that eventually caused their deaths).

He explained, "The German government has provided the tools and seeds to plant cotton, bananas, coffee and sugar cane. Getting the native workers to the fields every day is a monumental task."

Estanza could well imagine the difficulty of enslaving people who had always been free. She listened with growing horror as Ensign Schmidt related an incident described to him in a recent letter from his uncle.

"The Commandant of the plantation, faced with the reluctance of the workers to put in a full day's work, had them whipped for being tardy. The workers went on a strike. After a few days of watching the fields go idle, the Commandant ordered the wives of the strikers be brought to the military compound and whipped in public until the workers returned to their jobs. That ended the strike." Ensign Schmidt found this highly amusing and laughed out loud at the Commandant's cleverness in breaking up the strike.

It was with relief that Estanza realized they had finished walking their designated mile. She excused herself, attributing the queasy feeling in her stomach to seasickness, but she knew better.

Ensign Schmidt, still chuckling at the story he had just related, told Estanza that he would not be at the noon meal as it was his turn to stand mid-day watch on the Bridge. He wished her, "Bon appetit," and they both went on their way.

The noon meal was a festive affair since the crew had brought more than fresh water from Malaga. The Spanish town was famous for its rosé wines, and the captain had given orders to serve the sweet wine with lunch. It went well with the delectable rice dish, called paella, a specialty of that area of Spain. The fragrance of the spices reminded Estanza of the Turkish dishes her grandmother had served on special occasions, and her appetite was aroused in spite of herself. She breathed in the aroma as she neared the dining room and looked forward to tasting a little bit of home.

The wine was also delicious and a welcome change from the daily portion of beer. The doctor kept filling her glass and Estanza hardly noticed that she was getting drowsy.

After lunch Renée left quickly to pick up her charges from the upper dining room, where they ate with their mother. Estanza returned to her cabin. Carefully she braced the chair under the door handle, hung the black dress on the wall hook, kicked off her shoes and, half-clothed, stretched out on the narrow bed and promptly dozed off.

Chapter 13

The captain asked the doctor, the purser and the first mate to come to his quarters after the noon meal. Three men now sat around the dining table located in an alcove of his sitting room, waiting for the doctor to arrive.

"The subject of your sermon was well chosen today," the purser said, in an effort to make conversation.

The captain nodded and pointed to an open box of sweets that lay on the table. "That young woman, the one with a complexion like this caramel candy, is she the one who was supposed to be with Frau von Stahlenberg?"

"Yes, she is Fräulein Nikiolopolis." The purser smiled, remembering the vision of Estanza in the elegant black dress.

The first mate poured wine into the glasses on the table and passed one to each man. Just then the doctor knocked and came into the spacious sitting room. He apologized for being late without giving an explanation and sat down at the table. He drained a glass of wine and held it out for a refill.

Captain Holtzer had something on his mind that he wanted to discuss with the other men in the room but he did not want to reveal his indecision. He got up from the table and began pacing to the window and back again, but then stopped abruptly. The other three men watched him expectantly.

"Tomorrow we are to sail through the Strait of Gibraltar," he finally announced. "I must decide whether we pass through in daylight or wait until nightfall. The English have armed the fort with heavy artillery and make no bones about their hostility to the Kaiser. Last week they used a German navy vessel for target practice. The HMS *Lorelei* escaped unharmed by mere inches. If I decide to sail through in daylight, should I ask the ladies on this ship to stay inside?"

"Perhaps we would be safer if they were all on deck?" the doctor said.

The first mate looked thoughtful, the captain looked alarmed. The purser knew the doctor was being facetious and gave him a warning look while hiding a smile.

The captain, a man with little or no sense of humor, took the doctor's words seriously. Raising his voice several octaves he bellowed, "What a preposterous idea, Herr Doktor! Do you want the English to think we would hide behind a woman's skirts?"

The doctor remained silent, but the first mate suggested that a radio message asking for safe passage might be the best plan.

The captain bristled at this idea. He hated the English and their superior naval power. He hoped there would be a war soon so that, as commander of a naval ship, he could help sink their navy. However, at the moment, his mission was to get these females safely to Germany.

Finally the doctor spoke up. "We are on a peaceful mission and they gave consent for passage into the Mediterranean. Why would they make trouble for us getting out?"

"Because," said the Captain, "our relations with the English have deteriorated in the last few days. The Kaiser and King George have exchanged hostile words and sabers have been rattled. Who knows what that arrogant English bas…"

The doctor interjected, "Those two are first cousins. There is nothing worse than a family feud."

The first mate asked, "What do we have to lose by being polite or even deferential? It's not as if we could shoot our way out. We are not armed and we must think of our passengers."

He continued, "It would be best to send a message in English. It is a language that lends itself to diplomacy."

The captain finally agreed with the first mate, but as far

as he knew, none of the crew spoke English.

The doctor suggested they ask the governess who sat at his table; surely she knew English. The captain gave the doctor the assignment to recruit Madame Volant to write a diplomatic message asking for safe passage. He wanted to see it before it was sent, but since his English was limited he would take her word for its content. He also had to trust that she would translate the reply into German. Having settled the matter for the moment, and after drinking another glass of wine, the doctor excused himself to pursue his mission to find Madame Volant.

The three men lingered a while longer over their wine. The captain asked the purser what he thought of the doctor. "Can he be trusted?" asked the captain. "I heard a rumor that he is actually Jewish."

The purser mentioned that he had sailed with the doctor for nearly fifteen years, Then he added, "He has been a good friend to me and a loyal member of the Kaiser's navy as long as I have known him. As for his being a Jew, I don't think so."

"I have heard rumors that his maternal grandmother was half Jewish," said the captain. "Those rumors are usually true. We must stay alert." Then he added in a lowered tone, "Those people are money-grubbing cowards. Can you imagine suggesting that we ask the women and children to stay on deck to be shot at by those English fagots and fops?"

The purser knew better than to contradict the captain, who was well known for his anti-Jewish beliefs. He could also sense that the captain was about to start listing his grievances against the English. One of his main complaints was how the English coddled their colonial subjects by providing them with an education, medical services and even a legal code, instead of beating them into submission like the superior Germans did in their colonies. He could spend hours quoting Kaiser Wilhelm on the subject of subjugating inferior peoples.

To forestall a lengthy diatribe, the purser began to discuss the delicious meal they had just eaten. He explained that they had to put on a new chef because the old one and his assistant were needed to replace the bakers.

"The new man is actually Basque, an ethnic group that lives in the mountains near the French border. The Spanish say they belong to Spain, the French say they belong to France and the Basque don't want to belong to either one. They are sheepherders for the most part. I have heard that both the men and the women are great cooks. This one certainly is," the purser concluded.

Later that day a radio message came from the English fort on Gibraltar, in response to the one sent from the ship:

> THE HOHENZOLLERN IS TO REMAIN OFF SHORE -- PERMISSION GRANTED TO PROCEED THROUGH THE STRAIT AT A SPEED OF TWO KNOTS IN ORDER NOT TO CAPSIZE THE SMALL BOATS IN HER WAKE.

The captain was annoyed at the answer. How dare they tell him at what speed he was to travel! He sent for Madame Volant who came a half-hour later. "I needed to finish a lesson with my girls," she explained when she saw the captain's scowl.

"Are you certain of the wording in this message?" he demanded.

"Yes, it seemed quite clear to me," was her firm reply. "They are asking the ship to travel slowly through the crowded waters of this popular port."

The captain gave her a searching look, decided she was telling the truth, and was about to dismiss her when he had another thought. "This is the Sabbath, a day of rest. You should not require your students to do lessons on this day." He said this in the authoritarian tone he used with all women, with the exception of his mother.

Renée Volant drew herself up to her full height of five feet and two inches, and locked eyes with Captain Holtzer. Then she turned on her heel and, without waiting to be dismissed, stepped quickly out of the room, congratulating herself on having held her sharp and caustic tongue.

Chapter 14

After leaving the captain's quarters, the purser and the doctor spent the afternoon in the purser's cabin where they finished off two more bottles of the sweet, Spanish wine. Usually, they would have played a game of chess, but this afternoon their heads were not entirely clear. They let their thoughts drift in different directions, even dozing a little in their chairs. Finally the purser sat up, gave the doctor a questioning look, and decided to ask him something that had been on his mind since they had left the captain's quarters.

"Werner," he ventured in a neutral voice, "in all these years we have known each other, I had no idea that you had a Jewish grandmother."

"I didn't," was the doctor's quick reply.

"But the captain said there was a rumor . . ."

"Not again, not after all this time." The doctor sounded resigned as he went on. "My maternal grandmother's maiden name was Kohln. A clerk who filled out the nuptial paperwork for my parent's wedding left out the "l" which made it Kohn, an ancient Jewish name. No one noticed the error and whenever a copy of my parents' proof of marriage was replicated, the name Kohn appeared as my grandmother's maiden name. It was not until I enrolled in medical school that I found out about the clerical error that would drastically alter my life." The doctor sighed and closed his eyes.

"Surely such a minor error can be corrected?" The purser asked.

"Somehow it didn't seem to matter in grade school and

even in gymnasium, but when I wanted to go to medical school I was told that the quota for Jewish students was closed."

"Did you explain to them about the error?" the purser asked.

"It was a shock to me. It was the first I had even known about it," the doctor said. "Twenty-five years had passed and the forms had been duplicated many times. My grandmother's maiden name was on all the documents that concerned every phase of my life."

"But you got into medical school, didn't you?" It wasn't really a question.

"I went across the border and applied to the Basel University of Medicine. Anyone who has the grades and passes their entrance exam is accepted, providing they can pay the tuition—even women. Can you imagine?"

"So there is no Jewish connection in your past?" The purser sounded dubious.

"Not that I know of," answered the doctor. "However, I cannot practice medicine in Germany because of my Swiss degree or in Switzerland because of my German citizenship." He shook his head and added, "I fell in love with Switzerland and a Swiss lady. She married someone else, but I plan to retire there."

"You and I have been sailing on the Kaiser's yachts for fifteen years. How did you get this job?" The purser sounded puzzled.

"My mother's brother, a rear admiral, convinced the Kaiser that I would be just the doctor he needed on his yacht—someone who, of necessity, would be discreet." The doctor smiled knowingly at the purser, who nodded in return.

"There is a postscript to my story," the doctor continued. "A few years ago I went back to Basel to learn about some new developments in my field. A Zionist Conference was in session. There were hundreds of Jews from seventeen different countries. Several were doctors who had been fellow students from my University days. I had never bothered to deny being part Jewish so these men accepted me as such. In that capacity I was invited to an informal gathering and met the man who is responsible for developing the cure for syphilis. His name is Paul Ehrlich. You may have heard of him?"

The purser looked up with interest. He had experience with venereal disease. Many sailors were infected, incapacitated and eventually discharged each year. Since the discovery of the drug Salvarsan, most men were able to return to duty after treatment. "Was he the one who was awarded the Nobel Prize for Medicine a couple of years ago?" the purser asked.

The doctor nodded. "It turns out that our anti-Semitic captain owes his life to a Jew,"

Both men chuckled and the purser added, "If he found out, he might die of apoplexy, or prefer to die of syphilis." The men then toasted the irony with another glass of wine.

"One more thing I need to add about that stay in Basel," the doctor said. "The men I met in those three days of the Zionist Conference were totally focused on creating a Jewish homeland."

"That does not seem possible or practical," the purser said. "I have heard that no two Jews can ever agree on anything."

"They are determined, and their leaders are men of the highest caliber. If they succeed in forming a Jewish State it will be an extraordinary country. Like it says in the Bible, 'Zion will be as a light unto the nations.'"

The purser thought about this for a few minutes then asked, "I am curious, my almost Jewish friend, why are so many Jews involved in medicine?"

"I have done some research into that subject," replied the doctor. "It seems there are two main reasons: Jews are taught to revere all human life as a gift from God, and preserving it is a duty of the highest priority. Secondly, for thousands of years Jews have been periodically persecuted by the fanatics of the proselytizing religions and had to flee for their lives. The knowledge of healing transfers easily from country to country. After all, we humans all have the same anatomy."

The doctor's answer made sense to the purser, and although he had a few more questions about the Zionists, Jews in general, and anti-Semitism in particular, he sat in quiet thought for a few minutes.

The light from the window that faced the promenade deck was beginning to fade. The purser poured each of them another glass of wine, emptying the second bottle. Clearing his throat he said. "Given the captain's sexual predilection, wasn't it unlikely that he would contract a venereal disease?"

The doctor looked up in surprise, and realized that he had already said too much. His next words were even more revealing and in the back of his mind he blamed the wine. "Our Captain tends to swing both ways," he said, and tried in vain not to giggle.

The bell sounded for the evening meal. On their way out of the room, the purser asked, "Werner, are you Lutheran or Catholic?"

The doctor looked down at his shoes, "I am a lapsed Catholic. I had problems memorizing my catechism and the priest offered to give me very special, private lessons in his bedroom. I never went back to church."

"For similar reasons, I am a devout Atheist," the purser whispered as they entered the dining room.

Chapter 15

During the evening meal, the doctor thanked Renée for her help with the English message and mentioned that news had arrived from Palermo that the tall baker had not survived the amputation of his hand. "The Kaiser will be upset," he said. "The nuns are asking an exorbitant amount to be paid for burial expenses."

Renée lowered her head and concentrated on keeping her amused smile hidden from the others at the table. It was at that moment she noticed Estanza was absent from the meal. She remarked on this fact to the doctor, who speculated that Estanza might be seasick. "She also drank several glasses of wine at lunch," he added with a wink.

"I will check on her later," Renée said. "She told me her cabin is next to the infirmary."

A soft knock woke Estanza. She stayed on her back for a few moments, trying to orient herself. Why was she feeling so chilly? Then realized she was only wearing her chemise and underpants. The knock came again followed by a woman's voice calling her name.

"Estanza, it is Madame Volant—I mean Renée." The words were followed by a louder knock.

"One moment, please," Estanza called, putting on the wool shawl she kept at the foot of the bed. She moved the chair back under the table, and reached for the door latch.

Renée entered, still wearing her Sunday dress of dark blue silk. It took a bit of maneuvering for Estanza to retreat sufficiently to let her friend into the small space. Renée held back a sarcastic remark comparing the spaciousness of most jail cells to this little room.

"We missed you at the evening meal," Renée said, as she sat down on the chair being offered by Estanza. "Are you feeling all right?"

"I fell asleep after all that good food and wine," Estanza replied, while lighting the lamp on the table. She sat down on the bed and thanked Renée for coming to check on her.

"It was a delicious meal," Renée agreed. She then went on to tell Estanza that the ship would be traveling through the Strait of Gibraltar the next day.

"How exciting!" the young girl replied. "I've read about the huge cliffs and all the tension around who should be in charge of the 'gate to the Mediterranean.'"

"The English are in charge at the moment." Renée explained. "There is friction between the two royal households and safe passage for a German ship is not assured as yet."

The shawl had slipped from Estanza's shoulders while the two women were talking and, once again, Renée noticed the bruises on Estanza's upper arms. She could not help but wonder what had caused such contusions on her friend's otherwise flawless skin.

In a conversational tone, Renée went on to report the wording of the radio message from the English commander of the fort. Then, mostly to prolong her visit, she told about the message from Palermo and the death of the second baker who had been evacuated to the hospital there.

While telling this news, Renée noticed that Estanza crossed her arms and covered the bruises with trembling hands. Her eyes widened and began to fill with tears. At first, Renée thought they might be tears of sadness, but she sensed that there was another emotion involved. Quietly, almost in a whisper, Renée asked, "Estanza, how did you get those terrible bruises on your upper arms?"

A silence filled the little room. The walls seemed to contract around them. A choking sob escaped from Estanza's throat. She looked up and met Renée's kind, inquiring eyes. She knew the decision was hers to make and, once she told Renée, she could no longer pretend that the rape didn't happen. In a monotone voice, that Renée hardly recognized, Estanza told her about the attack. She did not tell about her revenge. That was one secret she planned to take to the grave and she felt no remorse.

"For the first time in my life I am terrified about being an unprotected woman," Estanza admitted to Renée. "Frau von Stahlenberg is angry with me. I was to travel under her protection. I don't know if she has withdrawn that protection permanently or if this state of affairs is only temporary."

"Do you know what has aroused her anger?" Renée asked.

"That's just it," Estanza replied. "I have no idea what I might have done to cause her to withdraw her protection. She only shouted at me to get out and of course I did."

"You have a right to be confused and frightened." Renée told Estanza. "I would offer to help, but her maid has already told me you are an untrustworthy thief and Frau von Stahlenberg has washed her hands of you."

"So you don't think it would do any good for me to try to talk to her. To, at least, find out what I have done wrong?" Estanza questioned.

"From what I have heard, she will not speak to you, so save your dignity." Renée replied.

Then she went on to ask, "Do you know anyone in Berlin?"

Of course Estanza thought of Konrad, but only said she had a letter from the foreign office that was signed by one of the directors.

"So you must send a message to the foreign office as soon as there is radio contact, telling them that you are arriving unescorted and need to have someone meet you and take you to your quarters. They did say they were providing an apartment as part of your employment?" Renée asked.

Estanza took a piece of paper and a pen from the carpet bag and began to write out a message, as Renée suggested.

"The ship should reach Cadiz in a few days. It's a Spanish port and more reliable for sending messages to Germany," Renée told Estanza, as she read over the short inquiry as to who would meet her at the ship and an address she should go to upon arrival.

"If there is no acceptable reply, I will book a passage back to Greece." Estanza said.

"Let's hope that is not necessary," Renée sighed in response. "Now let's see if we can get you something to eat. You must be hungry by now." She got up and headed for the door. "I have friends in the galley and will be back with a little snack for you." Before Estanza could object she was gone.

Renée came back with a tray of sandwiches and a glass of beer. In the meantime, Estanza had put on her nightgown and started to brush out her tangled hair.

The sandwiches were made with slices of Parma ham and the beer was not the strong, bitter ale the Germans usually drank, but a milder, sweeter type from Spain. Estanza finished it all and told Renée how grateful she was for her concern.

"I have spent my life taking care of young girls, and it just comes naturally to me," Renée said in response.

"Have you always been a governess?" Estanza asked.

"All my adult life," was Renée's brief answer.

"You never married, or wanted your own children?" Estanza felt she was prying, but she really wanted to know more about her new friend, and also what it was like to be a self-supporting woman.

"All of that is a long story—a sad one, with a semi-happy ending," Renée said.

"I am really interested," Estanza replied. "If you are so inclined, please tell me."

Renée began:

"I was born in Metz, a city in Alsace Loraine, a district that is disputed territory between Germany and France—although most of the people who live there are French.

In 1871 the Germans occupied the area and gradually began a campaign to Germanize everything. French was forbidden to be spoken in public, and the schools taught everything in German. After a few years it was forbidden to speak French even in our homes. To enforce this new rule and further subjugate the French people of the area, the Germans started billeting their soldiers in private homes.

The German soldier that lived in our house was a handsome fellow with the bluest eyes named Karl-Heinz Wentzel.

(Just by the way Renée said his name, Estanza surmised Renée must have loved him.)

He was eighteen and I was sixteen and we fell in love. For a year we secretly held hands and stole kisses. One day orders came for him to be shipped to the German colony of Kamerun in Africa.

On his last night he sneaked into my bedroom. It was not planned, but we made love all night, and the next day he joined his regiment. I never heard from him again. Many years later I learned that he had been killed in a native uprising.

My parents, who were both school teachers, were devastated when they found out I was pregnant. My father was furious and ordered me out of the house. My mother was no less angry, but more practical. She sent me to stay with her sister in Paris until the child was born. Her plan was to send it to an orphanage for adoption. But my aunt and I had other plans.

My aunt is a dressmaker, lives above her shop, and is self-supporting. After the little girl, whom I named Karla, was born, my aunt hired a nanny to help take care of the baby and made certain that I finished high school.

She taught me to sew, but we both agreed that my real talents were elsewhere."

At this revelation, Estanza had to smile and briefly interrupted the narrative. "I had the same problems," she told

Renée. "Everything I did with my hands always proved inadequate or insufficient. No matter how hard I tried I could never please my mother."

Renée sighed with understanding and went on with her story:

"I applied for a scholarship to the Sorbonne University and eventually earned a teaching degree but was too shy to teach in a classroom. At first I started tutoring students in German and English, but then I found that French governesses were in demand by German families.

I have had two other positions before this one. I must admit, working for the household of an ambassador has been the most interesting so far.

So there you have my scandalous story, as briefly as I could tell it."

"What has become of your daughter?" Estanza asked

"Karla is about your age. She lives with my aunt, Alicia, who has, for all intents and purposes, been a mother to her. Alicia tells me that my daughter has become a skilled dressmaker and hopes she will take over the shop someday. Needless to say, I am very proud of her and forever grateful that I didn't send her to an orphanage for adoption."

Estanza looked at her watch and saw it was getting close to midnight. "You have a full day of work tomorrow," she told Renée. "You must go to bed and get some rest. I will take the glass and tray back to the galley in the morning."

The two women embraced and bade each other goodnight with new warmth. They each held a confidence about the other and were aware of the bond they had formed. Estanza carefully adjusted the chair under the door latch before she got into bed, hoping to dream of Konrad.

Chapter 16

During the night the ship had passed the harbor entrance and was slowly making progress toward the Strait of Gibraltar. When Estanza went up on deck after breakfast she was astounded to see the ship surrounded by a fleet of small rowboats. Each boat held a colorful assortment of handmade goods. Mostly women occupied the boats. They held up their wares and shouted in English, German and Italian, describing what they were selling and offering at "good price." The reason for the orders to keep the ship "at a speed of two knots" became obvious.

Crew, passengers, and vendors were shouting back and forth, bargaining for the scarves, fans, shawls and embroidered tableware. Money and goods were exchanged with baskets strung on fish lines between the *Hohenzollern's* railings and the little boats. One enterprising man had a boatload of umbrellas. "If you don't have one you should buy one," Ensign Schmidt advised Estanza. "You can expect terrible rainstorms this time of year."

Estanza didn't have an umbrella but was hesitant about spending money unnecessarily.

"How much are you asking for the umbrellas?" she shouted down to the man in the boat. He yelled back an amount but not the type of currency.

Ensign Schmidt took a German mark out of his pocket, put it into a basket, secured it with a pebble that was in the basket for that purpose, and sent it sliding down the fishing line. Then he shouted at the man in the boat, "Send up one large umbrella for the lady!" Soon a colorful umbrella, tied to the basket, was being pulled up to the railing by Ensign Schmidt. He handed the umbrella to Estanza with a slight bow and the click of his heels. "This is a souvenir gift for you," he said, and added, "May you never need it."

At first Estanza wanted to protest his generosity, but he looked at her with such satisfaction on his handsome, young face, she decided that the best thing to do was to accept the gift gracefully and express her gratitude.

It was late afternoon before the little boats dispersed and the *Hohenzollern* passed under the guns of the English fort. The setting sun reflected brightly on the hundred or so cannons lined up along the sea wall. Just as the ship passed the last set of cliffs of Gibraltar, a cannon shot was fired to designate that the ship had passed out of the Mediterranean Sea.

Now they were in the open water of the Atlantic, and immediately the waves rose higher and fell lower. Before they reached Cadiz the next morning, almost every passenger and many of the crew members were seasick.

Although the *Hohenzollern* had sent radio messages about the need for the ship to dock in Cadiz to take on water and other supplies, the harbor master kept the ship beyond the mooring area for several hours. He requested a special tax for coming into the harbor without proper notice. Eventually the ship was cleared to dock, with instructions to depart before dark.

Estanza asked the purser about leaving the ship to send a telegram or make a telephone call to the German foreign office in Berlin. The purser, who spoke a little Spanish, offered to accompany her. They found a telephone exchange in a narrow street near the harbor. Making an international collect call proved to be infeasible. The purser offered to pay for the call in the local currency, and the lady in charge proved to be a little more accommodating.

After placing the call to a German exchange where it was

forwarded to the foreign office, they had to wait for a return call from the Germans. They were then advised that it would take about a half hour.

"To be certain of making contact, we should also send a telegram," the purser advised. So they went to the telegraph service across the street. Sending a telegram was much less complicated than making a telephone call. Estanza had written out her inquiry a few days ago and was ready to have it transmitted.

"We will see which of our modern methods of communication is the fastest," the purser told Estanza. "Let's hope one or the other of our messages is answered before we must leave Cadiz."

Next door to the telephone exchange was a pharmacy, and Estanza asked the purser to inquire about a remedy for seasickness. The pharmacist recommended little packages of candied ginger (Estanza's favorite sweets). "The seas north of Cadiz are usually rough and this candy must work, because many sailors come in here to buy it."

Estanza and the purser waited another hour before the telephone call came in. A clerk at the foreign office reported that there was no one there who could advise them about plans for Estanza's arrival in Berlin since everyone of any consequence had departed for the month of August. The telegram was answered with a similar message.

After leaving Cadiz the *Hohenzollern* headed out to sea, traveling along the coasts of Spain and Portugal and into the wild and turbulent English Channel. The ginger was helpful, but most days Estanza felt wretched, as did most of the other passengers. When some of them came to meals, their stay was brief. Walking on the promenade deck was not a possibility most days. When a passenger came on deck they might spend a few minutes retching over the rail, and then they were hurrying back to the salon or their cabin to get out of the wind-driven rain.

By the time the ship arrived in La Havre, the water supply

was running dangerously low.

The French harbor master was not inclined to give a German ship permission to tie up at the pier. After a day offshore, anchored in the turbulent waters, the *Hohenzollern* was finally given permission to enter the harbor and tie up at the furthest pier, usually reserved for tramp steamers. While the captain and the purser arranged for payment of the moorage fee, the crew pumped fresh water aboard. The officer in charge of the galley used the telephone in the harbor master's office to order a food delivery from the local market.

This was on a Saturday, so Renée had the afternoon free. She and Estanza went for a walk on the pier, and then took advantage of the almost motionless conditions to study Greek and French, respectively.

At the Sunday morning prayer service, the captain announced that the *Hohenzollern* would not be going all the way to Berlin as originally scheduled. He explained that the heavy rains had caused the rivers to rise and the ship would not clear the Spree River bridges. He added that the passengers would be taken as far as Hamburg and advised them to make their own arrangements for transportation to Berlin.

For the next few hours the ship to shore radio room was busy with attempts to reach family or friends who could bring cars, trucks, or even horse-drawn carts to Hamburg and provide transportation for the daylong drive to Berlin. The expected arrival day was uncertain, but the calculation was another week at the most.

Elisabet von Stahlenberg contacted her father, who assured her there would be vehicles waiting for her when she arrived in Hamburg. Her mother was already in Marienbad, the resort she frequented every summer, and Elisabet had orders to join her there.

The ambassador's family and Renée were also traveling to the same resort, as the ambassador was already there. When Estanza inquired if there were any messages for her, the purser told her that the Imperial Foreign Service had sent a message that they were aware that all passengers were to disembark in Hamburg, but no mention was made of her name or arrangements for transportation to Berlin.

The last week on the ship, the seas were calmer. It rained almost daily, but the sight of land was reassuring. Estanza missed the blue skies of Greece. She remembered being puzzled as to why so many Germans frequented her family's hotel. They were always critical of the sanitation; they didn't like the Greek food or the wines. The Germans didn't seem to like the Greek music, either, often drowning it out with their loud beer-drinking songs. Now she understood why they came to Greece with all its inconveniences. There was no way to export the wonderful climate to Germany, but they did their best to bring what they considered a much superior culture with them to Greece.

Chapter 17

The SMY *Hohenzollern* was greeted by a cheering crowd at the mouth of the Elbe River. It was a familiar sight to Captain Holtzer, but for the passengers, who were finally able to stay on their feet and wave back, it was like arriving in heaven. The passage over the bar went smoothly as the tide was in their favor. By the middle of the day the ship was docked in Hamburg and the debarkation began.

Estanza's belongings were packed in the green trunk and the embroidered carpet bag. Her straw hat and the umbrella hung on a hook, and she would be back after the noon meal to pick up her things and leave the ship.

Renée was already at the table when Estanza sat down next to the doctor. He handed her an envelope. "Here is my name and address, in care of the shipping company who handles my mail," he said. "In case you ever need a character reference."

Estanza took the envelope and thanked the doctor, who excused himself and left the table.

The meal was eaten in almost complete silence. Everyone at the table was already thinking about the next events in their lives.

The whistle blew for the debarkation of the passengers to begin, and Renée and Estanza hugged one last time, promising to stay in touch.

~

After entering her cabin Estanza read the letter from the

doctor. It was brief and referred the inquirer to contact Dr. Werner Heinemann at the address below, etc. A character reference for Estanza Nikiolopolis would be provided upon request.

While putting the letter back in the envelope, she noticed the scissors on the table. For a few moments she stared at them. Then a shiver went through her body. It must have been the doctor who removed the scissors from the baker's hand. How did he know they were hers? So he knew what she had done. What kind of a reference would he give her? Putting the scissors in her bag next to the letter, she called the cabin boy to help her with the trunk.

~

Private automobiles, commercial trucks and several horse-drawn wagons were assembled on the dock. Estanza watched as the women went gingerly down the steep gang-plank and dispersed into the private cars. Most of the luggage was piled into the trucks; some was loaded onto the open wagons and covered with tarps.

Konrad was not among the men waiting on the dock. Seeing no one who resembled him, or an official-looking person who might be from the Imperial Foreign Service, Estanza felt a slight quiver of anxiety in her chest. She followed the stevedore as he carried her trunk to the curbed sidewalk flanking the loading area. He set the trunk down near a light pole, bowed politely as she handed him a few coins, and walked back toward the ship. The gangplank was being raised while the departing whistle was sounded. In a few minutes, the *Hohenzollern* would be slipping away from the dock.

"Fräulein Nikiolopolis," a familiar voice said, as Estanza watched the ship disappear. It was Ensign Schmidt, who was standing behind her with a tall sailor at his side.

"We have a few days shore leave, and my friend and I are going to explore Hamburg," he said. "Are you also staying here?"

"No," Estanza explained. "I am to wait for a government car to take me to Berlin, where I will be working for the Foreign Service."

The sky was beginning to darken as black clouds rolled in from the North Sea. Ensign Schmidt gestured toward the sky. "I hope your transportation arrives before the thunderstorm," he said, tipping his hat with slight bow, while his friend followed suit. Both men turned toward the lights of a distant tram line and walked off arm in arm.

The dock used by the Kaiser's yachts was somewhat remote from the main terminals of Hamburg Harbor. Since the Kaiser did not need to go through customs to re-enter his own country, no customs house or other office building was located nearby. Estanza found herself totally isolated and alone on the expanse of the loading dock.

A loud clap of thunder was followed by a streak of sheet lightning that lit up the opposite bank of the wide river. In the next moment the rain came pelting down, drenching Estanza before she could open the umbrella. Her straw hat sagged into her eyes. She fought to open the umbrella while the stiff wind drove the rain against her. It was no use. The next gust turned the umbrella inside out and left her exposed to the rain. The thunder and lightning came almost simultaneously. The storm was directly overhead.

At first Estanza felt annoyed about having her hat and her lovely new traveling suit ruined, but the growing anger faded into pangs of fear as she realized her position. She was alone on a deserted dock in a violent thunderstorm, with night coming on. She needed to assess her options rationally. Above her head the street light came on, making a small pool of light around her, and showing the rain driving down to the ground like a solid sheet of water.

The pangs of fear gave way to mind-numbing despair. Estanza sat down on the trunk, her carpet bag between her legs, and tried to clear her mind. It took all her willpower to think clearly and to assess her situation. Each clap of thunder, each flash of lightning reflected the storm inside of her. She put her head down on her bag and, totally against her will, began to sob. She was as helpless in the throes of her emotions as she was powerless against the storm that churned around her.

She could hear her mother's voice above the howling wind: *You useless, foolish girl! Aren't you sorry now that you left your home for this unknown future?* She wasn't really sorry, only very frightened and unsure of what to do next. She tried to think what the Headmistress would advise her now. This cleared her head a little, but the fear was still lodged firmly in the pit of her stomach. Then she remembered some words from the graduation speech last spring:

> This school has provided you young women with the tools to overcome the vicissitudes of life in this modern and complex age. With the physical and mental skills you have acquired here you have the ability to reason and plan, and to be—if you so choose—self-sufficient.

The rain was letting up and the thunder was receding southward. Estanza shivered in her wet clothes, surveyed the wreck of the umbrella, and resigned herself to walking toward the far off light in the direction Ensign Schmidt had gone. She decided to sit for another minute to gather her strength and to wait for the overwhelming fear to dissipate sufficiently for her shaking legs to hold her up. With her head bowed and the soggy brim of her hat obstructing her view, she saw a pair of black boots standing next to her. The fear grew into near panic, since she had not heard footsteps.

"Fräulein Nikiolopolis?" a voice said. When Estanza started to look up the voice continued. "I have been sent to escort you to Berlin." The words were spoken in a manner and tone used by educated Germans. Estanza raised her head, pushed back the brim of the hat and saw a black chauffeur uniform, emblazoned with two rows of silver buttons.

She started to get up, but stumbled backwards over the trunk. A gloved hand steadied her by her left arm and another hand went out to catch her carpet bag.

A scream of sheer terror rose out of her throat when Estanza saw the face above the uniform collar. It was as shiny and black as the boots on the man's feet.

Fortunately the man in the chauffeur uniform had good reflexes. Still clutching the carpet bag, he released Estanza's left arm and stepped back out of the reach of the six-inch hat pin that was pointed at his left eye.

Standing about six feet away from the fierce weapon, he revealed his magnificent row of white teeth. It was difficult to tell if he was smiling or gritting his teeth in fear or anger. His eye lids were almost closed as he looked down at the frightened girl.

Sensing that he was not trying to attack her, Estanza lowered her arm to her side, still holding the hat pin by its jade handle. At the moment of crisis, she had remembered what to do.

Self-defense was a required class at school. The headmistress, over the objections of the principal, had hired an expert to advise the girls how to use the nearest objects for defense. The hatpins of that day were obviously a lethal weapon. "Aim for an eye," was one of the directives. "Or for the crotch," was another one.

"My name is Biku," the man said quietly. "I hope you are Fräulein Nikiolopolis?" Then he smiled, cocked his head to the side but kept his arms by his side.

Estanza was still breathless from the scream, but she nodded her head and waited to see what he would do next.

Biku unbuttoned several of the silver buttons, reached into his tunic and pulled out an envelope. "This is from Herr Konrad," he said. His cultured voice was reassuring, and hearing Konrad's name gave Estanza the courage to step forward and take the letter into her left hand. Her right hand still clutched the hat pin in case he made a threatening gesture.

With relief Estanza saw that it was indeed a letter from Konrad, written in his handwriting about a week ago. Finally exhaling, Estanza stuck the pin back into her hat, sat down on her trunk, and began to read.

August – 1910

Biku:

The ambassador and I are the reluctant guests of the local suzerain near the Bulgarian border. The German government has been notified and negotiations are underway to pay the necessary fees whereby we can continue our journey to Berlin. Inquiries about the yacht Hohenzollern II have revealed that all passengers are to debark in Hamburg because the River Spree is at flood stage and cannot accommodate the vessel all the way to Berlin. Due to heavy seas the arrival date is uncertain.

I have been informed that Frau Elisabet and the Ambassador's family plan to travel directly to Marienbad upon leaving the ship.

You are assigned to transport one of the passengers, Fräulein Estanza Nikiolopolis, from Hamburg to Berlin. She has been hired as an interpreter/translator for the Foreign Affairs department. Her living arrangements still need to be finalized, so take her to my rooms at the Hotel Bristol. She is to be rendered the same courtesy and service as I am when in residence at the hotel. All expenses are to be added to my account.

You are authorized to show this letter to the management or any of the staff to be certain that my request is carried out. Share this letter with Fräulein Nikiolopolis to assure her that her needs will be met.

Konrad Herman von Stahlenberg

Vice Consul, German Foreign Service

Estanza read the letter twice while Biku stood back. He needed to be patient and choose his words carefully. She had been nearly hysterical. Biku had read about female hysteria in a book by Freud, the Austrian psychiatrist. Considering the restricted life that women led in the European society of that day it was not surprising that they often became agitated to the point of hysteria. He smiled to himself and thought how, just being in those tight corsets, unable to take a deep breath, was reason enough to scream. Besides the restrictions of the corsets, many women wore those hobble skirts which shortened their stride and made it impossible to get onto a street car or even walk up a flight of stairs unassisted. He had only faint memories of his origins in East Africa, but he had seen pictures of the tribal life and couldn't help but compare the bodily freedom of the women there, compared to those he saw every day now.

Watching Estanza, Biku became aware that her skin was not the pale, almost white, color of the women in Germany. In his mind he searched for comparisons and decided almond was a good match.

Estanza read the letter from Konrad for the third time and Biku noticed that she had brought the page up to her lips, as if to kiss the words. He knew that Konrad had a preference for dark-skinned women, and surmised that this girl was more than an employee. He had made the right decision about where to spend the night.

When she finally looked up at him with expectation about what would happen next, he helped her to stand, picked up the green trunk and approached the Daimler at the curb. She picked up the carpet bag and allowed him to help her into the impressive German town car.

Chapter 18

While driving the eight hours from Berlin, Biku had formulated a plan of what to do with Fräulein Nikiolopolis when he found her. It was too late at night to drive the eight hours back to Berlin and it was imperative that he get some sleep before starting on that journey. Also, both he and the lady would need to eat. After ruling out the hotels in Hamburg where he would not be allowed to eat in the dining room, or to rent a room, he decided to take the Fräulein to the *Maison Sombre* (The Dark House). Frau Brauner was more than the proprietor of the brothel; she was a trusted friend of many years. It was a safe place to spend the night and the kitchen was open twenty-four hours a day. It was about a half-hour drive. On the way he would try to forestall any objections that Estanza might bring up about spending the night in a brothel.

He started to tell her that he was taking her to a rooming house, but he didn't need to disclose anything more about their destination because Estanza fell asleep. Upon their arrival he carefully took her in his arms and, followed by one of the girls who brought Estanza's belongings, carried her to the room Frau Brauner reserved for guests who needed to stay overnight. With utmost gentleness he laid her on the soft featherbed and matching pillow. He removed her shoes, the menacing hat pin, and her ruined hat, covered her lightly with the silk coverlet, and tiptoed out of the room, slowly closing the door behind him.

In the kitchen Biku was served pigs feet and sauerkraut

(his favorite meal since he arrived in Germany), which he washed down with several mugs of dark, Bavarian beer. Frau Brauner came in with apologies that there were no more vacant rooms.

"I can sleep in the car," Biku offered. "Don't worry about me."

"You look very tired," Frau Brauner observed. Then she added, "Maria Theresa, our devout Catholic girl, is away on a retreat. You can have her room. You really need a full night's sleep."

Biku sank gratefully into the soft, wide bed. The fragrance of rose oil wafted faintly around him. He remembered the first and only time he had spent a night with a prostitute. Her skin was a shade lighter than his, but their passion was a perfect match. Afterward they had talked until dawn. In the morning, after two hours of sleep, they had decided to get married.

He had introduced Lina to his mother, Ena, who welcomed her without reservation. Ena, who had come to Berlin from East Africa, with the five-year-old Biku, to cook for the von Stahlenberg's, had almost despaired of finding him an African wife. Biku and Lina explored literature, philosophy and science. After eight years she was also a match for his intellect.

From the age of five until they were eight years old Konrad and Biku were tutored at home. There was no doubt that Biku was the better scholar, but it was Konrad who was sent to school to be trained as a diplomat, and Biku stayed at home and did a lot of Konrad's homework. Konrad graduated from gymnasium and University with honors. Biku was sent to trade school and became a first-rate auto mechanic and chauffeur, which left him time to continue his studies. His latest interest was psychology.

Estanza slept most of the night, but near dawn she woke and needed to relieve herself. Thinking Biku had checked her into a hotel, she got up, found the bathroom and then looked around the bedroom. It was ornate with mirrors everywhere, but that was most likely the style in a city like Hamburg.

She realized that she was fully dressed. After getting her brush and other toiletries out of her carpet bag she went into the bathroom to go through the morning grooming process. Then she went out to the bedroom to find her shoes. While working on the arduous task of lacing up the high-button boots, she heard a knock on the door.

Biku came in without waiting for an invitation. "Good morning, Fräulein Nikiolopolis!" He smiled, his brilliant, white teeth reflecting in the mirrors. "We must be leaving for Berlin as soon as possible. Are you ready to go?"

Estanza nodded and then asked. "Is there time to eat some breakfast? I am so terribly hungry."

Biku picked up the green trunk while Estanza took her bag, pinned the ruined straw hat on her head and indicated that she was ready to leave. They went down two floors to the kitchen where Frau Brauner's head chef served them rolls and coffee. Before they went back up to the entryway he handed Estanza a heavy cloth bundle. "This is for your noon meal." He indicated the bundle. Then he added, "I already put a bottle of wine in the car."

The car rolled smoothly over the narrow road, passing fields of newly mown hay, orchards and small villages. The scenery was very different from Greece, where mountains dominated the landscape on all sides. Estanza was enjoying the variety of the landscape and beginning to feel less anxious about her future, when she was overwhelmed by nausea. She frantically rapped on the glass that separated her from the driver. Biku slowed down and looked in the rear view mirror. He saw Estanza's distorted face, and quickly pulled the car to the side of the road. Before he could open the door for her, Estanza had jumped out of the car and scurried to the grassy area beside the road. The coffee and rolls spilled out of her in one great heave as Biku held her by the waist. He handed her a white handkerchief after he was satisfied that her spasm had subsided.

"I am so sorry." Estanza sputtered. "I thought I was all through being seasick."

"Sometimes people get the same sensation from lengthy car rides," he said, sounding unconcerned. "I have a jug of water up front. Come and drink a little. People tend to get motion sickness in the back of the car. Come sit in the front for a while," he said, while she sipped some water from the clay jug.

Estanza climbed into the front seat and noticed that there were no side windows. The roof and windshield were the only protection from the elements. The motor and the passing wind made conversation difficult so they sat in silence for the next few hours. The sky was overcast with dark clouds, but it was warm if somewhat humid.

Biku said that this was typical summer weather for this part of Europe. "We get used to the frequent thunderstorms." He shouted over the engine noise. "In about an hour we will stop and eat. I know a perfect spot. There is shelter nearby in case it rains."

Strangely enough, Estanza was feeling hungry again. After eating the tasty little breads, spread with mustard and liverwurst, drinking a little wine and more of the water, Estanza climbed into the back seat where it was warm and much quieter. She had started to doze when a horrible thought she had fought to suppress clawed its way to the front of her mind: *Could I be pregnant?*

It was not impossible, but highly improbable. For the first time in eight years she had lost track of her menstrual cycle, which was very regular. Her body had developed early. She was eleven when men began to notice her. It was another five years before she understood the meaning behind those leering eyes.

The nausea returned, but this time she had the feeling that it was from anxiety. She fought it down as panic clutched at her middle. She felt that she couldn't bear it if she were pregnant.

Her first thought was of Konrad. If she could get him into bed with her soon enough, she might be able to convince him that the child was his. Could she deceive a man she loved? She hoped it would not be necessary to try. She had heard that there were ways to terminate a pregnancy. Where would she get the courage to inquire about such a thing? If it became necessary, would she have the courage to kill herself?

Biku had to take a circuitous route around Berlin to get to the Hotel Bristol, located on Unter Den Linden, the main street through the city. Every area of the city was being torn apart and dug up for the construction of the new subway. It took almost an hour longer than he had anticipated to bring the car to the front of the imposing structure.

The doorman recognized the late model Daimler and hurried to open the door for Estanza before Biku could get to that side of the car. Expecting Elisabet, the doorman recovered quickly from his surprise when he saw Biku.

"I will help the lady check in and escort her to her room," Biku told the valet, who had come out of the hotel to help with the luggage. "Leave the car here; I will move it shortly," he told the doorman. He carried the green trunk into the opulent lobby, followed closely by a still disturbed Estanza.

The checking in process went smoothly. The letter, written in Konrad's handwriting, expedited the matter, and within a few minutes Estanza and Biku were on their way up to the penthouse in the newly-installed Otis elevator.

The three-room apartment reflected Konrad's aristocratic taste. The salon, furnished with a couch, chairs and ottomans, was color-coordinated with shades of light-to-dark greens and accented with white. There was a library with floor to ceiling bookcases, and upholstered chairs with reading lamps and tables placed in strategic settings. The bedroom had a warmer feeling with rose-colored draperies and bedding to match. The whole arrangement was pleasing to the eye and much more than Estanza had expected.

After letting Estanza into the rooms and showing her around, Biku handed her the heavy key and a slip of paper with his telephone number. "The hotel staff is always available, so do not hesitate to call them," he said, and demonstrated the use of the telephone. She could hardly believe that each room in this hotel had a telephone. In the hotel in Distomo a telephone sat at the desk, but no one had ever thought to put one in the rooms. "You have my telephone number, so call if there is something I can do for you." He tipped his hat and headed for the door. Estanza felt a pang of loneliness as he disappeared into the hall.

For a few moments she sat on the bed, looking around; then she headed for the bathroom. Everything a person would need for a luxurious bath was neatly placed on wide counters, and the towel racks were hung with huge, soft towels.

While the warm water swirled around her and the fragrant bubbles teased her nose, Estanza smiled broadly and thought, *A girl could get used to this.*

An hour later, dressed in the black organdy dress, Estanza entered the dining room, let the head waiter take her to a table, and felt her mouth water as she perused the menu.

The Hotel Bristol served full dinners in the evening because their clientele was made up mostly of foreigners and upper-class Germans who often ate their large meal in the evening; only working-class people tended to eat their main meal at noon.

The waiter offered to order for her and she acquiesced, and then began to look around the dining room. Glittering chandeliers hung from the ceiling, palm trees waved their fronds in the breeze from the rotating fans near the walls. Estanza heard several different languages coming from nearby tables. A couple at the next table looked in her direction and she heard the woman say, "Look at that girl. I didn't know the Hotel Bristol allowed Gypsies into the dining room."

The man turned his head fully in her direction, gave

Estanza an appreciative glance and turned back to the woman. The man responded, "Obviously no decent girl would come in here without an escort." The implication was obvious and Estanza felt herself blushing.

A three-course meal arrived, course by course as one would expect in a French restaurant. She especially appreciated the spices and the garlic that enhanced the flavor of the venison. There was a different wine for each course and by the time she had finished eating she felt a little dizzy, as if she might be back on the ship. With great care she made her way back to the penthouse. She brushed out her hair and climbed into the soft, wide bed and fell into a dreamless sleep. The next morning she was filled with unutterable relief when she found blood stains on her nightgown.

~

Dark clouds shrouded the city for two more days. On the third day, a thunderstorm drowned out the sounds of cars, horses and construction with earsplitting claps of thunder. Sheet lighting streaked across the sky like constant fireworks. Rain pounded on the roof and flooded the streets below. Estanza hardly noticed the dramatic antics of nature. During her first day in the penthouse suite she discovered a shelf of books on the subject of sexual intercourse.

A Sexual Guide for the Groom was the first book she took down from the shelf. It was devoted to giving step-by-step instructions to the young man, about how to introduce his most-likely virgin bride to the pleasures of the matrimonial bed.

The author warned the new husband that his bride may have little or no knowledge of the male anatomy. Having grown up in Greece where nude statues, with all their body parts intact, were commonplace, Estanza couldn't believe that German girls were that sheltered and ignorant. She stifled her amused laughter but quickly felt empathy for any innocent girl who encountered a fully aroused, impatient, insensitive bridegroom. If the young man were unable to control himself, he would most likely ruin all hope of a truly happy marriage. No doubt many brides had to endure the indignity of marital rape.

In several recent works by such notables as Sigmund Freud and Krafft-Ebing, and in ancient texts like the *Kama Sutra,* the advice to husbands was graphic, detailed and enhanced by illustrations that made Estanza blush, while simultaneously arousing her.

When the week of thunderstorms finally let up, Estanza hardly noticed. She had no desire to go out into the flooded streets. Instead she ordered food to be brought up and kept on reading.

Chapter 19

Athens, July 1910

The main railway station in Athens was always crowded and chaotic. Finding the right track and train was problematic as the schedules were written in Greek and few foreign travelers could read the language. The timetables were useless since no one could remember when a train had actually been on time. The four men from the German Embassy finally found the train that would take them through what was left of the Ottoman Empire and on to the border of Bulgaria. Actually the borders of the Ottoman Empire were not yet defined and kept changing as the ruling warlords wrestled for control.

Konrad, carrying only a small valise of his own, carried a large, ungainly suitcase for the ambassador. The ambassador's valet, a huge man who also served as his bodyguard, carried the other suitcase and had a large duffel bag that looked like bedding slung over his bulging shoulders. The clerk who accompanied them was loaded down with several briefcases that hung from his body by leather straps. The men worked their way through the narrow passages on the train until they found their compartment. The valet stowed the luggage in the overhead bin and gently put his duffle bag on the floor, positioning his long legs in front of it. The train began to move north and the bundle of bedding gave a low moan.

"Eric, what is in that bundle?" The ambassador's voice was stern, commanding.

The valet/bodyguard looked down and then up at the three men who were watching him expectantly.

"My wife, sir," was the hesitant answer. He undid the cord at the end of the bag and carefully peeled back layers of featherbedding, linens and blankets.

The woman who emerged from the soft cocoon resembled a nymph, much like those depicted on ancient frescos. A thick, black braid hung past her slim shoulders, dark eyes dominated her round, olive-toned features. She barely reached the valet's shoulder, as he stood looking sheepishly at the ambassador with a protective arm around the slim woman at his side.

"Sir," he said quietly, respectfully, but with a firm tone. "This is my wife, Iona. We are legally married. She has the papers to prove it." He gestured to Iona to show the papers to the ambassador who quickly handed the official-looking scroll to Konrad. He verified its validity and handed it back to Iona.

"These two are definitely married, according to these papers," Konrad informed the ambassador then he spoke to Eric. "The best thing to do is to buy her a train ticket."

Eric nodded and looked embarrassed. "I only had funds for one ticket," he admitted. The ambassador was tempted to give the young couple a lecture on how Germans did not sneak onto trains to avoid paying the fare, but instead just frowned to show his displeasure, and then ordered Konrad to give Eric enough drachmas for another ticket. Eric took the money with a sheepish grin and left to find the conductor.

Later over bowls of lamb stew, Eric told their story.

> "In Athens there are numerous establishments surrounding the area below the Parthenon where handmade items, including knives and daggers, can be bought. A display of particularly artistic sheaths and hilts for daggers intrigued me one afternoon, and I went in to investigate. The boy I thought I saw at the counter turned out to be a girl who was very knowledgeable about various blades and their use.

I found out that Iona, the only child of a Greek couple, who had lived for a time in the Turkish-occupied part of Greece, became her father's apprentice. After her mother died, she also helped manage the retail store.

I courted Iona for almost a year. Her father was hostile to Germans, as allies of the hated Turks, and he was not inclined to approve of our marriage. When he leaned about my position as the German Ambassador's valet, his animosity toward Germans seemed to soften a little. He gave his permission for us to marry.

When the ambassador informed me that we were returning to Germany, Iona's father arranged a hurried but legal wedding. For a wedding present he made her a stiletto with a sheath made of Iona's own hair. It fit into the thick braid that hung down her back, making it virtually invisible to the casual observer. Her father also gave her minute instructions about the lethal use of the slim weapon.

There was not enough time to procure all the papers needed for Iona to leave Greece or for her entry into Germany. Also, I didn't have enough funds to buy a rail ticket for my wife. Hiding in the bedroll was her idea."

Konrad listened to this explanation and thought, *So he is starting out right away with blaming the wife for bad decisions.*

The local bey sent his troops to inspect the identity papers of the passengers at the Bulgarian border. Then he demanded a fee for allowing them to leave the Ottoman territory. Somehow the news had gotten to bey Kaliman that the authentic German ambassador to Greece was on this train. Obviously there was a traitor among the German delegation, since the ambassador had assigned four other men, who were traveling different routes, to carry identical papers indicating that each was the real German ambassador to Greece.

After a scrupulous search through all the luggage and possible hiding places in the compartment, the bey's men agreed that there was no gold or other valuables. Following orders they escorted the ambassador and his companions off the train and brought them under guard to the bey's palace, where the men were made to strip and their clothes were shaken vigorously by the guards. Eventually a few gold pieces fell out of ripped linings and secret pockets. Since Iona wore only a thin shift, a search was deemed unnecessary.

Bey Kaliman did not mince words. With the help of a translator who spoke very broken German, he explained that he was sending the valet, with a ransom letter, to the wealthy German Kaiser. The others would remain as hostages.

When Eric protested that the woman was his wife and he was not leaving without her, the bey gestured one of the guards to cut off her head. There was no need for a translation of his intent as the guard drew his scimitar. Eric quickly stepped in front of his wife, loudly proclaiming he would go alone after all.

The bey sat down at his ornate desk and wrote a ransom letter in Turkish. Konrad offered to rewrite the letter into German since the Kaiser would recognize his handwriting, giving the letter more credence. Eric took the letter and a stamped document that would, hopefully, assure him safe passage to Berlin. When the valet made a motion to embrace his wife before his departure, she turned away. He left feeling puzzled.

The men were taken to what were, by middle-eastern standards, comfortable quarters. Iona was sent to the bey's extensive harem.

Two days later a telephone call came for the bey from the German ambassador in Bulgaria. He informed the bey that, number one, Kaiser Wilhelm was somewhere in the Norwegian fjords on his yacht and unavailable for the duration and, number two, Eric had been intercepted by the Bulgarian border patrol and taken to the German consulate in Sofia, where he was awaiting further orders.

Konrad then persuaded the bey that a telephone call to his father-in-law might be helpful. After all, this was one of the richest men in Europe. His armament factories supplied weapons for all the important powers in the world, including the Sultan who ruled the Ottoman Empire. During this call, Konrad found out that the yacht *Hohenzollern* was landing in Hamburg instead of Berlin, that Elisabet was traveling directly to the spa in Marienbad where her mother awaited her, and that no arrangements were in place for getting Fräulein Nikiolopolis to Berlin. It was then that Konrad wrote the letter to Biku. Given every diplomatic assurance that this letter would bring the desired results, the bey allowed it to be sent.

A week went by and the bey began to doubt if there would be an answer from the Germans. It was then that he decided the woman might have some value. While he waited for her to be brought to his quarters, he remembered that she had seemed cold toward the man who said he was her husband. His five reluctant wives had only borne daughters. He hoped that this Greek woman would be docile and bear him a son.

The eunuch who came to get Iona did not address her by name, but just called out for the Greek woman. One of the maids understood who he meant; she handed Iona a veil for her hair and pushed her toward the man at the door. The eunuch did not look at or touch Iona, but motioned for her to follow him. She looked around the wide, marble hallway, hoping to find an escape route, but there were no doorways or windows on either side. Oil lamps were placed in sconces at short intervals, producing the effect of daylight. At the opposite end of the hallway a guard stood at the entrance to the bey's quarters. When he saw the eunuch he stepped aside to let him pass. He did not look at Iona as she stopped just inside the door. The eunuch stepped aside and Iona was facing the bey who sat on the foot of a huge bed. The door closed behind her and Iona stood very still, waiting for whatever would happen next.

The bey stood up, took a few steps toward her, and removed the veil from Iona's jet black hair. She noticed that he wore a loose, pastel green robe. It was made of very sheer fabric, almost like the veils worn by belly dancers in Greece. He might as well have been naked. Without his stately garments and ornate turban, the bey was not much taller than Iona and, except for his slightly rounded belly, he was in good shape for a man in his early forties.

"You are an attractive girl," the bey said in Turkish. To his surprise and pleasure, Iona thanked him for the compliment in the same language. "You speak Turkish?" The bey asked. His tone was suspicious.

"My mother grew up under the Turkish rule," she replied. "She was forced to speak that language." Iona spoke softly, fighting to keep the defiance out of her voice. "She spoke Turkish, even at home, as a precaution."

The bey reached out and took her hand, leading her to the bed. Iona began to breathe more quickly, indicating her excitement. The bey pulled the string that held her robe up around her neck, and it fell to her feet. Instead of shrinking back from him as he expected, Iona started to undo his robe in turn. Next she lay down on the bed, indicating he should come to her. He could hardly believe his good luck as she raised her arms above her head and spread her legs in a motion of welcome. In a moment he was upon her. Just as he started to enter her, Iona reached for the stiletto embedded within her thick braid. With a swift, practiced motion, she drew it out and inserted it into the bey's neck, just below his earlobe. He collapsed without a sound.

Iona struggled out from under him. Quickly she put on her robe, tying the veil around her waist. There were a few drops of blood on the bedding as she pulled the stiletto out of the bey's neck. She wiped it clean by inserting it and drawing it out swiftly from one of the many pillows on the bed. After replacing the knife into her braid, she examined her hands and found no bloodstains. She didn't see any on her face when she looked into the mirror at the head of the bed. Still looking into the mirror she practiced looking agitated, and then went to the door, calling out in Greek, "Help, help!"

The guard came into the room, went directly to the bed and bent over the bey. In a split second Iona had slipped the stiletto into the guard's neck, and then quickly withdrawn and sheathed it. Slipping the veil over her hair, she walked quietly toward the harem. The eunuch at the door didn't look at her; he just opened the door as she slipped in.

Iona had conjectured that no one would suspect a woman of killing the bey and his guard. Even if there had been some suspicion, not one of the men in the bey's service could actually identify one woman from another. A search was launched for the assassin and it was concluded that he had escaped.

Funeral plans were made immediately since their religion demanded a burial within twenty-four hours. Messages were sent to the neighboring suzerains whose leaders were expected to attend. Since the bey had no male heirs the ranking imam was temporarily head of the district until the sultan sent a replacement. However the most likely scenario would be a battle between the competing factions until the winning warlord named himself the new bey of Kaliman and sent word to the sultan about the change of command.

Everyone in the palace was expected to attend the funeral for the bey, even the German hostages. From what Konrad observed, every man in the huge hall carried a weapon. The officers of the guard and the military leaders were nervously fingering their side arms. After a lengthy sermon by the imam, the men got up stiffly, their knees aching, and hobbled out the arched doorway. Everyone stopped to put on their shoes; then they followed the plain wooden casket down the wide stairs.

The eunuch herded the women along at the very end of the procession as it wound its way through the palace grounds, to the graveyard just outside the high walls.

No one knew who fired the first shot, but it rang out just as the bey's coffin was lowered into the waiting grave. Within moments more shots were fired, swords began to flash, and even the eunuch drew a knife to defend himself. The women—all but one—scurried back to the palace.

By midmorning of the next day, Iona (disguised as a teenage boy) had hidden several gold pieces in her clothing and was well on her way back to Athens.

Chapter 20

Athens, July 1910

The German hostages, left unguarded, managed to work their way out of the melee. Taking advantage of the nearby wall, they edged their way around to the other side of the palace. Konrad led the way to a growth of shrubs that seemed to indicate the proximity of a river. It was only a small stream, but they followed it until sunset. Since no one seemed to be following them, the men decided to spend the night on the riverbank. Another half day of walking and the stream expanded to a navigable river. In the distance they saw a narrow bridge.

"I believe that bridge indicates the Bulgarian border," Konrad said, "but I can't be certain."

The sentry guarding the bridge called out, "Halt!" as the three men approached. Then he raised his gun. They stood perfectly still while he addressed them in a language which was not Turkish, to their great relief. The sentry saw that they did not understand his words so he gestured that he was asking for their papers. Since none of them had identification papers they held up their hands to show that they were not armed. Konrad tried to explain first in German, then French, and finally in his very inadequate Greek, that they had no papers and were escaping from the Turks. The sentry said some more unintelligible words, indicated they were to wait, and went into the sentry box to make a telephone call. When he came out he motioned the ambassador to speak to someone on the other end of the telephone line, and a lengthy conversation in German ensued.

Within an hour a staff car arrived and took the three Germans to a nearby town, where they spent the night as guests of the mayor. In the morning the three men set out on the bumpy road to Sofia where an anxious Eric awaited them. When he found out that his wife had been left behind in the quagmire that was the border area of the Ottoman Empire, he scarcely could hide his rage. Without a word he stalked out of the German embassy and headed back to find her.

Another week went by as the personnel at the German embassy tried in vain to contact someone with authority at the foreign office in Berlin. Everyone of importance was away for the summer. The state department was virtually shut down until the first week in September. Without proper identification papers it would be dangerous to travel through the Balkan countries and almost impossible to cross borders.

Konrad asked the ambassador to write and sign a letter of identity that might help him get across the Austrian border. The ambassador was reluctant, but he finally agreed to write a letter of introduction. He also provided Konrad with a small amount of Austrian kroner, which would allow him to continue his journey to Berlin.

After leaving the German Ambassador and his clerk at the railroad station in Sofia, Konrad bought train tickets for Marienbad, where he planned to meet up with Elisabet.

The ambassador had decided to head northeastward to Sibiu, a German enclave in Romania. He needed to find another German valet as soon as possible. It had been years since the man had tied his own shoe laces, buttoned a shirt or tied his own tie. Although the clerk had tried to help, the ambassador's untidy appearance made it obvious that he would never be an acceptable replacement for Eric.

~

The crowned heads of Europe descended on the sleepy, little Czech town of Marienbad throughout the summer months. The wealthy aristocrats, eager to be seen with royalty, followed them there. Konrad found Elisabet ensconced in a suite of rooms at the Grand Hotel. Reluctantly the maid had opened the door to him. Elisabet greeted him coldly, then she introduced an imposing, older woman as "my dearest friend, Sonia" and a young man named Kurt, who was, ostensibly, her bodyguard/butler/chauffeur, but was dressed like a gentleman of means.

There had never been an argument or harsh words between Elisabet and Konrad throughout their ten years of marriage. They had not cared enough about anything, or each other, to actually raise their voices, but now Konrad had a serious grievance.

"What has happened to Estanza?" he asked, trying hard not to sound confrontational.

"I really do not know," Elisabet replied, adding flippantly, "and I don't care."

Konrad wanted to remind her that they had promised Estanza's father that they would be responsible for her, but he could sense that this would be a waste of time.

"Konrad," Elisabet's voice was firm, "Sonia and I are traveling to America on a ship that is leaving Trieste in a week." Then she pulled a letter out of her dress pocket and handed it to him. "I was planning to mail this to you from New York. I hardly expected to see you again." With a motion of her hand she signaled Sonia toward the bedroom. The two women disappeared behind the closed door and Konrad never saw or heard from Elisabet again.

For a moment Konrad stood watching the bedroom door; then, with clenched fists and grinding teeth, he left the hotel to return to the railroad station. On the way he remembered that he didn't have enough money for even a third-class ticket to the next station. He spent his last kroner on a salami sandwich and washed it down with a Pilsner beer. *The Czechs do know how to make beer,* he thought, wiping the last of the foam from his mustache.

Chapter 21

The summer of 1910 left most of Europe a muddy mess. From Spain to the outer edges of the Austrian-Hungarian Empire, heavy rain—accompanied by almost daily thunderstorms—pelted the country side, washed out roads and railway embankments, and flooded the great cities.

In Paris people navigated the streets in rowboats. In Vienna the streets were so slippery with horse droppings mixed with the torrents of rainwater that tram cars slid sideways in their tracks. In Berlin work on the new subway system was halted because the excavations were turning into turbulent rivers.

All over Europe train departures were cancelled or, hopefully, just delayed. There were no trains going to Berlin from Marienbad in the foreseeable future. A train was available headed toward Frankfurt, but potential passengers were warned that they might need to transfer to other forms of transportation before arriving at their destination. Konrad was ready to take a chance on the Frankfurt train, when he remembered that he had no money for a ticket.

The ambassador's words about Germans not sneaking onto trains to avoid paying the fare was an ironic echo in Konrad's brain as he tried to figure out how to do just that. He decided to board the train and devise a plan while en route. The first class compartments were at the front of the train, separated from the coal burning engine by the luggage car.

Konrad entered one of the compartments, made himself comfortable on one of the plush seats while his brain worked feverishly on a plan that would get him to Frankfurt, and eventually on to Berlin. He watched the baggage handlers load the piles of heavy luggage onto the baggage car. The window was open and it was obvious they were complaining about the extra work caused by the overcrowded train.

In a few minutes he had worked out the details of his plan. The other passengers would be coming momentarily. He had to act quickly. He took off his coat, vest, and tie, rolled them into a small bundle, and pushed them under his seat. He unbuttoned his collar buttons, rolled up the sleeves of his immaculate, white shirt, and proceeded to the open platform between the passenger and the baggage car. He heard voices from behind him. He had left the compartment just in time. Looking back he got a glimpse of a tall man ducking his head as he waved two women and a little girl through the door. Konrad hoped they were getting off before the train reached Frankfurt; otherwise, retrieving his bundle of clothes might be a problem.

He wiped little dabs of coal soot that had collected in the corner of the platform onto his face and into his shirt, and then rumpled his hair with his sooty hands. He wiped his shiny shoes with more coal soot and scuffed them on the sharp edges of the metal railing.

The train was moving out of the station, speeding up as it traveled into the green countryside. Konrad tried to open the door of the baggage car. It was locked from the inside. A heavily mustached face appeared in the glass panel. "Let me in!" Konrad yelled as he banged his fist on the door. "I have been sent to help unload in Vienna!"

He could see the railroad guard, wearing an Austrian uniform, sitting on a trunk. He was armed with a pistol and a rifle leaned against some stacked parcels beside him. Realizing that the train was Austrian, Konrad knew he needed to change his demeanor in order to carry out his plan.

The months he spent in Vienna as a member of a trade delegation gave him some insight into the Viennese lifestyle.

Austrians tended to saunter, while Berliners strode with a purpose. In Vienna he heard street cleaners, lamplighters, even masons repairing cobblestones, humming bits of music from the latest operettas as they worked. Policemen walking their beats tended to sing snatches of familiar songs. There were coffeehouses in Berlin, but nothing like the coffeehouses in Vienna. These resembled a social club. Men sat for hours playing chess or cards or reading the newspapers that were displayed on rollers near the doors. Konrad reminded himself that the casual, relaxed manner was a front. After all, the Royal House of Hapsburg had pushed back the Ottoman Empire from the very gates of Vienna and now ruled a large part of Europe with an iron fist.

Austrians spoke a type of German that came out as a guttural drawl. Each district of Vienna had its own accent, and Konrad remembered that working class people had crude expressions that marked them as being from a certain area. He could hardly understand the porters at the train station, but now he would try to emulate their speech.

When the muscular luggage handler opened the door, Konrad stepped inside the fully packed luggage car. There was barely a space for the two men to stand.

"I'm to help unload the first class baggage when we get to Frankfurt," Konrad drawled in what he hoped sounded like working-class Austrian.

"Papers?" The guard, sitting on a box in one corner, held out his hand in expectation.

Konrad looked surprised, then said, "I left them in my coat." At the same time he put his hand to his forehead in a gesture of trying to remember something. "They are in the third class baggage car at the back of the train. "I'll go get them," he said and started toward the door.

"Let it be," the guard mumbled, and continued to doze.

Konrad saw a stack of boxes where he could sit with his back against a pile of suitcases. He leaned back, twirled each end of his mustache in turn, to show nonchalance. Lowering his eyelids to suggest sleep, he kept a careful watch through his thick eyelashes.

Since there would be several stops, the train should arrive in Frankfurt by early morning. Konrad had several hours to develop a plan for retrieving his coat and for finding a train headed to Berlin.

When the train stopped in the Frankfurt station, Konrad helped unload several pieces of baggage before disappearing into the first-class car. The passengers had left and he pulled his bundle out from under the seat, put on the vest and coat and, while tying his tie, made his way off the train. He headed for the men's bathroom, hoping to clean up a bit before trying to sneak aboard another train. One look in the mirror and he realized that he would never get away with stowing away on a German train.

At the freight yard a row of open cars were marked with the logo of a Berlin distillery. Konrad climbed up the rungs on the side of a car and saw it was half-filled with potatoes. Before he could climb down, the train began to move and Konrad decided to trust his fate to the potatoes. He knew the distillery was in the outskirts of Berlin and, once he got there, he could find his way to the Hotel Bristol. Lying on his stomach, the lumpy forms bouncing beneath him and his nostrils filled with the strong odor of fertilized soil, Konrad fell asleep. Late that night the train pulled into the distillery loading dock. When Konrad heard voices he sat up. Stiffly, he crawled down the rungs and walked to the nearby road. A truck loaded with vodka bottles stopped to pick him up. The driver was making a delivery to the Hotel Bristol.

Chapter 22

"Estanza, are you there?" Konrad called out and knocked again.

Estanza could hardly breathe as she opened the door. He came into the entry and reached for her. She stepped back from his outstretched arms. The voice on the other side of the door had been Konrad's and her heart had raced with anticipation, but the man that stood before her was a stranger. He was hatless with matted, dark hair. A black beard covered most of his face. His clothes were damp and muddy and he smelled like a wet dog.

Konrad dropped his arms to his side. With clenched fists he stood perfectly still, watching Estanza retreat into the room behind her. He sought her eyes and she finally stopped and looked up at him again. There was no mistaking Konrad's flashing, green eyes. She hesitated for another moment then moved closer. Overcoming her revulsion she threw her arms around his neck. He raised his arms and held her gently. They stood like this for several minutes. Estanza was crying softly when he slowly pushed her away.

"Please release me, my dearest, so I can clean up," he breathed into her ear.

A half-hour later, Konrad stepped out of the bathroom, clean shaven, his wet hair glistening in the late afternoon sun. He was wearing a white flannel bathrobe that came to his knees and his feet were bare.

Estanza had ordered a tureen of hot soup and a flagon of red wine. The chef had added a fresh loaf of bread, a bowl of grapes and plums, and a bottle of Konrad's favorite brandy.

Their conversation consisted of Konrad's description of his harrowing journey from Athens to Berlin and Estanza's brief interjections of sympathy for his ordeal.

The sun had set when Konrad got up from the table, poured each of them another glass of wine and led Estanza into the bedroom. They sat on the edge of the bed, toasted each other by clinking the glasses. Their eyes met, signaling understanding of what was to come.

Standing up, Konrad allowed his robe to fall away and expose his full erection. He waited for Estanza's reaction. Without looking up, she finished the wine in her glass, set it down on the nightstand and stood up. With her eyes still lowered, Estanza pulled the pins out of her hair. It fell in ringlets down her back and around her face.

Slowly and deliberately, Konrad unbuttoned her blouse. He was pleasantly surprised that she was not wearing a corset. With a few quick movements, she stood in front of him in her stocking feet.

Konrad inhaled deeply while his gaze moved down her slim, brown body, so reminiscent of the Hindu dancers that had aroused him in his teens. While he watched, the large dark areola of her breasts shriveled and her nipples began to pucker into glistening, black pearls. He ached to touch her, but instead he moved around to the other side of the bed, stretched out on his side and waited for her to lie down beside him.

Sitting on the bed Estanza removed her stockings, and then arranged herself on the bed, facing Konrad. For a minute they lay side by side, and then he began to stroke her hair, her neck, and kissed her softly on the mouth. When he touched her breasts she gasped with pleasure.

Their lips met with endless, soft, warm kisses while his hands caressed her back. He sucked gently on her hardened nipples while probing the moist area between her legs. Ripples of pleasure began to course through her body as she clutched at strands of hair on his chest.

Estanza smiled to herself, as she realized that Konrad was following the instructions in the marital guide. The ripples swelled into waves and she waited, breathless for the finale. It was then that she realized that for her body and mind to reach the longed-for release, she would need to conjure up the terror and total helplessness that she had felt during the rape on the ship. She had come to the point of no return, and the scenario of her first orgasm would have to be the catalyst. She raised her knees and Konrad slipped into her. Immediately she was engulfed in a tidal wave of ecstasy. Her scream of pleasure startled Konrad and he tightened his hold on her writhing body.

A few minutes later Estanza lay trembling and gasping beneath him. He felt a peaceful relief which blossomed into joyful triumph. After twenty years of sexual encounters, he had finally brought a woman to an orgasmic climax.

Konrad moved over to lie on his side and pulled Estanza into his arms. He held her like this until she started to move away. He kissed her tear-stained face, brushed her hair out of her eyes, and slowly released her from out of his embrace. She lay on her back with her eyes closed and smiled that dazzling smile that he loved so much.

Stretching her arms above her head, she looked up into his face.

"Konrad!" she almost screamed. "You shaved off your mustache?!"

"You mean you didn't notice all during dinner?" he asked.

Estanza felt a little embarrassed. "I was so busy just looking into your beautiful eyes," she managed to stammer.

"Let me know if you want me to grow it again," he offered. "But it was getting to be nuisance." Then adding," I think mustaches are going out of style in the twentieth century."

They slept for several hours, and just before dawn they woke up. Konrad touched Estanza's hair, and then her shoulder.

She moved closer and felt the hard lump of his penis against her thigh. Shyly she put her hand around it and felt it grow longer and thicker. To her surprise, her body responded with little thrills of pleasure. They started to kiss. Konrad waited until he determined that she was fully aroused. He took her very gently, with slow strokes. She was obviously enjoying his caresses, but neither of them felt the same passion as the night before.

~

Over time they realized there were different aspects to their sex life. Sometimes there would be passion, at other times their love was a sweet ache that needed to be satisfied at a more leisurely pace. From that day, on regardless of where they happened to be—at the breakfast table or across a room of chattering guests—when she met Konrad's deep green eyes, Estanza always felt a thrill, almost an orgasm.

Konrad called Biku later that day and found out that his father was in East Africa with a peace delegation. Then he left a message at the foreign office asking the minister to call him back at his earliest convenience.

For another twenty-four hours, the lovers ate and drank, bathed and made love. They lay in bed listening to the rain pound against the windows.

The next morning a brilliant sun shone in a cloudless, blue sky and they could hardly wait to get outside. Konrad was eager to show Estanza around the magnificent city of Berlin.

Chapter 23

The Goethe monument was right across the street from the Hotel Bristol, and since it was Estanza's love of the German poet's work that had brought her to Berlin, she chose this famous landmark to start their tour of the city.

Konrad gave Biku the day off and hired a horse-drawn carriage to transport him and Estanza through the colossal arches of the Brandenburg Gate and on to the Altes Museum to see the antiquities collection. He explained how the German government had decided that the collections of ancient artifacts of Western Civilization would receive better care and be more appreciated here on Museum Island in Berlin than in the chaotic city of Athens.

The carriage crossed the bridge to the Museum Island in the middle of the Spree River where they admired the facade of the Kaiser Friedrich Museum. The tour went back to the main street and past the Bristol. A chilly wind caused Estanza to shiver in her light summer jacket. Konrad waited in the carriage while she retrieved her black wool shawl from the hotel room before she and Konrad headed for the Luna Park. They planned to have their midday meal at the Terrace Restaurant overlooking the huge amusement park.

"Tomorrow I will introduce you to my mother's dressmaker," Konrad told Estanza, as the carriage made its way past the Berlin Zoo and into the birch woods that surrounded the amusement park. "You will need a new wardrobe for the cold German winters," he continued.

Estanza did not reply, only wondered how she would pay

for new clothes, or if she would need them, given that her family expected her to return to Greece shortly. The driver stopped in front of the multi-terraced structure that was aptly called The Terrace Restaurant and Cafe.

Estanza felt a twinge of regret as she watched the carriage disappear around a corner of the building. She had felt like a princess sitting beside this handsome man, being drawn through this elegant city by a white horse. Konrad guided her up to the third tier of the restaurant, where glass panes shielded them from the wind. It was still quite chilly and Estanza drew her shawl tightly around her shoulders while Konrad helped her into a gilded chair.

Although it was nearing two o'clock in the afternoon, the restaurant was crowded with well-dressed clients eating large portions of their main meal of the day. The menu was daunting. Estanza started to read the six pages of small print with descriptions of each dish, but gave up after the first page. She turned to Konrad. "Please order an appropriate meal for me," she asked, giving him an apologetic smile. "I am certain that a restaurant of this size has specialties that I have never heard of." Then she added, "I like to try different foods."

Konrad ordered sausages, potato dumplings, the ubiquitous sauerkraut, and a pitcher of beer. Estanza sighed with resignation. This was the food she had eaten almost every day on the ship. She decided that in Germany, "different food" meant hardly discernible variations of the same ingredients.

A couple and a young woman, presumably their daughter, were sitting at the next table. Estanza sat facing them, and was too far away to hear what they were saying. However, they kept looking at her and frowning, obviously with disapproval. She tried to think if she had said or done something to annoy them, but nothing came to mind. Konrad, on the other hand, was seated with his back to them, but close enough to hear their conversation.

"It's a shame that they let those people in here," The older woman was saying.

The man seemed to agree. "Decent people should not have to expose their children to them," he said, while looking around at Estanza.

The girl, who looked to be about twelve, kept her head down and concentrated on eating her meal.

The woman continued the conversation. "You would think that an obviously mature and affluent man, as he seems to be, would know better than to bring her here."

"Well," the man said, a slow smile spreading across his face, "she does look as if she hasn't washed her face in weeks." Then he chuckled.

Konrad suggested to Estanza that she might like to go to the washroom before the meal arrived. Gratefully she excused herself and left the table. He turned around and addressed the man sitting at the next table.

"My name is Konrad von Stahlenberg. I am in the foreign service of the Kaiser." He then showed his identification card to the startled gentleman who took it to show his wife and daughter. "The lady I am escorting is the daughter of one of the richest Maharajas in India. In order to blend in she chose to wear humble garments and not her usual rich attire. She speaks perfect German. I can only hope she didn't understand your low-class Berlin dialect." He turned back to his table and drained a full stein of beer in one gulp and set it down with a loud thump.

When Estanza came back to the table, the three people at the next table made a point of nodding at her with friendly smiles. She gave them a cold stare in return. She had heard what they had said before she left the table. It was not the first time, and hardly the last, that she encountered the German antipathy toward other races. She wondered what had made them change their demeanor, but she didn't pursue the matter with Konrad.

When they returned to the Hotel Bristol, Konrad ordered coffee, a tray of cheese with fruit for two, and brandy to be sent to their room. While they waited, he showed Estanza the letter Elisabet had given him in Marienbad. Estanza read it several times, thinking that perhaps she didn't understand what was meant.

> I am traveling to America to start a new life. You will not see me again.
>
> —Elisabet von Stahlenberg

"Her parents are making an effort to find her," Konrad told Estanza. "If she wants a new life, she will not be able to remarry without a divorce." As if it were a new idea, Konrad added, "Neither will I."

Estanza went into the bedroom, leaving the door ajar a few inches. She hung her shawl and jacket in the closet, removed her hat, and sat down at the dressing table. She presumed that a knock on the hotel room door was room service with their order. When Konrad opened the door it was obvious that he was greeting someone he knew. Estanza sat very still, hands in her lap, and listened to the two men in the next room.

Although he was surprised to see his father outside the door, Konrad set his mouth into a welcoming smile, put his arm around Kurt von Stahlenberg's shoulders, and drew him into the room. The two men had not seen each other for two years, but being Prussian, they did not embrace; just patted each other on the shoulder with one hand.

"I was having dinner in the dining room with colleagues from the foreign office," the older man explained, not taking his eyes off Konrad, who met his gaze with a shy grin. "The waiter mentioned that you were here. I couldn't resist coming up to take a look at you."

"I am so very pleased to see you, Father." Konrad smiled and waved Kurt to a nearby chair.

The elder von Stahlenberg laid his hat and cane on the

table by the door and took a quick look in the mirror. He patted his graying sideburns then took a few steps into the room. If he suspected that they were not alone he gave no indication of it. He sat at the edge of the wing-backed chair. "I just returned from a peace conference in East Africa." He began. "Our colonies on that continent are in a chaotic state. We are not good colonizers. When we took control of those uncivilized areas the plan was for Germans to emigrate and cultivate those fertile lands. Only a few families have actually gone there. It is truly not realistic to expect northern Europeans to work in that heat."

Konrad had seated his father with his back to the bedroom door and he hoped that Estanza would have the good sense not to come out. He was very tempted to step across the room and shut the door, but knew that would only call attention to the fact that someone was in that room. So he sat facing his father who was just finishing his description of how the army had to put down the rebellion of those lazy blacks. "The ones that survived the thrashing will not try to run away again." Kurt's voice rose in triumph at these last words.

"I also have just returned to Berlin," Konrad said. "The mission to Greece was recalled due to the hostile attitude of their King George." Kurt shook his head with displeasure at this news, then asked after Elisabet. Konrad showed him her letter.

"What does this mean?" Kurt sounded very disturbed and looked at Konrad expecting an explanation.

Konrad just shook his head. "She would not talk to me in Marienbad, just handed me this letter. Her parents have hired detectives to find her. I can't divorce her unless she signs the papers."

At these words Kurt stood up and pointed a finger at Konrad. "Divorce is out of the question! Think of your career."

Konrad stood up to face his father. "I know how the Kaiser feels. He won't even hire a footman who is divorced." As his father began to cool down, Konrad continued, "Let's wait and see what Elisabet has in mind."

Both men sat down again and Kurt said he was leaving shortly for the south of France.

"With your mistress?" Konrad asked in an even tone that hid his agitation. His parents, much like he and Elisabet, had lived separate lives. After his mother died, his father accepted many foreign assignments. He took Konrad along when he could, but most of the time he left his son in school or at home with Ena, the cook and nanny he had brought from Africa.

Kurt gave Konrad a long and knowing look, and then said evenly, "Lydia Gottlieb is not my mistress. A mistress is a woman who is kept by a man, a woman who drains funds away from his family. As you very well know, Lydia is a self-sufficient person with a well-paying career as part-owner and headmistress of a prestigious school for girls in Vienna. In fact, she is in Rome right now, at a conference for training educators in the Maria Montessori method. Perhaps you have heard of Dr. Montessori?"

"Yes, there was talk about her, even in Athens," Konrad offered. "Isn't she the Italian woman who graduated from medical school?"

Kurt nodded his head and added, "She gave up her medical practice, which, by the way, was doing quite well considering the reluctance of many people to go to a female doctor. She is now developing an education method for three- to six-year-old children that is revolutionizing the education system in Italy and has been adopted by Austria. It is rumored that Kaiser Franz Josef is a supporter and personal friend and Kaiser Wilhelm is considering it for Germany."

The men sat in silence for a few minutes then Konrad cleared his throat and softly apologized for his earlier remark. "I am very tired tonight," he offered as an excuse. "That makes me a bit irritable. As you know I am very fond of Aunt Lydia."

"Actually, I have plans to spend the winter in Provence," Kurt interrupted him. "I want to get away from the Berlin winter this year. However, it looks like I will be sent to Greece again soon. It is always summer there, which makes it one of my favorite assignments." He paused to smile knowingly at Konrad. "The food is delicious and so are the women." Kurt allowed himself a short chuckle.

A knock on the door was followed by a man's voice announcing, "Room service!" The waiter rolled in a serving table, unmistakably, set for two.

Kurt immediately understood the situation. With a meaningful glance at the slightly open bedroom door, Kurt, with the finesse of a true diplomat said, "It was thoughtful of you to order refreshments for us, but I have just eaten a large dinner with several glasses of wine. Besides, I have a long trip out to the villa and must catch an early train for France tomorrow."

At the door Kurt reminded Konrad, "Lydia and I have plans to spend the summer in Switzerland. We would be very pleased if you joined us once again this year."

When Konrad turned back into the sitting room, Estanza was sitting in the wing chair, wearing her flannel nightgown, her hair brushed down her back.

"We need to talk about our situation and, more precisely, about my position in Germany." Estanza's tone was serious and businesslike.

"First of all," Konrad countered her, "we will eat this scrumptious repast, drink some of the wine, make love, get some sleep, and then we will talk in the morning."

Their eyes met in total agreement, and they did all the things Konrad said—but not exactly in the order he suggested.

Chapter 24

Heavy clouds hung over Berlin, the threat of rain was in the cool, damp air of early morning. Estanza sat across from Konrad at the breakfast table. Her mood reflected the leaden sky she observed out of the Palladian window across the room. She felt chilly in her flannel nightgown and curled her fingers around her cup of coffee to warm her hands. For ten minutes she had been trying to catch Konrad's eye. Her need to talk about her situation was churning in her thoughts and went all the way into the pit of her stomach: *Should I make plans to return to Greece?*

Konrad, wearing his white, fluffy bathrobe was very busy buttering his roll, brushing crumbs from the table, and stirring his coffee for the tenth time. When he reached for the newspaper next to his plate, Estanza folded her napkin, got up, and went into the bedroom, closing the door. It was only then that Konrad looked up. He sat watching the door for a minute, then continued unfolding the newspaper and eating his roll.

He knew Estanza wanted to talk about future plans. The truth was that he didn't know what to say. The plans he had made in hopes of keeping Estanza in his house as Elisabet's secretary were gone with Elisabet. He needed to devise another plan to keep Estanza in Berlin. The bedroom door opened and he was startled to see a fully-dressed Estanza stride across the room. She stopped to adjust her hat in the hall mirror, shifted her carpet bag to her left shoulder, and then turned to look at Konrad who was coming toward her.

She put out a hand toward Konrad, in preparation for a farewell handshake.

"Good-bye my darling," she said with a forced smile. "I will be returning to Greece on the first available ship."

Instead of shaking her outstretched hand, Konrad caught Estanza around the waist and drew her back into the room, pressing her hard against his body. Even before he bent to kiss her lips, she put her arms around him, hugging him tighter to her. They stood like this for a long moment, losing all sense of time.

When they loosened their grip, giving in to the desperate need for air, their eyes met. There was no need for words, but they said them anyway. They knew they would stay together as long as they lived, bonded as any married couple. A sense of relief was palpable between them, similar to the feeling of having survived great danger. However given the nature of the society in which they lived, and worked, they knew the difficulties they faced and the need to find ways to circumvent rules—both spoken and unspoken—that were meant to keep them apart.

For several more minutes they stood, arms entwined, feeling the reassuring warmth of each other's bodies. Finally Estanza spoke. There was a tone of authority in her voice that Konrad had not heard before. "Go get dressed," she said matter-of-factly, "while I finish my breakfast."

When Konrad came back into the sitting room, the dishes had been taken away and Estanza was sitting in the wingback chair that Kurt had used the night before. She got up and motioned Konrad to sit beside her on the sofa. Taking his hand in hers she looked into his face then down at their hands. His hand, freckled with wisps of blond hair on the back, and hers, a smooth dark brown with long, pink nails, lay between them on the maroon cushion.

Without preamble she came right to the subject on her mind. "Presumably I came to Berlin to be a secretary and translator/interpreter for Elisabet. Since that position is no longer available I will need to find other employment. I have no intention of becoming a 'kept' woman." She paused, waited for Konrad to say something.

He cleared his throat, put his other hand over hers and stroked her fingers with a tender motion. Estanza kept sitting quietly, waiting. To fill the silence she related her father's advice about marriage, which he described as a three-legged stool. She explained: "One leg is love, one is trust, and the other is respect. You need all three to keep the stool level and useful. If one leg collapses the marriage is over."

Konrad, who up until that minute had only been thinking of his own needs, nodded his understanding of those wise words. He began to realize that Estanza was no longer a dependent school girl. Although she was half his age, she was a mature woman who had plans for her own future.

A queasy feeling began to form in the pit of his stomach. Although this girl had made love with a passion that proved to him that she truly loved him, she was not ready to devote her life to him. As he was not yet free to marry her, his right to control her depended purely upon her feelings for him. He remembered that during some of their Saturday afternoon conversations in Athens, Estanza had expressed doubts about marriage. It had come as a revelation to him that a woman could have ambitions beyond pleasing a husband. At the time he had thought, *Now that we are educating women, the world will soon be a very different place.*

Finally Konrad said, "I am not going to tell you that you do not need to go out and earn money. In fact, another income will be very helpful. My position as vice consul does not bring in nearly enough to pay for this penthouse. We will need to leave at the end of this month in any case, since Elisabet's parents have told me they will not be paying the rent any longer."

Estanza, who had anticipated an argument about her working, was pleasantly surprised to learn of this development. Konrad could clearly not afford a mistress.

"There is an opening at the Foreign Ministry for a

multi-lingual secretary—someone who can translate letters from Greek to German and vice versa." Konrad looked up at Estanza who gave him her dazzling smile. "There has never been a female in that position." He continued, "But in this case, you are uniquely qualified."

"It sounds ideal," Estanza breathed. "When do I start?"

"I'll try to get you an interview with the foreign minister." Konrad said sternly, "He hires the secretaries. It isn't up to me." Then he added, "First we need to be certain that you have a position. Then we will make plans about living arrangements."

As good as his word, Konrad telephoned the Ministry of Foreign Affairs; he was connected to the minister (who coincidentally was a personal friend of his father, Kurt von Stahlenberg) and asked about an interview for a prospective secretary. A date and time was set for the following week.

"We need some time to get your winter clothes ready," Konrad told Estanza, who looked crestfallen at having to wait a week for this interview. "Berlin gets very cold. It could start snowing any moment and you really need some warm things to wear and a good pair of fur-lined boots."

The next few days were spent shopping for boots, a fur-lined jacket, and a hat and muff to match. The tailor said it usually took a week to finish a wool suit, but he would try to have it ready in three days. The day before the interview, Estanza was admiring the little fur hat that sat at a pert angle on her tightly rolled up hair. It complimented the dark gray suit and she could hardly believe that the she was the fashionable lady in the mirror. When the tailor handed Konrad the bill, he signed it and handed it back to the frowning man. "Can you pay for a part of this now?" he asked, clearly annoyed.

Konrad shook his head with a sad look on his face. "My salary has been delayed this month due to disturbances in Greece. I will pay you next week." With these words he wrote an IOU on the back of the bill dated for the following week.

Biku was waiting for them when they came out of the tailor shop. "Ena is inviting you two for dinner at the villa," he told them, while helping Estanza into the backseat of the car.

~

For an hour they drove through tree-lined streets and then along the Spree River, until they reached the area where huge mansions, separated by acres of well-tended gardens, lined the shore of the river. Further along, smaller villas, separated by yards of grass, could be seen from the narrowing road. The von Stahlenberg villa had a circular drive that led to the covered portico and the front door. Biku ushered Konrad and Estanza out of the car and waved them toward the massive entry doors. Each had a huge brass lion head with a ring in its mouth. Konrad picked up one of the rings and banged it forcefully against the door.

A soft voice rang out behind the massive door. "I'm coming, I'm coming." The door opened and a very tall, black woman enfolded Konrad into her outstretched arms. Biku, who had come into the hall from another direction, stepped forward to help Estanza out of her heavy coat.

"Please follow me," Ena said. Her German was almost without accent. She led the way to a lower part of the house. It was dark by now, but the large windows revealed a lawn rolling down a slight slope toward the Spree River. Ena led the guests into a sitting room furnished with a pale green velvet couch and four upholstered chairs. Small tables near each seating area held electric lamps, ash trays and books. An arched doorway opened to a dining area. Six cushioned chairs were arranged around a table set with five places. An electric chandelier hung over the table. A dark-skinned woman stood in a doorway leading to a kitchen.

"Hello and welcome," she said in French-accented German. "I am Lina, Biku's wife."

She went to Estanza and asked if she wanted to freshen up after the long drive, and then led the way to the well-appointed bathroom which adjoined one of several bedrooms on that floor.

"Biku and I have a small apartment of our own on the top floor." Lina told Estanza as they went back to the dining room. "This floor is for Ena's use. The von Stahlenberg family uses the main floor and the bedrooms on the floor above that."

"Does Mr. Konrad live here with his wife?" Estanza asked.

"No," was Lina's quick response. "He and Mrs. Elisabet lived at the grand mansion with her parents. They have their own apartment there when they are in Germany. I believe she may have stayed in Greece to await his return."

Estanza didn't think it was her place to enlighten Lina about the von Stahlenberg situation. As they entered the dining room, the men were already seated at the table, talking animatedly. They broke off immediately and stood up while Ena pointed to a place for Estanza to sit across from Konrad. She then went to join Lina in the kitchen.

The meal was spicy and consisted mostly of green vegetables, rice and beans. But it was surprisingly delicious, and the five of them devoured every morsel.

Chapter 25

On a bitter cold morning in the middle of November, after a snowstorm had almost buried the central part of Berlin, Konrad and Estanza had to walk most of the way to the Foreign Ministry. They had an appointment with the foreign correspondence secretary about a position for Estanza in his department.

There was no motor traffic, the streetcar tracks were covered with a foot of snow. Many people were walking along the newly swept sidewalks. Horse-drawn sleighs were able to get around and Konrad was able to flag down one of these sleighs and pay the driver to take them to the government compound. The secretary and his assistant were waiting for them inside the front door of the massive building. The secretary apologized for bringing them out on a morning like this. He explained that the receptionist was unable to get into the city, and he would show them up to his offices.

"My assistant and I are accompanying the Kaiser to his summer quarters tomorrow," he panted as they climbed the wide, marble steps to the second floor. "If the fräulein will wait in this ante room for a few minutes," he continued when they reached the landing and pointed to a door on his left. Then he and the assistant waved Konrad into an adjoining room which was very cold. Estanza was glad of her fur coat and muff. Her boots were wet and some of the moisture began to soak into her stockings. There were no chairs in the room so she walked around the perimeter to keep warm. The windowless room was papered with red silk and featured another door that led into the next room. She heard voices and stopped to listen. Konrad was speaking, his tone level.

"What you are offering is only half of what the other translators are being paid. This girl passed all the required tests with the highest marks and has credentials that warrant a full salary."

"Be realistic" the secretary's tone was imploring. "You don't really expect us to pay a female the same salary as a man?"

"Actually, I do believe so. If she does the same work, why not?" Konrad asked,

No one spoke for a minute. Then the assistant cleared his throat and said, "Women do not have the same responsibilities as men. They do not need to support a family and keep up a household. Why should we pay this slip of a girl as much as a man? She will only spend her pay on pretty ribbons and baubles."

"Actually, I am reluctant to put a woman into a position that has such importance to foreign policy," Estanza heard the secretary say. And then he lowered his voice bit, but was still audible in the next room. "She is so dark, like a Gypsy. She seems more suitable for kitchen work. Are you sure she is Greek?"

Estanza wished she could see their faces, especially Konrad's. Was he becoming angry? She would have liked to do some bodily harm to the secretary and his assistant. She was tempted to storm in on the three men. She clenched her teeth and took a few more laps around the room. She was startled when the door to the next room opened and Konrad beckoned her to come in.

The secretary stood behind a desk, twirling his wide mustache. The assistant sat on a low sofa just beside the door. The tall window behind the desk was filled with glare from the white wall on the opposite building. Estanza blinked, barely able to make out the form of the secretary standing in front of her.

"Fräulein Nikiolopolis, we have decided to give you six months' probation on our translating staff," the secretary said to Estanza. "In June we all leave for summer vacation, and we will let you know our decision about hiring you on a more permanent basis when we return in September. Report to Herr Kestlring at eight o'clock on Monday morning. The receptionist will show you to his office when you arrive." In a tone that was like an order, he added, "Be here at least ten minutes earlier; we Germans do not tolerate tardiness."

Then he and the assistant strode toward the door leading to the hallway, giving Konrad a curt nod on their way.

Konrad and Estanza walked all the way back to the Hotel Bristol. It took two hours for a trip that usually needed only twenty minutes by car. Snow flurries blinded them, and it was too cold to talk. When they arrived at the hotel they went right up to their room and ordered hot tea laced with rum, smoked fish sandwiches, and a plate of dried fruits. Konrad turned up the gas fire in the fireplace and they began to peel off the layers of damp clothing.

After the meal and several cups of tea, Konrad finally told Estanza about the position and expected salary. He explained about the probation. "It is customary for every new Imperial employee," he told Estanza. Also there would be a raise in salary when she was hired permanently.

Sitting beside her on the sofa, Konrad gently stroked hair back from her temples. It was still damp from the snowflakes that had drifted down on their long walk. It was their last night in the luxurious rooms of the Hotel Bristol. The movers were coming in the morning to transfer all Konrad's many books and other belongings to the von Stahlenberg villa.

Konrad awoke near dawn. The bedding that covered him felt damp. He looked over at Estanza lying on her back next to him. She had kicked off most of the covers. Instead of feeling cold as he expected, her forehead was hot and sweaty. She seemed to be gasping for air. When she opened her eyes they were glassy and feverish. He went to the telephone and asked the operator if there were a house doctor available Then he called Biku, at the villa.

The roads had been cleared during the night and traffic noises could be heard from the street. Konrad covered Estanza but she kept pushing the covers away. Then she began to shiver, uncontrollably. To Konrad it seemed an eternity, but the house doctor arrived within a few minutes. He examined Estanza, and then told Konrad she would need to go to the hospital.

"She seems to have influenza. She cannot stay here in the hotel in that condition. We must think of the other guests." The doctor's voice was stern and his manner abrupt. "I will call for an ambulance," he said and went to the telephone.

"We will have transportation shortly," Konrad told him. "Please, no ambulance. We are leaving the hotel at the earliest possible time. Is there anything we can do to make her more comfortable? Do you have any medication we can give her?" He sounded very frightened.

Both men were aware that influenza was a dangerous condition and people all over Europe were dying from this illness. Konrad's mother had died as a very young woman, leaving him bereft until Ena came into his life.

The doctor suggested cold compresses to get the fever down, which he had measured at 103 degrees. "Such a temperature is dangerous for the brain and can stop other body functions," he warned Konrad. "Keep putting cold compresses on her forehead and neck." Then he was gone.

Biku arrived two hours later. He and Konrad bundled Estanza into fur-lined coats and Biku carried her to the car. The drive to the villa on the Wannsee took about an hour, but seemed to take forever.

Ena tucked Estanza into the huge bed that was Konrad's when he was single. For three days, Ena sat by her side and fed her herbal teas and other trusted remedies. Finally, on the third day Dr. Rosenbaum came to look at Estanza. After he took her temperature, felt her pulse and listened to her lungs and heartbeat, he talked with the frightened Konrad about what little could be done. "She is young and strong," the doctor told Konrad. "Most people die within a week. If she lives until next Thursday she will be out of danger." Dr. Rosenbaum went on to explain that the flu very seldom attacked strong, young people. "This girl is dark-skinned like someone from the southern Mediterranean area," the doctor remarked.

"She is from Greece," Konrad told him. "She is a very talented translator and it was I who urged her to come to Germany. I couldn't bear it if I were to be the cause of her death." Then his voice broke and he looked on helplessly as the doctor gathered up his instruments and got ready to leave.

"It will take a few weeks for her to get her strength back after such a high fever." He continued. "You seem fond of her, so urge her to go back home if she recovers. These dark people are not made for German winters."

Konrad sent word to the foreign office that he would be unavailable for another week. He spent the next few days at Estanza's bedside. Sometimes he bundled her in the feather bed and held her in his lap, rocking her in the rocking chair in which his mother had rocked him before she had died. He kissed Estanza's forehead as he remembered his mother doing to him, singing snatches of lullabies, and prayed for her recovery to a being he didn't think existed.

Chapter 26

By the end of December, Estanza was walking around the villa in nervous, impatient strides. She was eager to get on with her life. Lying in bed during her illness, she had time to think about what she wanted to do with her life. Dr. Rosenbaum's advice about returning to Greece went totally unheeded. She had no intention of returning to making beds at the hotel. When Konrad told her that he would be devastated without her, but that she should consider going back to Greece for her health, her answer was forceful.

"This is my life you are talking about," Estanza had finally said, after listening to his arguments about her health. "For the first time I am looking forward to being in charge of it. I am almost twenty-one years old, an adult person. Soon I will be earning my own money. It seems I should be allowed to make my own decisions."

"Estanza, you belong to me," Konrad started to say, but seeing the look on her face, he quickly added, "We belong to each other." There was a note of desperation in his voice.

Her reply was quiet, thoughtful, but firm. "I love you, Konrad. And in all matters of the heart and relating to sexual pleasure, I will always be totally faithful. But we must face our situation logically. Even if you were free to marry me, such a union would ruin your career. Although we are soulmates, tied by physical and emotional needs, on the surface, we must lead separate lives. Much like your father and Lydia Gottlieb must be doing."

"Yes," he answered softly. "You are being logical about an

illogical situation. But then, your countrymen invented logical thinking, so you come by it honestly. For a lovely, young woman, you are quite the philosopher." Estanza noticed and appreciated the respect in his tone.

"Besides, I am not inclined to get married," Estanza stated matter-of-factly. "Marriage offers protection for a woman, at the price of social restrictions and expectations, like motherhood. I have no patience for young children. I would be a terrible mother. My idea of work is in a quiet room with pencil and paper and possibly a typewriter." It had taken courage to speak those words, and Konrad was well aware of it. He sat down beside Estanza on the loveseat by the window, took her hands in his and gave her a long and loving look that told her he understood, and was even relieved.

~

Later, that dark December afternoon, they went up to Konrad's childhood bedroom. Finding the bed made up with clean linen they promptly undressed, slipped between the cool, white sheets. It was the first time Konrad had been in this bed since he went away on his honeymoon ten years ago. At first it felt strange having a real woman beside him. He told Estanza about how he had imagined her in this bed long before he knew of her existence. The Hindu dancers who had aroused his sexual desires looked like her.

Since he was sharing his fantasy, she wondered if she should share her secret. Should she tell him that she had to relive the rape on the ship in order to reach full orgasm, even while in his arms? No, she would never tell him. It was best that way; she knew her decision was the right one. Instead she said, "I can't wait to feel you inside of me. I missed you."

Their lovemaking was gentle but very satisfying and they finally fell asleep, cuddled spoon fashion, his left hand gently cupping her left breast, the fingers of his right hand tangled in her hair as it spread across the pillow. When Ena called them for a late supper, they didn't stir.

~

The next day a telegram arrived from Konrad's father. He was coming home to be with his son for Christmas and to celebrate the new year. A few days later Kurt von Stahlenberg arrived at the Berlin train station accompanied by a short, stout woman, dressed in a drab, brown business suit. Her dark brown hair was tucked into a large-brimmed, beige hat that hid her face. When she tilted her head back to greet Biku, her ruddy cheeks, brilliant eyes and friendly smile made it obvious what Kurt saw in her. Just looking at her made a person want to smile in return and become her friend. There was the promise of adventure, interesting conversations, and merriment in her lively, Viennese accent.

By the middle of the week Ena had decorated a small Christmas tree that stood in one corner of the library. She spent the next few days preparing favorite holiday dishes. Biku and Lina helped with setting out the polished silver flatware, the elegant porcelain, and the sparkling crystal for the festive meal. After dinner on Christmas Eve, Ena, Biku and Lina went to the Catholic midnight mass, while their employer and his guests spent the evening getting better acquainted.

Kurt explained that the missionaries had converted Ena as a child in one of the schools in her African village. She loved the Bible stories and wholeheartedly adopted the teachings of love, peace and mercy. "My Ena is a true Christian," he proclaimed firmly. "She lives the spirit of the religion in spite of the priests who converted her."

It was obvious that Kurt and Lydia loved each other dearly, even though they tended to tease one another about private foibles. They did not share their private jokes, but were generous about revealing how they met. "We were students at summer classes in Basel University and met while hiking to a lake in the vicinity," Lydia told Estanza. "It was understood that right after Kurt graduated he was to marry a woman his family had chosen for him." Lydia and Kurt exchanged quick glances. They knew that their situation might seem strange to these modern young people.

"We spent that first day together and I could hardly wait to see her again," Kurt added. "It didn't take long before we were completely in love." He let out a deep sigh.

"Marriage was out of the question," Lydia concluded, "so we made a promise to meet in Switzerland every summer."

"The fact is," Kurt chortled, "I was following von Stahlenberg tradition. You see, my father bought a lovely chalet outside of Basel when he was a young man and spent his summers there with his mistress. He often took me along while my mother went to Marienbad."

"I can't stand that place," Konrad interjected. "It's supposedly a health spa, but it makes me sick. All the nobility in Europe congregate there to show off the latest Paris styles, flaunt their jewels and exchange gossip." He grimaced.

The subject moved to New Year's Eve. The von Stahlenberg family had a standing invitation to the masquerade ball at the Kaiser's winter palace. "Lydia and I have decided not to go this year," Kurt said. "You young people should go. But you will need a very good disguise."

"The theme is 'famous couples, past, present or fictional.'" Lydia explained. "I was thinking of a Greek goddess for you," and she pointed at Estanza. "Apollo and Diana come to mind." Then Lydia shook her head. After a moment she jumped up and exclaimed, "I have it! Estanza will be Scheherazade. You remember—the storyteller from *One Thousand and One Nights.* Konrad can be the sultan. Those Arab women are completely veiled. Nothing will show except her expressive black eyes."

"There will be dancing, Konrad, and I have never learned to dance." Estanza sounded worried. "And where will we get costumes? We have not even paid the tailor for my suit yet."

"We have a whole week until the ball and I will teach you to dance," Konrad promised. "In fact, my father is the one to teach you the Viennese Waltz. He learned it from a true Viennese." He added with a wink toward Lydia.

~

Christmas morning everyone helped prepare breakfast and they all sat down to eat it together. Biku poured coffee, Lydia brought in the buttered gingerbread rolls, Estanza served the traditional Greek baklava she had made days before, Ena sat at the table and peeled fruit for everyone, Lina and Konrad set cheeses and breads on the table while Kurt supervised the whole process. When everyone had eaten their fill, and had at least three cups of coffee, they each spoke about being thankful for the blessings they had enjoyed. To Estanza's surprise, giving presents was not part of the von Stahlenberg tradition. To them, Christmas was a purely spiritual holiday to be celebrated with food, drink and family.

New Year's Eve was a success. Lydia created costumes from material she found in the house. Estanza learned to waltz and English two-step. She danced every dance and didn't even stop to eat. Besides she was reluctant to remove the veil that hid her dark face, to reveal she was not Elisabet. A few quick sips of champagne kept her going until two in the morning. Then Konrad reminded her that she was still convalescing from a serious illness and if she used up all her strength she could have a relapse. When Biku brought them back to the villa, he helped Konrad carry Estanza upstairs and quickly slipped out of the room.

~

The first day of 1911 went by quickly for the occupants of the von Stahlenberg villa. Everyone had slept until noon and it wasn't until late afternoon that they all gathered for a farewell meal. Lydia was leaving later that day. Kurt would accompany her as far as Vienna; then he would take another train to visit the German ambassador in Turkey. It was a secret meeting but he hinted that the concern would be Greece. "That country is a thorn in the side of the Kaiser," Kurt said in explanation. "We are hoping to persuade King George to distance his country from the English and ally it with Germany." Konrad nodded in sympathy but the others in the room tended to look away.

After dinner they went to have coffee in the library. Lydia and Kurt sat on the pink satin sofa, their fingers tightly intertwined. Konrad and Estanza sat on the loveseat facing them. They also managed to hold each other's hands in a gentle, but quite firm grip. Biku and Lina were perched on the upholstered window seat, their arms around each other's waists. Ena sat beside them, her long, slender hand across Biku's shoulder. They were all very aware that they would soon be going their separate ways without knowing when they would see each other again.

No one expressed it, but there was a mutual feeling of apprehension as they started out this new year. A discussion ensued about the differences between German and English culture. Citing Shakespeare versus Goethe, they all agreed that both poets were masters of their language and had achieved immortality by accurately portraying the timelessness of human flaws and virtues. Kurt, always the diplomat, pointed out that it was not a matter of who was better, but just that these men were from different cultures and that difference should be respected.

Estanza, who had studied both authors, spoke up. "For example," she said, "Goethe's tragic works are dour, dark, and humorless, while Shakespeare inserts comedy into even his most tragic works."

Biku chuckled. "Well, of course. He got his best ideas from the ancient Greeks," he said, with a quick glance at Estanza.

Estanza emboldened by this tribute, ventured further. "Also, Shakespeare's women are witty, courageous, wise, and have depth—passion."

Konrad tended to agree. "The women of Schiller and Goethe are sometimes depicted as shallow, naive, cruel, or the victims of ambitious, scheming men." He smiled, and then pointed out, "Of course, Shakespeare has some cruel women, too."

Lydia cleared her throat. Everyone looked at her expectantly.

"The German poets use their beautiful language to expound the superiority of the Teutonic culture—a culture that praises militant nationalism and glorifies death. Much of what they write frightens me." Her words were met with an ominous silence. Everyone in that room knew exactly what she meant and further comment was superfluous. For them war was always imminent.

It was Lina who made an effort to lighten the mood. "It is still very cold outside, so before we leave for the train station, I suggest we warm our insides with hot toddies." She had them ready in a few minutes and indeed they all felt warmer and more cheerful as they started out into the freezing wind and a flurry of new snow.

Chapter 27

It was barely daylight when Estanza arrived at the Ministry of Foreign Affairs that first Monday in January of 1911. She did not have far to go as her apartment was across the cobblestone courtyard from the government offices. The ministry was part of a group of buildings that stood back-to-back as part of a government complex. The front of the structures faced a main street and the back of each building opened to a large, cobblestoned courtyard. On that first day, when she had arrived with Konrad for an interview, Estanza had entered through the main door and walked through the opulent lobby with its two-story skylight, and up the curved stairway to the ministers' offices. As an employee, she would now be entering through the dimly lit, narrow hallway that led to the various clerical offices in the area behind the entry.

She was early and only the outer door was unlocked. While she waited in the cold, bare hallway, in front of the door marked TRANSLATOR/INTERPRETER, Estanza thought of the many obstacles that had to be overcome before she could take this position.

Recovering from the influenza attack had been the most important obstacle, but then came the problem of living quarters. The minor clerks lived in dormitories on the first floor. The supervisors and directors had one-bedroom apartments on the second floor. Hiring a woman for a translator position created a bit of a crisis. Eventually an apartment was made available for her, but she needed a suitable chaperon.

Estanza had tried to contact Madame Volant, but found

she had already left for Paris. Ena offered her services. Of course there were objections from Herr Kestlring, who felt that an African female did not have the proper qualifications to be a chaperon for a young lady. Ena assured him in her aristocratic German that she was not an uneducated savage straight out of the bush. Finally he had relented, as long as it was understood that the position was temporary and the government was not paying her a salary. So Ena had come into Berlin to cook and clean for Estanza until a more "suitable" person could be found.

Finally Herr Kestlring arrived at the ministry with the keys. As he bent down to open the door, two young men came strolling up. They nodded to Estanza and then walked past her into the long, narrow room. Herr Kestlring hung the key ring on a hook near the door, his coat and hat on a coatrack below the hook, and motioned for Estanza to do the same. He then pointed to where her desk would be. Three desks were lined up in a row below the high windows on one wall. A fourth desk was separated from the other desks with a tall, white screen. All four desks could be seen at once from the entry door.

"This is your desk," Herr Kestlring motioned Estanza toward the screen. "The screen was my idea. It will keep the men from becoming distracted."

Estanza noticed that there were no drawers, or even shelving, for the desks. Across the room from the desks and next to the door stood a filing cabinet with four numbered drawers.

Herr Kestlring explained that all materials were to be put into the drawers each night after work. "The translators are welcome to bring dictionaries and any other supplies they might need. Everything must be placed into the drawer before they leave for lunch and after the work day," he barked out, as if giving military orders.

A third man came into the room rolling a cart loaded with folders. Each folder contained correspondence that needed translating into German or replies to be translated into foreign languages.

"Before we start on the material that is on the cart," Herr Kestlring said for Estanza's benefit, "we must finish the work left from yesterday which is in the drawers. There may only be supplies in your drawer, which is number 4, so look at the folders on the cart and see if any of the letters are in Greek. They should be your first choice." He gave Estanza a questioning look and went on. "You are familiar with other languages?"

"Besides German, I am fluent in French and familiar with English," Estanza said softly.

She went to drawer number 4 and looked inside. It contained several pencils with erasers, a very dog-eared Greek/German dictionary, and a thick layer of dust. She made a note to herself to bring a dust rag when she came back to work.

The young men were all seated behind their desks by now, with folders open and pens at the ready. It was then that Estanza noticed the typewriter on a table next to her desk. She was relieved to see it because she had always had a barely passing grade in penmanship. Her relief was short-lived. It seemed that she would be doing all the typing for this office. The translating of Greek letters would actually be a secondary chore.

"The men do not type," Herr Kestlring noted. "Some jobs are just done best by women. They are good typists because they have smaller fingers and they are good telephone operators because they have softer, clearer voices," making reference to the dozens of young women who worked in the basement of the building in twelve-hour shifts.

Estanza was thinking that if a job is boring and repetitive, it is considered "women's work," whether it is in the home or in commerce. And they are paid half of what a man would be for the same chore (or paid nothing at all if she works at home). She tried to set aside her annoyance and reminded herself that she would now have her own income.

For the first few days there were only mundane letters of lading, contracts for goods, and revisions to customs regulations that came across Estanza's desk. She spent most days typing what the young men had written. It was very seldom that bills of lading, contracts and other mundane business correspondence from Greece came into the office, but when they did, Estanza always felt a twinge of nostalgia.

The apartment was sparsely furnished with just two chairs and a table in the kitchen area, where a small coal stove served for cooking and heating. It was primitive compared to the kitchen at the Stahlenberg's grand villa in Wannsee, but Ena cooked delicious meals in the cramped space. After all, she had come from cooking on an open fire in her village at the edge of the Serengeti Plain, to cooking over a fireplace in the colonial governor's house, and then found herself in the villa of a German aristocrat in a suburb of Berlin. Cooking just for Estanza and herself was like a vacation for her. The sitting room also served as her bedroom and Ena rolled her bedding under the wide daybed each morning.

One day when Estanza came home at noon, Konrad was sitting at the kitchen table. Ena turned her back as the two lovers embraced. They clung to each other for several minutes, until Ena cleared her throat to remind them that lunch was ready. She served them a sweet and spicy stew that reminded her of the monkey stew she used to cook for her masters in East Africa. She told them it was wildebeest, but she found that pork gave the stew a similar flavor.

Still holding hands as they sat across from each other at the little table, Estanza said, "You told me we would need to wait months before getting together. You said that we could not afford rumors and an ensuing scandal, because you could lose your position and I could lose my job."

"There have been developments that I needed to tell you about," he replied. Konrad's tone was serious.

While Konrad and Estanza ate the meal, Ena went into the sitting room, ostensibly to do some mending, but she heard everything they said.

The latest news was that Kurt von Stahlenberg was selling the villa to a member of the Rothschild family. It was a difficult decision. The first Baron von Stahlenberg had built the structure two hundred years ago. Now the high taxes, mandated to pay off war debts, made these huge properties difficult to maintain. In fact, all of Europe was still recovering from the war with Napoleon. Konrad had counted on an ambassadorship in his future, but since Elisabet's disappearance, this was unlikely. Kaiser Wilhelm only appointed married men to be ambassadors of Germany—"because it shows stability" was his pronouncement on the subject.

"For the time being I will live with my father," Konrad said. "He is renting an apartment in the center of Berlin. We are still looking for Elisabet. Her father has traced her to New York. Her disappearance has left me in limbo. It affects my position in the government as well as socially."

Estanza and Konrad exchanged knowing looks. They both realized that their relationship must remain clandestine as long as he was an employee of the German government. After only two years, he could sue Elisabet for desertion. However, a divorced man would find himself edged out of any important or lucrative position in the government or even in the business world. If he didn't hear from Elisabet for seven years he could have her legally declared dead.

"Konrad, I have told you that I plan to maintain myself," Estanza explained. "I have a good job now. I can buy food, pay Ena a small salary, and I am paying off the tailor for the clothes he made for me."

Konrad looked uncomfortable at these words, as he tried to adjust to this new world of independent women. The relationship between his father and Lydia Gottlieb had always seemed so strange to him. They were two totally independent people, but in their presence he sensed that they were emotionally and spiritually together. He fervently hoped that he and Estanza could be able to maintain such a bond, but that they would be able to spend more physical time together than just a few months in the summer.

In February, Klaus, one of the young men in the office, greeted Estanza with his usual, "Good morning, Fräulein," then went on to say, "I have an invitation to the *Fasching Ball* ("Mardi Gras") at the French embassy, where I did some interpreting work during the year. It would be an honor if you would allow me to escort you to this event." Her first reaction was to decline, but when she told Ena about the invitation, she urged her to accept.

"It is a masked affair and one never knows who might show up," Lena said. "What is the theme?" she asked, sounding very interested. "There is usually a theme."

"I don't know about a theme, and I did not accept the invitation. I said I needed to check my social calendar," Estanza told her.

"You should accept," Ena urged. "Find out the theme, and I will make you a costume."

The theme was figures in French bucolic paintings, which were romanticized versions of milkmaids, shepherds and shepherdesses, woodcutters, hunters, and various farm workers. Preparing a costume was not difficult, and a suitable mask of brown silk almost matched Estanza's own skin color.

So in the middle of February, just before Lent, Estanza dressed as a sixteenth century peasant girl and found herself twirling around in quadrilles and other country dances in the elegant ballroom of the French embassy in the heart of Berlin.

Toward the end of the evening the orchestra played a waltz. A man dressed as a swineherd, with the rubberized boots and sow prod on his shoulder, asked Estanza for a dance. Klaus reluctantly relinquished her. Just before he whirled her away, she looked up into the green eyes behind the black mask of her new partner. He gave her a mischievous smile and held her tightly to him. She stopped herself from saying his name out loud, but her lips formed it with a silent kiss. Before he surrendered her to her escort he kissed her hand, thanked her and disappeared.

Later that evening she told Ena about the encounter and her eyes twinkled with knowing amusement.

Chapter 28

In early March a letter written in German that needed to be translated into Greek came across Estanza's desk. It concerned the cancellation of the promised trip to Berlin for Polonia Arthenis. The Foreign Ministry sent regrets that the diplomatic relations between Greece and Germany had deteriorated to such a degree that a visit was not auspicious at this time.

Estanza thought how ironic that she was here in Berlin writing this letter. Polonia would be very disappointed, and denying her this visit would only serve to worsen the growing animosity between the two countries.

Very late that evening Konrad came for a visit, and she told him about the letter. He agreed about the irony and that there was some justice in life after all, since he had thought Estanza should win the trip in the first place.

They talked briefly about the Fasching Ball, and she told him that her highlight of the event was that last waltz. He asked her if her partner had been a good dancer, and Ena joined in the laughter before she left the lovers alone. She told them that she planned to spend the night with Biku and Lina, as Lina was not feeling well.

Toward morning, Konrad got dressed and told a sleepy Estanza that he would be going away for several weeks. He was not at liberty to tell about his mission, but he explained that he would be back by the beginning of April. "We will spend the summer in Switzerland," he told her before he slipped out of the apartment just before daylight.

Time seemed to creep by during the rainy, dark days of March. The weather was getting warmer, but Estanza had only the navy blue travel suit she had brought from Greece. There was neither time nor money to shop as she worked five days a week and every Saturday morning. One Saturday afternoon, she went to see the tailor near the Hotel Bristol to make the final payment for the winter suit he had made, and he showed her a pale pink blouse that he suggested would go well under her navy blue traveling suit. He said he had made it for a customer who cancelled the order and he would sell it to Estanza for less than half the cost.

She felt extravagant, but she bought it anyway. She wore the new blouse to the office on Monday and Herr Kestlring, noted her appearance with a backhanded compliment. "Doesn't our little Greek peasant look elegant this morning?" he asked, with a sideways smirk to the other men in the office.

So Klaus had talked about the Fasching Ball at the French Embassy. Had he guessed who had waltzed with her? She wondered how much these men knew about her life. Klaus had only given her friendly nods since that evening and had not offered any further invitations. This was a great relief, as she had no intention of going out with him or anyone else.

Her job was getting monotonous since she spent the day typing long, wordy contracts and by afternoon it was hard to stay awake. Then a letter in Greek came across her desk. It was from the Greek Department of Antiquities. It read:

> It has come to our attention that German archeologists are transporting Greek antiquities to a German museum without the required permits. Persons involved in this activity are subject to a fine based on the value of the objects that are illegally transported.
>
> Henceforth, all ships leaving Greek ports will be inspected by the Greek harbor patrol, and all illegal

goods will be confiscated until fines are paid in full and the required permits are obtained.[1]

Estanza was pleased and surprised to find out that someone had obviously read the letter she had sent to the Greek government. She translated the letter into German and sent it on to the director of the Altes Museum in Berlin. A reply to the letter came back within a week and was placed on her desk to be translated into Greek and then sent on to Greece.

The gist of the German letter was this:

Germany is a center of Western culture and Greece should feel honored that the leaders of the German Empire have deigned to provide space in their world-acclaimed museums for the display of the best of ancient Greek culture.

We urge you to revoke these restrictive regulations immediately.

Estanza changed a few of the words in the above letter to read as follows:

The leaders of the German Empire are honored that the Greek government entrusts us to display the artwork that was created in the birthplace of Western Civilization.

With this letter we agree to pay for all required permits.

Sending that letter was one of the more gratifying moments of Estanza's career in the translations department of the Foreign Ministry. She could only hope that the changes would go unnoticed and never be traced back to her. Actually, small payments were made until the start of hostilities three years later cut off all contact, and friendly relations between the two countries were never fully restored in the twentieth century.

~

In early April, after dark, Kurt von Stahlenberg came to visit Estanza and Ena. He had news of Konrad, who would be returning to Berlin in a few days. He also told about his new apartment on the prestigious Pariser Platz. The address was actually on Eberstrasse number 23, but it was in the same building as the apartment of Max Liebermann, the famous expressionist painter.

"At the moment, Herr Liebermann is the president of the Art Academy and the Sezession Group of artists—the German branch of expressionists," Kurt explained. "The Liebermanns are on the second floor, just below my penthouse. Max painted a portrait of my mother when she was young. It is in the Kunst Museum in Vienna." His voice took on a respectful quality as he spoke about his mother, a distant relation to the Empress. Then he sighed and added, "The Kaiser does not like Liebermann, or his art. He feels expressionist art is too French and Max Liebermann is too Jewish, even though his paintings are exhibited in the most respected galleries and museums in the world. Given my position in the government, I haven't told the Kaiser about my mother's portrait and, unless he asks me directly, I won't tell him my new address either."

After Kurt left, Ena told Estanza more about the Liebermann connection with Kurt von Stahlenberg. It was Max Liebermann who had introduced Kurt to Lydia Gottlieb when they were university students in Basel. This was long before Kurt was married. He and Lydia had shared a secret affair. Neither of their families would have approved of a marriage. They promised to meet every summer in Switzerland, no matter what else happened in their lives.

"So, for over thirty-five years," Ena explained, "they have spent their summers in the chalet near Basel that Kurt's father had originally bought for his summer retreat." Ena folded her hands and her eyes took on a faraway look as she gazed out the window. She sighed deeply and turned to Estanza. "The Stahlenberg men have not had good luck with their marriages. The story goes that Kurt's father built the Chalet so he could meet *his* mistress there each summer. He even took his son, who was only a boy, along to meet her. Then Kurt did the same thing—taking Konrad to Switzerland each summer to be with Fräulein Lydia."

"Was Lydia ever married?" Estanza asked

"No, she is dedicated to her work of educating young children," Ena replied.

"Lydia is such a pleasant person; I can see why Kurt is so fond of her," Estanza said.

"It is good you like her, because you will be spending time with her at the chalet this summer. Konrad has already made plans for you to go there in June." Ena smiled encouragingly at Estanza and even produced a little wink.

Thinking about the summer in Switzerland made the days more bearable for Estanza. The men in the office were distant, but not hostile. Herr Kestlring stopped at her desk each day just as he did with the other translators. Usually he rested a hand lightly on her shoulder while he glanced at her work. The first time he did this, she wanted to shake his hand away. But she quickly noticed that he did this to the men as well so she let it pass and endured his touch, though it made the hairs stand up on the back of her neck.

~

One day at lunchtime Estanza was in the middle of typing a letter and decided to finish it before leaving. The other translators had already left when Herr Kestlring came up behind her and placed his hands on both her shoulders. Then, ever so slowly, he moved his hands down the front of her blouse, cupping her breasts. At first Estanza was too shocked to move. Herr Kestlring must have thought this was acquiescence, because he began to squeeze, pushing his fingers into the soft flesh of her breasts. Then he began to rub her hardening nipples with his thumb.

Estanza grabbed his hands away, pushing herself to a standing position. She faced Herr Kestlring. "Don't you dare touch me again." Estanza's voice came out in a low growl, like a dog defending a bone. She gathered her skirt into her tight fists and turned to leave when he put out a hand to stop her.

"Or what will you do, you dirty, Gypsy whore?" he sneered at her.

Estanza's mouth was dry, but she managed to bring a few drops of spittle to her tongue. She spat them into Herr Kestlring's smirking face and again turned to leave, clutching her dress up a few inches in preparation to ascending the stairs near the door. Before she could take a step, his left hand came up and struck her, backhanded across the face. The burning pain spread through her cheek all the way to her ear. Herr Kestlring stood with his hands on his hips, watching her reaction with an amused grin on his boorish face.

Estanza raised her skirts and with all her strength sent her right knee into Herr Kestlring's groin. His eyes widened, his mouth clamped shut to stifle a scream. He sank to his knees and then, holding his hands between his legs, he toppled over onto his side. Stepping around Herr Kestlring, who lay whimpering on the floor, Estanza went to the coatrack, took her shawl and hat, and crossed the courtyard to her apartment.

She walked hurriedly, her heart beating up into her throat, the blood roaring in her head, and her eyes unfocused. She clutched at her hat as the warm April breeze tore at her shawl and teased strands of hair out of the bun at the nape of her neck. She strode blindly to the entrance of the apartment building.

Ena had been watching her progress across the uneven cobblestones. Now she stood at the open apartment door as Estanza stumbled inside. Without a word, Ena put her arm around Estanza and helped her sit down on the nearest chair by the door. Ena sat down opposite Estanza on the day bed and waited while the girl covered her face with her hands and began to sob.

"Tell me what happened," Ena coaxed in a soft voice. She gasped when she saw the red marks on Estanza's cheeks, and then repeated her request for information.

In a flat monotone, Estanza told Ena what had transpired in the translator office.

"No one saw or heard what happened." Ena said in a level tone. "When you go back to work this afternoon, you act natural. Sit down at your desk, and finish that letter you were typing."

Estanza looked at her in amazement. "What if someone sees my face?"

"I am putting some salve on it right now and in half an hour it will be almost normal," Ena said reassuringly. "Come wash up, comb your hair, and straighten your dress." She pushed Estanza toward the little bathroom and turned to the kitchen to warm up the chicken and rice dish she had prepared for their midday meal.

They ate in silence. Then Estanza laid down for about a half-hour. The pain in her cheek was getting faint and the arnica cream had dispelled the red marks. By the time she was ready to return to work, she felt calmer and more secure. Fingering the long hat pins before sticking them into her hat, she hoped she would never have to use them. In fact, she was beginning to feel a little remorse about what she had done to Herr Kestlring.

~

Two of the translators were already at their desks when Estanza came into the office. They greeted her with their usual friendly nod and continued working with the papers on their desks. Estanza hung up her hat and shawl and resumed typing the letter in her machine. A few minutes later Klaus came in with his colleague and Estanza, thankful to be behind the screen, overheard the men talking about Herr Kestlring's ostensible seizure.

"It was very much like an epileptic attack I have witnessed." Klaus was telling the others. "He could not move or talk. I sent for the ambulance." He looked in Estanza's direction and lowered his voice. "Dr. Schuster ordered them to take him to that private clinic where they all go with their venereal diseases."

Chapter 29

The pain was almost bearable when Horst Kestlring woke up in the hospital bed. A cold compress between his legs helped to alleviate the burning sensation that emanated from his groin. Despite the numbing effect of the cold compress, sweat was dripping from Horst's forehead. When he tried to move he found his legs were strapped down spread eagle. He was wearing a hospital gown that covered most of his body. His head began to clear and his eyes were able to focus. Klaus, his senior translator, was sitting in a chair facing the bed. The young man was watching him.

"Klaus, where are we?" Herr Kestlring asked, hoarsely.

"We took you to St. Benedict Clinic; it was the closest medical facility."

"Who is 'we'?" Herr Kestlring sounded very agitated.

"The foreign minister's private secretary has an automobile. After I went to his office to use the telephone to call an ambulance, he offered to take you to this place in his own car."

A nursing nun came into the small room. By the light of the narrow window on the wall opposite the door, Horst could see that she was young. In her hand was a basin with a fresh compress and when she lifted his gown to replace the old compress, Herr Kestlring had to bite his lips to keep from screaming, not so much from the pain, as from embarrassment. No woman had ever seen him since his mother had disappeared when he was four years old.

"Who is in the office?" Horst Kestlring asked. "How long have I been here?"

The nurse finished placing the new compress and covered the area with the gown.

Klaus walked over to the window and looked out at the garden while the nurse was replacing the compress, turned around and said reassuringly, "You have been here about four hours. The men and Fräulein Nikiolopolis all promised to stay until closing time. The foreign minister himself asked me to stay here until you recovered consciousness and then report back to him about your condition."

Just then the doctor, a short, bald man with very thick glasses, came into the room. "I am Dr. Schultz, and you are Horst Kestlring?" he asked the man on the bed. Peering over the glasses he waited for an answer.

It was Klaus who answered the doctor's questions about the identity of the patient. "He is the director of the translator/ interpreter department of the Foreign Affairs Ministry," was his answer. "We found Herr Kestlring on the floor, unconscious, when we returned from our midday meal. One of my colleagues has an automobile, and the foreign minister suggested we bring him here to this clinic."

"I examined Herr Kestlring earlier. His bruises are serious, but not life threatening," the doctor addressed both men, but again, only Klaus gave any indication of having heard him. "I suggest he spend another day here, because moving him would be very painful. I know these rooms are small; they were cells for the monks before the abbey became a private clinic." He waved his hand around apologetically to indicate that he knew the space was inadequate for such an important personage. "I will be back tomorrow afternoon. We will make a decision about your discharge at that time." With a curt nod in the patient's direction, the doctor left the room.

Horst Kestlring unclenched his teeth and summoned Klaus to come sit in the chair next to the bed, and gave instructions: "Report to the foreign minister that it is urgent that I speak to him personally. Ask him to come here with you tomorrow."

With a wave of his hand he dismissed Klaus and closed his eyes. He wanted to sleep, to dream of raping that Greek bitch. He thought of the women he had groped over the years. He had not particularly liked any of them. In fact, he had felt a hostility toward women all of his life. He did like touching their private parts, kneading their soft breasts, squeezing their buttocks. Some enjoyed his attentions, but most stayed out of his reach. He had never consummated a liaison. At thirty-nine years of age, he was an eligible bachelor, and would remain so till the end of his life. His parents had turned his desires away from marriage.

Horst's father fought in the Franco-Prussian war of 1871 and had come back with one leg. His young wife did not seem to mind his disfigurement and they had a son a year after his return. By the time young Horst was five years old, he had learned to stay out of his father's reach. His mother, who endured years of verbal abuse, had managed to elude her crippled husband's attempts at beating her.

However, one day Horst's father had caught her off-guard. She was standing by the window, drawing the drapes when the enraged and drunken man picked up a hot poker from the fireplace and smashed it against her arm. She was so startled that she didn't seem to feel the pain. So he raised the iron rod again and hit her more forcefully. "You bitch!" he yelled as she screamed in pain and ran from the room. "I saw you signaling your lover. I'll teach you to run around with other men." He followed her to the open door and watched her run down the street. Horst never saw her alive again.

For years Horst's father ranted about how he had known that she would run off with another man someday. After all, what woman wanted to be married to cripple? Two weeks later, the body of Horst's mother was dragged out of the Spree River. The five-year-old Horst went with his father to identify the body. The face was unrecognizable after all that time in the river. Even so, both of them knew it was their wife and mother, respectively, because of the burn marks on her arm where she had been hit with a heated fireplace poker.

"That other man must have thrown her out," Horst's father said. Then he added, "Serves her right for abandoning her child and crippled husband."

For twelve years, Horst and his father lived on the meager "disabled veterans" pension. Horst excelled in his high school studies and earned a scholarship to a good university, where he showed a talent for languages. After university he started work in the basement of the foreign ministry, supervising the dozen women who worked the telephone exchange.

His father had instilled in him a deep rooted hostility against women, yet Horst desired them. He was conflicted and angry at himself for being so weak. The young women in the telephone exchange had been easy targets. Most of them endured his groping and fondling because they could not afford to lose their job. On rare occasions he had to dismiss an operator who objected to his rough advances. He was not looking for a relationship with any woman. For one thing, he was not certain if he could actually please a woman, or sustain an erection. He preferred to create his own pleasure in the privacy of his bedroom.

Eventually he was promoted in the foreign affairs ministry to be director of the translator/interpreter department. Estanza was the first woman to work there and Horst could not resist touching her.

She had no right to spit into his face and to so viciously attack him. She would regret these actions for the rest of her life—which, if he had his way, would be very short.

At the end of the second day of Horst's stay in the hospital, his legs had been freed from the constraints and he was allowed to sit up for a few minutes each hour. He was still swollen and very sore, but on his way to recovery. When Klaus came to see him after work that day Herr Kestlring gave him stricter orders to bring the foreign minister himself to the hospital. "It is an urgent matter and you must persuade him to come here. It cannot wait until I return to work." The tone was indeed very sinister and Klaus promised to do his best.

The next afternoon Klaus, the foreign affairs minister and his secretary crowded into the small hospital room. They stood next to the bed and waited for Herr Kestlring to reveal his urgent message.

He began by swearing them to secrecy. They must never reveal the source of the damning information he was about to reveal. The gist of the information was that Estanza was a Greek spy. She had tried to remove classified information from the files. Kestlring had caught her, she had attacked him, and she had left him for dead.

"Fräulein Nikiolopolis came to work as usual that afternoon as well as all day yesterday and today," Klaus reported. "It doesn't seem likely that she would do that if she thought you were dead." He looked innocently at the other men. "In fact, she seemed to act quite normally. Are you sure it was she who attacked you?"

"She may have had an accomplice," Herr Kestlring mused. "I didn't see who hit me when I confronted her holding the stolen papers." For a few moments the light green walls of the tiny room seemed to close in on him. "She must not get away," he spat out in a hoarse whisper. "She deserves the firing squad."

"We need to investigate the situation before we detain the young woman," the minister said, sounding dubious.

"You must have her arrested immediately," Kestlring came close to shouting.

"All the employees have gone home for the night," the minister said, in what he hoped was a reasonable tone. "There is a protocol to arresting people. I will see about getting the proper warrant and proceed from there."

Klaus waited for the minister to finish speaking then added, thoughtfully, "It would be best to arrest Fräulein Nikiolopolis at the office. I have met her African companion.

She looks dangerous and it might be best not to involve her. Those people have magical powers."

"Yes, that would be best," Herr Kestlring said. "Arrest her at the end of the day. That way she will have put in one more day of work."

"I will do my best," the minister said, and he prepared to leave.

"It must be done tomorrow," Herr Kestlring said firmly. "Another day will be too late."

The doctor came in at that moment. Seeing the agitation on the patient's face he turned to the foreign affairs minister. "Sir, we cannot allow the patient to become so disturbed. Please do whatever you can to placate him. His condition is very delicate and any emotional arousal could damage him for life."

"Tomorrow!" Herr Kestlring yelled from the bed.

"Yes, yes," the minister called back over his shoulder.

As the three men filed out the door, the doctor gave the patient a sedative to drink, took his pulse, and then shook his head. "You need to stay quiet for another day or two," he said and left the room.

Horst Kestlring soon went to sleep with a broad grin on his full lips. He dreamt about seeing Estanza in prison, then full of bullet holes from a firing squad.

Chapter 30

The three men and Estanza stayed in the office until closing time and Franz, who filled in for Klaus, checked that all the work was locked up. Then they all four left and went their separate ways. Estanza went back to her apartment. She admitted to Ena that she was a little uneasy about what would happen when Herr Kestlring came back to work, but there was no use worrying about it until then.

Not worrying about what would happen when Herr Kestlring returned to work was harder than expected. Estanza and Ena lay awake until very late. It was near dawn when they finally started to doze off.

If they had been sleeping soundly they would not have heard the soft knock on the door.

"It is Klaus Bauer," a familiar voice whispered on the other side.

Ena, who was fully dressed, got up from the bedroll in front of the door. "Wait," she whispered and lit the gas light in the wall sconce.

When she unlocked the door, Klaus slid into the room, quietly closing and locking the door behind him. He looked at Ena with interest. "Are you going out?" he asked, noticing her clothing. She did not answer, only looked at him inquiringly. Then he saw Estanza sitting up in the bed. "You are in great danger," he whispered fiercely. "You must leave right now. Herr Kestlring is accusing you of being a spy. He wants you shot."

Estanza, her eyes wide with surprise and fear, pulled the covers up tighter around her. Ena seemed to understand what the young man was saying. "Get up," she ordered Estanza, "and get dressed in the bathroom. Hurry!" Then she turned to Klaus. "Where can we go at this hour?" Her tone was more an accusation than a question.

While Estanza was getting dressed, Klaus told Ena to pack everything they could carry. The small, green trunk was standing in a corner of the room and Ena began to fill it with clothing and shoes. She left the winter coat out on the bed for Estanza to wear. When Estanza came out of the bathroom a few minutes later she was wearing her navy blue traveling suit that she had brought from Greece along with the matching shoes. Her hat was already pinned firmly to her rolled up hair.

Klaus turned to the women and, with an air of authority, told them to follow him, to be totally quiet, and lastly, that he was helping them escape because he owed Konrad von Stahlenberg a great favor. "You must trust me," he said, after seeing the expression on their faces. "Your lives depend on it!" He spat out the words, hoping he sounded convincing.

The three of them tiptoed down the narrow stairs. Estanza was carrying her carpetbag with all the papers and books. Ena carried the bedroll, her jacket pocket stuffed with bread and cheese. Klaus led the way with the green trunk on his shoulder. Instead of turning right to go out to the main foyer of the building, or going straight into the courtyard that led to the office building, he turned sharply to the left and opened a door that the women had not noticed before. An even narrower staircase led down to the basement of the building where the coal furnace was throwing an eerie orange light on one wall.

Klaus led the way past the furnace and the coal chute. Two steps up led to a low doorway that opened to an alley between two apartment buildings. The threesome filed out into the cold morning air. In the dim glow of a street-light from the main street beyond the alley they saw a black delivery wagon. A black horse stood patiently in the harness, his hooves covered with thick felt pieces that were laced around his fetlocks. The wheels were also covered with a thick rubbery substance.

"Get in the back." Klaus ordered and helped the women into the wagon. "Let's go!" he said to someone in the coachman's seat at the front of the wagon. Then he climbed in and they all three sat on a box that resembled a coffin, the women clutching their belongings.

The wagon moved noiselessly into the main street and Klaus finally revealed his plan. "We are in a death wagon." He began. In the darkness of the wagon he couldn't see if the women looked frightened or startled, but he immediately regretted his choice of words. Yet that was what this type of conveyance was called. It was used by the undertakers to pick up corpses to prepare them for burial rites. Since this process usually was done in the middle of the night or very early morning, it was important to be as silent as possible while passing through the sleeping city.

"I am taking you to the establishment where I worked while I was still in school." Klaus kept his voice low and even, while the women listened quietly. He had hoped to keep Konrad's name out of any explanations about the plan he had devised to rescue Estanza, but he realized that to be successful he would need her to trust him. He cleared his throat several times in order to gain time and to collect his thoughts. He asked himself, how much he should tell them, how far back did he need to go? Their continued silence was unnerving. "I am a friend of Konrad von Stahlenberg," he began. "In his name, I need you to trust me," he concluded.

Finally Estanza spoke, "You know Konrad von Stahlenberg?"

It would be an hour-long ride over the bumpy cobblestones of the oldest part of the city, giving Klaus time to reveal the whole story and reassure the women of his motives. So Klaus began:

"Although I was only ten years old, I was the man

in the family and had to accompany my father's body to the undertaker after he died of the influenza that raged through Berlin that year.

It happened that Konrad von Stahlenberg's mother had died that same night. We met at the undertaker's establishment. Konrad was a bit older but he was also feeling totally bereft at the loss of his mother. My mother had to stay home with my little sister, and Konrad's father was out of the country on a diplomatic mission. It was up to each of us, the eldest and only son, to sit watch that night. We talked about our mutual affinity for learning foreign languages. Konrad was headed for Gymnasium but I, being a working-class student, would be sent to a vocational school, regardless of my grades or abilities. In fact, I was to be apprenticed to the undertaker, since my mother could only pay a small portion of the cost of my father's funeral.

I began to meet Konrad at a coffeehouse on Petristrasse in the working class neighborhood where I lived. We studied English, Greek and Russian together. We both were learning French in school. Often he brought Biku to join us. He was the one who bought the coffee, because he was earning money as a chauffeur and he helped us with our homework."

"So you have known Konrad since you were boys?" Estanza sounded curious. "You have remained friends even now?"

Ena's voice rose softly out of the darkness. "Konrad is a special person. He sees past skin color, uniforms, titles, or social class. He just sees another human being and is unfailingly polite and respectful to every decent person who happens to cross his path."

Although they could not see each other, all three people in the wagon nodded their heads vigorously in agreement with Ena's quiet statement.

"Your son does the same, Frau Ena," Klaus chimed in.

While the black wagon lurched and bumped over the cobblestones, Klaus continued:

> "It was Konrad who started me on the path to civil service, and since he and his father worked for the foreign ministry, they were instrumental in getting me the job I have now.
>
> The undertaker treated me well, and after a period of my being an errand boy, he taught me the business and even offered to make me a partner. I in turn offered to train another man to take my place, since I now had other plans. My mother enrolled me in a trade school for office workers. I was learning how to use a typewriter, a very useful skill for both men and women."

Estanza interrupted his narrative. "Klaus, was Konrad behind the invitation to the dance?"

"Yes," Klaus answered reluctantly. Then he added, "It was his idea and my very great pleasure."

"I enjoyed it too," Estanza said. In the darkness no one saw it, but Klaus was certain she was smiling. But instead, Estanza was struggling to keep down the nausea rising in her throat.

Just then the wagon stopped, and the driver, a short, stout man, opened the back door. The sky was still dark, but the stars were fading and a rosy glow showed in the East. The portly man touched his cap then helped the women down. Ena was surprisingly spry for a woman in her sixties. Estanza, who had been suppressing waves of nausea for most of the bumpy ride, now vomited up her breakfast into a nearby bush. Klaus gave her his handkerchief, and then turned to pick up the belongings, while Ena guided Estanza up a gravel path behind him.

The front room of the mortuary looked like the living room of any upper-class Victorian family. Overstuffed sofas flanked the walls and small tables, covered with brick-a-brac, were scattered around the room.

Klaus put down the things he was carrying and guided Estanza to a loveseat near the window. He closed the heavy velvet drapes, tucked a silky afghan over Estanza's trembling shoulders, and showed Ena to the kitchen area, where he filled a glass with water for Estanza.

After eating a few bites of the bread Ena had brought along, Estanza gratefully drank the water. Then she closed her eyes. "I was seasick like this on the ship coming from Greece," she murmured. "I'm so sorry to be so much trouble." Her words trailed off, as fatigue overcame her. An hour later Estanza woke, feeling her energy restored. She looked around the strange room and saw Ena sitting in a chair next to the sofa. She looked tired and worried.

"I'm feeling much better," Estanza assured her. "But I do need to find a bathroom." Ena showed her to the water closet at the end of a long hallway. To her complete surprise, Estanza threw up the bread and water she had just ingested. She didn't say anything about it to Ena, who was waiting for her in the hallway.

On the way back to the parlor, Ena told Estanza that Klaus had left to go to the office as usual. He planned to tell the other workers that Estanza had notified him with a note that she would be absent this morning due to official business and would come in after lunch. "This will give you more time to get away from Berlin," Ena added.

Before they could resume their seats, Biku came into the room and announced that the car was ready to take Estanza to Stettin.[1] "It's about a four-hour drive because the roads are still muddy and rough from the winter rains." His tone was urgent as he hurried Estanza to the car. He placed her green trunk at her feet, tucked a blanket around her legs and told her to lie back and enjoy the ride.

"I will tell you about the plans as we drive," he said as he got into the driver's seat and started the car. It was a new model, manufactured in Germany, and did not need external cranking. "Listen," he said to Estanza. "You can hardly hear the motor. Now *that* is German engineering!" His voice was full of pride.

Estanza tried to relax, but her mind was racing with questions and trepidations. She saw that Biku was busy navigating through morning traffic, so she waited—but not exactly patiently—for him to tell her what was planned for her escape. Eventually they were at the outskirts of Berlin and the road, though rough, was clear and straight ahead for many miles.

"Biku," Estanza tried to keep her voice level, though she was fighting down another wave of nausea. "I only kicked Herr Kestlring. Do they shoot people for that in Germany?"

Biku stifled a chuckle, and then tried to reassure her that she would soon be out of Germany.

Estanza continued to question him: "Where are we going? What are the plans for my escape? Am I going to be sent back to Greece?" Her voice was rising.

"Please be patient," Biku said in a calming tone. "I only know that I need to take you to a place where you will be safe. The less you know right now, the safer it will be for you."

Chapter 31

St. Nikolas, the Greek Orthodox Church in the port city of Stettin, was flanked by a rambling warehouse on one side and a five-story apartment building on the other. The gold plated onion dome of the little church was topped with a Greek cross that pointed defiantly into the sky. Inside, the decor made up for the drab exterior that faced the Kanalgasse near the Stettin waterfront. Originally, the church was at the very outskirts of the harbor, but as the dock kept expanding to accommodate more and larger ships, the commercial area began to grow outward. Soon the taverns, brothels and warehouses of the port began to encroach on the open space and surrounded the stately little church.

The church's actual history was shrouded in time, but it went back to before the area was ruled by Sweden. The story was told that a wealthy Greek merchant founded the church after his son was saved from drowning by some fishermen when his ship floundered off the coast near Stettin. Over the centuries, the church had acquired many lovely gifts from grateful patrons. There were gold-plated icons, silver candle holders, richly embroidered altar cloths, and frescos of bible scenes covered every inch of the walls.

The area called Ohber Slesien by the Germans had, for ages, been passed back and forth between several countries, sometimes by trade agreement, often by treaty, and several times by violent conquest. Miraculously, through all the centuries, the Church of St. Nikolas survived unscathed. The city of Stettin had a mixed population of German, Polish,

Russian, and many other ethnic groups, which were involved in the shipbuilding and other services related to shipping. It was, and still is, the largest port to the Baltic Sea.

Father Amiridis served a small and mostly transient congregation of Greek sailors who came ashore from merchant and passenger vessels. Sometimes Greek shipbuilders, designers or naval attachés would come to a service.

However, these more affluent Greek residents usually traveled to Berlin to the prestigious cathedral for holiday celebrations. Occasionally a sailor brought in a baby to be baptized or a girl to be converted so they could marry. The handsome, young priest asked that everyone call him "Father Ami" as this was easier to pronounce. "*Ami* means 'my friend' in French," he told new congregants and friends. "I want everyone to think of me as a friend."

The first time his mother brought five-year-old Spyros Amiridis to a local church, he fell in love with everything he saw and heard. Compared to the barren fisherman's hut he shared with his seven older siblings, this was his idea of heaven. He had fallen asleep during the service, for when he woke up in his own narrow cot the next morning, he thought he might have dreamt the whole experience. The next Sunday he again accompanied his mother to church, and after that the church became his second home.

Although he spent the next six years learning how to read, write and do fundamental math, and then another five years at sea in his father's fishing boat, his real life was lived in the Church. It was his good luck to meet a girl who shared his passion for beauty and service to God. They were both seventeen, but certain of their love for each other and what they wanted to do with their lives. The local priest took Spyros under his wing, blessed his marriage to Helena, and taught the young man everything he needed to know about leading a congregation. For seven years he served as deacon for the village. A few days after his twenty-fifth birthday, Spyros was ordained by the Bishop of Athens. The whole village attended the ordination ceremony at which he became Father Amiridis.

The art and music was what had brought Father Ami to his faith. Long after he had developed doubts about the existence of a deity that interferes in human affairs, he was still devoted to the visual beauty of the church. He endured the rituals and routines in order to stay surrounded by the art, decor and architecture of the Church. He also enjoyed the prestige and privilege of being a priest. If his wife suspected his true feelings, she did not show any signs of it. The subject of faith was never broached between them.

With his black curls that were always falling over his forehead and into his dark, twinkling eyes, his shy grin, and generally self-deprecating manner, Father Ami gave the impression of being one of the older altar boys. At their first meeting, people often had to be reassured that he was actually the priest. He still had the broad, muscular shoulders of a man who spends much time rowing a boat. He often rowed out to the ships that were anchored outside the harbor in order to perform services for quarantined sailors, give last rites, or act as interpreter for on-ship disputes. Father Ami and his wife, Helena, had come to St. Nikolas almost ten years ago, at the behest of the Bishop of Athens and had seen much of human drama unfold among the congregants.

As one of the few Greek Nationals in Germany at that time, Father Amiridis was sometimes called upon to translate port and customs documents. In this capacity he had made friends with the harbor master who informed him when a Greek ship was due in Port so he could be ready in case his services were needed. It was due to his desire to be as accurate as possible in his translations that Father Ami met Klaus Bauer in the language section of the University Library in Berlin.

Klaus was seeking to improve his command of Greek, while Father Ami was researching commercial terminology and vocabulary in German. Sharing the same work table one afternoon, the two men began a conversation. These men, from different worlds, found they were about the same age and shared a similar philosophy about how a good life should be lived. They also shared a curiosity about each other's religious practices and found that their core beliefs were identical.

Their friendship proved to be mutually beneficial on a personal level, as well as furthering understanding between the two different cultures they represented. On several occasions they were able to defuse international hostilities when a misunderstanding arose between ship commanders and crew members who spoke different languages, or between merchants and customs officials. Their efforts toward this end garnered praise from Kaiser Wilhelm for Klaus and funds for repairs to the church dome from the Bishop of Athens for Father Ami.

While Biku was driving the well-worn road from Berlin to Stettin, Father Ami was reading and then re-reading a telegram from Klaus Bauer. During the ten years of their friendship, the two men had devised a code. When either one of them used the word "urgent" in a message, it meant a personal meeting would be required. When the wording "personal messenger" was sent to Father Ami, it meant Biku was bringing someone to see him. He remembered the time he received such a message, and an adviser of his Majesty himself had arrived on his doorstep. He needed a carefully worded letter to forestall a court scandal. Father Ami smiled to himself, remembering how frivolous it had seemed to him. In anticipation of an important guest, he went to find his wife in the rectory behind the church.

Helena was in the small vegetable garden that adjoined the living quarters. Father Ami did not show her the telegram, but told her that they would be having company for their midday meal. With a smile of anticipation, Helena smoothed her skirts, picked up the basket of vegetables she had just gathered, and followed her husband into the rectory kitchen. She instructed their cook to prepare a festive meal as they were expecting company. Without questioning him about who was coming, she followed Father Ami into the sanctuary and started on her chores of replacing wilted flowers on the hidden altar, dusting the icons on the iconostasis, sweeping and then mopping the marble floor until it gleamed in the morning light coming in through the stained glass windows. Next to her husband, her second earthly love was this beautiful building and all it stood for.

Chapter 32

Biku drove the black car into the stable next to the vegetable garden of the rectory. Father Ami stepped to the back door of the car and, trying to not show his surprise, helped Estanza to step out.

"I am Father Amiridis," he said in greeting.

"May I introduce Fräulein Nikiolopolis," Biku cut in.

"You are Greek?" There was pleasure in Father Ami's voice.

Estanza, still a bit groggy from having slept most of the way from Berlin, smiled at the handsome man who was now holding her by the elbow and guiding her into the little house nearby.

Within minutes, Helena, Father Ami and Estanza were chattering together in Greek. Biku reluctantly interrupted them with a reminder that he had to drive back to Berlin as soon as possible. He wanted to explain Estanza's presence at St. Nikolas and the plans that had been made for her departure from Germany. He told the priest and his wife about the danger Estanza faced and that she was a friend of Konrad von Stahlenberg. This revelation was met with broad smiles, as Klaus had filled them in on the connection.

Helena showed Estanza to the austere, yet warmly welcoming, guest room at the back part of the rectory. The high, narrow window opened to green rows of the vegetable garden and the daffodils around the edge of the red brick wall. A narrow table painted a cobalt blue, which reminded Estanza of the roof tiles in most Greek villages, stood against one of the starkly white walls. Between the table and the narrow bed was a ladder back chair, painted a deep, satisfying red that reminded Estanza of the roses in her grandmother's garden. A blue and white quilted bedspread covered the crisp, white sheets on the bed. The bright yellow of the daffodils in a jar on the table were reflected in a small mirror across the room. Estanza felt instantly at home. At Helena's urging, she stretched out on the bed and was half asleep before Helena reached the door.

Estanza was the latest of a conglomeration of people who had found refuge, comfort and peace in that very bed. Helena provided competent and compassionate care to whomever arrived at her doorstep. She was equally available to the beggar women who needed a warm place to recuperate from pneumonia, the sailor recovering from a broken limb, the prostitute who was dying from a button hook abortion, or the young mother who needed a midwife.

For two nights Estanza stayed at the rectory in the small, but spotless, room. The Greek cook prepared special dishes in her honor, and the two women talked for hours about their memories of Greece. They agreed that German culture had much to offer, but they missed the warm sun and water of their homeland.

On the third day of her stay in Stettin, a letter arrived at the church addressed to EN. It had been slipped under the door of the sanctuary and Father Ami had found it after morning service. He took it to Estanza who was having breakfast with Helena in the bright kitchen of the rectory. The letter was from Konrad. After a fond greeting, he informed Estanza that a Greek tramp steamer, The *Spirit of Pythias,* was expected in Stettin that very day. Konrad had arranged passage for Estanza under another name. She would find the new documents enclosed in the envelope, as well as funds for her journey. The steamer would take her to Le Havre, France, where she could debark after three days at sea, and Konrad would be waiting for her. If she decided to return to Greece, she should just stay on the ship until the final destination,

Piraeus. He closed with loving words, but wrote nothing about what he hoped her decision would be.

While Estanza and Helena finished their breakfast that morning, the cook was pouring coffee for her son in the kitchen. She had left Greece almost thirty years ago to follow a German sailor to Stettin. Theodora and her sailor were married in St. Nikolas and soon thereafter she began to cook for the parsonage. The couple had a son who was now a policeman. Each morning he came to have coffee with his mother before he went to work at the local station. This morning he had just finished his coffee and was about to leave when Estanza came into the kitchen carrying a tray of dishes from the breakfast room. She had seen the young man leave the house each morning, but this was their first encounter. He nodded briefly and started out the door.

In the sanctuary Father Ami was making preparations for the morning service. It was a weekday and he didn't expect more than a handful of worshippers. Just as he was starting, Helena and Estanza slipped in through the rectory door. After the service Father Ami started to walk to the harbor master's building to answer a summons sent the night before. As he came near the customs building he saw the reward poster with Estanza's image on the door. At first he was almost paralyzed with shock. Then he gathered his wits and strode swiftly back to the church.

It was that very morning when "Wanted" posters with a prominent image of Estanza appeared on the walls of post offices, government offices, and police and railway stations, all over northern Germany. The smaller print revealed the woman depicted on the poster to be a dangerous spy and a generous reward was offered for information leading to her capture, dead or alive.

The poster was the first thing that the cook's son saw as he entered the police station. He recognized Estanza immediately, and then ran into his superior's office with the good news. The conversation in the rectory breakfast room had been in Greek, and Theodora's son had grown up with his mother speaking Greek to him. At the edge of his consciousness he had overheard much of the conversation, and now some of the words came back to him. He remembered the name of a ship and, vaguely, a time of sailing. Late afternoon, he thought.

The police captain made some quick decisions. He sent two men to the church, and if the spy had already left, they were to find the Greek ship in the harbor. "Take your pistols," he ordered the two eager officers.

At the church, all the doors were locked. The policemen knocked on the rectory door and banged on the sanctuary door. Then they crawled over the garden wall, trampled through the vegetable beds, and pounded on the kitchen door. When Helena answered the door, she looked startled. No one ever came to the kitchen door, because to reach it, one had to crawl over the wall. She said as much when she saw the policemen. The two men insisted on coming in and searching the house. They found no trace of a guest on the premises and then began to question Helena.

Her answers were blunt and to the point. No one had been visiting. Father Ami had gone on a mission for the harbor master. The cook, Theodora, had gone to the market, and she had been in the laundry room in the basement and had not heard the knocking. The sincerity in her tone was irrefutable and Theodora's son began to doubt his own eyes.

The two officers decided to follow their orders and drove quickly along the harbor front, examining each ship along the way. The *Spirit of Pythias* was docked at the very last space on the pier where captain-owned, tramp steamers were relegated. Her cargo varied from season to season, and the ship could double as a fishing trawler when that was a more lucrative activity. The trawler aspect explained why heaps of fishing nets were kept handy on the deck near the rails.

The coal delivery wagon had just dropped Estanza and her baggage off near the *Spirit of Pythias* when the police car drove up to the widest part of the dock. The gangplank was ready to lift as soon as Estanza boarded the ship. She was nearing the gangplank with a sailor stepping up ahead of her, carrying her green trunk, when they heard the shrill police whistle.

Two policemen were running toward the ship, yelling, "Halt, halt in the name of the Kaiser! Halt!" This part of the pier was too narrow for the car so the officers had to proceed on foot. Just as they came along beside the ship, a cloud of fishing nets dropped over their heads. At the same time the gangplank clanged shut, the ship's horn gave a loud, long bellow, and the *Spirit of Pythias* moved away from the pier.

The two police officers spent a half-hour untangling themselves from the fishing nets. Punching their fists in the air and cursing loudly, they watched the tramp steamer sail out of the harbor, into the Baltic Sea.

Boarding the ship with her small trunk and carpetbag brought back memories of her last voyage on the Baltic Sea almost a year ago. Estanza was already feeling queasy just thinking about it. She hoped the fresh ginger from Helena would help her.

The *Spirit of Pythias* was nothing like the Kaiser's yacht. The cargo must have been coal, because black dust covered everything on the ship. Her cubicle of a cabin was clean enough, but bits of black floated in the water that she found in the basin. A chamber pot under her bed indicated that there were no facilities for females aboard.

The seas were fairly calm and they reached Le Havre without incident. There was never any doubt in Estanza's mind that she would debark there. Konrad was waiting on the dock, as promised, and for the first time in many days, Estanza took a deep breath. With a pounding heart, she flung herself into his arms. They spent the night in Le Havre at a hotel near the railroad station. The whistling and rumbling of trains would have kept them up all night, but they didn't sleep or hear the trains.

The next day they were finally on a train to Switzerland. Estanza had dreamed all winter of this trip with Konrad and the Chalet in the meadow, the cows, the snowy mountains, and the fields of flowers. Before they knew it, the train pulled into the station in Basel, Switzerland. Bertram, the hotel manager, was there to meet them with a horse-drawn buggy. It had begun to drizzle and the cover was up, so Estanza missed the lovely view driving to the guest house, which Konrad's father had named "The Chalet." When they arrived, Berta, Bertram's twin sister, was there to welcome them. She hugged Estanza warmly and made a fuss over Konrad, whom she had practically raised.

"You call us Berti and Berta," she told Estanza. "I apologize about the rain, but we need it. Tomorrow will be blue sky and sun," she said in her strange German. The next day was as promised. The Chalet stood in the middle of a flower-covered meadow. The pinks, blues, reds and luscious greens were dazzling. In the distance loomed the snow-covered mountains, while the deep-blue dome covered the picturesque and peaceful scene. Estanza breathed in the crisp, clean air and decided right then and there that she wanted to live in Switzerland.

Chapter 33

In August, Kurt arrived with Lydia and they joined Konrad and Estanza as they hiked the mountain trails, went into Basel to visit the museum and the university libraries, and attended plays, concerts, and fondue parties, which were so popular in that part of Switzerland. That month was like a long, enjoyable party, and it went by in a flash.

Estanza knew that she needed to make plans for after the summer, but it floated by so quickly, nothing was done. In the middle of September, she stopped getting nauseous every morning. It was imperative to make plans for her life—and Konrad's child. She made a decision guided by the example of Renée Volant.

"My skills are in languages," Estanza told Konrad. "If I am to make a living and provide for my child, I will need to pursue my profession."

"You mean 'our' child," Konrad responded, sounding concerned. "I plan to provide for both of you," he stated firmly.

Estanza was thoughtful for a time. Then she went to him. She stroked his hair and kissed him on the cheek. "Konrad," she said quietly, "we will accept whatever you give us, but I *must* live my life as I see fit. I want no chain links to bind us except our love for each other." His respect and admiration for this young woman grew even deeper at these words. He would have never admitted it out loud, or even to himself, but he felt enormous relief.

It was decided that Estanza needed to move to Basel since the Chalet was often snowed in for months at a time.

Also, the twins had no time for catering to guests during the winter. After the cows were brought down from the high meadows and lodged in the lower part of the house, they became a major source of heat for the inhabitants above, but they needed a constant supply of fodder.

Besides feeding the cows, Berti and Berta kept very busy making cheese, carving decoration for cuckoo clocks, cleaning and repairing the decor and furnishings for the guest rooms, and replenishing the pantry with preserved foods for the next summer season. In those long, dark, evenings, the siblings read or played cards by candlelight.

Before Konrad left on a new assignment he ensconced Estanza in a small two-bedroom apartment within walking distance of the University of Basel Language Center and the railway station. He spent a few days helping her furnish the flat and find a doctor for pre-natal care. After promising to be back for Christmas and the birth of their child, he was gone.

At first Estanza was busy getting enrolled into the classes she was required to take for certification as a licensed translator/interpreter. Although Konrad had advised her to destroy her original Greek passport, she had kept it. In the registration process, many of the forms asked for personal history so she thought it best to use her original identity. She kept the forged papers, but well-concealed.

One Saturday in late October, Estanza looked around the Victorian decor of the apartment and found it depressing. She had a fleeting vision of the bright, friendly room at the rectory of St. Nikolas that reminded her so much of home. *Something is missing here,* she thought to herself. Then she remembered the Greek cross that hung over the door in the rectory bedroom. She decided to buy one she had seen in a wood carving shop along Hutgasse, just off Marktplatz.

Her clothes were getting tight and she needed to shop for a stylish smock-like dress for her condition. First, she would look for the Greek cross, and then she would find a dress.

Estanza found the shop where she had seen the Greek

cross. There were several versions, and she had difficulty making up her mind which one to buy. Fortunately, she didn't need to worry too much about the cost. Konrad had left her ample funds in a nearby bank to last her for at least a year or until she was able to earn money as a translator. She finally chose a design she liked and stepped out of the store and on her way to the dress shop, when she heard a familiar voice call her name. She stopped and slowly turned around, hardly able to believe her ears or her eyes as she stood face to face with Renée Volant.

Both women were obviously surprised and delighted to see each other. In a part of the world where people tend to be reserved in their demeanor, even in the privacy of their own homes, the sight of two well-dressed women hugging and laughing in the street drew attention from passersby. Estanza and Renée were oblivious to the smiles and frowns they had elicited. For a few minutes they stood in the middle of the broad sidewalk exchanging information about themselves. Then they became aware of their surroundings and moved into the doorway of a nearby apartment house.

It turned out that Renée had married Dr. Werner Heinemann, the doctor from the Kaiser's yacht. He had come to Paris to court her and persuaded her to join him in his retirement in Basel. He was now on the board of the university, where he worked part-time in the medical research department, and they lived in a chalet near the campus.

Estanza related her situation and how Renée's life story had been an inspiration, and that she intended to keep her independence, since marriage to the man she loved was not an option. "You showed me that being a single mother does not need to be the end of the world." Estanza told Renée, "Marriage is not for everyone. However, in Greece, I would need to leave home in my condition and my family would feel I disgraced them."

They were both silent for a few minutes thinking of their mixed feelings. Renée, as well as Estanza, missed her family, but both women acknowledged that living in a foreign country gave them a sense of freedom because of their anonymity.

That afternoon they parted with promises of meeting again the next week. Estanza went on to the dress shop and found a smock to fit over her growing belly, then bought yellow chrysanthemums at the flower stand near the railroad station. The air was getting chilly as she hurried on to her apartment, but there was a warm glow in her heart as she thought of Renée and their friendship. How wonderful it was to be seeing Renée again, and how happy she felt that her friend had found a person with whom to share her life.

The leaves turned red and gold, then suddenly the trees were bare and snow was covering the branches and blanketing the landscape. Basel became a winter scene, but even in November the cold was softer, gentler, than in Berlin. Estanza and Renée visited each other through the next few weeks, and their friendship resumed as if they had never been apart, as if they had known each other forever. Dr. Heinemann was also happy to renew his acquaintance with Estanza. They found that they appreciated the same music and often talked about the great German writers. It was gratifying to know that Goethe had also loved Switzerland. Throughout the rest of their friendship they never talked about the voyage on the Kaiser's yacht.

~

Late one afternoon, when Estanza was just rousing herself from the nap she now seemed to need every day, she heard a knock on her door. The light had faded from the window and the room was dark except for the glow of the street light outside. Estanza groped her way to the newly installed electric light switch, and went to the door. A familiar voice came from the other side. "Estanza, it is me, open the door please." At first Estanza thought she might still be asleep—that this was a dream. But when she opened the door, Ena's warm and smiling face was very real and joyously welcome.

After getting settled into the second bedroom, Ena told Estanza that Mr. Kurt and Konrad were in Morocco where there was some trouble with the French. They hoped the dispute could be settled peaceably and before the Christmas holiday. Biku and Lina were on their way to Africa. The British Colonial government, in a place called Kenya, was offering teaching positions to educated Africans in schools for native children, and they were accepted, had a five-year contract, and would be provided with living quarters. "So, since no one in Germany needed me, I thought I would come to Switzerland." She grinned at Estanza, her white teeth flashing in her black face.

"I am ecstatic that you have come." Estanza's voice was warm with gratitude. "I do need help. As you know, I am not much good at being a homemaker. Even if I didn't need to study eight hours most days, I would rather read than cook, and rather write than clean."

They chuckled together, remembering some of Estanza's unappetizing culinary creations. Then Ena put on her apron and started to find her way around the little kitchen.

~

Konrad appeared a few days before Christmas. He had arrived on the early morning train from Paris. When Ena opened the door, he was delighted to see her, and was pleased to find Estanza still in bed. He tried not to show how startled he felt to see her in such an advanced condition of pregnancy. The emotional shock of waking up in Konrad's arms might have been the catalyst, but that morning Estanza started to have labor pains. By late afternoon she and Konrad were the parents of a black-haired, green-eyed girl with skin the color of raw hazelnuts. They decided to combine their names and call her Konstanza.

Part Two

Chapter 1

Basel, Switzerland, 1919

The first eight years of Konstanza's life were mostly happy and carefree. The turmoil of the Great War that was tearing Europe apart had very little effect on the lives of the Swiss people; but Konstanza, even at five years old, had felt the tension in the air around her. She didn't understand the conversations, but the worrisome tone of voice used by the adults was disturbing. They talked about their mixed feelings about Greece siding with England instead of Germany, and she saw aunt Renée weep one day when news came of the Germans conquering Paris. Uncle Konrad became less jovial and was away for long periods of time. Berti and Berta never talked about the fighting; they were the constant in her young life.[1]

Berti and Berta opened their Chalet to men from France, England and Germany. For four summers Estanza and Konstanza were the only formal guests, and Estanza's language skills came to be very useful. Some lasting friendships resulted from the Swiss hospitality to these wounded soldiers. Many of them came back after the war to vacation with their families, and Switzerland became a synonym for international understanding.

Konstanza spent those wartime summers at the chalet with her mother and Uncle Konrad. They often left her with Berti and Berta while they went into Basel for cultural events. She missed Ena, who took this time to visit her children in Africa. Even before Konstanza was four years old, she had learned how to milk cows, and in the following years she learned to cook Swiss dishes. In fact, the milkmaids, kitchen help and chambermaids at the Chalet were beginning to wonder if this little girl was after their jobs.

Ena came back from Africa every year, just as the leaves were turning, to clean the Basel apartment before Estanza and Konstanza returned from the country.

While Estanza attended classes and studied for her translator/interpreter certification, Ena taught Konstanza how to read, write and do basic arithmetic. She also took her grocery shopping every day and taught her how to pick the best ingredients for the spicy, African dishes that were her specialty.

During Konstanza's eighth summer, her mother became part of an international team of translators scheduled to work in Geneva at a peace conference and at the newly organized League of Nations. Only a few women were assigned to work at this important gathering and everyone in her circle, including Konrad, urged Estanza to accept.

It was Lydia Gottlieb who suggested boarding school for Konstanza. "It is time she went to school with other children," Lydia said in a mild, persuasive tone. As director of several Montessori schools, she felt qualified to give advice on education. She suggested a prestigious girls' school in Freiburg across the Rhine River in Germany. "It is a respected school. I happen to know the head mistress and the dean of education," Lydia assured Konrad and Estanza.

When Lydia saw their hesitation, she continued: "This school is just across the river from Basel and you could visit whenever you wanted. The school closes during the summer and the girls go home, so we could all meet at the Chalet as we always have." She smiled reassuringly.

Konrad, who had himself been sent to boarding school when he was eight years old, expressed relief at having the problem of Konstanza's education solved. Estanza knew that boarding school was expected for children of the German and the English aristocracy, but had misgivings about sending her child away. However, in the end, she agreed it was the wise and necessary course.

Konrad made certain that Estanza and Konstanza had sufficient funds for living, but he also urged Estanza to contribute as much as possible of her pay to a separate account that only she controlled.[2] Swiss bank accounts had a unique attribute: they used only numbers—one number for making deposits and another for making withdrawals. Only a very highly placed executive of the bank knew the name that was connected to the number and was sworn to secrecy by the government sector that controlled the banking system. Estanza followed Konrad's advice and her account grew steadily.

"It is time for you to see your mother's homeland," Estanza told Konstanza one day. "You have grandparents, aunts and uncles, and many cousins that you have never met."

Estanza knew she was taking a chance of losing her family by bringing Konstanza to Distomo. If they found out her true situation they would ostracize her and her daughter.[3]

At the suggestion of Kurt von Stahlenberg, Konrad used his diplomatic connections to obtain documents that allowed Estanza to create a phantom marriage, which had left her a widow with a young child. In Europe, during the postwar years, this state of widowhood was very common.

Fortunately Estanza had spoken Greek to her daughter for the last eight years so she was fluent in the language. This would assure the family that the girl had a Greek father, whom she didn't remember, because he had ostensibly died when she was about three years old and was just beginning to talk.

Letters went back and forth during the winter of 1919 and 1920. Finally, in midsummer of 1920, plans were in place for Estanza and Konstanza to travel to Greece. From Paris onward, they were to take a newer version of the Orient Express, which had been reinstated after the war. This luxury train stopped infrequently and they were in Athens within a week.

Estanza's father came to meet them with the station

wagon he used to pick up hotel guests. The train station was very crowded and confusing, so her father hustled Estanza and her daughter out of the building as soon as possible. It was not until they arrived at the parking area and started to climb into the car that he took the time to hug his daughter and take a good look at his "new" granddaughter.

Nick Nikiolopolis stepped back a pace before helping the young girl climb in and then studied her. She resembled his daughter with her black curls and tawny skin. Her angular face would never be considered classically beautiful, but in the next few moments she gave her grandfather that dazzling smile that could light up a whole room.

"You look just like your mother at your age," he finally said and grinned with satisfaction. "What grade are you in at school?" he asked. He was pleased and a little surprised, when she answered in the Greek dialect used in the mountains around Distomo.

"I'm starting school in the fall," she said. Then added, when she saw his questioning frown, "I was being tutored at home, and I know everything I need to know to start third grade."

Then Konstanza climbed into the back seat of the car and closed her eyes against the brightness of the afternoon sun and the dazzling blue sky. She began to doze but was much too excited to actually fall asleep.

Estanza tried to keep awake and talk with her father as he maneuvered the car up the winding road to Distomo. He had to concentrate to avoid the rocks and keep the car on the road around the sharp curves, but during a straight stretch he relaxed a little and looked over at his daughter. "Estanza, your mother will be so very happy to see you. She will love your little daughter, mostly because, from what you wrote about her, she is more like your mother than like you."

Nick looked around to the back seat and noticed that Konstanza seemed to be asleep. He turned to Estanza, his face severe and stark. "She has Konrad von Stahlenberg's green eyes. She is his daughter."

Estanza gasped, but she knew there was no point in denying the fact. Her father continued, "Your mother never met him, so she will not question the child's parentage. I will not tell her. She need never know your shame."

Estanza started to say something to express her gratitude for his help and understanding, but he cut her off, sharply. "After this visit, you and your bastard daughter are never to come back to Greece again. Do you understand me?" He bit off the words and began to concentrate on the road ahead, which had become quite narrow, with a wall of rock on one side and a steep cliff down on the other.

For Konstanza, the hotel that her grandmother ran with thoughtful efficiency was like a life-sized playhouse for the eight-year-old girl. She worked with the chambermaids making the beds, and helped the cook chop and stir. Milking goats was similar to milking cows, but the goats seemed friendlier, and she loved the feta cheese that she learned to make from the milk of her pet goat.

Konstanza liked doing the things that were needed to keep a hotel running smoothly; thus she was a delight to her grandmother. Everyone at the hotel—the staff, guests and vendors who made deliveries—loved the green-eyed girl from Switzerland. The grandfather was pleasant enough, but seldom present.

Every night during that summer, music and dancing filled the air, either on the hotel terrace or at the cabaret next door. On Sunday mornings, Konstanza dutifully went to church with her grandmother. At the church she met her aunts and numerous cousins. She never questioned why her mother, grandfather and uncles didn't come along. While the adults stood in rows singing and praying, the younger children wove in and out among them playing a quiet game of hide and seek.

After church the family gathered at the home of one of

the relatives. Each week it was a different home. The food was plentiful, delicious and varied. Each household seemed to have a different specialty. Konstanza adored everything Greek. Suddenly, like the blink of an eye, the summer was over.

On the long ride back to Athens, Estanza's father did not speak to her, but only to Konstanza to point out the sights that tourists came to see in the area. When they arrived at the train station he helped them arrange their luggage into the train. He settled Konstanza in a window seat, gave her the lunch that his wife had prepared and guided Estanza to the door of the compartment, carefully closing the glass panel.

Outside in the corridor, he put his arms around her, hugged her tightly and whispered in her ear, "Remember, do not ever come back to Greece." Slowly he released her and their eyes met. Estanza saw the pain and sorrow, but also the resolve in her father's eyes. He had put on a superb act to shield his wife from scandal, but he was now giving up his favorite daughter just as he had sacrificed a life by the sea for the woman he loved.

Only once during the conversation in the corridor had the adults glanced at Konstanza, who was seen looking out the window. But after her grandfather had slid the compartment door shut, she had inched her way toward it. Keeping her head turned toward the window, Konstanza moved the door back just enough to hear what was being said in the corridor. She quickly moved back to the window as her mother entered the compartment. It was obvious that her mother was weeping softly.

Pulling a lacy white handkerchief from the big bag on her lap and dabbing her eyes, Estanza sniffled, "I have a cinder in my eye." Then she sat back in the seat and closed her eyes.

It was then that Konstanza remembered the words she had overheard in the car on the way to Distomo. She had been only half-listening, and thought that perhaps she had misunderstood what she heard. But this time she had heard clearly. Her grandfather was warning them not to return to Greece.

Chapter 2

Before she left for her assignment in Geneva, Estanza brought her daughter to the Freiburg Girls Academy, a boarding school for the daughters of diplomats, aristocrats and wealthy industrialists from all parts of Germany. The tuition, as one would expect, was exorbitant, and Konrad von Stahlenberg had made it clear to the director that he would be responsible for all costs related to Konstanza's schooling. In a lengthy letter he had explained that she was the daughter of a colleague who had died of his wounds from the war and that Konrad had promised to help his widow. He further informed the staff at the school that Konstanza's mother was an interpreter at the League of Nations conference in Geneva and would be coming to enroll her daughter within the next week.

Driving up to the palatial structure that was the main building of the institution, Konstanza was suitably impressed. Beyond the three smaller buildings were acres of beautiful gardens. Her eyes wide with wonder and her mind full of questions, Konstanza, mercifully, was not yet aware of the eight-year nightmare that would engulf her.

Hand in hand with her mother, Konstanza walked up the marble steps of the building, clutching her stuffed rabbit in her other hand, while her mother carried a small suitcase. Estanza rang the bell and a uniformed maid opened the door. She was tall and blonde with very white skin. Her round face was pulled into a frown.

"The employment office is in the back," she barked. Then she added, "Madame does not employ women who have young children."

Before the maid could slam the door in her face, Estanza was able to say, "I am here to enroll my daughter in the school. I need to see the director."

Reluctantly, the maid stepped back and opened the door. "Wait here," she ordered and disappeared into one of rooms that opened off the wide foyer.

For several minutes, Estanza and Konstanza paced the shiny marble floor. They walked around the center table where a huge vase displayed a bouquet of hothouse flowers. The maid reappeared and gestured them to a door that was at least ten feet high and almost as wide. It was Konstanza's first glimpse of that ornate room, which would become the most dreaded place in the world for her and her fellow classmates.

The director of the school—a descendant of a prince of the realm whose family had once owned the present district of Freiburg—was a short, dark-haired man of about fifty. He had never married but lived in the palace with his mother, a housekeeper, several maids, and a valet who rarely left his side. He took his duties as a father figure to the sixty girls in his care very seriously. He knew each girl by name, the net worth of their family, and how they were connected to the other people who ruled the realm. Sitting behind his massive, paper-strewn desk, he gazed at Estanza and her equally dark-skinned daughter as they entered the room. Then he looked down at the papers on his desk.

"Frau Nikiolopolis?" he asked, sounding a bit doubtful. Estanza nodded and he continued. "So this is your daughter, Konstanza?" getting another nod from both the figures standing in front of him. Then he touched a buzzer on his desk and a large, gray-haired woman appeared in the open doorway. "This is Frau Waldheim. She is the headmistress of the school," he told Estanza as she turned around to look at the woman. "She will take your daughter to her quarters."

Leaving her daughter with strangers was difficult for Estanza. The headmistress waited patiently while the mother and daughter extricated themselves from each other, and finally Konstanza was standing, quite alone, in front of the woman who would rule her life for the next few years.

Frau Waldheim loomed over the little girl. With a small, cold smile she glared down at Estanza, leaving no doubt as to her authority over her. Konstanza looked up at the mean, narrow face, the close-set, dark eyes under the white cap of hair, and shivered with fright and foreboding. Cold fear trickled down her spine as she followed the black-clad form down a long, dimly-lit hallway. When they stopped in front of a door, Frau Waldheim turned to Konstanza, grasped her upper arm and pushed her into a bare room. "This will be your home for the next few years," she said.

There were three narrow beds forming a U, one against each wall. A little nightstand stood near the head of each bed. Under a wide window stood a worktable with three low chairs beside it. A bare lightbulb hung from the ceiling. The switch for this lightbulb was out in the hall. It was used at the discretion of the house mother, Frau Mindler, a small, round woman, who came bustling in just as Frau Waldheim started to leave.

Konstanza stood in the middle of the room clutching her stuffed rabbit in one hand and her suitcase in the other, and in spite of her heroic effort, she began to sob hysterically. Frau Waldheim stepped in front of her and slapped her hard across the face. "Control yourself!" Frau Waldheim ordered, as Konstanza, shocked into silence, sank to her knees. Frau Mindler started toward her, but Frau Waldheim motioned her back.

"Show her where to put her things," she ordered the red-faced Frau Mindler, pointing to Konstanza. Then she turned and left the room.

In all of her eight years on earth, Konstanza had only experienced love and kindness from the adults who surrounded her. Occasionally someone had been annoyed with her, scolded her, or reprimanded her for something she had done or had not done, but no one had ever struck her. She knew people did such things in other families. The children in the park sometimes told stories of being spanked, but Konstanza could not imagine someone in her family actually hitting her.

Frau Mindler picked up the suitcase and put it on the bed closest to the window. A dark brown dress was spread out near the foot, covered with a white pinafore apron. Next to the dress were black, woolen stockings and several pieces of white cotton underwear.

Konstanza stood up and began to examine the objects on the bed. Frau Mindler had opened the suitcase, exploring the neatly folded contents. She found a handkerchief and handed it to Konstanza. "Wipe your face," she said, not unkindly. "Now, let's put your things away." Deftly she began to arrange the clothes and shoes on the shelves in the wardrobe next to the door. There were three compartments, each with shelves and a few hooks for garments that needed hanging.

When the suitcase was empty Frau Mindler closed it and pushed it under the bed. "See?" she asked Konstanza. "It just fits." Then she pulled a chamber pot out from under the bed. "This is for use during the night," she said, as she pointed to the lidded vessel, and then pushed it back under the bed, next to the suitcase.

Footsteps sounded in the hallway and Frau Waldheim pushed two very pale girls into the room. A man stood behind her holding two suitcases. He put them down and disappeared back into the hall.

One girl had golden braids; the other had thin, stringy strands of almost white hair. They both had gray eyes and looked to be sisters. "This is Else, and this is Erna," Frau Waldheim said, pointing to each girl in turn. "They are cousins from Munich and will be your roommates this term," she told Konstanza, and then she turned to Frau Mindler. "Get these girls organized and then come to my office. The rest of the new ones will be arriving any minute." Before going out of the door she turned around to face the three girls. "We allow only one stuffed animal per girl, so if you brought any more of them, they will be confiscated and sent to a nearby orphanage." She closed the door behind her, and they heard her steps clanking on the shiny, hardwood floor.

Frau Mindler pointed to the garments lying on each bed. "Those are your school uniforms. Put them on and hang your clothes in the closet. You won't need them until you go home for the summer." The three children were each sitting on a bed, looking at each other with wide, curious eyes. "Get going," Frau Mindler ordered, her round body vibrating a bit as she shook her finger at them. "You need to do something with your hair," she said, pointing at Konstanza's unruly, black curls. "A bell will ring when it is time to come to the dining room for dinner. One of the older girls will come and get you this first time and show you the way." With one swish of her full skirt she was out the door, and the girls were left alone.

Konstanza began to undress in preparation for putting on her required school garments. Her roommates began to giggle and point at her. "She is brown all over," Erna proclaimed in a high-pitched voice.

"It looks like she is dirty," chimed in Else. "You need a bath," she shouted, pointing a wiggly finger at Konstanza, who didn't know what to say.

This was only the beginning of the ordeal Konstanza endured during the next eight years. Her hair refused to be tamed. Even when severely braided, curls managed to escape and look untidy. Her hands were never clean enough and were often red for days after being smacked with a ruler, over and over, for being "brown."

Each week the girls were ordered to write a postcard to their parents. Konstanza's first postcard, after a week at the school, was a heartfelt lament, asking her mother to please allow her to come home as soon as possible. "If you do not come to get me this week, I will kill myself before your next visit," she wrote in Greek.

That very afternoon she was called to Frau Waldheim's office. "You must write correspondence in German," Frau Waldheim explained to a surprised Konstanza. "We cannot send this card the way it is written."

Konstanza was inclined to argue about this, but the look on the woman's face stopped her. Frau Waldheim handed her another card and mentioned that the cost of the second card would be added to her tuition account. That gave Konstanza an idea.

"Please, Frau Waldheim," she said, mustering up a respectful tone that she hoped hid her loathing. "It is so wasteful to write another card. Sufficient space is here between the lines for me to write the German translation." Frau Waldheim was duly impressed with the frugality of the eight-year-old girl. Konstanza had her first sweet taste of triumph that can be gained by deception. She carefully wrote a German word under each Greek one, indicating how happy she was, how she liked the food and her teachers. The card was sent, but it was over a month before Estanza came back from Geneva and read it. By the time her mother could come for a visit, Konstanza had called Ena and told her not to worry, she was going to stay alive. Eventually she found ways to smuggle sealed letters out of the school.

~

Her roommates were usually blond, pale, blue-eyed girls from affluent, aristocratic families. The only dark people these girls had encountered were servants, gardeners or delivery people. They either teased Konstanza about her looks or ignored her. Making friends with them proved to be impossible.

There were a few exceptions to the stream of self-centered, arrogant and rude girls who attended this school. One of them was Hilde Jagger, the girl who shared her room the third year. She had black hair, large brown eyes, and her skin was almost as dark as Konstanza's. Her family lived in

Vienna, Austria, and her father was in the banking business. Germans looked down on Austrians as lower species; thus the girls made fun of Hilde's accent, although she spoke the classic German of the region. She and Konstanza became friends, and the next five years at the Freiburg School were more endurable for both of them. Konstanza and Hilde were exposed to similar treatment from their fellow students and the staff. Often they consoled each other as humiliating words were hurled at them.

During the summer of 1923, Estanza was appointed director of the female interpreters at the League of Nations. Konstanza and Ena, along with Uncle Konrad, went to the promotion ceremony in Geneva. The president of the fledgling organization made a speech that impressed Konstanza and she began to have more respect for her mother after hearing his words:

> The position of translator/interpreter carries grave responsibilities. The right words uttered with the wrong inflection or tone of voice can produce hostility and make the difference between hostile and peaceful negotiations. Often the calamity of war can be forestalled and prevented by the use of words and how they are perceived.

Following that powerful ceremony, Estanza was sent to Lausanne to help with the negotiations between Bulgaria, Greece and Turkey to settle the borders for modern Turkey and the dismantling of what was left of the Ottoman Empire. It took almost two years to hammer out the final version of the Treaty of Lausanne. During that time, Konstanza was in the care of Berta and Berti during the summer and in the clutches of the Freiburg boarding school staff the rest of the year.

Chapter 3

The summer of 1923 Walter Mannheim came into Konstanza's young life. He was two years older but an inch shorter than Konstanza. At age eleven, she had reached her full height and developed the body of a young woman; Walter, at age thirteen, was awkwardly chubby and still had five more years of growth ahead of him. He had protruding front teeth and sandy-colored hair that constantly fell into his faded blue eyes, which looked enormous behind his thick glasses. Every inch of his exposed skin was covered with rust-colored freckles. He made up for his lack of good looks with intelligence and an insatiable curiosity about the world. And he was extremely fond of Konstanza.

Walter was also attending a boarding school near Freiburg and spending his summers in a pension on the outskirts of Basel. The two met one day while hiking one of the many mountain trails near Basel. The friendship was instant and soon became a teenage romance.

They told each other about their experiences at school and found that they were quite similar. The teachers at both schools struck their pupils with willow sticks and seemed to enjoy seeing the pain they were causing. Walter described the terrible thrashings that were dealt out to the boys. He even showed her the welts on his own backside, while she showed him the dark bruises on her upper arms. Neither of them had ever told their parents about the beatings, mostly because they were told by the school staff that if they told about the punishment, they would need to explain what they had done to deserve it; most likely their parents would be very angry about their misbehavior. Walter told Konstanza that his father beat him for every trifle and sometimes slapped his mother. "I would never treat the woman I loved that way," he told Konstanza one day.

Gradually the friendship became warmer. They held hands while sitting together on park benches or in the fragrant meadows, reading poetry or adventure stories. One evening near dusk, while walking back from a long hike, Walter asked Konstanza if she would like to go to a movie in Basel.

"I read that the new Plaza Theater is showing movies now," Walter said. "My parents do not approve of those films from America, but I have heard they are quite entertaining."

Estanza had a feeling that her mother would not approve of those films either, but she had the allowance that Uncle Konrad sent her each week. She agreed to go to Basel with Walter when he found a film he wanted to see. Toward the end of the summer a Charlie Chaplin movie was playing, and the two of them made plans to go.

They walked the mile to the end of the streetcar line that went into the city center, got on the streetcar, proudly paid the five pfennig fare, and a half-hour later they were in the center of town where they walked on opposite sides of the street to the new theater. They were not sure why they didn't want people to think they were together, and they did not discuss it. They walked, separated by the busy street, to a block past the huge, red town hall. The marquee was ablaze with electric lights. Walter stood behind Konstanza while they each bought a ticket. They were just in time for the first performance of the day. It was dark in the theater and there were many empty seats. Konstanza walked down the first aisle and Walter went to the next door and went into the darkened room down a different aisle. They met in the middle of a row near the back of the theater.

The movie was just starting as they sat down next to each other. The piano player at the front of the hall played furiously as the credits rolled by and then changed the tempo as the little tramp came down an alley strewn with garbage.

Walter put a tentative arm around Konstanza's shoulder and when she turned her head to look at him, he kissed her on the lips. For a long moment they sat there with their lips touching, exploring the feel of the soft flesh. Konstanza felt a twinge between her legs. It was a pleasant feeling and she didn't want it to end.

The movie lasted two hours. After it was over neither Konstanza nor Walter could have said what it was about. When the houselights came on, the two young people got up and went out of the theater as if they had never met. They had not talked about it, but they returned to the streetcar stop on opposite sides of the street; yet when the car came, they sat down side by side in one of the back seats. They rode to the end of the line, paid the fare, and started to walk back to the Chalet where Konstanza lived with Berta and Berti. It was nearly time for the evening meal and the two moviegoers were starving. Berta asked Walter if he wanted to stay for dinner and he nodded a yes with enthusiasm.

No one asked where the young people had been or enquired if they had eaten anything during the day. After downing a hearty cheese fondue, sliced pears and a small piece of chocolate, Walter made his way back to the pension where his parents rented a flat each summer. By then it was getting dark and the ringing of cowbells heralded milking time.

Walter's mother looked up as he came into their rooms. "You are too late for any food," she snapped. "We pay for the meals whether you come and eat or not," she added. She didn't ask Walter where he had been, but returned to the book on her lap.

Walter started up the narrow stairs to the attic room where he slept under the eaves. Before he reached the top, his mother called to him. He came back down and stood waiting for her to tell him what she wanted.

"Your father has gone to a conference in Munich," she

told him. "He is coming back next week, and we will return to Germany." Walter waited to see if she was going to say anything else. After a few minutes he started up the stairs again. He sat on his hard, little bed and thought about Konstanza. Her lips had been soft, warm and welcoming. This evening she had escorted him out to the veranda and kissed him goodnight. He was enveloped in love for this girl. It warmed his very soul to think that, finally, someone on this earth loved him.

In early September, all the guests left the alpine villages and returned to their various countries and winter homes. Konstanza and Walter wrote long and loving letters to each other. In order to get them sent out they resorted to a variety of schemes. Konstanza had made friends among the kitchen staff as she spent much of her free time watching them work and sometimes even helping with meal preparation. The young kitchen maids loved romantic intrigues, and they were delighted to help smuggle letters out of the school for a small fee and for Konstanza to use their return addresses for Walter's replies. Walter was equally well-connected and bribed various delivery people to mail and receive his correspondence with Konstanza. The two of them used fictional names. Ostensibly Konstanza's letters were addressed to a girlfriend while Walter wrote to a male cousin. They were both good students, or had been, but now they were both a bit distracted, and it began show in their grades. They used to take pride in their studies; now they could hardly wait for school to be over. They lived for the summer and only felt really alive when they were together.

Each fall Hilde and Konstanza fell into each other's arms like long-lost sisters. They spent many sleepless nights exchanging stories of their summer adventures.

Konstanza told of the long hikes with Walter, the amusing films and plays, and—best of all—that she was now "in love" just like the ladies in these stories.

Hilde, who led a sheltered life in spite of living in one

of the cultural centers of Europe, had little to talk about. The strict routine of her life had few variations. There were daily walks in the Augarten park with her mother, coffee at the Hotel Sacher, the midday meal with her father, followed by a rest and reading until four o'clock. Then her mother and father went to the bridge club, while Hilde visited with cousins, went to one of the many museums, or attended a concert.

In the summer of 1926, Hilde's life became more interesting. Hilde's cousins, three girls about her age, persuaded her parents to allow Hilde to stay with them for a month. With them she joined a health club and went swimming in the Olympic-sized pool, wearing the new scandalous, abbreviated, Jantzen bathing suits. One of their friends even talked about competing in the next Olympic Games.[1]

An aunt took her along to an outing at the Prater Amusement Park. Her parents frowned on such "working class" diversions as beer halls and also forbade her to go to the cinema. "What your mother doesn't know will not distress her," her Aunt Trude, her mother's younger sister, commented one day.

Hilde returned to school that fall and was a very different person. Her exposure to the more liberal and varied lifestyle of her cousins would serve her well in the future. It helped her navigate the nightmare that would envelope her country in the next decade—and eventually even saved her life.[2]

Chapter 4

For Konstanza and Walter, the summers drifted along with little variation to their daily activities. They had each other and only felt truly happy when they were alone together. They had a few friends who came and went out of their lives without being very memorable. One day while exploring the trail around an alpine lake near the village, they were caught in an unexpected summer shower. Looking around for some shelter they discovered a grassy area under a weeping willow tree. The low hanging branches trailed their tips in the clear water of the lake and brushed along the grass-covered area beneath the tree.

As they ducked under the green canopy of the tree they found a dry spot and sat down to wait out the rain. The willow tree provided a curtained sanctuary and they came back to the spot many times. They would lie in the grass for hours talking about the natural world and expressed wonder at the miracle of growth and decay around them. Sometimes they just lay in each other's arms, enjoying the warmth and the feeling of being loved. During the summer of 1927 their kisses grew more passionate. When Walter touched her budding breasts, Konstanza became breathless with the pleasure that flowed through her body.

The first time Konstanza opened her lips to receive Walter's tongue, he felt an electric shock pass through his whole body. He wondered if she noticed his erection as they pressed against each other. With an incredible effort he controlled his desire. After that encounter, Walter tried to keep their embraces from lasting longer than a few seconds. If Konstanza noticed his cooler behavior, she did not comment on it. They seemed to know instinctively that they were not ready for sexual intercourse.

The summer was nearly ended when Walter's mother told him to invite Konstanza for a midday meal that coming Friday. "We are returning to Munich next week," she announced one day. "Before we leave, your father and I want to meet this girl you have befriended."

Walter noticed that she had not smiled and her voice was harsh. Her invitation was actually an order. He knew better than to question his mother when she used that tone. He said his usual, "Yes, Frau Ma-ma," and added, "So Herr Pa-pa will be joining us?"

"That is his plan," Frau Mannheim snapped. Walter knew from her frown that she doubted he would show up. He often changed his plans at the last minute. Sometimes appearing when he was not expected and not appearing when he was. "Let me know by Wednesday if she is coming," she continued in the same clipped tone. "I need to make reservations with the pension staff."

Konstanza accepted the invitation readily. She was curious about the mysterious Herr Mannheim, who traveled back and forth to Munich all summer. The pension where the Mannheims spent each summer was like a little German enclave at the very edge of the village of Alpernschloss. Although summer visitors came to this area from all over Europe, and were scattered in a variety of hostels, hotels and chalets, the Germans gathered only in the large pension known as the Kaiser Wilhelm Colony.

A few minutes before noon, dressed in her best dirndl dress—the one with the green leaf design that complimented her eyes—a pale green cloche hat holding down her unruly, black curls, Konstanza met Walter and Frau Mannheim in the parlor of the pension.

Although it was a hot August day, Walter wore a three

piece suit of pale blue linen. Frau Mannheim was dressed in a stylish, gray shift, with satin shoes to match. Her reddish, blond hair was severely parted in the middle and twisted into a braided knot at the nape of her long, white neck. Her lips were a narrow slit beneath her straight nose and pulled back to simulate a smile.

Konstanza noticed how much Walter resembled his mother. He had her snowy white skin and pale blue eyes. That year most of the women in Europe used henna to get the shade of red that came naturally to mother and son.

They moved to their table which was set for three. "Herr Mannheim was called away unexpectedly," Frau Mannheim told the two young people.

Walter held his mother's chair while Konstanza seated herself without waiting for him to seat her. She looked around at the other five tables. Everyone sat stiffly upright, hands on the linen napkins on their laps. Konstanza unfolded the paper napkin, which was provided for non-resident guests, and did the same. She watched the two serving girls come out of the kitchen pushing a double-tiered cart. They quickly served each table with bowls of steaming soup. When all the guests had been served someone hit a spoon against a half-filled beer mug. In unison, which produced a loud clash of silverware on porcelain, everyone in the dining room began to eat.

The main course was Fleisch Roladen. The room filled with a delectable odor of spices and baked beef. To make this dish, paper thin slices of beef were spread with a thin layer of mustard and aromatic spices like clove and nutmeg, and then rolled up around a sliver of dill pickle and tied up with string. These rolls had been baked with slices of new potatoes sprinkled with chopped onions and garlic. Konstanza found that her mouth was watering before she had even tasted the food on her plate.

The serving girls kept the beer mugs filled and the conversation was at a minimum for the first few minutes after the main course was served. Then the complaints began.

"The food is too spicy."

"The mixture of flavors is not to German taste."

"Where is the sauerkraut?"

It turned out that the chef was newly hired that summer and not German. The rumor was that she was Hungarian or from some other Eastern European country.

"She came highly recommended by the owner of a 'foreign' hotel," someone sneered at another table.

Konstanza could hardly believe her ears.

It wasn't until the bland streusel cake was served with the milky coffee that Frau Mannheim spoke to Konstanza. She asked her a stream of questions about her father, her mother, and her plans for her future.

"Surely you do not mean to remain in Switzerland?" Frau Mannheim asked when she heard Konstanza say that she would continue her schooling in Basel University.

"You and your mother should return to Greece when you finish school here," Frau Mannheim declared. "Your German education will be a valuable asset for such a backward country," she continued.

Walter nodded and smiled at every proclamation coming from his mother. Konstanza listened with growing wonder and unease as Walter and his mother declared how all of Europe would soon benefit from the orderliness, punctuality and morality of their superior German culture.

Through all the entire diatribe, Konstanza had been thinking about how, actually, Greece and then Rome had been a model for Western Culture and Civilization. Most of the laws, manners, mores, art, literature and science in all of Europe had their foundation in Southern Europe. She sat quietly, eating the bland and greasy pastry, washing it down with the flavorless coffee, and then excused herself to find the powder room.

Frau Mannheim took advantage of her absence to hiss at her son. "Are you crazy running around with this fatherless mongrel? Your father is in line for an important position and you must limit your associations to people who come from respectable families. From her looks, this female could even be a Jewess."

Walter started to object to this last statement. His mother stopped him in mid-sentence and continued in the same low tone, "I forbid you to see her again."

Just then Konstanza returned to the table.

A week after that meal, which was memorable for the delicious food and the icy coldness that Walter's mother displayed toward Konstanza, Walter announced that he was going to Munich with his father. "I will be away for the rest of the summer," he told Konstanza. "After this important conference my father is enrolling me in a military academy. I am to be an officer."

The two young people were walking around the mountain lake, expecting to rest, as had become their custom, under their willow tree. The lake was a favorite after-dinner strolling site for the villagers, and they heard voices from nearby paths. Konstanza tried to imagine Walter as a military officer. He had grown several inches above her head by now, his freckles had faded and, after several years of painful braces, his teeth were almost straight. Although Walter had never been very athletic, he had distinguished himself on the school swimming team. The years of training in the water were reflected in his broad and muscular shoulders. The eyeglasses he wore now made him even more handsome and dignified.

"I will be staying here in Basel," Konstanza told Walter as they lay on their backs looking up at the green canopy of the weeping willow. "My mother and Uncle Konrad want me to go to university here in Switzerland," she sighed. "I had hoped to travel. I don't like staying in one place all the time. Aunt Lydia said I should follow my mother into the foreign service field, but I don't have the knack for languages and would prefer a job on a steamship."

Walter chuckled, "You have such strange ideas. Women do not work on steamships."

"I have heard that Russian ships have female cooks and even female deckhands," Konstanza countered. "Besides, if you are going off to be in the army, I should have a chance to see the world also." They were quiet for a few minutes then embraced before getting up to resume their walk. They strolled, side by side, holding hands. In some places the path was flanked by bushes, or a large boulder would reduce the space and they had to walk single file. While his back was toward her during one of these narrow spaces, Konstanza asked Walter why his mother did not like her. He turned abruptly to face her. She had lowered her eyes to see the trail, and as always happened when she raised her eyes to his, Walter experienced a little thrill of surprise and pleasure to see such clear, green eyes in her tawny complexion.

He took Konstanza's hand again and as they continued walking he explained his mother's attitude. "She asked me if you were a Jew," he said. Konstanza let out a little gasp. "When I reminded her you were of Greek origin and did not profess any organized religion, she just told me that you looked Jewish. She forbade me to see you again."

For a few minutes Konstanza and Walter stood facing each other. The voices of nearby strollers floated over their heads as they searched each other's faces in the waning light. They found nothing more to say and in the next few minutes they kissed warmly, pressing against each other with arms entwined. Although they never spoke of it, Konstanza sensed that Walter, like herself, felt happier and more secure in the world when they were touching like this. After a few more hugs they walked to the Chalet and kissed again. "I will try to see you before I go off to the academy," Walter whispered between kisses. Then he was gone.

Chapter 5

In the fall of 1927, Konstanza and Hilde started their last year at the Freiburg Girls' Academy. Their reunion was bittersweet. They promised to stay friends and see each other often, but knew that this was unlikely, given the different lives they would be living. Hilde's parents were sending her to a finishing school in Geneva for the next two years. When she graduated she would be an eligible young debutant. Several young men had been designated as possible husbands and she would be obliged to pick one before her eighteenth birthday. Although Hilde's family was not observant, they were still Jewish and the custom was for the family to hire a matchmaker to provide several eligible, acceptable and willing men from which the young woman must choose a husband.

Konstanza found this custom barbaric. Hilde was resigned and even grateful that her life would be planned for her. Once she chose one of the men her parents had approved for her, she would not need to make any further decisions.

The atmosphere in the school changed that year. Several new teachers were hired. They were younger and more strict than the ones who were retiring. There was more emphasis on German history and the superiority of German culture to the rest of Europe. Some of the advanced mathematics classes were cancelled. Girls didn't need to study calculus, they were told. Better to learn how to raise children and run a well-kept household. There were new classes in nutrition and personal hygiene. The fact that the older girls already knew most of the information was ignored, and strict rules were implemented about hairstyle, dress length and deportment.

On the last day of school before the two-week winter holidays the new history teacher distributed fliers to the departing girls. "Take these brochures home to your families," Frau Schultz ordered in her brassy voice. Her blue eyes blazed with zeal as she almost shouted, "These words are excerpts from an important book, written by a great man. Read them and learn the truth about our enemies." In a quieter tone she wished them all a Happy Christmas and dismissed the class.

On the train from Freiburg to Basel, Konstanza had time to read the ten-page brochure with excerpts from *Mein Kampf* written by a man named Adolf Hitler. She gasped in horror at the lies and half-truths about why Germany was in such dire economic straits. His remedy for Germany—and eventually all of Europe—was to deport all Jews after confiscating their property and all their funds. According to the author, it was obvious that the Aryan[1] race was superior and preordained to rule and exterminate all the inferior races as they saw fit. Clearly (in his eyes) Jews should be exterminated if they refused to leave German soil.[2] When Konstanza showed the vile publication to her mother, Estanza didn't just throw it into the waste basket. She tore it into little pieces and then burned it in the fireplace. She had not said a word, but her expression of outrage stayed in Konstanza's memory.

~

To celebrate Konstanza's fifteenth birthday, Uncle Konrad and Estanza hosted a party at a casual restaurant in Basel. They invited Renée, Werner, Kurt and Lydia. An invitation had been sent to Hilde, but she had to decline because of the distance from Vienna. She sent a small gift of embroidered handkerchiefs and a letter containing all her best wishes. A similar invitation had been sent to Walter, but there was no reply. Konstanza was hurt by Walter's snub, but in her mind she made excuses for him: *He was busy with his military training school. He didn't get the invitation due to the snowstorms. It was lost in the mail. A mean student destroyed it before it reached him.* She had included a personal note with Walter's invitation, telling him how much she missed him during the long winter and that she thought of him every day. She did not mention how disturbed she was that he had not answered her weekly letters. She had hoped for a reply up to the day of the dinner party. There was no mail for her that day and she lost hope.

As the train pulled out of the Munich station that December morning, a heavy snow began to fall. Walter watched the flakes whirl around the window, obscuring the landscape beyond.

He soon gave up his effort to remain calm and detached. His stomach was churning with rage at his cousin for her betrayal and his mind was ablaze with the anticipation of seeing Konstanza again.

It was clear from the note she had inserted into the birthday party invitation that she had not received his letters which he had entrusted to his cousin Gisele to mail for him. It was only now, as he sped along on the train, that the realization came to him that Konstanza's letters to him had also been intercepted. He knew his mother was behind the deceptions and betrayal. She had forbidden Walter to see Konstanza again after this last summer, explaining that the son of a Nazi official could not be seen with such a dark-skinned, foreign girl. "She looks Jewish" had been his mother's last word on the subject.

The envelope with the invitation to a dinner in honor of Konstanza's fifteenth birthday had been mailed from Basel, Switzerland, and not from Freiburg, Germany, where Konstanza went to school. So finally Gisele had some mail for him. She had handed him the envelope without comment, probably thinking it was from one of the Swiss schools he was hoping to attend.

Much to the disappointment of his father, Walter had not been accepted into the military academy as planned. Working-class boys were not usually accepted into prestigious officer training schools. His father had served in the Kaiser's infantry and was now a very highly-placed official in the Nationalist Socialist Workers Party (better known as Nazis), but that meant nothing to the aristocratic establishment. The Kaiser and his family were gone, but German institutions still clung to their class distinctions. So Walter had spent the fall traveling to Nazi rallies with his father, who was charged with introducing the dynamic, persuasive men who told lies and half-truths to the working class audience. They stirred up discontent and promoted hatred for Jews, who had lived among them for generations. After a few months of exposure to one diatribe after another, Walter, who had just had his eighteenth birthday, began to believe the far-fetched lies.

The Nazi propaganda and philosophy had nothing to do with his feelings for Konstanza. He began to reminisce about their idyllic trysts. For hours they would lie in a loving embrace, under the curtained branches of their favorite willow tree. When they had kissed that last time they were together, she had opened her lips. Now on the speeding train, Walter was aware of the swelling in his crotch as he remembered how their tongues had touched and the ecstasy that had flooded through his body.

The train pulled into the Basel station just before seven. He was almost an hour late for the dinner. No one knew he was coming because he dared not mail a reply. He was certain the Giesing (a suburb of Munich) postmaster would show it to his parents. He was almost at the restaurant door when he became aware of the snow in his rust colored hair. He had forgotten his hat on the train. He had planned a flourishing salute to impress the birthday girl and her guests. Part of that gesture was a sweeping motion with his hat.

The Blue Parrot restaurant was famous for excellent food at reasonable prices and an international clientele. The waiters were multi-lingual and the menu items were listed in the language of their country of origin. Even at individual tables the guests spoke to each other in several languages, switching back and forth as they addressed one person and then another. An example of this practice could be heard at a secluded table at the back of the room. Estanza and Konstanza spoke Greek to each other, German to the men at the table, and French with Renée and Lydia.

The eventful year of 1927 was coming to a close and people had a lot to talk about: the flight of the American across the Atlantic, the decision to allow women to compete in the Olympic games to be held in Amsterdam next summer, the actors now talking on the cinema screens, shortwave radio broadcasts bringing symphonic music right into the homes of people who would never have attended a concert, and the ability to talk directly across the Atlantic Ocean by telephone. Konstanza's birthday party guests tried to steer the conversation away from the terrible economic situation and the rise of the Fascist party in Germany.

Eventually they could no longer avoid it. Kurt von Stahlenberg mentioned that he was returning to Berlin, after escorting Lydia back to her home in Vienna. "It is becoming difficult to know whom to trust," he said, when he was questioned about the state of the Reichstag. "Berlin is a nest of intrigue and every face has at least two sides." His chuckle was half-hearted and his expression was dire.

Halfway through the meal, Walter Mannheim strode into the restaurant. He approached the table, saw that there was no chair for him, reached over to the next table and drew a chair up next to Konstanza who was sitting at the head of the table. He glanced in her direction, swept the table with half-closed eyes and sat down beside her. "I see I am in time to wish you a Happy Birthday," he said in a pleasant tone, but offered no apology for not replying to the invitation or for coming in near the end of the meal.

Konstanza tried to meet his eyes, but Walter looked

everywhere but at her. When he did turn his head in her direction she could not see his eyes because the light from the ceiling lamp was reflected in his glasses. Konstanza's emotions were in turmoil. Her heart was pounding and there was a large lump in her throat. Unable to speak she turned away from Walter to hide the tears rising to her eyes.

"We are having Black Forest cake for dessert," Konrad said as he turned to Walter. "I hope you like chocolate and cherries."

"I can only stay for a few minutes," Walter replied. "So now I will drink a toast to the birthday girl." He finally looked into Konstanza's shining eyes. She returned his steady gaze for a moment then looked away. Something was wrong—different. A quivering of apprehension began to flutter in her stomach. It would become a familiar part of her life from that day forward.

While they waited for the cake and coffee, the conversation resumed to the subject of politics. Kurt suggested the Nazi Brownshirts were just a manifestation of a few men who couldn't get over the humiliation of losing the war.

"My father is an organizer of those Brownshirts," Walter announced. "Hitler may be Austrian, but he has a German soul. He knows what is best for our Fatherland." Since no one spoke, Walter continued speaking. "We must rid ourselves of the rich, parasitic Jews."

Lydia looked Walter in the face and tried to see his eyes, but they were darting around like restless flies. "Do you know any such people?" she asked him, fighting to keep her voice even.

"No," was the quick reply, "but my father has told me about them." Walter stared across the table at Lydia with half-closed eyes and a grim expression.

"What does he say?" Lydia, asked, her dark eyes flashing, She tried to sound curious and interested, though she knew what was coming. The brown shirt he was wearing said it all.

"Those Jews take up most of the places in medical schools, own all the big stores, and exploit the rest of us who are forced to work for them."

It was Kurt who stared across at Walter and replied, "All the same, we must admit that these same Jews have shown themselves to be generous philanthropists. Many hospitals, cultural institutions, and scientific projects would not exist without their gifts to Germany."

"They think they can buy their way into our superior, Aryan society," was Walter's quick reply. He looked imploringly at Konrad and Werner for corroboration, and then went on with his rant. "If we allow these Jews to dilute our Aryan blood with their inferior, racially-mixed blood, we will lose our natural superiority as the master race. They must be eliminated from German soil." Walter stopped short. He had meant to add the words "from European soil" but the expressions on the faces of the people around the table stopped him. He had thought they would agree with him and cheer him on.

But this was not a Munich beer garden rally. These people just sat in stunned silence. They looked at him in disbelief. This young man, whom they had known since his early childhood, was a stranger, an aberration. He looked normal, but he was speaking complete and utter nonsense with such sincerity—as if he really believed what he was saying.

Lydia rose slowly, and bowed to Konstanza. "Happy birthday, my dearest girl," she said, smiling a frozen smile. Kurt had also risen and now cupped Lydia's elbow in his hand and guided her away from the table.

Walter stood up and turned to Konstanza. "Again, I wish you a happy birthday and a healthy year," he said in a formal, distant voice. He picked up her trembling hand from the table and kissed it. He tried to see her face but she was bent over her plate and didn't look up at him. He turned her hand over, cupping it in his and pressed his hot lips into her palm, and brushed it with his tongue.

It was then that her eyes met his. As always, he felt the little shock of surprise to see those emerald green eyes behind the long black lashes. For a split second he saw disdain—or was it disgust?—distorting her lovely, young face. His heart lurched in his chest. His blood ran cold. He dropped her hand and walked toward the door. If he heard her whisper his name, he did not acknowledge it.

Konrad summoned the waiter for the check while Estanza helped her daughter gather up the parcels that were her birthday presents. A small box contained a pink satin half-slip and matching lace trimmed panties that Renée had brought from Paris. There was a suede-covered diary with a lock and key from Lydia. Its inscription admonished Konstanza to "write down your hopes and dreams, your frustrations and disappointments. Treat this diary like your best friend and you will gain insight, acquire knowledge, and discover yourself." Uncle Konrad and her mother gave her a narrow gold bracelet. The words carved into it brought tears to Konstanza's eyes: "Our love encircles you without end." Uncle Kurt, the practical one, gave her a receipt for a sizable deposit in her own numbered Swiss bank account. "I will add a bit each year," he told Konstanza. "It is easier than trying to find a suitable gift." Then he wrote a number on a scrap of paper he tore from the dinner check. "Memorize this number; you will need it to withdraw funds. Then tear up the paper." He told her, "It will be our little secret."

~

Walter strode out of the Blue Parrot restaurant with the same heavy tread he had used to enter. The air had become colder and he missed his hat. Shivering, he entered the train station and walked across to the information counter. The clerk handed him his hat in a deferential manner, bowing his head slightly to signify respect. Walter liked that gesture. So there were people in Switzerland who agreed with the Nazis. He felt a little better.

The third-class cars on the Munich-bound train were not heated, and the wooden slats of the benches were hard and splintered. Walter kept his hat on as he noticed that there were only a few men in the car. He found an empty bench and began to stare stoically out the window. For the next eight hours there would be little to see, since the sun would not rise until an hour after the train arrived in Munich. His parents would be worried about him if they discovered that Walter had not been home all night. With luck he might get into the apartment and into bed before his mother got up. (He didn't need to worry about his father, since he usually slept until noon.)

Totally unbidden thoughts of Konstanza went through his mind. He admitted to himself that he loved her. She had given him the attention, the physical affection, the caring love that he missed from his parents. Neither of them had touched him since he was a baby; never hugged him or ever shown any appreciation for his efforts to live according to their rules. He had been an obedient son, rarely argued with his father, seldom lied to his mother, but today he had openly defied them. They had forbidden him to see Konstanza again and had convinced his favorite cousin to help with the plan to keep them apart. Now, after the scene at the dinner party, he began to think his parents were right. He must forget her.

In his mind he had fabricated a story about his whereabouts last night, but now he resolved to tell his parents the truth, admit that he did wrong and face the consequences like the man he wanted to be. For hours he sat very still trying to control his mind and feelings, but a deep pain stabbed his heart, constricted his chest and throat. In spite of the chill in the train car, his clenched fists were damp with cold sweat.

By the time the train had reached Munich he was exhausted from emotion and lack of sleep. Walter had stumbled off the train, caught one of the first trollies headed to the working-class district at the edge of the city, and quietly made his way through the apartment to his bedroom. Lying in his bed he buried his face in the pillow to stifle the sound of the wracking sobs that shook his body.

Chapter 6

After the winter holidays a new seating arrangement was implemented in all the classrooms. The teachers who might have objected to the new rules had been dismissed over the holidays. Heretofore, the students at the Freiburg Girls' Academy had been seated in alphabetical order. The new rule would seat the students according to Aryan purity. Blonde girls with blue eyes were to use the seats toward the front of the room. Those with darker hair and eyes were to be seated in the next rows. A row was assigned for girls who were from a mixed marriage. Without asking them about their parentage, the new history teacher ordered Konstanza and Hilde to clean out their desks and move to the last two seats in the back of the room.

As the two girls walked toward their new seats, the surly-looking teacher snarled at them when they moved by her. "Your kind shouldn't even be allowed into a racially-pure school."

There had been sufficient propaganda in the newspapers and on the radio so that Konstanza knew that some people hated Jews. The reasons they gave for that animosity didn't make sense to her. Hilde was Jewish and a decent, trustworthy friend. Lydia was Jewish and one of the nicest people Konstanza had ever met, and she had been a good friend to her mother for many years. How was all this hostility toward other nationalities and races going to help Germany revive from the economic depression? She had no one to ask about this question. The school administrators and staff seemed convinced of the truth of the vile propaganda, but they would scarcely speak to her.

The school year seemed endless and by March Konstanza was desperate to get away from the toxic atmosphere. She found solace and friendships in the kitchen. The girls who worked there had helped her mail letters to Walter in the past, and she often helped them with food preparation when they were shorthanded.

The head chef, Filomina, was Italian and oblivious to politics. All she cared about was providing nourishing and tasty meals for the students and staff of the school. Every morning before daylight she went to the local farmers' market so she had first pick of the fruits and vegetables she would be using that day. Adjoining the produce market was an area where chicken and pork farmers sold their goods, and Filomina spent another half-hour haggling with the vendors about the high price of their protein. On Friday mornings she went to the fish market where she bought freshly-caught trout from streams that flowed through the Black Forest.

One of the kitchen maids usually accompanied Filomina on these expeditions, but lately they were shorthanded. Many young girls preferred to work in stores and factories now, and the kitchen crew was down to two girls. They needed to be in the kitchen to prepare breakfast while Filomina went shopping. One afternoon while visiting the kitchen, Konstanza heard her complain about having to do this chore alone. Konstanza offered to go along the next morning.

"Well, I just need help with the carrying of the purchases," Filomina said. "Even a student can do that much." After that, Konstanza went with her each morning and still managed to get back in time for classes.

Those early morning outings were the highlight of Konstanza's day. She loved the smells and sounds of the market and watching Filomina pick and choose the various products. It was an education to hear her haggle with the vendors. Somehow each side always felt they had made a good deal.

The market was about a half-hour walk from the school,

which was located near the edge of a grove of beech trees. The gravel road that led to the market area was dusty on dry days and muddy after a rain, so Filomina chose to cut across a meadow to get to the produce market. In the predawn the air felt crisp, and Konstanza took special pleasure in watching the sky at sunrise. While they walked Filomina talked about her adventures in Paris. She had been a student at Le Cordon Bleu, a cooking school founded in 1895 that specialized in training female chefs. This was a revolutionary idea, but eventually other cities in Europe opened their culinary institutes to women.

The more time Konstanza spent with Filomina, the more she wanted to become a chef. It would be difficult to convince her mother that she would be happier preparing food than sitting in an office, and Konstanza spent many hours trying to find the right words to tell her. In the meantime she would learn as much as possible from her friends in the kitchen.

~

The April rains provided opportunities to go mushroom hunting in the Black Forest that bordered the small city of Freiburg. In just a few minutes a person could be deep in the leafy canopy of the old trees. Filomina was even more knowledgeable about mushrooms than Berta had been, and she enjoyed teaching Konstanza about the rich variety that grew in these German woods. The poisonous mushrooms were difficult to distinguish from the edible variety. It seemed that the more attractive and colorful the growths were, the more likely they were to be poisonous.

Filomina pointed out the barely-discernible difference between the death cap and the delicious toadstools and fluted red caps. The variety seemed endless and there were only a very few poison ones among them, but a mistake could be fatal. Filomina told Konstanza that the deadliest of the mushrooms didn't kill people instantly. Many varieties could make one sick, but the fatal doses of the death cap would take six to twelve hours to shut down the vital organs, depending on how many mushrooms were consumed.

At last it was June, and Estanza and Konrad drove to Freiburg to help Konstanza bring home her things from the eight-year ordeal of boarding school. She had not told her mother that she did not want to go to University in the fall, but wanted to enroll in a culinary institute instead. She decided to wait until later in the summer.

On the drive back to Basel, Konrad told Konstanza that he was taking his two favorite girls on a tour of Europe this summer. It would be a vacation and a learning experience about the ancient and modern culture that had shaped the continent. Getting ready for the tour was an experience in itself. Konrad and Estanza drew Konstanza into the planning process. Auto tours through Europe were not that common in 1928, and decisions needed to be made about roads to take, places to stay, and sites that just had to be seen.

Konstanza hardly ever thought about Walter. When he came to mind, she reminded herself that he was not the same person she had loved. She missed the former Walter, but he no longer existed.

The European tour started out in France, and they worked their way up through Italy seeing the scenery, artwork and ancient historical sites that had provided the source of Western Civilization and attracted visitors for a thousand years. On the way to Vienna they drove through the lake country in Kernten and visited ancient castles, ate schnitzel washed down with Pilsner beer, and enjoyed the affable hospitality of the Austrians in this truly beautiful countryside.

In Vienna they visited Lydia, who told them that Konrad's father was thinking of moving there from Berlin. "Kurt is getting ready to retire from the foreign service and we intend to make a life together," she told them.

Konrad was delighted. "It is about time," he told his

father's lover of thirty years.

Konstanza enjoyed a brief reunion with Hilde. She lived in the very center of Vienna near the area called The Graben (the ancient moat around the city), in an apartment on the Juden Platz. From her window she could see the Vienna Culinary Institute and, knowing Konstanza's desire to be a chef, Hilde pointed it out to her. "My father knows the man who runs it," she told Konstanza. "They now take females in their classes, but they can only become assistant chefs."

"I have plans to go to Le Cordon Bleu in Paris, where Madame Martha Distel had been training women to be chefs since 1895." Konstanza replied.

The day after this visit Konrad bought the last four tickets for the afternoon performance of the Lipizzaner Horses at the Spanish Riding School. The seats were not together with two seats in the lower middle row of the stadium and two other seats further back. Konrad suggested that Lydia and Estanza take the lower seats and he and Konstanza would climb up to the two seats above. He seemed eager to be alone with Konstanza and she was pleased with the situation. She planned to take advantage of their privacy to tell him her plans for culinary school. Konstanza was reluctant to tell her mother first. She knew that Estanza had practical, sensible and well laid-out plans for Konstanza's education. Like most European parents of that era, she expected her daughter to follow her mother's profession. Konstanza had always been able to talk more freely with uncle Konrad. She wanted him to help her convince her mother that she was serious about having a different career.

Before she could begin on this topic, Konrad took her hand and said, "You seem strangely sad, my little treasure." Then he looked at the watch he carried in his vest pocket. They had fifteen minutes before the show would start and he hoped to find out why Konstanza had been so subdued on this trip. "Please don't tell me that it is nothing. I can guess it has something to do with Walter Mannheim." She nodded and looked out over the expanse of the arena. Horses and trainers were practicing dressage routines in the far side of the staging area, and a small band was rehearsing in the pit. A few rows below, Lydia and Estanza were talking animatedly. Finally Konstanza turned to Konrad.

"I loved him so much," she whimpered. Her voice was so low, Konrad barely heard her.

"Walter is no longer the person you loved. That Walter has disappeared. I have seen it happen many times. My own wife changed into another person after ten years of marriage." Konstanza's eyes widened and Konrad asked her, "You knew I was married, didn't you?" She nodded. (Although no one had ever actually told Konstanza that Uncle Konrad had a wife in America, she had overheard conversations on the subject.)

Konrad continued: "To live a satisfying life, one must learn to accept disappointments and tragedy. I have a mental happiness box. I keep all the happy memories in this box. When I start feeling sad about someone who has gone out of my life, I open the box and take out one of the happy memories. I allow my mind to play with it, to remember the good times until I feel better. Then I put it back in the imaginary box until the next time I need it."

Konstanza nodded; she understood.

"Try to be thankful that you were allowed those wonderful moments of love and pleasure. Many people don't even have those memories to enjoy. Also, Walter is young. He may return to who he was."

Konstanza shook her head, but there was a tiny spark of hope that flared up in her heart.

A few minutes before the show started she spoke to Konrad about her dream of becoming a chef. He was surprised at her choice of career, but not at her determination. "You are a lot like your mother, my little treasure." He chuckled.

She smiled knowingly. He would help her get her wish and convince Estanza that it was the right plan for her daughter.

~

After hiking in the Vienna Woods, taking a cruise on the Danube, and visiting the ancient Abbey of Melk, the three travelers decided to spend a day at the world-renowned amusement park in the heart of Vienna called The Prater. They rode on the giant Ferris wheel with gondolas the size of railroad cars. Konstanza thought about how she would have loved to share this once-in-a-lifetime experience with the former Walter.

That evening they left the rental car in Vienna and boarded the overnight train to Berlin. The plan was to stay with Konrad's father who had returned to Berlin a week ago. Both men were eager to show Konstanza the wonders of this ultramodern city, the museums, the world famous zoo and the parks, and to take her on a river cruise along the River Spree.

Chapter 7

Berlin, 1928

On a warm evening in September, a few days before they planned to return to Basel, Konrad, Estanza and Konstanza were walking home from the customary Sunday concert in a nearby park. The cool breeze from the river was a welcome relief. They were passing by a low wall, over which they saw a lovely garden between two stately houses. Konrad began to hum the refrain from the last march of the outdoor concert. Konstanza had her hand tucked into his left elbow. His brass-handled walking stick was tucked under his right arm and he held Estanza's hand up against his chest. The three of them walked briskly, keeping time with the music.

Three men came sauntering across from the other side of the street. Abruptly they stopped in front of Konrad and the two women. The men were hatless and dressed in shabby work clothes. The taller man in the middle spoke to Konrad in a working class dialect. "Where is a gentleman like yourself going with these Gypsy whores?" he smirked. The two shorter men on either side of him were grinning broadly.

Before any of them could make a move to get around the menacing trio, the shorter man on Konrad's right pulled the walking stick out from under his arm. He raised it to tip Konrad's hat off. It fell behind him and when Konrad turned to retrieve it the taller man grabbed the walking stick and bashed it against the side of Konrad's head. He sank to his knees and Estanza screamed.

The tall man then started to swing the stick at her. With one smooth motion of her right hand she pulled the hat pin out of her hat and thrust it into his left eye. He dropped the walking stick within an inch of her head, clutched at the hat pin, and then, with a gurgling growl, he fell to the ground beside Konrad. Estanza started to bend down to Konrad, who lay very still, when she heard a muffled cry.

The other two men had grabbed Konstanza and hoisted her over the low garden wall. Estanza picked up the walking stick at its narrow end and jumped up to sit on the wall. She swung around to face the other side. Just before she jumped down she saw her daughter on the ground with her dress pulled up around her waist. One of the men was sitting on her chest, trying to stuff her silk panties into her mouth. The other man was kneeling between her legs; his pants were unbuttoned and drooping around his hips. One of his hands was holding up his erect penis, the other was clutching Konstanza's bushy, black pubic hair.

With the strength born of madness, Estanza swung the solid brass head of the walking stick against the side of his head. He fell forward against the man sitting on Konstanza's chest, blood spurting from his ear. Estanza raised the stick, ready to swing again, when the other man ducked out from under his unconscious accomplice, stumbled to his feet and ran into the bushes at the back of the garden.

Konstanza was barely conscious when her mother finally got her to sit up. Her face was beginning to swell from multiple bruises and the rest of her body would be sore for several weeks, but otherwise she was unharmed.

The two women knelt beside Konrad. He was breathing and his eyes were beginning to open. Estanza took off her coat and put it under Konrad's head. As she gently lowered his head to the coat, a few drops of blood fell on her hand. For a few moments she couldn't decide whether to try to find the wound and bind it up, or to hurry away to get help. She decided to go get help.

She straightened her clothes, found her cloche hat, pulled the hatpin from the tall man's eye and wiped it clean on his pant leg, and stuck it back into her hat. She assumed he was dead, the long hat pin having penetrated his brain. With an effort she held back the urge to kick him in the ribs. "Stay with Uncle Konrad!" she ordered the weeping Konstanza, and she started toward the nearest house, where she noticed telephone wires. After repeated knocking, a portly, middle-aged man opened the door a crack. He was wearing a dark velvet smoking jacket, so he was not the butler.

Before the man could speak, Estanza explained, as calmly as she could, "We were attacked on the street. Please telephone the police and ask for an ambulance."

The man opened the door a little wider, looked Estanza up and down with suspicious, searching eyes. From past experience, Estanza surmised that he thought she might be a Gypsy. It was certain that he would not let her into the house.

"My daughter is badly hurt. Please hurry," she said and stepped back, to show that she had no intention of forcing herself into the house. He closed the door and Estanza could hear the lock click. She waited to see if he would really use the telephone she had glimpsed in the entry hall.

"Operator, connect me to the police station," she heard him say. He gave the address and listened for a few seconds, then continued speaking. "A woman that looks like she might be a Gypsy said she and her daughter were attacked on the street." This was followed by a short silence, and then Estanza heard the man chuckle. "Yes, most likely some man trying to keep them from picking his pockets. She said to send an ambulance."

Estanza went back to Konrad and Konstanza. A small crowd had gathered around the crime scene and she heard murmuring among the assembled group.

"The two corpses look like ordinary workers. Poor devils."

"The girl sitting with the gentleman looks like she could be a Gypsy."

"She must be a whore, see how beat up she looks."

"Look, here comes another one. Dark like a Gypsy, but

she is wearing such stylish clothes."

"Did you hear? The young one called her 'Mama.'"

"I bet they were trying to rob the old guy when the workers came along to help him."

"That's what you get, trying to be a Good Samaritan, the poor slobs."

The German police had an inflexible routine when they were called to a street crime scene.[1] Badly wounded victims were taken to a prison hospital ward and questioned as soon as they were able to talk. The dead bodies were delivered to the nearest morgue, and anyone else who might be under the slightest suspicion was arrested on the spot. At the first sound of the police siren the crowd disappeared and no one came out of the nearby houses.

Konrad was taken away in the ambulance, the two dead bodies were loaded onto the lorry (called "the meat wagon"), and Estanza and Konstanza were unceremoniously handcuffed and shoved into the police van. When they arrived at the police station, the two women stood briefly in front of a high desk, gave their names to an invisible person behind it, and were then told to sit on a bench against the bare brick wall in the entry hall. Suddenly a man in tall black boots stood in front of them. A grin crossed his fat face. "Take the murdering thieves to the lower cells," he said to the arresting sergeant. Then under his breath, "That name, Nikiolopolis, sounds familiar."

Estanza and her daughter were led down a steep, stone stairway. The two officers held them firmly by the arms to keep them from stumbling in the dark. At the bottom were rows of cells with straw strewn on the bare concrete floors. A small slit near the ceiling let in a sliver of daylight, which was fading quickly. A kerosene lamp burned on a small table at the end of the cell block.

A man rose from a chair, dangling keys from a large ring. His face was hidden in the gloom, but his voice was harsh, derisive. "What have we here?" he bellowed. He picked up the lamp to see the faces of the two prisoners. "This way, ladies," he said, and the officers pushed them into a cell, the door clanged shut, and they heard the key turn in the lock.

Estanza and Konstanza stood there for a few moments, trying to take in what had just happened to them. One of the officers told them to put their hands out through the section of bars in the door, so he could remove the handcuffs. They did as they were told. The two policemen who had brought them down to, what can only be called, a "dungeon" started toward the stairs.

Estanza finally found her voice. "Please come back," she called out through the small, barred square in the door.

One of the men turned to look at her.

"Call Kurt von Stahlenberg and tell him we are here." She waited a second to see if he was listening. "Please—please!" She felt her voice cracking. "My daughter is only a child. You can't leave her here all night."

There was no response, and the two men went out. The guard went back to his chair by the table, taking the lamp with him.

After their eyes adjusted to the dark, the women could see that there was no place to sit in the small cubicle. The stench from the straw was almost unbearable and Konstanza began to gag helplessly. Estanza called out to the guard that they needed to use a toilet and that they had not eaten since noon. He came over to the cell. "This is not the Ritz Hotel!" he shouted. "We feed you vermin once a day in the morning—and you should be grateful for that," he continued and returned to his chair.

Estanza began to shiver. She remembered having left her coat under Konrad's head. Konstanza had a light jacket over her summer dress which was no help against the chill. The cell smelled musty and the straw was damp from moisture running down the walls into one corner where a puddle of urine had accumulated. They felt around and found a corner that was almost dry and huddled together until they finally saw daylight coming through the slots near the ceiling.

Early Monday morning, Kurt von Stahlenberg entered the rotunda-like police station near the Spree River Park area. He was accompanied by the legal attaché from the Swiss Embassy. The two distinguished-looking men stood facing the raised admittance desk. The high ceiling and expanse of white marble floor were meant to impress and intimidate.

"What do you want?" the officer behind the desk growled languidly.

For a moment Kurt debated with himself if he should remove his hat and decided to leave it on his head for now. He noticed, with annoyance, that the Swiss lawyer had taken off his hat already. Kurt knew that approaching German police hat-in-hand was not a good idea. Any show of deference seemed to goad them into more arrogance and rudeness. Lately he had the feeling that the country was becoming a "police state." In the year 1928, he had no idea how prophetic his thoughts were.

In his best diplomatic style Kurt said, "I understand that two foreign women named Nikiolopolis are being detained in this facility." It was not a question, but a firm statement of fact.

The officer behind the desk gave the two men in front of him a disdainful look, and then jerked his head to the area behind him. "I gave yesterday's roster to the captain. He is inspecting it now," he said and pointed to the glass-paneled office behind him. The captain could be seen sitting at a desk leafing through paperwork. Then he got up and went to the filing cabinet against one wall.

Kurt tried to think of what he should do next. There was a time during the Kaiser's reign when just the mention of his name would open doors and even the gates of prison cells. The von Stahlenberg men had faithfully served the government of Germany for generations. They were not the richest, by any means, but they had influence. Kurt himself had been a valuable member of the foreign service, starting as an assistant attaché, as well as a spy, and eventually had attained the rank of ambassador and served as such in several powerful countries.

He was still connected to the government, which was now called The Weimar Republic after its first president. Like many of the aristocrats he was reduced to a near destitute condition. The lands he had inherited from his father had been confiscated and distributed among the tenant farmers, who now paid their rent to the government. On a civil service salary, Kurt von Stahlenberg was not in a position to offer the captain "temporary enhancement of his finances" (more crudely called a "bribe"). Kurt tried another tactic, often successful with lower-ranking officials—the subtle questioning of their authority.

"I don't suppose that you have the permission to take me to see the women in question?" Kurt proposed.

The sergeant looked a bit startled at this remark, but replied, "No one is allowed into the cell blocks."

"So you don't even know if the Nikiolopolis women are at this station?" Kurt asked in an even tone.

The officer looked up. "They are here, all right," he snapped.

"You were not certain a few minutes ago." The Swiss lawyer had found his voice. "It might be best for all concerned to bring them here so we can identify them. That way we will not waste any more of your time." All three men glanced toward the office where the captain was moving away from the filing cabinet and toward his desk.

The suggestion made sense to the sergeant who had come on duty that morning and, if truth be told, was curious to see the women in his custody. He called to the two officers standing near the street door and sent them to "fetch the prisoners in cell number 4," handing each a pair of handcuffs.

In a few minutes a disheveled pair of women shuffled into the reception area, awkwardly holding their handcuffed wrists in front of them. When Estanza saw Kurt she cried out his name and asked about Konrad in one breath. Then she began to cough uncontrollably. Konstanza gave Kurt a pleading look and moved toward her mother. The guard near her reached out and pushed her back. Her tear-stained face gave witness to the night's ordeal.

"Are those the women you are looking for?" the sergeant asked gruffly.

"Yes, they are," Kurt replied, in an even tone that belied his outrage.

The sergeant was waving his arm, indicating that the guards should take the women back to the cells, when the captain emerged from his office, carrying a large piece of yellowing paper. He turned to the sergeant. "I found the 'Wanted' poster," he crowed, and waved the yellow sheet with Estanza's picture for all to see. "There is no statute of limitations for espionage. We'll see that she doesn't get away again."

Everyone in the hall turned to look at Estanza. She was oblivious to the staring eyes, as her coughing had drowned out the captain's words.

"Take her to the cells," the captain barked, straining to be heard over the wracking coughs that echoed throughout the cavernous space. "The commissioner will be here tomorrow to set a court date."

Kurt raised his voice to command level. "This woman is very ill. She needs to go to a hospital, not a jail cell."

The captain moved to stand in front of Kurt. "Von Stahlenberg, you would do well to keep your voice down and your temper in check." He hissed, "This female has killed two German citizens and is wanted for spying on the state." He paused for effect and looked around the room.

During a brief respite in her coughing, Estanza put her hands up in a gesture of imploring an unseen presence, and then she turned to the captain. "Don't put her back in the cells. She is just an innocent child," she rasped out between coughs.

"You can take the girl," the captain said, pointing to Konstanza.

One of the guards removed her handcuffs and she began

to scream, "No, no!" Kurt stepped to her side. Estanza also made a move toward her daughter.

The guard closest to Estanza lifted the leather covered, wooden truncheon from his belt. It struck Estanza between the shoulder blades with the heaviest part coming down at the base of her skull. A loud crack echoed through the hall. Emitting a low gasp, Estanza sank to the floor, blood spewing out of her mouth.

Chapter 8

Rain streaked across the windows of the train as it sped through the drab countryside. Konstanza looked at the blurred vista with unseeing eyes. She was barely aware of her surroundings but the click-clack of the wheels on the track reminded her that she was leaving Germany behind. In a few hours they would be out of that hateful country. She knew nothing about Poland but it had to be a better place.

The events of the past two weeks had left her emotionally drained. She felt numb and empty of all feelings. The horrifying scenes came flashing into her mind like postcards viewed through a Victorian era stereoscope. The thugs who tried to rape her. The night spent in the police dungeon. Her mother lying on the white marble floor in a pool of blood. Her beloved uncle Konrad in a coma while she sat by his bedside, and then dying in her arms. Being told, at long last, that he really was the father she had longed for all her life.

Thinking of the ugly scene at Konrad's funeral aroused a rage in her that overshadowed the deep sorrow. It all played out in her mind like a scene in a movie.

~

The small contingent of mourners had stood around the ornate casket for a brief service before it was carried into the elaborate von Stahlenberg crypt. At the conclusion of the service a tall, blond woman had stepped in front of Kurt von Stahlenberg. She raised her black veil to reveal a pale face, twisted into a mask of malevolence.

"You old reprobate"—she spat out the words—"have you no respect for your son's memory? How dare you bring his bastard child to mock me at *my husband's* funeral?" She then had moved in front of Konstanza and stared at her with disdain, and then at Lydia, who had her arm around the girl's waist. "I see you brought your dirty Jewish whore to round out the insult!"

Lydia's hand had moved with lightning speed, seemingly without her own volition. It left a dark, red mark on Elisabet's cheek. Elisabet staggered backwards. The woman behind her put out an arm, with a swastika armband, to steady her.

Konstanza looked across the train compartment at the half-dozing man whom she would be calling Uncle Marcus. Her thoughts went back to the dinner party that was to be the catalyst for a new life.

Lydia and Kurt had allowed Konstanza a two-week period of mourning without interruption. Kurt was mourning the loss of his son and, like Konstanza, spent much of that time just sitting in his room, looking out the window with unseeing eyes.

During the second week a telegram arrived from Marcus Mandel, announcing his arrival in Berlin. Kurt's friendship with Marcus went back to their university days in Torun. This city was in Prussia when the men studied there and it was now, once more, in Poland as it had been when the famous astronomer Nicolas Copernicus was born there several centuries ago.

With some trepidation Lydia approached Kurt with an idea about how to bring Konstanza out of her deep depression. "You and Marcus usually go to a fine-dining restaurant when he comes to Berlin," she had started a tentative conversation at breakfast one morning, "but if we had a guest here perhaps Konstanza could be persuaded to join us for a meal." They both looked at the empty, ornate Biedermeier chair that stood waiting next to the other five chairs around the table.

Kurt put down his coffee cup and gave her a dubious

look. She continued: "You two men have not met for over a year and you have much to tell each other. You know that in these times you cannot speak freely in public." With relief, Lydia saw that Kurt was not averse to her suggestion. There was indecision in his face, and he gave her a questioning look.

Kurt replied, "All the servants will leave tomorrow in preparation for my move to Vienna. Who would prepare a meal? You and I hardly know how to boil water for coffee." He forced a smile to lighten his words.

"I have an idea, Kurt." Lydia's tone was light and excited. "Please hear me out."

Kurt took a bite out of the crusty Kaiser roll, and then put it down on his plate, to show Lydia she had his complete attention. She was persuasive; although he had his doubts about the outcome, he agreed to her plan.

At first Konstanza listened to Lydia with a frozen expression and empty eyes. She gazed distractedly out the window across the spacious bedroom. Slowly her attention focused, as Lydia explained how she needed her help.

"Kurt wants me to prepare a meal for him and Marcus, and I do not even know how to boil water," Lydia confessed

"You have never cooked anything?" Konstanza asked in disbelief. It was the first full sentence she had uttered since Konrad's funeral.

"Cooking was not a part of the curriculum at medical school." Lydia chuckled, and said, "None of the women on my mother's side of the family knew how to cook. They were seamstresses, secretaries, bookkeepers, telephone operators, and ran retail stores. They left the meal preparations to the experts." Lydia tried her best to look forlorn and helpless.

"I can help you if you want," Konstanza had said without much enthusiasm.

"Would you please?" Lydia sounded relieved. "I have made up a menu," she added, and she proudly held up a wrinkled piece of notepaper. Gradually Konstanza began to show an interest as Lydia asked questions about recipes, where to get the ingredients, and the actual process of getting a cooked meal to the table.

Konstanza rose to the challenge. She and Lydia went shopping at the farmer's market and the KDV department store food section. They decided that dessert was a little beyond their expertise and stopped at the Ankor Bakery on the famous Unter den Linden Boulevard to buy a Linzer Torte. "I can whip cream for the top," Konstanza offered, when Lydia asked about where to get the customary topping for this light, berry-filled cake.

The meal for Kurt and Marcus was a great success. The dinner conversation started with family news. "My nephew, Paul, and his wife had a baby girl last March," was Marcus's home-front news.

"We were at his wedding in Vienna last year," Lydia remarked. "They didn't waste any time procreating." Everyone chuckled at this observation.

"Yes, he married the younger Menkes girl," Kurt chimed in. "The older one lives in Egypt."

"Mathilde is beautiful, like one of those American movie stars, and an excellent secretary," Marcus continued, "but she is helpless around the house." Marcus looked at Lydia who was frowning at him from across the table.

"Not all women are born competent homemakers." Lydia's voice was cool and a bit sharp. "I never learned to cook, or to run a household. In my family, we hired professionals to do that."

The subject changed to more serious matters. Being able to talk freely was a relief, and the three adults discussed the dire economy and the dangerous political situation—all the while downing the delicious four-course meal.

Although Lydia had offered to help Konstanza prepare the meal, the only real contribution was her vague recipe for chicken soup (a handful of this and a pinch of that). Konstanza had learned to make noodle dough from Filomina. To Lydia's astonishment, the strips of dough were hung to dry over the backs of the kitchen chairs. When the hot, savory soup was served as the first course, the men sighed with satisfaction, remembering their mother's soup.

The schnitzel inside its golden crust was tender and tangy, with spices that Ena had used to give the veal more flavor. The side dish of Swiss-type spaetzle was just the right texture. Even Berta would have been proud to serve it. The creamed spinach had just a touch of garlic, reminiscent of the Greek version that was served in Distomo. The third course was a crispy and colorful salad, also of Greek origin. Lastly, the Linzer torte, topped with whipped cream, was a light dessert that complimented the meal.

By the time the four of them assembled in the parlor for coffee and brandy, Konstanza had proven her potential as a chef. Lydia and Kurt beamed proudly as Marcus, a recognized gourmet, praised the table setting, the competent and artistic presentation, and most of all, the tasty food.

The discussion turned to Konstanza's future. "She wants to be a chef." Kurt tried to keep his voice neutral to hide his bias against female chefs.

Lydia mentioned that they had visited culinary institutes in Vienna and Berlin, but at sixteen Konstanza was too young for admittance. "They are reluctant to allow females into their classes and, besides, the tuition is prohibitive," she sighed.

In the well-appointed kitchen, Konstanza washed the dishes. She welcomed the change from the cramped area in the Basel apartment.

The chatter from the parlor continued late into the night. To Konstanza, it was evident that the two men, who came from totally opposite backgrounds, had a deep and special friendship that was based on shared values, humor, and a realistic view of the world.

~

Now sitting in the train across from Uncle Marcus, Konstanza tried to remember what had persuaded her to come to Poland. It wasn't just the words that had been spoken. He had warmth, gentleness, and a sincerity that had impressed her and influenced her decision.

"My nephew has a spacious apartment overlooking an ancient castle and a tree-lined park," he had said in a tone that revealed his pleasure at the location. "There is a modern kitchen where you will have full reign of all food preparation." These words had intrigued the young girl more than any others. She was also curious about the new baby. Konstanza had never seen a real baby. "Her name is Hedwig, but we call her Hedy," Marcus had said as further enticement, "and although there is a nurse, you could help take care of her."

The station in Gdansk was almost as huge as the one in Berlin, but Marcus guided them expertly to the right tracks just as the last local train was ready to depart. As they traveled south the setting sun flooded the sky with spectacular shades of pink and orange. Konstanza watched the glow of bright light and it started to lift her spirits. Gradually the pain in her chest began to ease and a tingle of anticipation began to flutter in the core of her being.

Chapter 9

Like autumn leaves in the wind, the years drifted by. Each year Konstanza thought about leaving her position with the Mandel family, and each year she postponed her departure.

When little Hedy began to walk, the nurse gave notice because, as she explained, she only cared for babies, not toddlers. So Konstanza became the nanny as well as the family cook. She was more than fond of Hedy, and the Mandels treated her like an older sister to Hedy and sometimes like a younger sister to Mathilde.

They took Konstanza along to Austria where they went each summer. Vienna was hot and humid, so the whole family usually rented a small villa on a lake in the southern district of Austria known as Kernten. Konstanza enjoyed the scenery which reminded her of Switzerland, but the constant German in her ears made her uneasy. In Austria the family really didn't need a nanny. There were aunts, cousins, and a doting grandmother to care for Hedy.

"This summer I am not accompanying you to Austria," Konstanza announced in the spring of 1933. "I would like to avoid Germany and the German language. This summer I would like to see Switzerland again."

"I understand," Paul Mandel said, "but we will miss you. Do you have funds for such a trip?" he asked with real concern.

"My uncle Kurt has already sent me extra funds because he wants me to visit him and Aunt Lydia in Basel this year. We kept missing them in Vienna because they had already left for the summer when we arrived." Konstanza still referred to Kurt von Stahlenberg as her uncle, although by now she knew he was her grandfather.

Returning to her birthplace was a bittersweet experience. The apartment in Basel, where she had lived with her mother, had been sold after Konstanza had gone to Poland to work for the Mandel family. At the Chalet, Berta and Berti were delighted to have her back. Kurt and Lydia were finally married after thirty years of clandestine trysts in the Swiss Alpine village. They were a comfort and helped to alleviate the longing for her mother and her father—whom she still thought of as Uncle Konrad. But it was walking around the lake, sitting under the willow tree, and climbing their favorite trails that made Konstanza's heart ache for her Walter. However, for the next few years she returned to the Chalet and found a modicum of peace in the beauty of the landscape and the warmth of her family.

While other young girls filled their diaries with gossipy secrets about boys, clothes and social successes or failures, Konstanza had filled her diary with recipes, instructions on food preparation, and where to find the freshest ingredients and why to use them. She had made illustrations of plants, fungi and fish. She had listed the names of countless herbs and spices and their use.

That fall when she returned to Poland, she told the Mandel family, "Hedy will be starting school next year and she will no longer need a nanny. It is my intention to enroll in a culinary school and finally become a chef."

"But you can cook anything you want in our kitchen," Mathilde pleaded. "Please reconsider for just one more year." Then Hedy began to cry, and no more needed to be said. Konstanza couldn't stand her darling's tears. She gathered five-year-old Hedy into her arms and promised never to leave her—knowing perfectly well that, one day, it would be Hedy who would choose to leave.

For four more years, the Mandel family went to Austria and Konstanza spent the summers in Switzerland. Even though she grieved for her parents and still missed Walter, it was the best time of her life.

In the fateful year of 1938, the dark clouds of death began to gather for Konstanza and for all of Europe. Her beloved grandfather/uncle Kurt died in January. His wife, Lydia, blamed his heart attack on the political situation in Germany and the threat of the Nazis coming into Austria. Marcus Mandel traveled to Vienna for the funeral. He came back to Poland with a terrible cold, which developed into a fatal bout of pneumonia.

In the middle of March, the Nazis marched into Vienna and were greeted with wild jubilation by most of the Austrian people. The country was renamed Ostmark and became a part of the new Germany. All the laws regarding Jews in the Third Reich were now enforced. Jews were forbidden to practice any profession, use any public facility, meet with more than five people at a time, be on the street after dark, or shop for food before four o'clock in the evening. They were also forced to divest themselves of all property by selling it as soon as possible to an Aryan buyer for a minuscule amount.

A tear-stained letter arrived in the Mandel home asking Mathilde to come to Vienna. Her father was dying and her mother needed help. Almost all of her relatives had emigrated to other countries all over the globe, and Frau Menkes was desperate. Jewish doctors were not allowed to practice and non-Jewish doctors were not allowed to treat Jews.

By the time the letter had arrived, her father had died and Mathilde's mother sent a telegram begging her to come to Vienna to help with the funeral arrangements.

"You can't travel to that hell-hole." Paul Mandel had tried not to raise his voice to keep Hedy from hearing his desperation.

"I need to go to my mother," Mathilde said firmly. "She is all alone by now. Even Konstanza's aunt, Lydia Gottlieb von Stahlenberg, has left for Melbourne, Australia. It was the farthest place from Germany she could find."

There were a few more days of arguments, but Mathilde left for Vienna at the end of the summer. According to her last letter to Paul, she had found her mother in a terrible state—half-starved and almost incoherent. There was a problem with paperwork and she would need to stay in Vienna until things were settled.

He never heard from her again.

At the end of October of 1938, Paul took a desperate chance. "I am going to Berlin," he told Konstanza. "Kurt von Stahlenberg introduced me to some influential people on my last business trip. I know it was over five years ago, but they might still be able to help me with the authorities in Vienna."

Konstanza had grave doubts about his traveling into what she considered was the mouth of the dragon. She wanted to dissuade him but could not find the words. She still refused to speak German and her Polish was not fluent even after ten years. So Paul left for Berlin. She and Hedy waved him off at the train.

A few days later the terrible pogrom, called *Kristallnacht*, was unleashed in every town in Germany, even in the smallest villages. If a store was owned by a Jew, the windows were broken and the place was looted by the Brownshirt thugs with swastika armbands. (Many non-Jewish stores were looted as well.) In the morning thousands of Jewish men were rounded up and sent to Dachau concentration camp. All the Jews left in Germany were held responsible for the damage done by the SA (or "Stormtroopers") and were being held for ransom.

With sufficient funds their female relatives could bribe the right Gestapo officers and gain the release of their family member. This person had to leave the country within forty-eight hours or faced being re-arrested.

If there was no inquiry about the fate of a man in Dachau within a certain time, he did not survive for very long. Those without any funds, which included most of the men there, were eventually starved or beaten to death to make space for the men who were soon to be sent there from all over Europe. Paul Mandel disappeared into the maw of that beast that would soon take over almost all of Europe.

For twelve years the people of Europe lost their moral compass. In the countries occupied by the Germans the Christians enthusiastically rounded up the Jews in their midst and sent them away to be brutally murdered. Although this action was totally against their own self interest, there was almost total cooperation in deporting skilled doctors, teachers, scientists, craftsman and all productive, decent, patriotic citizens who happened to be Jewish.

Chapter 10

Konstanza lost track of the days after Hedy had been taken away. She paced the floor of the apartment much as Paul Mandel had done after Hedy's mother had disappeared. Thoughts of recrimination flooded into her mind, and she thought of all the things she should have done to save Hedy. I could have hidden her. *I could have taken her away to Switzerland. I could have brought her to a convent.*

But none of those plans had occurred to her. What had she been thinking? That Hedy's parents would come back? That the Germans would overlook a twelve-year-old girl, especially one who looked totally Aryan? She had miscalculated, and her remorse went deep into her very being. Once again the terrible pain of loss filled her chest, made her stomach churn, and caused nausea in the back of her throat.

One morning as she was fighting dizziness, caused from a lack of nourishment, she heard a pounding on the apartment door. Two German soldiers grinned at her as she opened it a crack. In broken Polish, one of the young men told Konstanza that she must leave the apartment that very day. She tried to tell them that she had nowhere else to go. He shrugged his shoulders and repeated the order.

Her dizziness receded as she was consumed by a helpless rage. She was very aware that her only choice was to obey the order or be shot. Over the last months she had seen what happened to people who showed even a twinge of reluctance in obeying an order from the German occupation forces.

A cloud of dust rose into the room as she dragged an old

suitcase out from under her bed. She had not used the elegant leather suitcase since her last trip to Switzerland five years ago. The memory of that last trip came sharply into focus. She was overcome by her longing for the kind people and the wondrous vistas of that peaceful land.

For a few minutes Konstanza remained on her knees by the bed, not seeing the sunny day through the window. Instead she saw a green slope, speckled with red poppies and snowcapped mountains in the distance. Without a conscious effort on her part, Walter Mannheim's face floated into her vision. She had lost everyone she loved, but losing Walter had left a deep void in her life.

Other loved ones had changed from friend to foe overnight after the Nazis came to power in Germany. These betrayals had been painful, but nothing like the piercing agony of losing Walter's loving companionship. She allowed herself a few tears and it was the last time Konstanza gave in to the luxury of self-pity.

She began to fill up the suitcase with her few pieces of clothing and her extra pair of shoes. She left space for the large wooden cigar box that held several small jars of exotic little waxed paper-lined boxes filled with dried herbs from her window box garden. On top, she folded the black wool shawl from her mother.

The Germans came back an hour later to make sure she was packing. One of the burly men saw Konstanza place a miniature figurine into a small space left in the suitcase.

"No take!" he bellowed. "Take clothes, papers—nothing more." To give emphasis to his words he took out his pistol and waved it menacingly.

"I am not Jewish," she protested. Konstanza felt a twinge of shame the moment the words came out of her mouth. Then she remembered how she had admonished Hedy to do whatever she had to do to stay alive. Proclaiming she was not what the Germans described as "subhuman" could save her life. Her emotions were of no importance now. With a numb, empty feeling she left all the things that mattered to her and to the Mandel family in the apartment and started down the stairs.

A man was standing in her way as she entered the foyer. He wore a different uniform from the regular German military. Konstanza recognized him as member of the special "occupation forces" that took charge after the army had subdued the population. These black-clad men were a branch of the Stormtroopers who were in charge of policing the civilians in occupied territories.

Their orders were to round up all Jews, and deport them as quickly as possible. Anyone who made the slightest objection to this "Aktzion" was summarily shot. Whole families were mowed down with machine gun fire if one person in their midst tried to resist. Crying babies were snatched from their mother's arms and had their heads bashed against the nearest wall or were thrown up into the air and shot before they reached the ground. The terror-stricken mothers did not dare to cry out for fear that the rest of the family would be shot.

Konstanza had resolutely watched this spectacle from her window one morning. At first she wanted to look away, close the blinds, and cover her ears with her pillows, but then she decided to watch, and someday testify as an eyewitness to these atrocities.

To her horror and shame there were Polish bystanders who cheered the sharpshooting skills of the death squad as the bloody little bodies fell to the ground. *So,* she thought to herself, *the brutality of the Germans has infected the Poles. A terrible plague has spread all over Europe. Morality is dead. Those men in black had first choice of looting the homes of the deported Jews and when they were done the Poles rushed in taking what was left.*

"Do you speak German?" The tall, boyish looking officer asked Konstanza.

She, who had not spoken the hated language since she had arrived in Poland over twelve years ago, stared mutely into space. The officer began to shout at her, but she shrugged her shoulders and said, "Polish only."

The German occupation forces had been given a few lessons but for the most part they used their hands to motion what they wanted people to do. If there was non-compliance due to a misunderstanding the errant person was shot and dragged away. Now the officer motioned for Konstanza to follow him to the Command Headquarter in the city hall.

"I will take your suitcase, madam." He said politely and grabbed toward the handle. He repeated the offer and when she did not comply he stood very close in front of her, holding out his hand for the suitcase. It was now obvious that she did not have a choice.

Fortunately Konstanza had the foresight to hide her identification papers and other vital documents, like her Swiss passport, a wad of Swiss francs, and her birth certificate. If they took her purse, they would only get a few Polish zlotys and a wrinkled handkerchief.

The man carrying her suitcase followed her along the narrow street to the cobblestone square in the center of the town. He kept following her as she ascended the steep, marble stairs to the carved oak door of the City Hall. He reached around Konstanza and opened the heavy panels, holding the door for her. Inside, a guard in a regular army uniform stood waiting for her.

"Follow me," he said in German, then seeing her empty face he gestured to her.

When Konstanza turned around to take her suitcase from the soldier behind her, he had disappeared. She followed the guard along a hallway, their shoes making a heavy clanging sound on the marble floor. They passed several doors with glazed-over panels which let some light into the hallway, but obscured whatever was behind them.

The soldier stopped at a door at the end of the hall, marked "PERSONNEL" and knocked on the glass pane. A man called out in Polish, "Come in." It sounded like a military command.

The soldier opened the door and motioned for Konstanza to enter. She started to do so, then turned to the soldier.

"What has become of my suitcase?" she asked in Polish. He shrugged and turned to leave.

"Come in." The man behind the desk barked again. Konstanza suppressed the urge to back out the door and run out of the building. She was not frightened, but instead was filled with revulsion as she recognized the neighbor who had helped the Germans find and drag away twelve-year-old Hedy.

Seeing her reluctance the man behind the desk repeated, "Come in, come in," in a softer tone. He seemed to be smiling but to Konstanza it looked very much like a sneer. "The German officials have asked me to find suitable workers," he explained. "The commander of the Occupation Forces requires a housekeeper who can cook. I remembered the delightful smells coming from the Jewish apartment. You must be a good cook."

Konstanza steeled herself to keep a neutral expression while she seethed with loathing. When the man came out from behind the desk she backed up a little, hoping he would not come any closer or reach out to touch her. A ring she recognized as having belonged to the mayor gleamed on his finger as he held out his hand toward Konstanza. With the other hand he handed her several sheets of paper. "Fill these out so we can issue you a work permit—although we should arrest you for colluding with Jews." Konstanza took the papers, not knowing what else to do. "I have arranged for you to work for Gruppen Feurher Habermann at the old Heller house."

The Polish neighbor pointed to a nearby table. He brought her a chair and a pencil and went back to his desk. She sat down and then filled out the forms. When she was done, she returned them to him. He glanced at them briefly.

"Give me your papers," he commanded. She handed him the identification papers issued by the Polish government, but not her Swiss Passport, which she kept concealed in her undergarments along with the Swiss francs that Kurt von

Stahlenberg had pressed into her hand so many years ago, admonishing her to save them for a dire emergency.

After a few minutes of stamping and signing, he came around the desk again and thrust the work permit out to her. Konstanza took the folded permit and somehow got the courage to ask about her suitcase.

"Your belongings will be inspected and possibly returned to you," he said curtly and stepped back behind his desk. "You know the Heller house. You are to report there at once."

Walking back down the long hall, Konstanza thought about the fate of the mayor who had lived there. He had been arrested and deported, along with his wife and two daughters. The stately mansion, named for the founder of the textile mill that had provided most of the employment in the area, had been built in the eighteenth century. The mayor had said he wanted to keep the original character of the building intact for prosperity. He had allowed a few concessions to the twentieth century, like indoor plumbing, but only for the second floor; electricity with one wall switch in each room, but only on the second floor. A telephone was installed in the front hallway but no central heating. Each of the rooms had a fireplace, complete with woodbox and bellows. Keeping the fires lit, especially in the cold Polish winters, was a full-time job.

Years ago, when she had first come to this village at the outskirts of Torun, the mayor gave a party to celebrate his first year in office. Konstanza had been hired for the evening to help with the catering. She remembered the elegant furnishings, the crystal chandeliers, lit by a single lightbulb hanging from a cord in the ceiling of each room. She had been impressed with the floor to ceiling bookshelves with rows of leather-bound books in many different languages, even Greek.

A pang of sorrow, followed by a blinding rage, flashed through her thoughts as she remembered that most of those books had been thrown onto the huge fire which had followed the house-to-house search for literature banned by the Fascist fiends. Only books that lauded the psychology and beliefs of the Third Reich were allowed to be read.

Suddenly a cold chill of fear went down her spine, as Konstanza tried to remember if she had packed any books into her suitcase, besides the book of poems by Heinrich Heine, a gift from Walter. It was difficult to keep track of what the Germans considered suitable literature. But owning a book about any subject that did not aggrandize the regime in Berlin, or was written by a person suspected of having Jewish ancestors (which was true of Heine) was very dangerous.

It was a long, two-mile walk to the Heller Mansion, but the streetcar had not yet been reinstated after the wanton destruction wreaked on the town by the German army. When Konstanza finally found herself at the front door of the Heller Mansion, a soldier, standing guard motioned her to go around to the back door. She retraced her steps down the driveway and left the shelter of the portico just as it began to rain. Reluctantly she walked around the house to the back door.

Chapter 11

A scuffed up wooden door opened into a small entry hall. Konstanza stood inside the door for a moment, letting her eyes grow accustomed to the dark space. A narrow slit of a window above the door let in some daylight and she could see the outline of a small table against the back wall and a rack of hooks on the wall to her right. A narrow bench was discernible along the left wall with a few shoes scattered underneath. Next to the bench was the open kitchen door, and Konstanza stepped into the long, narrow room. She started to look around the area when a soldier stepped in behind her.

"Wait here!" the soldier barked. Konstanza wondered, not for the first time, if all Germans had forgotten how to speak in a normal tone of voice. Since they had occupied this small town in Poland, the soldiers had only screamed orders at the inhabitants, bellowed insults at people they perceived to be Jews, and usually shouted to each other as if they were deaf.

For a little while Konstanza tried to remember her father's voice, which had always sounded calm and comforting to her. And also Walter's tone as they had talked about mundane matters like the last movie they had seen or the taste of a food they had eaten. Then she remembered his loud and stringent diatribe against Jews when she had last seen him. He had sounded like a stranger. She sighed.

A tall, thin man came down the stairs that led into the kitchen from the dining room above. He had to bow his head to clear the lintel at the bottom step. A soldier, carrying

Konstanza's suitcase came down behind him.

"This will be your workplace," the tall officer said in strongly accented Polish, and waved a hand around the drab room.

Konstanza nodded to show she understood and looked around. Counters took up one wall; the door leading up to the dining room was on another. A large sink with an old-fashioned water pump was under the window that looked out at the outhouse and the dense forest beyond. A long, narrow table with a chair at either end stood in the middle of the room. Beside the door to the entry, a large wood stove with six fire rings took up the rest of the wall space.

The two men came into the center of the room and the officer towered over Konstanza as he spoke. "Through there are your quarters," he shouted at her, pointing to the door across from the kitchen door. "Latrine for you," he continued gesturing out the window toward the little shack at the edge of the woods.

"The commandant wants to eat his midday meal at one o'clock," he said. Then he turned around and made to leave.

Konstanza stood in the small splash of light that came in through the window and looked around the bare kitchen. It was obvious that no one had cooked here for some time. The counters were dusty; the greasy stove was stone cold and showed no outward sign of use. "I will need supplies," she said in broken Polish. After twelve years in the country she spoke the language fluently, but she had decided not to let the Germans know that. She pretended to only speak Greek, barely understand Polish, and have no knowledge of German. "No can cook meal with no food," she stammered.

The tall officer looked down at Konstanza with contempt. "You probably can't cook anyway," he sneered. Cracking his riding whip in the air he turned again to go up the stairs.

The soldier put down the suitcase and followed him.

Picking up her suitcase, Konstanza walked through the kitchen door, into the cubicle that served as an entry hall and coatroom, and into the next doorway. It opened to a square room with a floor to ceiling window on the wall that faced the forest. A cot was against the opposite wall and a small table, with a kerosene lamp on it, was next to the bed. Another table, behind the door, held a wash stand, with bowl and ewer, and a towel rack on one side. The mirror above the washstand was cracked in several places and was hanging by a string from one nail. An armoire loomed against the wall next to the washstand.

Trying to decide what to do first, Konstanza sat down on the hard cot and stared out the window thinking about her situation. Should she try to escape? But from what she had heard and read in the bulletins that were posted daily by the Germans, all of Europe was now engulfed in the Fascist nightmare. All conquered people were treated as slaves with all Germans as their masters. She looked longingly at the forest outside the window. Could she find freedom among those tall trees? Perhaps she could make it during the summer, but the Polish winters were dire and, without food and shelter, no one could survive.

Reluctantly she made her way to the latrine. It was as filthy as she had expected. Hurrying back to the kitchen she found some fairly clean rags under the sink, along with a stiff floor brush and a bucket. Searching behind a narrow door next to the stove, she found a broom and dustpan and a small container of lye. From the janitors at the boarding school she had learned that a few drops of the lethal liquid would make the water in the bucket an effective cleaning solution. As she proceeded to clean up the latrine she thought of how her time in that school had not been wasted after all.

After giving the latrine and the double seats a thorough cleaning, Konstanza used the facility and headed back to the kitchen. She glanced at the clock on the kitchen wall. Someone had thought to wind it because it was showing the same time as Konstanza's little wristwatch, a present from her mother. She had three hours to prepare a meal for the Germans. For a brief second she contemplated just walking out of the house, down the road and possibly all the way to Switzerland. In a flash she could see the consequences of such an action. She would be shot just as she had seen others being executed summarily for showing even a hint of defiance. By now, mostly women and small children were left in the small mill town. She had admonished her beloved Hedy to stay alive at all costs, and she must do the same.

Konstanza threw her suitcase onto the bed, rummaged around for her apron, and started to look around for the makings of a meal. In a flour bin, she found a cup's worth of flour. In the little pantry area under the stairs she found a head of shriveled garlic in the otherwise bare cupboards. An icebox under one counter contained a finger-sized chunk of salt pork. On her way to the latrine she had seen mushrooms growing beside the muddy path, and she hurried outside to pick an apron full. After careful examination Konstanza discovered that some of the mushrooms were the poisonous "death cap" variety. Carefully, she separated the deadly specimens and laid them out on a piece of newspaper she had found with the thought that they might be useful as a pesticide someday. Then she thoroughly washed the good mushrooms and set them aside.

The firebox of the stove was full of ash and had to be cleaned out with the scoop hanging from a nail above the stove. She had watched Berta perform this chore numerous times but had never done it herself. Dust flew everywhere so that her face was soon covered with ash. She tried to wipe it off with the hem of her skirt, leaving streaks around her chin and forehead.

Making pasta dough with only flour and water was tricky. Eventually, it was ready to be rolled out. Fortunately, someone had left a rolling pin in one of deep kitchen drawers. Judging by the style and worn condition, it was at least as old as the two-hundred-year-old house. A few dull knives were in another drawer, but they were sharp enough to cut the pasta dough and chop up the sauce ingredients. Reluctantly she took her box of spices out of her suitcase. After using a few sprinkles of the appropriate flavorings, she put the box on the top shelf of the kitchen pantry.

By one o'clock, fettuccini with mushroom sauce was ready to serve.

Before venturing up the stairs to the dining room to set the table, Konstanza took some precautions. She covered her head with a large bandana, folded it across the forehead so not a wisp of hair would show, and tied it under her chin. Then she removed the belt from her dress, which allowed the hem to come to her ankles where it met her high-topped shoes. A few quick strokes with her ash covered finger added to the disguise. A quick look in the mirror showed a wrinkled, old woman, which made Konstanza feel a little safer.

Cooking for the half-dozen Germans proved to be easy. They ate mostly pork and potatoes which they requisitioned from nearby farms. The Polish sauerkraut was different from what they were used to in Germany, but it was usually the only vegetable they allowed on the table.

The main meal was served at one o'clock, and in the evening it was customary to have a lighter fare which might be made up of a slice of bread, cheese, hard-boiled egg, or a bowl of soup.

During the first summer at the mansion, Konstanza planted a small kitchen garden along the path between the latrine and the kitchen door. Her work permit had been stamped, showing that she was allowed to go to nearby farms to collect seeds. Commandant Habermann had also given her verbal permission to go into the forest to collect berries, mushrooms and herbs, but she must stay where the daytime guards could easily see her.

"If you disappear from their view they will come into the forest and shoot you," he had said with a broad smile on his face. "Of course there is a good chance that you would be shot by that partisan scum before my men even found you." The thought that she might go into the forest at night did not occur to him. Not even his guards ventured into that dark area in back of the house at night.

The garden thrived and produced many root vegetables as well as a crop of small, but tasty, potatoes. One morning while hoeing weeds, Konstanza noticed that several plants were missing from each row. She examined the area but saw no signs of rabbits, or deer tracks. Strangely, only the carrots, radishes, and turnips were being pulled up when they were only half ripe.

Usually Konstanza took the kerosene lamp with her to the latrine. But one night in late August when a brilliant full moon flooded the landscape with light, she left the lamp in the house. On her way back to the house a slight movement caught her eye. Standing very still in the shadow of a tree she saw a small child among the row of beets, pulling up plants and stuffing them into a coat pocket.

The next night Konstanza left a plate of cooked food among the vegetables. In the morning the bread, potatoes and vegetables were gone. The only things left on the plate were the pickled pigs' feet. She had heard the Germans talk about the bands of Jewish children that had escaped from the camps and ghettoes. Could they be the vegetable thieves?

"The people in this town know better than to hide or feed Jews," Commander Habermann had commented at the midday meal one time. "Some Poles try to protect that vermin. I can't understand it." He shook his head, indicating bemusement, as he crammed little boiled potatoes into his mouth.

There was a murmur of agreement from the men at the table. Konstanza looked around at these men. They appeared so human, some were even handsome, and they all seemed too young to be officers. She listened with growing revulsion and rage as they discussed the various techniques involved in the murder of human beings just like themselves and their wives and children.

"I prefer shooting the children first," she heard one of the men say in a tone that might be used to describe a tactic on the soccer field.

"Don't the women get hysterical when they see their children die?" asked another man.

"Yes, but they tend to want to protect the little bastards from having to watch their mother die," was the pragmatic answer.

"Killing the children first is the best method," a third man inserted his agreement. "A large group of hysterical children can be difficult to control."

"Sometimes the little bastards jump into the pit before we can shoot them," a man from the other side of the table observed. "They play dead and crawl out at night and escape. I heard that some of them are hiding in the forest."

A man sitting near the middle of the table poured himself another shot of vodka then filled the glasses for the men near him. "Not in my command," boasted the man in charge of the vodka. "As the officer in charge, I walk around the pits and shoot every moving body in the neck."

While gathering up the dishes after the meal, Konstanza had to work hard at controlling the urge to stab these men with the sharp, stainless steel knife in her hand. She sighed deeply as she thought it was regrettable that many of them looked like Walter.

Every night before she fell asleep, in spite of her resolve to forget him, she thought of Walter and wondered if he was with these occupation forces, murdering innocent people, or if he was fighting in the war that the Germans had recently started with Russia. Imagining him in danger produced a cold knot of fear in the pit of her stomach.

Chapter 12

Walter Mannheim had spent many of his student days traveling with his father, an organizer for the Fascist Party. They held rallies in large cities like Munich and Frankfurt, as well as in small villages all over Germany and Austria. When the Fascists were voted into office and the Nazi Party took over the German government, Walter's father allowed him to return to the university in Munich. His main interest was in the medicinal uses of the plants that grew in abundance in European forests. The professor who had been in charge of that department had a worldwide reputation for his successful experiments in that field. To his disappointment, professor Hildebrandt was gone and, when Walter asked why some of the most competent staff members were no longer there, he was told, "They are Jews"—as if no further explanation was necessary.

After six years of traveling with one of the leading organizers of the Nazi Party, Walter was still puzzled by his father's hatred of all Jews. He had been led to believe that Germany and, subsequently, all of Europe and, eventually, the world needed to be freed from the greedy bankers and other Jews who were undermining the greatness of the Third Reich. He had doubts about the utility of eliminating all Jews. There were some very good doctors, scientists, musicians and even generous philanthropists among their number. In fact, the doctor who had doubtless saved his eyesight during a severe bout with measles was Jewish.

Walter kept his doubts to himself. He did not want to wind

up in a concentration camp like some of his less circumspect friends. After uttering comments that sounded like a criticism of government policies and a mild defense of some Jewish workers they knew, two of Walter's colleagues had disappeared. Months later their families received notification of their untimely demise, along with a box containing ashes. The return address was Sachsenhausen Concentration Camp.

During this time of uneasy peace in Europe, Walter's mother began to complain of a pain in her abdomen. Dr. Scholke, their family doctor was still allowed to practice medicine as long his clients were Jews. When her Aryan doctor failed to diagnose any physical problem, she went to see Dr. Scholke who had a sophisticated medical laboratory connected to his office. After examining Walter's mother and samples of all her bodily fluids, he told her that she had a form of cancer that could be successfully removed by a colleague who was no longer in Germany, but was practicing in Vienna, just across the border.

Walter's father was skeptical of Dr. Scholke's diagnosis. "He is a Jew and so is that surgeon in Vienna!" he shouted when he was told the news. "They only want to make money."

He then ruled out a trip to Vienna. Walter stood by helplessly as his mother became weaker and was often in pain. Risking arrest for being out after the Jewish curfew and treating an Aryan, Dr. Scholke often came to their apartment in the middle of the night to administer morphine and sooth her fears.

When his mother died, Walter listened in disbelief as his father ranted about how it was the moneygrubbing Jew's fault. Remembering the many nights that Dr. Scholke had sat by his bedside administering fever-reducing, or pain-alleviating, medication, Walter began to feel a smidgeon of shame start to grow somewhere in his being. As for the accusation of the doctor being moneygrubbing, Walter knew that was absurd. He was well aware that the doctor often was not able to collect his fees. After his mother died, Dr. Scholke had sent a note of condolences to Walter and waived all the fees he might have collected had he not been a Jew.

Mandatory army service was enacted and Walter was drafted before he could finish his studies of medicinal plants. After a year in training he came home for a month of furlough. He began to notice that his neighbor, Else, had grown into an attractive woman. The last time he had seen her she had been a plump, buxom teenager with long blonde braids. She was still a bit plump, but she had put her hair up into a stylish roll, wore short dresses that emphasized her hips, and knew how to flash her blue eyes to attract attention.

She was the type of girl his mother would have approved for a wife. The Fascists had engulfed her totally. She had no ambition except to serve her man, provide children for the Third Reich, and attend church as long as the pastor supported the regime. Many Protestant ministers had questioned the benefits of marginalizing Germany's most decent and productive citizens just because they were Jews. These men were quickly removed from their pulpits, incarcerated, and soon murdered.

Else was sexually available and, although he knew in his heart that he would always love Konstanza, Walter had human needs. He took Else to the movies, to dinner, for walks in the park, and to his apartment wherever his father was away on government business.

Their sexual encounters were brief and unsatisfying. Since both of them had been virgins, they were not able to compare experiences. Walter felt something was missing but had no words to describe his desolation after he should have been satisfied. He liked Else well enough, but to reach ejaculation he had to conjure up a vision of Konstanza. The green depth of her eyes, the feel of her body pressed against his, and the faint smell of exotic spices that came from her jet black curls. The terrible pain that came with this pleasure drove him to the edge of despair. He began to distance himself from Else.

Six months went by and everyone expected an engagement

to be announced during Walter's next furlough. Try as he might, he could not say the words that would make Else his wife, yet he felt regret about disappointing her.

In late December of 1938, Walter's father was away helping to round up the few Jewish men who had somehow evaded the round-up of November the ninth, known throughout Europe as *Kristallnacht.* In Munich, the majestic main synagogue and several smaller ones had been looted and burned to the ground, along with the religious artifacts that were left. Thousands of Jewish men had been sent to concentration camps that night. Walter's father, being a high ranking official of the SS by then, had come home in the morning and bragged about how he had been part of the "Aktzion" of beating Jews into abject submission as they entered the train stations. Those who happened to be in a respected profession were severely beaten: twenty blows with the cudgel for a lawyer, thirty for a professor, twenty-five for a doctor, five for common laborers, ten for store clerks. Walter's father had been disappointed at the lack of bankers and store owners.

Now Walter and Else were alone in the apartment. Else was in the kitchen preparing the evening meal. Her father was a butcher, and she and her mother were adept at boiling the flavor out of every cut of meat. Walter sat near the bridge lamp in his father's favorite chair, trying to read a book on poison plants. He was distracted by the odors coming from the kitchen and the smell of his father's aftershave in the chair. The sharp ring of the doorbell brought him to his feet.

In three steps he was at the door and was surprised to see Dr. Scholke's daughter, Susie, standing in the doorway. She looked disheveled and her hands were trembling. Walter had not seen her for several years but, as always, her dark hair and olive skin reminded him of Konstanza.

"Come in," was all Walter could say for the moment. She walked into the small sitting room and stood awkwardly looking at Walter with her deep, dark eyes.

"Walter," she began as he motioned her to sit on the other chair beside the lamp, "this is so hard for me, but I must do it." Twisting her fingers in front of her, Susie continued. "My father and I have a chance to leave Germany in the next week on a ship going to Shanghai."

Susie had lowered her eyes as she spoke, but now raised them to meet Walter's concerned gaze.

"We need money to buy the train tickets and get the papers that will allow us to leave the country. The government has confiscated my father's bank account and requisitioned all his supplies and instruments. We have nothing left to sell." Her voice was calm, but her twisting fingers gave away her agitation.

As their eyes met there was no more need for words. "Wait here," Walter said quietly. He knew that, like so many former patients, his family owed Dr. Scholke more than just money. As he went toward his father's bedroom, Walter remembered how Dr. Scholke and then Susie, as his assistant, had come to the apartment every day to put drops into his eyes during a measles epidemic after the war. Many children had lost their eyesight that year, but due to the medical care he was given, his eyes were saved, even though he had needed glasses. (His father had managed to blame Dr. Scholke for that defect.)

Without hesitation, Walter opened the drawer where he knew his father kept wads of paper money, as well as gold coins he had undoubtedly stolen from the hapless Jews who had come into his clutches. After a few moments he had gathered a handful of bills of large and small denominations and a velvet bag of gold coins. Returning to the sitting room he saw that Susie had risen and was moving toward the door. He did not see Else standing in the kitchen doorway staring at Susie.

"Take this," Walter said to Susie, and holding her hand open, he put the money and coins into it and closed her fingers around them.

"Thank you and God bless you," Susie whispered and stepped out the door, closing it behind her.

"I saw you give money to that Jewish sow!" Else screamed at Walter when he turned around and saw her. "What kind of extortion was she using on you?"

Walter was too startled by her angry outburst to reply. He stared at her in silence, as Else continued her diatribe. "How can you be so foolish as to give your father's hard-earned money to that Jewish scum? Have you no sense of shame, stealing from your own father?" She went on, her voice getting more shrill with every word.

Turning his back on Else, Walter started for the coat rack. He planned to put on his coat and hat and go out into street to get away from the sound of her voice but when she started accusing him of sexual relations with Susie, he lost his self-control. Walter Mannheim, who had never hit anyone before in his life, now turned around, raised his right arm and with a powerful back-handed blow across her open mouth, knocked Else backward into the kitchen.

He heard her screaming obscenities as he grabbed his hat and coat. Her voice got louder as he left the apartment, so he knew she was not badly hurt. After walking the dark streets for several hours he reported back to his barracks at the outskirts of Munich. He never returned to his father's apartment or saw his father again.

~

Else sat on the kitchen floor fuming, her mind racing on how she would get revenge. Her anger was not directed at Walter. In her experience, men often hit the women in their lives because they were angry at themselves. She blamed that Jewish bitch for his anger. She got up, straightened her hair and made a decision about her next move.

Putting on her hat and coat and locking the apartment door carefully behind her, she ran as fast as her stout legs would carry her, to the nearest police station.

"I want to report a theft," she hissed at the gray-haired man behind the desk. He looked at the panting girl with steady brown eyes; his bushy mustache hid a small grin as his gaze took in the cheap, little hat, her worn coat, and the run-down pumps on her swollen feet. She didn't look like a credible robbery victim. He pulled a piece of paper from his desk drawer and asked her to tell him the details.

"Gauleiter Mannheim's apartment was robbed by a Jewish whore named Susie Scholke. I saw her carry money and a velvet bag from the apartment just as I was coming in to clean the place. She ran away before I could catch her." Else's voice rose higher with every word.

The officer kept writing and eventually asked Else for a description of the Jewish female.

"I know where she lives." Else added after describing Susie as tall and dark-haired. She gave the address and watched with a feeling of satisfaction as two armed men were dispatched to arrest the thief.

When the armed men arrived at Dr. Scholke's clinic they found only broken glass and vandalized cabinets. The apartment on the second floor was now the home of Gauleiter Ludwig Lumner, who had been a secret member of the Nazi Party for fourteen years. He was also the owner of the car he used to drive as Dr. Scholke's chauffeur. The policemen questioned the neighbors and talked to Ludwig's mother, who had been the housekeeper for the Scholke family for twenty-four years. Then the policemen walked slowly back to the station.

After leaving Walter's apartment, Susie had hurried back to the small room in a nearby neighborhood where she had been assigned to live after her father had been dragged away to Dachau.

Upon his release, which had cost Susie every last penny she had been able to hide from the looters, Dr. Scholke had wandered the streets until he had finally found her. He told her they had to leave the country within forty-eight hours or he would be sent back.

Within hours Susie had managed to collect the money to buy passage to Shanghai, China, the only port open to Jewish refugees. Walter had given her just enough money to buy train tickets. As she entered the drab, little room, she had heard Ludwig's voice.

"You must listen to me," he was saying in his south German accent. "Herr Doktor, your residence permit has expired. If you try to get on a train you will be sent back to Dachau."

When Ludwig saw Susie come into the room he stood up from the narrow bench and took off his hat. "Fräulein Susie," he said in a deferential tone. "I found your father on the street. He must not go out. His permit has expired."

Susie, who was almost as tall as Ludwig, tried to meet his eyes, but they darted nervously around the room. She noticed that his hair was plastered to his head with sweat. He seemed highly agitated. Susie fought down her revulsion as she looked at the young man in his full regalia Nazi uniform. He continued to talk.

"I have a plan to get you over the border and to the ship in Trieste." He was pleading with her and Susie was puzzled. Dr. Scholke, who was crouched in one corner of the room, his head in his hands, raised his blank eyes to his daughter. Wordlessly he was asking, *Can we trust this Nazi thug?*

Susie knew she had to make a decision. It was a matter of life and death and she could only hope that she was making the right choice.

~

An hour later, Ludwig was helping Susie into the Daimler while her father put the two small suitcases into the trunk of the old car. Ludwig jumped into the driver's seat and turned to look at the two huddled forms in the back seat. "Just like the old days." He smirked in an effort at levity and set the car into gear.

At the Italian border, the German guards took a few minutes to examine the official travel papers, which showed that Vice Consul Scholke and his daughter were on their way to Rome for a conference with Mussolini. Noting the diplomatic sticker in the windshield, the captain waved the Daimler through without further delay.

As much as Susie wanted to ask Ludwig why he was helping them to escape, she could not bring herself to speak to him. She sat stiffly in the familiar old car, holding her father's ice-cold hands, staring blindly out the window.

Six hours after leaving Munich, Ludwig was driving the Daimler along the docks of Trieste until he found the S.S. *Graf Waldersee*. The huge luxury liner was scheduled to depart in an hour for Shanghai, China. Ludwig drove right up to the side of the gangplank, helped Susie and her father out of the car, and then handed the suitcases to the stevedore.

Dr. Scholke started up the ramp to the ship without a backward glance but Susie turned toward Ludwig. Grateful as she was for his help, she could not get the words out to thank him. Instead she had to swallow hard to keep from spitting into his face. She finally reached out as if to shake his hand. He curled his fingers around her outstretched wrist and bent his head down to kiss the back of her hand. Susie's eyes widened in surprise as he straightened up and she caught a glimpse of Ludwig's tear-filled eyes. Gently she took his hand and placed the small, velvet bag with the gold coins into his palm and, quickly turning around, she hurried to catch up to her father.

Chapter 13

Poland, 1942

A thunderstorm was gathering momentum and the air was heavy with the scent of rain. Sudden flashes of lightning illuminated the sky just above the forest, and Konstanza decided to make a quick trip to the latrine. She threw her wool shawl over her thin nightgown, quickly stepped into her felt slippers, and hurried out, hoping to make it back into the house before the rain started.

She had finished using the latrine and was wiping herself with the damp cloth she had brought with her, when she noticed a pile of rags in the corner of the hut, just at the edge of the lantern light. Straightening her clothes she lifted the lantern to inspect the heap of clothing. Carefully she lifted a threadbare coat and saw a shock of blond hair attached to the head of a small child. Setting the lantern on the edge of the seat, Konstanza reached down and picked up the ragged bundle. She could see the feverish face of the unconscious child as she retrieved the lantern and started back to the house.

A light drizzle, the precursor of a drenching rain, started to descend just as she entered the foyer. The door to her bedroom was slightly ajar so she could proceed into the room without putting down the child. She gently put the small bundle on the bed and set the lantern on the nearby table. The ragged garments fell away as the child stirred, revealing what looked like a five-year-old girl.

The feverish girl began to murmur, "Mama? Mama?" As she became more aware, she raised her voice. Konstanza made light shushing noises, putting her finger gently over the girl's lips, then picked her up and cradled her in her arms.

No doubt her parents had been murdered by the Germans and, if they found her, she would also be killed. A thin gold cross hung around the girl's neck, but that could only be a decoy to hide her Jewish identity. Given the right coloring and command of language, a girl could pass for being Christian. Boys were not as easily disguised; the Nazis only had to expose their genitals to prove they were Jewish.

Rocking the girl in her arms and telling her in broken Polish that she was safe for now, Konstanza shed a few tears while she thought of her darling Hedy. It was unlikely that anyone would be taking care of her if she were ill. She began to think of how and where she could hide this child, but first she needed to get her fever down. With that in mind, she went to the washstand and brought back a wet towel. All night she sponged the hot little body with cool water. Toward morning the fever seemed to break and Konstanza wrapped the girl in the black wool shawl she always kept near her bed.

A plan was forming in Konstanza's mind about where to hide the girl. The huge woodboxes, the armoire in her bedroom and the latrine where she had found her came to mind. She never thought to send her back out into the forest. Toward dawn the girl fell asleep and Konstanza went to the kitchen to prepare breakfast for the German soldiers. After she had served the men and brought all the dishes down to the kitchen, she spread a bit of jam on a thick slice of bread, poured milk into a cup, and brought it into the bedroom.

The girl seemed to be asleep, so Konstanza put the bread and milk on the bedside table and returned to the kitchen. A few minutes later Konstanza was standing at the kitchen window when she saw a small black form walking into the vegetable garden. With the half eaten piece of bread in one hand and clutching the black shawl around her with the other, the blond figure was headed toward the latrine.

At that moment the six men from the night patrol came marching up the road toward the house. One of the men pointed to the small figure starting to cross the narrow clearing toward the forest. Konstanza held her breath as the patrol leader called out, "Halt!" One of the men raised his rifle, and someone called, "Halt!" for the second time. The child was now running and had almost reached the trees, when from an upstairs window Commander Habermann called out "Fire!" Two men raised their rifles, aimed at the lower limbs of the trees and fired. The black shawl disappeared into the undergrowth while Habermann could be heard shouting obscenities about the poor marksmanship of the men.

That morning Commander Habermann signed his death warrant. Almost from the first day she had met him, Konstanza had thoughts of ways to kill this evil man. Now she made it her mission to actually do it.

During the next few nights she perused an old textbook about medicinal plants. In the back of the book was a section about how to make pesticides from household products. Nicotine was suggested as being especially effective against rodents and the instructions for extracting pure nicotine from cigarettes were explicit. The process was lengthy but not complicated. During the final stages a teaspoon of lye was added. After that, it was advisable to wear gloves, because even a drop of the syrup on bare skin could be fatal.

The German soldiers were heavy smokers and collecting a bucket of cigarette butts took less than a week. Once she had harvested the tobacco from the cigarettes, Konstanza began the process of turning it into pure nicotine syrup.

It would take about thirty days for the water in which the tobacco was boiled to evaporate and leave the syrup in the bottom of the bucket. Konstanza kept her mind busy thinking of the various ways to get the poison into Commander Habermann. She needed to do it soon. There was a constant turnover of German soldiers as their numbers moved eastward to the Russian front. Konstanza wanted to dispose of this fiend before he might be replaced. Although she had no compunction about poisoning his successor, she first wanted to dispose of Commander Habermann.

Konstanza had harvested many different herbs that grew wild around the edge of the forest. She replenished and added to her containers of dried dill, fennel, horseradish and several types of mushrooms on the narrow shelves of the pantry that adjoined the kitchen. When she ran out of glass and clay jars, she used the shell casings that the Germans left on the ground after the mass executions that were almost a daily ritual in the town square.

The declaration of martial law meant that there were no restrictions on the military and the commander of the soldiers stationed in the town had complete jurisdiction over the population. An accusation was tantamount to an indictment. There was no court or legal recourse and, besides, all the judges and lawyers had been sent to concentration camps or summarily shot. The townspeople who had enthusiastically cooperated with the German *Einsatz Gruppen* (the special forces assigned to eliminate all Jews) were now faced with the prospect of helping to round up other groups the Germans decided to eliminate.

After all the Jews had been murdered or deported, an *Aktzion* began to round up the teachers. They were accused of being Communists or Capitalists and deported or shot—depending on the mood of the local commander. Some teachers took up other jobs and tried to blend into the population. But the same people who had been eager to help round up the Jews were now reporting their neighbors—especially those who seemed more educated—to the German occupiers in hopes of getting more food rations or being exempted from deportation. No one was safe.

From the washer woman who came to pick up the linens every two weeks, Konstanza learned about the German edicts. There seemed to be a new one every week. One of the first was a closure of all schools. Education was not to be wasted on Slavs (i.e. Poles, Russians, and people native to the

Balkan states) since they were members of an inferior race and only fit for manual labor.

Then the "Work Order" edict was enforced. Families were separated according to age and gender. Men were sent to labor camps where they were worked to death in harsh outdoor conditions. Women and children over five years old were sent to work in factories in Germany since every able-bodied man in that country was now in the military service. Most of the people left in the Polish villages were the elderly or young children.

A few farmers were allowed to stay on their land and produce pork, dairy products, and a few vegetables, all of which had to be delivered to the German High Command of the area. A farmer who tried to keep a piece of meat or an ear of corn for his family met with dire consequences. Hoarding food, even small amounts, from your own farm was considered treason, punishable by death for the whole family. The Germans conducted surprise searches, questioned the children to expose their parents, and soon the farm population dwindled to a handful. The louts that had gleefully watched as their Jewish neighbors were dragged away or shot were now being shot for myriads of transgressions or dragged away to work as slaves in Germany.

Groups of young children were aimlessly wandering the streets scrounging through the garbage dumps for food. These children would have previously been cared for by the nuns who had who had run the local orphanage for many generations. However, only a few months into the German occupation, a zealous Christian reported the sisters to the Gestapo for the crime of hiding Jewish children. The Reverend Mother of the convent was shot that very day, along with any children who could be identified as Jewish. The other nuns were sent to concentration camps in Germany. The Romanesque convent stood empty and neglected and served as a reminder to the town of what they had lost.

Konstanza found the young children were useful for

gathering up the containers she needed for her growing spice collection. A small jar was worth an onion, a shell casing a piece of raw potato. She gave a whole wreath of garlic to the girl that brought her the screw top jar which now held the nicotine syrup and was stored on the highest shelf in the kitchen.

Chapter 14

The household of the German headquarters in the small Polish town was dependent on firewood for heating and cooking and the supply was running low. Konstanza began to wonder about plans to refill the huge woodboxes that dominated the main hallway and the kitchen and the smaller woodboxes located in the many bedrooms. The woodpile next to the house that had reached almost to the eaves at the beginning of the summer was now only waist high.

As if on command, a wagon load of wood, pulled by two horses, appeared at the backdoor one day. Konstanza heard the elderly driver call the horses to a halt and could hardly believe her ears.

"Good girl, Gaia, nice work, Sybil," he said in Greek as he climbed down from the seat, with surprising agility, considering his shock of white hair. He patted each horse on the rump and walked around to the back of the wagon where he unloaded a large wheelbarrow and began to fill it up with pieces of cord wood, just the right size for the fireplaces in the house.

Approaching the kitchen door he saw Konstanza standing just inside, wiping her hands on her apron. He stopped and put down the wheelbarrow, stepped back a pace, a startled expression on his sun tanned face. Standing stock still he raised one hand to smooth down his graying mustache, all the while never taking his eyes off Konstanza.

"You are just in time," Konstanza said in her broken Polish. "We will need this load of wood."

The man had not moved. He kept staring at Konstanza as if she were an apparition.

Finally Konstanza broke the silence. "You speak Greek?" she asked in that language. "I heard you talk to the horses and call them by ancient Greek names."

"Forgive me, young lady, but you resemble a girl I met many years ago." He smiled and continued. "I am Father Ami, the local woodcutter. I have been bringing wood for the people in this house for the last three years. Are you the new cook? Are you Greek?"

Konstanza answered in the affirmative to both questions. She wiped away the tears that were welling in her eyes at hearing the language she had not heard since her mother's death almost twelve years ago. They unloaded the wood from the wagon, and Father Ami, with surprising stamina for a man in his mid-sixties, stacked it expertly along the back wall of the house. While they worked, he told her that he had been born in Greece, but spent most of his life in Germany.

When all the wood was neatly stacked Konstanza invited Father Ami into the kitchen for a cup of tea. The old man pushed his graying curls away from his damp forehead, wiped the sweat from his brow with his shirt sleeve and smiled his acceptance. While they sipped the herbal tea that Konstanza had concocted from the various herbs in her garden, Father Ami savored each bite of the caraway filled pastry he remembered from his homeland. He paused to wipe his eyes and clear his throat. He began to tell Konstanza the heartbreaking story of what had brought him to these Polish woods.

"I had rowed out to a Greek ship anchored in the harbor to administer last rites to a dying sailor. My beautiful Helena was alone in the rectory when she must have heard a noise in the sanctuary. When I got back in the morning I found her on the floor, her head bashed in and all the silver candlesticks gone. Later I discovered that several of the precious icons were also missing."[1]

Father Ami was openly crying as he lowered his head and clutched Konstanza's hand as it lay on the table. Patiently she waited for him to recover his voice. After a few minutes he continued in a low tone, almost a whisper. "After that night I could not go out into the streets. Every man I saw could have been my Helena's murderer. I sent a note to the Patriarch in Berlin, requesting a position in another country. He sent me to Poland, just over the German border, where many of the people are of German descent."

"So you wound up with German people around you, after all," Konstanza inserted.

"Yes," Father Ami sighed. "But they all spoke Polish and were not involved in the atrocities committed by the Germans in Germany." For a few more moments Father Ami looked past Konstanza, his eyes wandering toward the window, where he could see birds flitting between the tall trees of the forest beyond the garden. He sighed again and added, "Those birds are the only free beings left in Europe now."

After loading the wheelbarrow back on the wagon and harnessing the two draft horses that had been allowed to graze in the meadow, Father Ami turned to Konstanza. "I must tell you that you remind me of a girl I met about thirty years ago. I will tell you about her when I come back next week."

Konstanza reached out a hand to shake, but to her surprise Father Ami pulled her into a warm and lengthy hug. Konstanza's heart gave a pleasant thump in her chest. She had not felt a man's arms around her since the last time she and Walter had embraced.

"I come once a week during the fall and winter," he said, "so we will have time to talk more. You will tell me your story next time. I am curious what a Greek girl is doing in northern Poland."

He climbed up to the wagon seat, took up the reins and started to turn the horses back out toward the road. "Wait," Konstanza called out. "Who pays you for the wood?"

Father Ami gave a short, mirthless laugh. "The mayor

used to pay me in zlotys, the Nazis said they would allow me to keep my life if I continued being useful to them." With these words he waved farewell and in a few moments the wagon could be heard rumbling along the graveled road.

Before the first snowfall, Konstanza had harvested a variety of vegetables from her garden, as well as edible plants that grew wild at the edge of the forest. She found dill, mint, fennel, tarragon, and rosemary and fragile stems of basil, which she brought into the kitchen to grow on the window sill.

The small pantry was soon filled with dried berries, mushrooms, and a variety of root vegetables that would keep for winter. Garlands of garlic hung from the beams, and sacks of onions and potatoes took up space on the floor. Although abandoned years ago, the apple orchard on one side of the house bore small, wrinkled fruit that, after the worms were extracted, made excellent applesauce.

The weather turned cold overnight and a light snow covered the evergreen trees like a dusting of powdered sugar glistening in the morning sunlight. Later that same day the biting wind and black clouds brought warning of the coming winter.

Within a few days the woodpile was visibly lower. As he promised, Father Ami showed up the next week. This time he had a young boy of about twelve on the wagon with him.

"This is Janush," he told Konstanza by way of introduction. "I found him starving by the side of the road."

Janush, dressed in a light jacket and trousers that looked like they had been cut down from a much larger size, jumped from the wagon, his long blond hair flying out behind him. He gave Konstanza a quick nod and made himself useful, unloading the wheelbarrow and starting to fill it with the cut wood. "This wood is not quite ready for burning." Father Ami told Konstanza. "Like Janush here, it needs a bit of seasoning before it will reach its potential."

While Father Ami and Janush unloaded the wagon, Konstanza went into the kitchen to start preparing the midday meal for the German soldiers who were quartered in the old house. Except for commander Habermann, who had replaced Gruppenführer Schwartz, most of the men only stayed a few days before being deployed to the Russian front.

Early that morning one of the soldiers had brought her two rabbits he had trapped while on night patrol. Konstanza skinned and cut them up for rabbit stew, a dish she had learned to make from Ena. Soon the aroma of garlic and frying onions filled the house. Just as Father Ami and Janush were coming into the kitchen with their arms full of seasoned wood, they heard footsteps on the stairs coming from the dining room.

Janush dropped his load of wood on the floor and jumped into the half empty woodbox beside the stove. Gently closing the lid, Father Ami put his finger to his lips and gave Konstanza a stern look. Commander Habermann stepped down into the kitchen and began to draw his gun as he saw Father Ami.

"Oh, it's you," he said in German, and holstered his pistol. "It smells good down here. Is the meal ready soon?" He turned to Konstanza as he spoke, and then looked at the pile of wood on the floor. "This is no place for wood." He barked at Father Ami, "Put it in the box where it belongs." Adding in an even louder voice as he started up the stairs, "At once!"

With exaggerated slowness of an old man suffering from aching bones, Father Ami began to pick up the pieces of cordwood from the floor, holding his back with one hand as he, even more slowly, straightened up and walked to the woodbox. By the time he lifted the lid of the woodbox, Commander Habermann was safely out of sight.

Janush, looking sheepish, climbed out of the woodbox and quickly went outside to the back courtyard.

Father Ami finished filling the kitchen woodbox and rolled his wheelbarrow back to the wagon where Janush helped him load it. Konstanza came out of the kitchen with a small basket on her arm. "Could you use some applesauce and blueberry jam?" she asked the old priest in Greek. By the broad smile on Janush's face she could tell he understood her.

"I taught him some Greek," Father Ami explained when he saw Konstanza's questioning look. "Especially the names of foods. Boys are always hungry so learning about food is a good way to teach a language." They both chuckled knowingly. "Janush is afraid of German soldiers." Father Ami said in quickly-muttered Greek. "He told me they shot his mother, and tortured him because they think his father is a Polish Partisan, and he knows where to find him."

Father Ami saw Konstanza observe the boy as he walked around the wagon to get the horses. "Yes, he has a limp," he said in a low tone. "They pulled out his toe nails, broke his leg and burned him with cigarettes. But even if he knew where his father was, he would never tell them." He gave a deep sigh and added, "One day soon he will disappear into the forest to join the Partisans—perhaps to join his father."

Father Ami hugged Konstanza and she felt the familiar warmth throughout her body. "Take care," she whispered in Greek and walked quickly back to the kitchen.

Chapter 15

The winter of 1942 was one of the coldest and most dismal of Konstanza's experience. The Germans were sending wounded soldiers back from the Russian front. Most of them were suffering from frostbite. The army doctors, mostly young men with little medical training, were busy amputating extremities and extracting bullets from men who would soon die in any case.

The food in her larder was running low, but Konstanza always found scraps to leave outside on the stone steps leading to the latrine. One night she decided to hide in the kitchen doorway to see who it was that came to get the food. Near midnight, a small figure approached the plate of food, started to reach for it, and fell into the deep snow. Konstanza waited for a few moments to see what would happen next, but the figure remained still.

Pulling her winter coat around her, she moved slowly toward the dark spot in the snow. When Konstanza touched the shoulder of the boy who lay on his side, he moved slightly, clutching his stomach. Without thinking of the possible consequences, Konstanza half-carried, half-dragged the frozen boy to the house and into the kitchen. She set him down next to the stove, took his cold hands into hers, and rubbed the fingers until he could move them. As he got warmer, he started to get up. "I must go," he said in a Polish accent that identified him as a Jew.

Without a word, Konstanza indicated that he was to get into the woodbox next to the stove. The box was half empty and the boy just fit so she could put the lid down. "I will bring the food," she said in Polish. Then she went to retrieve the plate.

After the boy had eaten, Konstanza threw a piece of tarpaulin she had used in her garden over him and put several pieces of wood on top. "Are you comfortable?" she asked in a whisper. There was no answer. "You can stay until dawn." She continued, "But then you must leave. Wait for me to let you out." A slight knock on the side of the woodbox seemed to indicate that he understood.

The small boy with the black curls was only the first of many boys whom Konstanza saved from the freezing nights of that winter. One night there were two boys who came to the kitchen door, and she put one in the woodbox and one in the armoire in her room. When three boys showed up during an especially cold night, Konstanza was up to the challenge. She put one boy into the kitchen woodbox, one in her armoire, and snuck the third one up the stairs and into the woodbox next to the front door. That night she didn't sleep, and just before dawn she let the boys out; they left the house one by one, running into the forest a few minutes apart.

That night of the three boys was the most stressful of her rescuer episodes and Konstanza hated the idea of sending them back into the freezing cold. There had to be a way to save them from what must be a terrible hardship.

Salvation came in the shape of the woodcutter. Father Ami had switched the wagon wheels to sled runners, covered the horses with warm blankets and the wood with an old rubberized sheet, and made his deliveries every week, despite several snowstorms.

"We are so grateful that you have come today," Konstanza told Father Ami after a particularly stormy night. "We are getting low on seasoned wood." After filling all the woodboxes in the house, there was enough wood left over to stack along the outside wall.

"I'll chop some kindling for the stove before I leave," Father Ami offered. "But first I need to come in and warm up a bit." Konstanza made tea and offered him a piece of bread with jam, and then sat down opposite him at the kitchen table. "You have not yet told me who or what brought you to this remote area of Poland," Father Ami mused as he chewed on the stale, dark bread and slurped his tea with gusto.

Konstanza took a deep breath, and in the hope of changing the subject, asked about Janush, who had not come along on this day. "He has vanished, just as I knew he would," was the curt reply. "Now, stop stalling and tell me your story."

In a low voice, Konstanza told about her years of misery at the German school, the prejudice she encountered, and the true details of her mother's murder. Her voice began to tremble when she told about her father. Then she added in a quick whisper, "I hate the Germans, but I know they are not all evil fiends. My father was a kind and loving man." Then in an even lower tone, as if talking to herself, she added, "I know there are others."

They sat in silence for a few minutes. The only sound was the crackling of the fire in the wood stove behind them. "I have a confession to make," Konstanza blurted out. "For years I have been telling the people here that my mother went back to Greece after my father died. It seemed easier than telling them of the police brutality we encountered."

"Perhaps that fantasy was a comfort for you." Father Ami's voice was soft, gentle.

"My darling little Hedy began to ask questions about my family. She was a caring and curious child. I could not tell her the brutal facts, so I made up a story that I wanted to be true. You are the first person I have told what really happened."

"I am honored that you trust me with this revelation." Father Ami smoothed down his mustache as he was wont to do when he needed time to think about what he would say next. "Now, I will tell you about my encounter with your mother."

He then told Konstanza, who sat in rapt attention, about the Greek girl named Estanza who had stayed at the rectory for a short time while her friends found a way for her to escape from Germany. "Those few hours of her visit were a warm, bright interlude in our lives, like a short and memorable visit to our homeland. Her dazzling smile reminded me of a sunrise over the cliffs of Santorini." The old priest sighed and gazed fondly at Estanza. "Except for those startling green eyes, you look just like her." He reached out and patted Konstanza's hand. Then he watched sympathetically as she wiped tears from those much admired eyes.

Konstanza decided to trust this man whom she had learned to love and told him about how she had hidden the boys from the forest. "I hate sending them back out to endure the cold and hunger."

Again, Father Ami stroked his mustache as he began to think about the situation and how to best resolve it. "I may have a plan. I need to work out the details," he half-murmured to himself. Then, more firmly, he asked, "Could the boys go stay in the latrine instead of running back to the forest?"

"I am the only person who uses it." Konstanza replied. "I suppose they could spend the day in there. But they might not be willing to be in there while I use the facility."

Father Ami smiled a rueful smile. "Yes, in a civilized society it would not be suitable. However, we are no longer living in a civilized world. Look, Konstanza, I have a plan to get the boys into the wagon, but it cannot be done from the house. I will come on the same day each week. You can depend on that. So we will plan accordingly."

On his next visit, Father Ami left the wagon between the house and the latrine. It was a suitable spot, since there was a pathway in the snow for easier access to the house with the wheelbarrow. He didn't unhitch the horses as the grass was covered with a blanket of snow, but he fed them a few strands of straw that he brought for them.

Three boys were concealed in the wagon bed during the unloading of the wood, a trip to the latrine by Konstanza, and then Father Ami as he also used the latrine. Then Father Ami went into the kitchen with one last load of wood, sat down at the table for a hot glass of tea, and shared the exchange of small talk with Konstanza. After that, Father Ami wheeled the tarp-covered wheelbarrow to the back of the wagon and, with Konstanza's help, hoisted it up under the oilcloth sheet.

The wagon slid up the road, and Konstanza waved it out of sight. She returned to the kitchen, put the pieces of wood that were lying next to the stove into the box, but did not fill the box completely. If someone needed to warm up that night, there would be space for them.

Eventually Father Ami and Konstanza were able to get the message to those hiding in the forest that once a week, on a certain day, three boys could be smuggled into the woodcutter's wagon and be on their way to freedom. It was an arduous journey, involving transport on a raft to the mouth of the Vistula, to a port on the Baltic Sea. Sometimes the boys got on a ship as stowaways; at other times, they were hired as cabin boys or even crew members. There was the constant danger of someone turning the boys over to the Germans.

~

For almost two thousand years the leaders of the Catholic Church skimmed over the fact that Jesus was a Jew and taught their followers that Jews were evil. Now, the Germans had the mechanism in place to destroy all Jews and they even offered valuable rewards, like a loaf of bread or a bottle of wine, to anyone who helped them find a hidden Jew. The promise of a reward, plus the teachings of the church leaders, culminated in the fact that, all across Europe, people who thought themselves to be "good" Christians enthusiastically cooperated in perpetrating the destruction of Jews. The enormity of the crimes committed in the era that would be called "The Holocaust" cannot be absorbed by the human mind. Even those who were victims and eye witnesses could not adequately describe the brutality and carnage perpetrated by the Germans and their allies.

Yet there were some brave and righteous men and women

who risked death to help these children get to a safe place. Konstanza and Father Ami were only among the first links in a long chain of love and decency. Once the boys were in a neutral country—like Sweden—Zionist organizations smuggled them past the British blockade into Palestine.

Chapter 16

The aggression against Russia ("Operation Barbarossa") began with great success, but as the winter of 1942 progressed from a freezing hell to a muddy bog, the tide began to turn. There was a shortage of everything that an army needs. There was much grumbling about the lack of ammunition. Some of the soldiers even dared to speculate that too much of it had been wasted on killing Jews.

Frostbite was as common as bullet wounds among the Germans, who were not equipped for the Russian winters. By now, there was also a shortage of eligible men. Even the lower-ranking SS officers were being sent to the Russian front.

Walter Mannheim was among those officers who never expected to see a battlefield, but now at the advanced age of thirty-two, he found himself in a basic training camp, being prepared to fight the Russians.

He unrolled his blanket on a cot in the crowded barracks and sat down on the hard surface. He watched desolately as the young men, half his age, filed into the barracks. Then a man close to his own age sat down on the bunk next to his. The two men stared at each other, and then the new arrival smiled in recognition.

"You are Obergruppenführer Mannheim's son," he remarked enthusiastically. "I remember you from some of the rallies. Your father is an inspiring speaker." He paused, waiting for Walter to agree or at least acknowledge his eager compliment.

Instead, Walter bent down and slowly untied his boots. He was playing for time with the hope that he would remember the man on the other bunk. He looked familiar but Walter could not place him. So he decided it was best to admit his lack of memory and let the other fellow fill him in. "You look familiar," Walter said, then added, "I am certain I have seen you before, but I can't remember where."

"My name is Ludwig Lumner," he offered. "I was Dr. Scholke's chauffeur and drove him to your house to see your mother. Sometimes you sent me to the kitchen to have your maid make me tea," Ludwig said, and prepared to shake hands with Walter, who was uncertain about what to do next.

Walter and Ludwig lived in the same working class neighborhood and spoke a similar dialect, but would most likely never have had social contact. Walter had a few grades of higher education and was the son of a high-ranking Nazi Party organizer, while Ludwig was a chauffeur and the son of a widowed domestic servant. But now that Germany was a police state, the lines between the different levels of working class people gradually blurred. Uneducated day laborers, as well as petty criminals, could aspire to positions of authority. It was a matter of life and death to show proper respect toward those of higher rank and just the right amount of arrogance when addressing those below one's current station.

Walter's dilemma of whether to shake hands with Dr. Scholke's former chauffeur was short-lived, as he remembered that Ludwig had outranked him in the SS. Both men were now noncommissioned officers in the *Wehrmacht* (the regular army). Because of their last names, they spent the first part of their military training side-by-side, and because they were a good ten years older than most of the other recruits, they were unpleasantly surprised at being subjected to the rigors of basic training. Ludwig was an excellent mechanic who expected to be assigned to the motor pool, while Walter, with his knowledge of medicinal plants, had thought he would be sent to the medical corps. But after basic training, they found themselves on a long train ride with the final destination being the Russian front.

Walter and Ludwig had their second-class compartment to themselves. The troop train headed for Berlin that morning was half-empty. The night before their scheduled departure, a bombing raid by the British Air Force had made a shambles of a large section of Munich's working-class neighborhood. Half of their battalion was ordered to remain in the city to help with the rescue work and cleanup of debris.

Even after several weeks of the camaraderie resulting from the military training, Ludwig and Walter were careful about their conversations. A word or phrase that might contain a hint of criticism about the regime or a perception of a complaint about a policy could result in dire consequences. No one could be trusted. Children were ordered to report their parents to the authorities if they overheard an unflattering comment about the fascist leadership. Whole families disappeared when it was rumored that one of them had spoken well of a Jew. However, Walter's curiosity overcame his trepidation and he decided to ask Ludwig what had happened to Dr. Scholke and his daughter.

"Do you happen to know the whereabouts of Dr. and Susie Scholke?" he began tentatively. Ludwig, who had been gazing out the train window, turned around abruptly, with a strange look in his widened eyes.

Ludwig examined Walter's expression carefully and decided that lying was the safest answer. "I don't know where they are," he said, his face reddening.

"Susie came to see me a few weeks ago. She asked for money to help them get to Shanghai." Walter's voice was flat and conversational. "I thought you might know if they had left the country."

"Did you give her any money?" Ludwig asked in the same tone. Now it was Walter's turn to be careful about his answer.

There was something in Ludwig's expression and how his fists were clenched in his lap that made Walter decide to tell him the truth and hopefully gain his trust. "I gave her all the money I could find in the house. I know it was not enough payment for what her father and she did for me when I had the measles and, later, for how they helped alleviate my mother's painful death."

For several minutes the two men sat in silence looking into each other's eyes. The clicking of the train wheels was the only sound in the compartment. Suddenly the train whistle blew as it neared a crossing, breaking the tension. Walter cleared his throat.

"I remember you came to the door with Susie on several of her visits," Walter said. "You carried her medical bag into the apartment and handed it to me." He smiled at the recollection and how glad he had been to see Susie, who was acting as her father's assistant after her mother died. Her father had taught her how to give injections and to help him in his laboratory.

Both men knew that Walter had admitted to a crime that could send him to a concentration camp or worse. Speaking well of a Jewish person was bad enough, but to give money or any help was a serious violation of the law. Walter had trusted Ludwig with his life. Now it was Ludwig who had to make a choice.

"It was against the law for Dr. Scholke or Susie to treat an Aryan," Ludwig mused. "I helped them do it." He smiled ruefully.

"We had no idea there would be such an acute shortage of doctors after Jews were forbidden to practice," Walter said. "I have sometimes wondered why so many doctors were Jewish."

"There is a good reason for that," Ludwig said. "The Jews have a long history of being driven from one country to another. Medical knowledge is easily transferred, even when one does not speak the language." He paused, looked out the window for a few moments then said, "The human anatomy is the same all over the world, and there have been no new models for centuries." He added, "Not like automobiles."

Walter looked thoughtful then spoke again. "That can't be the only explanation for Jews pursuing the medical profession. There are so many of them that the universities had to enact a quota to give some Aryan men a chance to become doctors."

"The Scholkes were not very religious, but they attended services at the Reform Synagogue in the old city several times a year. When I drove them there in the winter, Dr. Scholke insisted I come inside to stay warm. I couldn't help but overhear the sermons. They sounded a lot like our priest's, except that the Jews emphasized how precious life is and that saving one life is like saving the world." Ludwig stopped talking to see if Walter understood the connection. Then he continued: "There was no talk of an afterlife, like in our church. Jews are admonished to enhance life for everyone here on earth."

Walter knew that they were on dangerous ground discussing Jews in a favorable light.

It was a strange feeling for the two SS officers, but they had begun to trust each other. A few minutes later they each unpacked their small bundles of bread and cheese, spreading out the sparse meal on the seat between them. For a while they ate in silence, watching the gray landscape spin past the window. Finally Walter asked his original question, as if Ludwig had not answered it the first time. "Do you know where Dr. Scholke and his daughter are?"

Ludwig looked out the window again, though by now it was dark and he only saw his own reflection. "It would be nice to have a mug of beer with this bread," he said, avoiding Walter's eyes. Walter said nothing but it was obvious he was waiting for an answer. Finally Ludwig made a decision. "They are in Shanghai," he whispered hoarsely, pushing his voice around the lump in his throat. "I drove them to Trieste and watched them board the German liner *Graf Waldersee* bound for China."

While Walter breathed a sigh of relief, Ludwig lowered his head to hide the tears that flooded his eyes. "I loved those people," he whispered. "I loved Miss Susie. I didn't realize what would be done to them and I helped do it." His shoulders were shaking and Walter stared in disbelief.

"I was all for getting rid of the bad Jews," Ludwig explained, "but I didn't think that we would be persecuting *all* Jews, even the decent ones like the Scholkes. They hired my mother as a young war widow, with an eight-year-old son to support. Not many people wanted a housekeeper with a child. Miss Susie was thirteen, and she treated me like a little brother right from the start. I fell in love with her the moment I laid eyes on her."

Ludwig drew a deep breath and continued: "Dr. Scholke sent me to a trade school to learn auto mechanics and I loved working with motors. When I was eighteen, he bought the Daimler and taught me how to drive. I was ecstatic when he asked if I wanted to be his chauffeur. My mother and I had a good life. He paid us well and always on time. Many of his patients didn't do the same."

The train stopped in Dresden, where a large number of soldiers got on and two officers came in to share the compartment with Ludwig and Walter. For another hour the four men sat in silence, busy with their own thoughts. Then, while the other three men in the compartment began to doze off, Walter realized that the train had stopped, and then began to back up. Curious about what was happening he went to the end of the car, hoping to step outside, but the door was locked. Waking along the corridor past the compartments he could see that the troop train had been side tracked to allow a freight train to pass. A long row of cattle cars rumbled by on the southbound tracks. Walter wondered what could be more important than getting soldiers to the front.

The sun was setting behind the nearby hills when the troop train started to move forward again, In the dusky haze of evening Walter saw an eerie sight on the platform of the suburban station called Grunewald. Hundreds of seemingly abandoned baby carriages were crowding one end of the platform.

At first he was puzzled at this bizarre array, but then he

realized, with a sickening feeling in his stomach, the ominous significance of the freight train that had just gone by.

He recalled his father coming home, gleefully recounting how he had overseen the loading of cattle cars with as many as a hundred of those "dirty Jews" in each car. Walter knew from what his father said that most of the unfortunate wretches in those windowless and airless containers were women and children.

Before the troop train resumed its speed, he observed a dozen women going back and forth, wheeling the trams to waiting trucks on the street side of the platform.

An hour later, the train entered the central station of Berlin. No one was allowed to get off, but vendors walked along the track, passing food and bottles of beer to any soldiers who had the funds to pay for them. Walter had lost his appetite, but he bought two hardboiled eggs and a bottle of beer which he later shared with Ludwig as the train hurdled eastward into the night.

Chapter 17

When Walter arrived at the Warsaw Central Station, a car was waiting to take him to the General Headquarters building facing the main plaza. The clerk at the front desk looked at his orders, and then, not hiding the smirk that accompanied his words, he said, "You are to report to the clerical department on the third floor, Lieutenant Mannheim. You are lucky to have bad eyes." Then he muttered under his breath, but loud enough for Walter to hear, "And a father who is an important official in the party."

With several other bespectacled men, Walter sat on the hard benches in the waiting room of the head office of the clerical department. Men came and went through the glass-paneled door to the hallway holding paper folders. Some looked pleased and some looked worried. Walter wondered what he would feel when he got his orders.

Finally, someone called his name and he went into the next room and saluted the high ranking officer behind the desk. "We are sending you to keep records for one of the German Einsatzgruppen," the officer told Walter. Seeing the puzzled look on Walter's face he went on to explain, "It is a special squad assigned to eliminate unsuitable elements from the towns that are now occupied by the German army."

When he saw that Walter still didn't understand, the officer gave Walter a stern look, "You are a scientist, right?" The officer asked and not waiting for an answer he continued, "So, you should be able to keep an accurate count of the corpses. Don't look so shocked. This is a war and people get killed."

"I was told I would be doing clerical work," Walter said.

"Don't worry; you won't need to kill anyone. Just write numbers in this ledger." The officer handed Walter an attaché case. "There are a dozen sharpened pencils. You will find they work better than ink pens when you are in the field."

Carrying his backpack, attaché case, and orders in hand, Walter slowly descended the broad marble steps of the imposing General Headquarters building which had formerly been the Warsaw City Hall. An army truck was at the curb with an officer standing beside it. He addressed Walter with the customary salute, arm outstretched over his head. "Are you Walter Mannheim?" the officer asked. When Walter answered in the affirmative, the officer asked to see his papers. After a few minutes of perusing the folded sheets, he motioned Walter into the truck.

Getting into the back of the truck, Walter noticed that boxes of ammunition were stacked to the roof along the back wall. He picked his way around the half-dozen machine guns on the floor and found a space on one of the benches that lined the side walls. He squeezed in between two soldiers who looked to be about half his age. Through a split in the canvas curtain that was hung across the back of the truck, he saw an officer approach the truck and draw back the curtain. The officer handed a bottle of vodka to the man nearest the opening and said, "Pass it around. Make sure everybody takes a big drink." Then he pulled the curtain closed and could be heard getting into the cab of the truck.

The truck moved along on a smooth road for about an hour. By the time they started along an unpaved road the vodka bottle was empty. Several of the soldiers started singing while others closed their eyes and dozed. Walter, who had taken only a small sip of the vodka, sat stiffly on the hard seat, clutching the attaché case to his chest and keeping his legs wrapped around the backpack.

For several hours more the truck bumped along the unpaved road. Just after midnight they stopped for a few minutes. The men got out and scattered into the nearby field to relieve themselves. When they were all back in the truck, a basket of sliced bread with a thin coat of butter was passed around, followed by another bottle of vodka. Walter heard one of the men whisper, "I'd rather have a beer or two," and was certain that most of the men would have preferred it too.

It was a cool night, but the inside of the truck was getting warm, so the man nearest the back opened the canvas curtain a few inches to let in some air. In the gray light before dawn, Walter could see a group of about twenty men stumbling along the side of the road in the direction from which the truck had just traveled. The men were moving very slowly while four soldiers with rifles under their arms, in a ready position, walked beside them. Just before they were out of sight one man seemed to stumble and fall behind. The guard bringing up the rear stopped to shoot the fallen man in the head and moved quickly to catch up with the others.

At first Walter was shocked by the brutality, but then he told himself that there was a war going on and he needed to accept the fact. This time, when the bottle of vodka came around, he took a big gulp. A few minutes later they arrived at their destination.

A dozen men carried the machine guns about half a mile to an open field and set them up twelve feet from the edge of a wide, deep pit. It looked like a huge grave. When he saw the pit, Walter realized that the shovels he had seen stacked beside the road were the ones that had been used to dig this giant grave, and the retreating men must have done the digging.

While the men loaded the machine guns, the officer showed Walter where to stand so he could get a good view of the execution. Holding a movie camera, the truck driver stood next to Walter.

Just as the sun began to peek over the horizon, a group of twenty naked women and children came trudging out from behind a brush-covered knoll just beyond the pit. They walked in single file. Some of the women held babies, others led toddlers by the hand. As they moved closer, Walter could see that two of the shivering women were pregnant.

The soldiers guarding them ordered the women to line up along the edge of the pit facing away from the waiting machine guns. When the guns began to roar some of the women tried to shield the children, one woman held up her baby toward the officer, screaming in a language Walter didn't understand, but it was clear that she was asking him to spare her baby.

The whole scenario was over in five minutes. Walter stood frozen in horror. He saw the officer draw his sidearm and walk slowly around the pit. If he saw movement he shot the woman in the neck. When one of the unfortunate creatures tried to crawl out the officer ran up to her and shot her several times in the back; then he ordered one of the machine gunners to throw her back into the pit.

"Twenty adults and eight juveniles," the officer called out to Walter. "That's the first batch of Jewish sows today. Write small; there are about one hundred more. We have a full day's work ahead."

With a shaking hand, Walter gripped the pencil until his fingers ached and he began to write in the ledger. Fighting down the nausea, he looked up to see that the guards who had brought the women out to be murdered were going back behind the knoll, while another bottle of spirits was being passed among the machine gunners. Just as the next group of naked, shivering, frightened women and children was being marched to the edge of the pit, Walter lost control. The ledger dropped from his shaking hands and he began to vomit, falling to his knees in helpless convulsions.

Everyone ignored him. The truck driver kept looking through his camera lens, snapping pictures; the machine guns began to roar again; the guards who had brought the women and children to the pit went back behind the knoll to bring the next group. When the machine guns were quiet, a child could be heard whimpering, and the officer's gun exploded sporadically.

Walter, now on all fours, tried to crawl away into the tall grass behind him. He was stopped by a violent kick into his ribs. Falling onto his back he saw the officer standing over him, gun in hand. Certain that he was about to die, Walter closed his eyes. Instead of shooting him, the officer, joined by the truck driver, kicked in all his ribs, then stomped on Walter's stomach until he lost consciousness.

It took a year before Walter could walk upright. The army offered to send him back to Munich but he opted to do research at what was left of the University in Danzig, but soon the British bombed the city and the university buildings were destroyed. Walter, with his newly issued glasses, was sent to Stutthof concentration camp to keep track of the daily death toll in the gas chambers.

In 1944 the Germans had such a shortage of officers that even sensitive intellectuals with bad eyesight, like Walter, were promoted to command positions. One day in early spring, Walter was sent to replace the commander of a small town on the Vistula River, fifty miles south of Danzig. The roads were still impassible except for the panzer tanks, so he traveled up the river in a small cargo ship that was used to ship farm animals. The smell and the noise of the goats, pigs and the diesel engine deadened all of his senses. By the time Walter arrived at his destination, he was a nervous wreck. It was near midnight when he climbed out of the motorcycle side car and stumbled up the steps of the elegant mansion that served as the German headquarters.

Chapter 18

Commander Habermann was scheduled for a furlough, which was summarily cancelled when the tide began to turn on the Russian Front. To drown his disappointment he began to drink several shot glasses full of brandy every night. He kept the bottle next to his chair in the room he used for his private office. Where he got the French Cognac was a mystery, but a man in his position had "connections." Cigarettes were also getting scarce, but he was seldom seen without one between his thin lips.

It was near midnight and Konstanza was preparing a sauce for the next day's meal when Commander Habermann came out of his study. "I need more wood!" he called from the top of the stairs. "Bring some up to my study, and make it quick! The fire is about to go out."

Gathering up as much wood as she could carry, Konstanza made her way to the study. She opened the empty woodbox and dropped the wood inside. "Put some wood on the fire, and then bring up another load." Commander Habermann barked at her. Turning around to leave the room, she saw the half empty bottle of brandy and the darkly-stained glass on the little table beside the armchair.

"I clean the glass for you?" she offered, pointing to the sticky glass beside the bottle. "I bring back with more wood." If he heard her he gave no indication. She took the glass and put it in her pocket.

When Konstanza came back with the load of wood, she poked up the dying fire and put another log on the grate. The glass she took out of her pocket still had a little brown stain on the bottom, but the rest was clean to the rim. Commander Habermann was half asleep in his chair, so without a word Konstanza poured the glass full of brandy, set it back on the table and left the room.

Konstanza was cleaning up the kitchen after the midday meal when she heard raised voices from the rooms upstairs. No one actually came to tell her that Commander Habermann had died during the night. But she overheard the conversations among the soldiers that the "old" man had died of a heart attack. Sergeant Schultz, who was barely out of his teens, was now in charge. He tried to radio headquarters but communications were constantly interrupted by thunderstorms and partisans who jammed the radio waves. He decided to send two men on motorcycles to Danzig to inform his superiors about the situation, and then detailed two others to dig a grave for the deceased commander and prepare the body for burial.

Sergeant Schultz then ordered his corporal to gather up Commander Habermann's private effects while he wrote a note to the widow. Informing wives of the death of their husbands was the unpleasant chore that normally fell to officers, but the young man was determined to do his duty. He decided that a glass of brandy would be helpful, so he finished off the half empty glass that was still on the table in Commander Habermann's study and sat down to write. Later that day, Sgt. Schultz had a fatal accident when his motorcycle hit a tree. Since there were no doctors or other medical practitioners in the vicinity, the cause of death was ascribed to a bad road.

So now, only a very young, inexperienced corporal was in charge of the men who were the victorious occupiers of the village near Torun. Fortunately for him, he did not like brandy.

Two weeks went by before the men returned from Danzig with word that a new commander would arrive as soon as the roads were passable.

The sun was getting warmer, but the nights were still freezing cold. Each morning there was a white layer of frost on the landscape. Almost daily, huge panzer tanks roared through the village turning the roads into a sea of mud. They rolled over the fields around Torun but kept well away from the dense forest.

Konstanza had become so used to the noise of the tanks that she slept right through the arrival of a motorcycle during the middle of the night. In the morning, there was talk at breakfast about the new commander who had arrived the night before.

"He is an old man," one of the men said. "I helped him out of the side car and he had some gray hair already."

"He told me that he had been traveling from Danzig for two days," said the young corporal, who was very glad to be relieved of his duties. "He also told me that we are all leaving for the Russian front in a few days. Headquarters is sending replacements who are not qualified for frontline fighting."

"We have strict orders not to disturb the new commander until he comes down from his rooms," the corporal told Konstanza as she served the midday meal.

The temperature fell below freezing that night, and since the woodcutter was due the next morning, Konstanza knew that there would be a boy or two in the latrine. On clear, moonlit nights she left the lantern in the house, but this was a particularly dark night. Clouds were gathering for a late spring thunderstorm. The rumble of thunder was off in the distance, but it was definitely moving closer. Lantern in hand, Konstanza slid quietly into the latrine.

After using the facility she opened her coat and tucked a shivering little boy underneath and quickly went back to the kitchen. Setting the lantern on the table, she helped the youngster into the woodbox, covered him with a blanket, set a few pieces of wood on top, and closed the lid. She took off her coat, pulled the scarf from her head, shaking out the still mostly-black curls that cascaded to her shoulders. Then she turned to pick up the lantern and was startled to see the outline of a man in the archway that led to the stairs. She gasped, then froze, holding the lantern, her heart pounding in her throat. The man did not move. He slowly lifted his hand, put one finger over his lips to indicate silence. Then he stepped forward, took the lantern out of Konstanza's trembling hand and held it up to reveal both their faces.

"It really is you," the man whispered. "Konstanza, don't you recognize me?"

Konstanza had not heard him. Her head was whirling with speculation about how much this man had seen, who he was, and what he would do.

He repeated her name and this time she heard him. Just then thunder shook the house and a bolt of lightning lit up the kitchen like daylight. In the momentary flash, Konstanza saw the face she had been seeing in her dreams for over twelve years.

"Walter!" She stifled the scream with her fist, then stepped back and held up a trembling hand. "It can't be," she whispered. "It can't be."

Walter set the lantern back on the table, reached out a hand and gently touched Konstanza's arm. She lifted her arms; their embrace was fierce and lasted several minutes. It was Walter who loosened her grip and held Konstanza at arms' length.

"My dearest darling," he whispered, "I can hardly believe what I am seeing."

Konstanza stepped back and waited for what Walter might say next. He just stood there gazing at her face, one arm on her shoulder. Then she noticed the tears streaming down his face and that his hand was trembling as he wiped them away from under his glasses. She stood back and took his hand off her shoulder and into hers. Picking up the lantern, she led the unseeing Walter out of the kitchen, through the little coatroom and into her bedroom. All the while, her heart racing with trepidation, wondering what she would do if

Walter betrayed her and the hidden boy.

She guided Walter into her sparse bedroom, closed the door behind them and, still holding his trembling hand, she pulled him down to sit on the bed beside her. Gently, she let go of his hand and pulled off his glasses, with the intention of cleaning them, but Walter grabbed both her wrists and stared into her eyes.

"I have so much to tell you," his voice a barely audible croak. Releasing her wrists he slid off the bed onto his knees, wound his arms around Konstanza's waist, and pressed his head up against her belly. He began to sob and his words were muffled into her dress, but clear enough for her to make them out. "I am so sorry—so, so sorry—so ashamed. Were I not such a coward, I would have killed myself long ago." He kept weeping uncontrollably, his body heaving with convulsions.

Automatically Konstanza raised her hand to stroke his hair. She noticed a few gray strands among the reddish waves. Every part of her being was caught up in conflicting emotions. She felt love for Walter, even pity at his condition, but also fear that he would betray her.

After a few minutes he regained control of himself, sat down on the bed next to Konstanza, who was still holding his glasses. He took them from her and put them on.

Konstanza had not spoken German since she arrived in Poland but now she used it for the first time in twelve years. "So you are in the army?" she ventured to ask Walter. He nodded but remained silent for a long time.

"I am the new commander of this occupation district," he finally whispered. I came to replace Commander Habermann."

Konstanza gave a little gasp to hide the smile that started to cross her face. She waited to see if Walter would say anything about the boy in the woodbox. But Walter began to ask Konstanza about how she had come to be in this Polish village.

She answered his questions briefly, never mentioning that her employers were Jewish or that her young ward had been dragged away. She was still waiting for him to mention what he had seen in the kitchen.

The thunderstorm was moving away, and now a pelting rain began to descend on the roof, making a splashing sound as it gurgled down the drainpipes. For a long time Konstanza and Walter sat side by side on the bed, holding hands, much as they had during their summers in Switzerland.

Konstanza was still waiting for Walter to reveal his plans for her, when he slid his arm around her shoulders and whispered into her ear. "I saw the boy get into the woodbox," he said. When she jerked back a bit he held her more tightly. "Please trust me. I will not betray you."

Something in his tone persuaded Konstanza to trust him and she got up, put on her coat and went to get the other boys in the latrine. When she got back, she was chilled to the bone, her coat dripping, her shoes and stockings wet from the rain. She carefully and quietly tucked the boys into their safe hiding places, and then went to her bedroom. Walter was still sitting on the bed.

"You will get sick if you don't get out of those wet clothes," he said, real concern in his voice. He got up and, much to her surprise, started to unbutton her dress which was also damp, but not from the rain. Slowly, carefully, he removed Konstanza's clothes then he sat her on the bed, took off her high topped shoes and gently rolled down her wet stockings.

Her teeth still chattering, Konstanza gave herself up to being treated like a helpless child. Walter tucked her under the feather duvet that covered the bed. Konstanza watched him remove his shirt and trousers, hang them over the chair and place his glasses on the wash stand.

For the first time since she had known him he stood before her naked. She had thought about what this phenomenon must look like, but she had only seen drawings and sculptures, never a fully erect penis in real life.

Without a word, Walter gently pushed Konstanza to make space for him in the narrow bed. He gently began to caress her, fondle her breasts, softly kiss her lips, which still had the familiar softness that he remembered from their trysts by the lake near Basel.

She didn't withdraw from him, but something in her shy behavior indicated to Walter that Konstanza, now over the age of thirty, was still a virgin. He began to rub her nipples then suck on the hardened knobs. He took her hand from around his neck and guided it to his penis. She allowed him to fold her fingers around the stem. Then he began to explore the area between her legs. His fingers encountered moisture but he wanted to make certain that she was ready for him. Using the same slow and careful movements that he used to peel back the petals of a fragile flower bud or to uncurl the leaves of a young fern, he touched and probed, finally inserting one finger into the warm sleeve of her vagina. With his lips locked on hers he managed to adjust their position so he lay on top of her. Konstanza let go of his penis and wound her arms around Walter's neck. She had heard that there would be pain during the first penetration and she did feel a sharp twinge. Then he moved inside of her and for a few moments ripples of pleasure engulfed her whole body.

A feeling of peace and euphoria filled Walter's whole being. For years he had wanted Konstanza, thought about holding her in his arms again. For a few minutes they clung to each other. He whispered words of endearment while she shed tears of happiness and for the loss of her virginity. "My darling," Walter whispered, "I have longed for you all these lonely years. I love you so much and even when I tried, I could not love anyone else."

"I can hardly believe you are really here." Konstanza replied. "I have dreamt of you so often. I've imagined you in my bed, just like this. I think I must be dreaming."

Walter smiled in the dark, and then covering Konstanza with the blanket, he got up to dress. "Do not be alarmed if you find a few spots of blood on the sheet in the morning. I know you were a virgin, and I was careful not to injure you, but I could sense that there was pain." He sat down on the bed and smoothed the hair from Konstanza's damp face. "I will stoke up the fire in the stove," he said. Then seeing her eyes widen in alarm he assured her. "I will use the pieces lying next to the stove." His smile was mischievous, conspiratorial. Then he quickly left the room.

Chapter 19

Lying in the dark and listening to the rain, in spite of the shock, anxiety and excitement of that stormy night, Konstanza fell asleep. Just before dawn, as was her habit, she got up to start breakfast for the soldiers upstairs. She remembered the events of the previous evening, but she began to think it had all been a dream—until she saw the cup with cold tea on the kitchen table. Her heart leapt in her chest, and she hugged herself with elation she had not felt for years.

Quickly she cut thick slices of bread from the bread she had baked last week and took it to the woodboxes where the boys were hiding. "Stay till I get you," she whispered each time she passed the bread along. The two small loaves of stale bread that were left were barely enough for the rest of the day. The baker had been sent to Germany with all the other able-bodied men, so the villagers had to bake their own bread in the small ovens of their iron stoves. Konstanza began the preparation for baking the bread that would need to last all week. Her mouth began to water as she recalled the fragrance of the large, round loaves that came out of the brick ovens every day.

The soldiers were sitting around the table when Konstanza brought up the tray of bread and butter. She went back downstairs to bring the hot, brown water, flavored with chicory that was a substitute for coffee. A small pitcher of milk provided a few drops into each cup.

There had been several dairy farms around the village, but the Germans had killed many of the cows for meat, and sent the stout farmers to Germany to work in the munitions factories. One elderly farmer was allowed to keep two cows as well as two chickens, and one of his daughters. (His wife was shot for hoarding an egg, and his sons were sent to Germany.) The two of them provided the garrison with a pitcher of milk, and one or two eggs every day and a small clay jar of butter each week. Before the war most of the soldiers drank their coffee with sugar, a luxury now reserved for senior officers.

The men stood at attention when Walter came into the dining room from the front hallway. He saluted them and quickly sat down. In the commotion of shuffling feet and scraping chairs, Walter met Konstanza's eye. He would not have recognized her except for the flashing green eyes he remembered so well. A black scarf came down over her forehead; gray smudges resembled wrinkles on her face; her black dress hung loosely from her stooped shoulders. The image was that of an old crone.

A familiar tingling sensation went down Konstanza's spine when she saw Walter come into the dining room. She remembered the sensation from when she saw him again for the first time after a winter at school. Although he was a little taller, fuller and had gray strands in his reddish hair, his blue eyes behind the thick, gold-rimmed glasses were the same as she remembered them. After that brief glance, Konstanza kept her eyes down as she usually did when serving a meal. As unobtrusively as possible, she cleared the plates and cups and disappeared down to the kitchen.

Just as she was putting the first batch of bread loaves into the oven, Konstanza heard Father Ami's wagon rumbling into the back courtyard. Wiping her hands on the ample apron she wore for baking, she went out to meet the wood cutter. To her surprise, he was unloading a wounded man from the back of his wagon. He called out to Konstanza to get him some help and she ran upstairs to find a soldier to send down to the courtyard. One of the guards who kept watch on the front door followed her down to the back. He carried the wounded man upstairs and tried to find a place to put him down. All the beds upstairs, as well as the couches in the parlor area, were occupied by wounded soldiers from the retreating German army. The wounded man was breathing but unconscious, so the soldier put him on the floor and went to find the medic.

Father Ami told Konstanza that he had been bringing wood to a house just east of his usual route when he saw the man beside the road. He put him on top of what was left of the wood he was bringing to Konstanza. The man had been conscious at that time, and had told Father Ami that he had been left for dead by his platoon as they retreated from a Russian attack. With a severe wound in his shoulder, the man had walked several miles but had not caught up with his platoon.

"So the Russians are getting closer?" Walter had soundlessly come up behind Father Ami and Konstanza. They turned, startled by the presence of a German officer in the back courtyard, which was reserved for menials.

"It seems so," Father Ami said neutrally, and then unloaded the wheelbarrow and began filling it with wood, all the while keeping his back to Walter. Konstanza followed him to the existing wood pile near the house and helped him stack the new pieces. She did not turn around to look at Walter and he went back into the house to tend the numerous wounded men who had been left behind by the retreating Germans.

Konstanza told Father Ami the new commander was Walter Mannheim but nothing more. When they were finished with the wood, Konstanza invited Father Ami into the kitchen where she cut him several slices of the freshly baked bread. He ate one and gratefully drank a glass of water. Tucking a loaf of bread into his jacket pocket, he signaled Konstanza that he was ready to leave.

"Wait, I want to give you some of the vegetables I have stored in the pantry. I am planting a new crop soon and need the space," Konstanza said. A few minutes later they emerged from the back door carrying a bushel basket between them.

It was filled to the brim with turnips, carrots and onions. Father Ami hoisted the load onto the back of the wagon and covered it with a tarp. Konstanza pulled her oversized rain coat tightly around her as if she were suddenly chilled. Then she leaned over to kiss the old man's cheek, stepped back a pace and returned to the kitchen.

That night and for several nights in a row Walter didn't come down to Konstanza. She knew he was busy with the wounded men and with organizing burial details for the soldiers who were brought in already dead and for those who died shortly after arrival. When Walter finally came to her well after midnight one night, he was exhausted and overwrought. They were both too tired for lovemaking so they simply held each other. Eventually, Walter said. "I have to get away from all this death and destruction. I am a coward and don't have the courage to do what I know I should do. Early on, I should have protested but was afraid of being arrested. Now, I want to desert but I am afraid of being shot," he confessed.

When he began to cry again as he had done on the first night they had been together, Konstanza tried to console him. "Have you killed anyone?" she asked, feeling fairly certain that he was not capable of perpetrating the atrocities she had witnessed.

"I was sent to concentration camps to make the lists of murdered people to send to Berlin. There were thousands of names with birthdates and former addresses. Thousands and thousands, and most were women and young children." Sniffling, he wiped his nose on the featherbed cover. "It was a cushy job. I wasn't sent to the front because of my eyes and my father's rank."

Walter buried his face in Konstanza's soft, round breasts and she held him to her for a long time. It was early morning, but still dark outside, when they began to kiss and this time Konstanza felt no pain, only waves of all consuming ecstasy.

The German wounded were being evacuated in the military ambulances that shuttled back and forth from the hospital at Danzig and further back to Berlin for the more drastic cases. Each day there were more casualties from the front lines, but as the garrison became more organized during the spring and on into the summer, Walter managed to spend most nights with Konstanza. He began to bring a bottle of wine with him and drank most of it before getting into bed.

They did not talk about the war raging around them, or make plans for the future. They reminisced about the summers in Switzerland. A favorite topic was the food; just the memory of the taste and aroma of foods they enjoyed made their mouths water. Taking turns, they described dishes like Berta's spätzle, the fondue at their favorite bistro, and the savory stew at the pension where Walter's family stayed in the summers.

Chapter 20

Konstanza was in the kitchen garden when the rumbling of thunder reverberated through the forest. A cloudless sky gave no indication of a coming storm. She bent to her work of digging up weeds and harvesting the few vegetables left from last summer's crop when the booming sounds began again.

She straightened up and looked around, and to her surprise she saw Father Ami's wagon approaching from the road. He was not due to bring wood until later in the fall and seldom came by in the spring and summer. "Whoa Gaia, whoa Sybil," he shouted to the horses, who showed signs of wanting to move the wagon along toward the lush grass in the meadow beyond the courtyard. Always pleased to see her friend, Konstanza greeted him in Greek fashion, with a hug and a kiss on both cheeks. He returned the greeting, took her arm, and guided her toward the house. In the foyer, Konstanza took off the heavy boots she wore for gardening, put on her regular high-topped shoes, and went to the sink to wash and fill glasses of water for Father Ami and herself. She could see that the old priest looked disturbed.

"Did you hear the thunder?" she asked as she set a glass of water down on the table for her friend. "It is strange. There is no sign of an approaching storm."

Father Ami took a long gulp of the cold water, carefully set the glass down on the table, and looked directly at Konstanza who was now sitting across from him.

"The Russians are approaching the East bank of the Vistula. Those were German guns you heard. You must get out of here right now. Get your most vital things together, identification papers, passport, and any other documents that you brought with you from Switzerland." His tone was even, matter of fact, but there was no mistaking the urgency with which he spoke.

"I can't just leave." Konstanza protested, thinking of Walter, her garden, and—most of all—that she needed to be there in case her dear Hedy came back. She also thought of the boys in the forest and how they would need her again in the winter. She mentioned these things to Father Ami, but left out her reluctance to leave Walter, now that they had found each other.

"Listen to me," Father Ami said in a low, stern voice. "I am going to tell you something so horrifying that you will try not to believe me. But it is the truth. I overheard the German plans for their strategic retreat."

Father Ami began to tell her what was in store for the women and children left in the small town, but Konstanza covered her ears, shook her head in disbelief, tears rolling down her face. Father Ami stopped talking, stood up, and started toward the door. Konstanza went to him and, with a pleading look in her eyes, asked him to give her a little more time.

"Until tomorrow, then," He said. "I will be back in the morning. You must be ready just before daybreak. Do you understand?" He searched Konstanza's face for a sign that she understood that she was in mortal danger. He reached out and stroked her hair. "Please, please be ready to leave when I come. Time is running out."

While serving the noontime meal of sauerkraut, brown bread, thin slices of pork roast, and the local beer (the Polish brewer had been allowed to keep his brewery going to make beer for the Germans), Konstanza overheard the soldiers talking about the plans for the retreat. She could hardly believe that the British and American troops had landed on a beach in France. According to the men at the table, the fighting was fierce; the mongrel Americans and cowardly British would soon be pushed back into the sea.

Toward the end of the meal, when Konstanza was gathering up the empty dishes, Walter stood up, called for silence and read the latest orders from headquarters in a loud voice:

> All civilians in the district, without exception, are to report to the main church in each town, before dawn on Monday morning, where they are to remain so as to avoid congestion on the roads, and guarantee an unhampered retreat for the heroes of the German Army.
>
> The commander of each garrison is to deploy troops to ensure that this order is fully obeyed. Any resistance will be met with lethal force.

In a more conversational tone and after Konstanza had cleared the table and returned to the kitchen, Walter continued reading the orders.

> After all the inhabitants of the town are in the church, a contingent of soldiers is to set fire to every building. The Russians will find only ashes on this side of the Vistula River.

Konstanza had indicated with a gesture to Walter before she left the dining room that he should come to the kitchen. She hoped that after she told him about the new life in her body, she could persuade him to come with her.

While cleaning up the kitchen her thoughts went to the suitcase which was packed with two blouses, a black skirt, a suit jacket, a brightly colored scarf, some underwear, her flannel nightgown, and an extra pair of shoes. She was looking forward to wearing attractive and flattering clothing again. Her plans included getting to Paris to find a culinary school that would take women. French women dressed stylishly, and her first purchases would need to be new clothes.

In the back of her mind she was waiting impatiently for Walter to come to the kitchen.

He stood in the kitchen doorway, just as he had that first night. Konstanza reached out to him. His hands were icy as he took hers and tried to see her features in the dimming light. "I have something to tell you," he said.

She interrupted him by whispering his name and the desperation in her voice made him listen. "I am leaving in the morning. I wanted so much to stay and wait for my Hedy to come back. But from what I have heard that is not going to happen. I must save myself and the new life that I carry."

Walter was quiet for a few moments then he asked in a hoarse whisper, "You are pregnant?" When she nodded he kissed her forehead and pulled her toward the bedroom. They sat on the side of the bed and he told her about his orders and that other towns had been ordered to do the same. "It seems so senseless to burn up those people in the church." He paused, and then added, "They aren't even Jewish."

With those few words, Konstanza's love for Walter was snuffed out like a candle flame in a sudden draft. The blood rushed to her head, filling it with a buzzing sound.

Without a word Konstanza got up from the bed and walked out into the backyard hoping that the fresh air would clear the fog from her mind. As she walked, the fog dissipated and she searched deep inside of herself. But where her feelings for Walter had been, an empty numbness now settled in. She admitted to herself that she would miss the pleasurable feelings the very thought of him had engendered, like the butterflies fluttering in her stomach while waiting for him, and the anticipation, the ecstasy of their sexual encounters. The Walter she had loved no longer existed and perhaps he never had. The Walter of her dreams would never have committed atrocities, no matter who had given the order.

Walter sat on the bed, waiting for Konstanza to return from, what he surmised, was a trip to the latrine. When a half-hour elapsed, he went back upstairs to his quarters. He had much work to do before dawn the next morning. Organizing a retreat was as complicated as a battle plan.

Konstanza was relieved to see that Walter had left her bedroom. While walking into the kitchen, she remembered that she intended to take along some of the herbs and spices that she had collected over the last three years. Climbing on a chair to reach the top shelf of the pantry, she saw the dried death-head mushrooms she had laid out on a newspaper, planning to use them for killing mice that sometimes invaded the sparsely stocked pantry. The mushrooms, along with a drop of the nicotine poison from the small vial, also on the top shelf, would guarantee the demise of any creature that swallowed them.

Konstanza spread the old newspaper with the mushrooms on the kitchen table. She glanced at the headlines which were about the glorious Axis military victories.[1] Now that the Allied powers were advancing on the evil Axis, Konstanza hoped that sanity would be restored to the world.

She remembered the rumors that the Russians were as bad as the Germans; that their secret police, the KGB, was every bit as bad as the Gestapo. Yet she hoped this was an exaggeration, as nothing could be worse than the German fiends that ruled Europe now.

With a deep sigh Konstanza began preparations for the evening meal. She would make her signature dish, mushroom soup.

All the soldiers in Walter's command were at the evening meal. Even the night patrol came in for a bowl of hot soup before starting on their watch. Konstanza went around the table filling each bowl.

Chapter 21

An hour before sunrise Konstanza picked up her suitcase and walked out the kitchen door into the backyard of the eerily quiet mansion. She had stuffed her overcoat pockets with bread and cheese. The Swiss francs and important papers were hidden in her clothing and in her high button shoes. Father Ami was waiting for her by the gate that led to the road.

"The wagon is a half-mile up the road," he said. "I had to leave it there, since the road is clogged with people fleeing the Russians."

They walked in silence, while villagers carrying large bundles and small children passed them on the muddy road. When they came to the wagon, the horses were nowhere in sight. Father Ami gave a low whistle, Sybil and Gaia came trotting out of the woods. Quickly, he hitched them to the wagon, helped Konstanza up into the back, and started to cover her with the tarp.

"No need to hide me," she told him, her lips twisted into a wry, sad smile. She got up on the seat beside Father Ami, who looked at her with a puzzled frown. Placing the suitcase between her legs, she asked matter-of-factly, "Where are we going?"

He did not reply, but looked straight ahead, trying to guide his horses between the crowds of refugees on the road.

Father Ami soon turned off the crowded road and drove his horses through forest paths that wound around thick underbrush, dense growth of trees, and hills that were too steep for the two horses.

Twice they stopped to pick up passengers. Each of the obviously deserting, young soldiers crawled under the tarp, without acknowledging the presence of anyone else.

It was full daylight when Father Ami stopped the wagon and told his passengers to get out. The men crawled out from under the tarp, and Konstanza climbed down from the seat. "Leave your suitcase," Father Ami ordered, and pushed it down to where Konstanza's feet had been next to the driver. In German he said to them, "Walk into the forest about one hundred yards. You will see a small cave. Get in it and stay hidden until I come back."

"Father Ami, when are you planning to return?" Konstanza asked in Greek

"I'll be back just at sunset," he answered. "Listen for the wagon, and come out to this spot."

Konstanza looked at the two men standing beside the wagon. One was tall with dark hair and eyes to match, the other one was shorter, with light brown hair and blue eyes. He looked like a teenager. Then she looked back at Father Ami sitting on the wagon seat, ready to leave. She gave him a pleading look, but he smiled and nodded to her.

"It's going to work out, my dear girl," he said in Greek, and waved her along to follow the two men who had already started to walk into the underbrush.

In a few minutes, they saw the cave Father Ami had described. It was little more than a big hole in the hillside, but it was well hidden behind bushes, and if they had not had a description of what to look for they might not have found it.

The three of them managed to fit themselves all the way inside by pressing their backs against the wall and stretching their legs out until the soles of their boots met in the middle.

Konstanza asked their names and reluctantly they told her. (The tall one was Franz and the boyish-looking blonde one was Johan.) Writhing around in the cramped space, Konstanza pulled some of the bread and a hunk of cheese out of her pocket. She offered to share the food with the men and they made quick work of the pieces she handed them. With their mouths full they grunted their thanks and continued chewing.

Hearing the strangely-accented German, Konstanza was curious about the origins of the two young men. "Where are you from?" she asked them by way of making conversation.

For the next few hours, in the strange accent that she could barely understand, the young Austrians told Konstanza about their background.[1]

"My family is scattered around Europe," Franz told Konstanza after she had asked about them. "My youngest sister was beaten to death for breaking formation to pick a roadside flower, during a marching exercise." He stopped to wipe the tears from his cheeks. "She was five years old." He added in a barely audible voice then began to sniffle, as if he had a cold.

"The fiends shot my mother when she wouldn't hand over my little sisters to be sent to Germany to be adopted," Johan said in the same low whisper.

"And they drafted you into their army and expected you to fight for them?" Konstanza asked in disbelief.

"It was not as if we had a choice," Johan said.

"Well, yes. We did have a choice," Franz said slowly. "We had the option not to join the army and to be shot as deserters. I actually thought about it, but they told us that if we chose to desert all the members of our family would also be shot."

"I wanted to live and eventually take revenge on the bastards." Johan growled.

The sun was almost down to the far horizon when Konstanza heard the creak of the wagon wheels coming from that direction. Franz and Johan, who had gone out to relieve themselves, had heard it also. Cautiously, bent over in a crouch, they came out from the underbrush.

The wagon was piled high with hops cones used for the brewing of beer. For most of the summer, Father Ami chopped and stacked wood, which he began to deliver in the fall. But during harvest time, he helped to harvest hops cones. His high-sided wagon was well-suited to take the crop to a small brewery in the vicinity of Danzig. With the tarp he had made a cave-like hollow under the hops, and now the escapees crawled into the opening. The cones had a faint, not unpleasant, fragrance of beer.

Konstanza sat beside Father Ami, her suitcase between her legs, and shivered in the evening chill. The sound of cannons in the distance meant the Russians were advancing. Eventually the thunder of the big guns faded away as they traveled northward toward the outskirts of Danzig. The road was still busy with people (mostly women) walking and pulling small carts piled high with household goods.

Near midnight the wagon pulled into the courtyard of the brewery. Several men came out to help unload the hops cones into rolling bins that they took inside the building. The deserters were introduced as farmhands that had come along to help Father Ami load and unload the hops. Since the brewers were Poles of German descent, they spoke German with Father Ami and didn't ask any questions. When the wagon was empty, one of the men from the brewery brought out a tray with five mugs of beer. Father Ami, Konstanza and the deserters drank gratefully.

In a conversational tone, Father Ami asked the brewery worker if he knew of any ships leaving the harbor in the near future.

"The harbor has been demolished by British air raids," the brewery worker said. "No ships, not even a row boat, can get near the place. Everything along the waterfront is in ashes."

"Is the city itself intact?" asked Father Ami.

"Some neighborhoods are totally destroyed, like the government buildings and the area near the docks," the worker answered. "But luckily the business district, where most of the taverns are, is still standing."

"That is certainly a piece of luck for you guys." Father Ami gave a short chuckle. "I need to get these workers back to their farms," he said, and ordered everyone back onto the wagon.

The foreman came out from the brewery and handed Father Ami an envelope, which he tucked inside his coat without a word, and climbed up into the seat beside Konstanza. With a wave of his hands he turned the wagon around. When they were a few yards down the road he told the deserters to get back under the tarp.

Much to Konstanza's surprise, Father Ami headed back along the road they had just traveled. The horses made very slow progress against the traffic. The German tanks, Jeeps, and motorcycles took up the middle, while the people carrying bundles and pulling carts were pushed into the gullies that ran beside the road. She wanted to ask where they were going, but the creaking of the wagon, the distant roar of the cannons, and the wind in the trees made conversation impossible without shouting.

After an hour of struggling along at the outer edge of the crowded road, Father Ami guided the horses into a wooded area and onto a narrow, serpentine trail. A dense morning fog rolled into the forest from the nearby river. Konstanza could not see beyond the next tree, but the horses seemed to know where they were going.

Later that morning, when the fog began to lift, Father Ami stopped the wagon in a small clearing and unhitched the horses. He led them to a narrow stream nearby and then allowed them to graze for about half an hour. When Konstanza climbed down from the wagon and began to stretch it became obvious to the three men that she was pregnant. They pretended not to notice her condition although they were surprised and curious. They asked about their destination, but Father Ami warned them that the less they knew, the better. After a few minutes, Franz helped Konstanza climb up on the wagon and took his place under the tarp.

The wagon jostled along at a slow, but steady, pace. As the day became warmer Konstanza began to doze off. Father Ami steadied her with one arm as her head rested on his shoulder. Her scarf slipped and her black curls floated out behind her.

Father Ami remembered vividly the first time he had seen Danzig. Fear had been in the very air of the city.[2]

Chapter 22

A few days before Christmas 1938, Father Amiridis stepped off the train carrying two large suitcases, and went to the platform to claim his steamer trunk. It was full of icons and altar cloths that he had rescued from the fire which had destroyed his church in Stettin, on *Kristallnacht* (November 9, 1938). His wife of thirty years had been murdered that night by the Nazi thugs who mistook his Greek Orthodox Church for a synagogue.

The Patriarch of the Greek Orthodox Church in Berlin had assigned the distraught priest to a village near Torun, Poland. Since the train only went as far as Danzig he needed to find a means of getting his belongings and himself to his destination.

Several wagons were lined up near the platform but most of them looked too small for the father's luggage. Standing a little apart from the other vehicles was a dray, with sides the height of a man, hitched to two energetic-looking horses. Father Ami inquired if the wagon was available for a long-haul job. After bargaining a bit, the men agreed on a price, and Father Ami offered to pay half the fare now and the other half after they arrived. The men hoisted the heavy trunk and suitcases into the wagon bed and climbed up to the driver seat.

"My name is Herr Moeller," The drayman said.

"I am Father Amiridis, but everyone calls me Father Ami," the priest replied. "Do you speak Polish?"

Herr Moeller nodded and said, "Since you came on the train from Stettin, I assumed you would speak German. By the way, *ami* means "my friend" in French. Did you know that?"

"Yes, I know," Father Ami said, slightly surprised to find a drayman who knew French. "I will be living in Poland and I need to practice that language."

"In Danzig most people speak German as well as Polish. The city has a toe in each country. The Nazis have forbidden the use of Polish, so be careful. They arrest people on the slightest pretext, but they do not even need a pretext."

The drayman drove the wagon toward the street then pulled the horses to a stop. "To get to that village could take five hours, even with these frisky horses," he said.

"And much longer, if it starts to snow. You had best plan to spend the night in the city." Seeing that his passenger looked a bit dubious, Herr Moeller added, "I know a place where you can rent a room for the night. It's near the train station."

"It will be dark in an hour. I had best stay here for now," Father Ami agreed, and then asked about where he could store his baggage.

"You can leave your large bags and the trunk on the wagon," Herr Moeller said. "The stables are nearby where I stay with the horses and I lock up the wagon." He clucked at the horses and the wagon moved into the city streets.

In the course of their conversation, Herr Moeller mentioned that he needed to sell the horses and the wagon as soon as possible. He had steamship tickets for America but needed money for the train fare to Bremerhaven.

"Whoever buys this wagon and the horses can take over my delivery business," Herr Moeller said. "I have a loyal clientele that would appreciate the continued service."

"If you have such a good business, why are you leaving for America?" Father Ami asked.

"The Nazis are arresting people whom they suspect of being Communist. I'm no longer a member, but they will get to me soon. They are deporting all able-bodied men to Germany to work in their factories. Right now they are busy with suspected Jews, Polish intellectuals, and active Communists. When they run out of those they will start on former Communists, and any Polish men they can find."

"How much do you want for the wagon and the team?" Father Ami asked.

"Four hundred Reichsmark," was the curt answer. "Anyone who wants to take over my business will recover their cost in a month. Are you interested in buying the horses and wagon?"

"I have only two hundred and fifty Reichsmark to my name," Father Ami said. "Priests don't get paid very much."

"School teachers don't either," said Herr Moeller. "That is one reason I resigned last year. Besides, it was getting impossible to comply with the demands of the regime. My arrest was imminent." He cleared his throat and in a low voice continued. "I hope your papers are in order, because it is forbidden for anyone to enter or leave the city without a police permit."

The wagon pulled up in front of a three-story building with two storefronts facing the street. One was an abandoned restaurant, the other had a sign above the door reading "Meltzer Printing" and a large swastika flag covered the window. Father Ami followed Herr Moeller into the print shop. A petite woman stood behind the counter.

"Frau Meltzer, this is Father Ami, Father Ami this is Frau Meltzer, a customer and friend." Herr Moeller waved his arm to indicate the shop. "She also rents out rooms to weary, and less than wealthy travelers, like yourself." Then he stepped back out into the street. "I'll be back at daybreak!" he called over his shoulder.

Frau Meltzer and Father Ami stood looking at each other for a few moments. Her deep blue eyes narrowed and she put up a hand to push back a strand of her graying blonde hair that had come loose from the bun at the nape of her neck.

Father Ami stroked his gray mustache with one hand, and tipped his felt hat with the other. A graying curl fell over his forehead, giving him a boyish look.

He followed her slim form up the steep stairs to the room

at the end of a hallway. The window faced a cobblestoned courtyard where two trees strained their bare branches for a ray of the setting sun.

"The washroom is there," Frau Meltzer said, pointing to a door midway down the hall.

Father Ami had expected her to ask for his passport or identification papers, but she only told him the price of the room for the night and went back down the stairs.

The bed was covered with clean linens and a feather comforter. The pillow was filled with eiderdown feathers and softer than any Father Ami had ever slept on. He woke to the smell of the chicory-blended coffee and freshly baked bread. He followed the scent down the stairs and into the back room of the print shop.

If Frau Meltzer was surprised to see him she did not show it. With a soft, "Good morning," she gestured for Father Ami to sit down at the table covered with a blue checkered cloth, brought him a cup of hot coffee, and set down a plate with slices of buttered bread.

Neither of them remembered what they talked about that morning, but whatever it was, they wanted to talk again soon. Father Ami's decision to buy the horses and wagon from Herr Moeller surely had something to do with his wish to continue to see Frau Meltzer.

By the time the Germans occupied the rest of Poland, Father Ami had established himself as a dependable delivery service. Since his small church and rectory were in the midst of a forest, he decided to augment his income by providing fire wood for the nearby villagers. Cutting down trees and chopping them into cord wood is hard labor. However, after years of rowing out to ships in Stettin harbor, he had developed the muscles and the stamina of men half of his sixty-some years.

Twice a month he drove into Danzig, hauled cargo from the ships to their destinations, and spent the night at the print shop. Frau Meltzer and Father Ami talked for hours about their lives (she had lost her husband during the war, his wife had been murdered by Nazi thugs). During these conversations it became clear that she was not a Nazi sympathizer. Explaining the swastika flag in the window she said, "It is a cheap curtain and fools the vermin that walk the streets."

One day, Father Ami asked about the abandoned restaurant next door. Frau Meltzer told him the sad story of the couple who had started it. "He had graduated from a prestigious culinary institute. She was a seamstress for the local theater. They rented a room here. They saved every zloty until they could open the restaurant." Frau Meltzer sighed deeply and wiped her eyes. "I printed the menus and the advertising flyers. It was a popular place. When the Nazis came to power they sold the restaurant to a local chef and left the country. He did pretty well until last month when the Nazi thugs ran along the street smashing all the windows of businesses that were owned by Jews. I never asked them, but the couple who started that business might have been Jewish. But the new owner was a prominent member of the church. As you can see, he just abandoned the place and disappeared."

One day in March of 1939, the whole city of Danzig was buried in a snow storm. After feeding the horses, Father Ami fought his way to the print shop in the blinding blizzard.

Sitting across from each other at the table with only the kerosene lamp to light the room, Frau Meltzer took Father Ami's hand. "I am very grateful for your friendship," she said. "If you ever want to take our relationship to another level, you will need to take the lead."

Father Ami had often felt the stirring of sexual desire when in the presence of this soft-spoken, innately kind woman. Without a word, he stood up, pulled Frau Meltzer to her feet, and kissed her with all the ardor of a young lover. She returned his kiss and led him into her bedroom next to the kitchen. Holding hands they sat on the edge of her wide, brass-framed bed, listening to the crackling of the fire in the pot-bellied stove in one corner.

Then she asked him, "What did your mother call you?"

"Spyros," he whispered. "And what did your mother call you?"

"Trudchen," she giggled softly, then whispered his foreign name. "Spyros."

Hearing her say "Spyros" made the old priest feel warm and safe.

He decided to call her "Gertrude" because it sounded dignified and respectful, though he always added words of endearment, like "darling" or "sweetheart."

Their lovemaking was slow, deliberate, and filled with memories of other experiences. Each of them felt a deep satisfaction from the pleasure they gave each other.

That night Father Ami brought the eiderdown pillow down to Gertrude's bed and he used it whenever he was in the city.

They agreed that they felt better when they were together, but Father Ami did not want to give up his congregation and Gertrude didn't want to leave the city. "I need tall buildings, street cars, stores, and crowds of people," she told her dearest Spyros.

It always amazed Father Ami that the two of them could talk openly and comfortably, about any subject. He remembered the one time he had tried to talk to his Helena about religious beliefs. She had been appalled that anyone could doubt the existence of God.

"If there is a righteous God, how can so much evil be committed in the name of this Deity?" Father Ami had asked.

"You can't blame God for the terrible things humans do," Helena had countered.

After that exchange Father Ami was careful not to speak about religion with his wife. He had loved Helena, but he was more comfortable with Gertrude.

One day he told Gertrude about Konstanza and how amazing it was to meet someone who spoke Greek in German-occupied Poland. He also told her about the boys she was hiding in the woodbox overnight, and how reluctantly she sent them back into the forest at dawn.

It was Gertrude's idea that Father Ami bring the boys into Danzig, and she would hide them until he found a ship that would take them to safety. She hid them in plain sight. When one of her frequent customers remarked on how she found so many different boys to do the typesetting, she explained that typesetting was tedious work and few boys had the patience to do it for long.

"These boys all come from the orphanage. Heaven knows, there are so many orphans now." She sighed, "The typesetting job is just a stepping stone for them. Once they know how to do it, they go looking for a better position."

Gertrude had gone to a prestigious art academy in Berlin. She knew her way around paint, ink, brushes, and calligraphy pens, as well as how to run a mimeograph machine and how to use engraving plates. Each boy in her "employ" had authentic-looking identification papers to show that he was in the city legally.

Over the last three years, with the cooperation of various ship's captains, Father Ami, Gertrude and Konstanza, had helped hundreds of boys to freedom and safety. It was a dangerous project, but even under the direst stress, Father Ami and Gertrude found they could occasionally joke about their situation. Who would ever suspect the swastika-waving widow and the pious old priest of smuggling Jews?

Chapter 23

Even after five years Father Ami felt a tingle of happy anticipation whenever he came near to the city where he would soon see his beloved Gertrude. Just thinking about her produced a warm feeling in his chest. Now he was jolted out of his reverie as the wagon left the dirt road and began to bounce on the cobblestones of the deserted city streets. The citizens of Danzig were at home, eating the main meal of the day. Father Ami turned the horses into a narrow alley. The high sides of the wagon scraped the walls on either side.

"You will need to get out one at a time," he told the men under the tarp. "We are entering the city and will soon get to a checkpoint. I can't take a chance on having them search the wagon."

"I'll get off first," Johan said. "I know the city, since our platoon was billeted near the town square." He jumped down and quickly hid in a doorway. The horses drew away and the wagon barely cleared the walls at the other end of the alley.

The wagon crossed an intersection and lurched sideways on a loose stone. Konstanza swayed first toward Father Ami and then to the other side, nearly falling off the seat. She struggled to hold onto the suitcase between her knees, but it began to slip out of her grasp. As she bent down to straighten it, she felt a sharp spasm in her back. She gasped, and then stifled a scream as pain shot through her whole body. The sounds she was making startled Father Ami and brought Franz out from under the tarp.

It was evident that Konstanza was in agony. Sweat was

streaming down her face as she gripped Father Ami's arm in vice-like fingers. Franz came around to her side of the wagon and took the suitcase out from between Konstanza's legs and tossed it into the back of the wagon. It was then that he saw the pool of blood at her feet. A policeman came up to the wagon on Father Ami's side and asked what was wrong with the woman.

"She needs to go to the hospital. She is having a miscarriage," Franz said. Then in a voice ringing with authority, he added, "I am an army medic and have been assigned to take her there. Her husband is the commander of the retreating Panzer division and he can't leave his post."

The policeman went to the other side of the wagon to get a better look at the nearly unconscious Konstanza. Seeing the pool of blood at her feet and the growing stains on her dress, he stepped back from the wagon and addressed Franz: "It is not far to the hospital. Just follow this street." The policeman waved his nightstick in the direction of the harbor.

Franz got on the seat beside Konstanza and put both arms around her, holding her tightly as the wagon bumped over the ancient cobbled streets.

Father Ami had no intention of taking Konstanza to the hospital. He knew every bed was taken up with wounded soldiers and that there were no competent doctors left in the city. (The Jewish doctors had been expelled from German territory years ago and the non-Jewish doctors had been drafted into the army or sent to concentration camps.)

He guided the wagon to the area near the train depot and pulled up in front of the Metzler Printer sign.

To his dismay a German staff car was standing at the curb. He pulled the wagon as close to the door as possible and quickly climbed down to help Franz with Konstanza.

"You need to go now, if you want to get away," Father Ami whispered to Franz as they lifted Konstanza down between them. "There must be Germans inside. They will ask questions, ask for papers. Go while you can," he repeated.

"I will stick to the story I told the policeman." Franz replied "Besides, it is not a total fabrication. I really did serve as a medic and Konstanza's lover could have been a German officer."

The pain receded and Konstanza looked up at the building in front of her. She and Franz saw the swastika flag across the window and exchanged fearful looks. Father Ami kept them moving toward the glass-paned door. He reached toward the doorknob when the door opened from the inside and Gertrude stepped aside to let them enter. A German soldier sat in the only chair near the counter. He got up quickly and stared at the trail of blood that followed the three people into the printing office.

Before the soldier could ask questions, Franz shouted at him in the same tone of command that he had used on the policeman: "Go get the suitcase out of the wagon and quickly!"

While the soldier went out the door, Franz and Father Ami followed Gertrude into the back of the print shop. She ran to the bedroom and motioned the men to put Konstanza on the bed. She had quickly thrown a blanket over the bedspread and was ready to tuck a pillow behind her head. Then she went into the kitchen and returned with a basin of water and an armful of towels which she handed to father Ami. He quickly told the ostensible identity of Konstanza and Franz. Gertrude nodded her understanding and went back out to the store front.

The soldier was standing inside the door holding Konstanza's suitcase waiting for further orders.

"Thank you for your help." Gertrude said. She then handed him the stack of flyers that he had been waiting for. "I will send the bill to your headquarters," she said. He started to leave, but he turned at the door and looked as if he was about to ask a question. Gertrude spoke before he could utter it. "The lady is the wife of the commander of the panzer tank battalion. He is in charge of the retreat. He sent his orderly to take his wife to safety. She is having a miscarriage. They tried to take her to the hospital but there is no room and no doctors."

When she stopped to take a breath the soldier nodded. "I am aware that I must report to the police for overnight guests. I will see that everything is in order and report to the station in the morning." Gertrude assured the soldier who looked doubtful. "Please go now and take those notices to the station. They need to go up immediately."

Again the soldier nodded, clicked his heels, gave the Nazi salute and went out.

Gertrude put a "closed" sign on the door and went to the bedroom to see what could be done for Konstanza. The men had removed her shoes and bloody garments, placed several towels in her groin and were washing the blood from her legs.

Franz lifted Konstanza while Father Ami turned down the bed covers and placed her back down on the clean sheets. She was almost as white as the pillow under her head and her hands were cold and trembling.

"She is going into shock. We need to keep her warm," Franz said. He turned to Gertrude, asking, "Do you have a hot water bottle?"

"Yes, I will start heating more water right away," Gertrude answered. Opening Konstanza's suitcase she found what she was looking for. "In the meantime, put this flannel night gown and these woolen socks on her."

Konstanza was like a rag doll as the men worked to get her into the thick flannel gown, the warm cozy socks, and the soft feather duvet. It took most of the night and many towels before the bleeding began to taper off. Toward morning, Franz checked the towels in her groin. There was no new blood. All three of them sighed with relief to see color coming back into her face.

"Franz, you had best wait until it is dark to make your escape," Father Ami advised. Then he turned to Gertrude. "Franz is a deserter from the German army. They brutalized his family in lower Austria because they are of Slavic descent and then expected him to fight for the Reich."

Gertrude looked hard at Franz. "You performed well as

a German officer—the arrogance, the rudeness, the guttural barking commands."

Franz gave a rueful smile. In his soft, accented German he said, "I had lots of time to learn that dastardly demeanor."

Gertrude then asked if he had identification papers and he shook his head. In a hard, decisive voice, Gertrude said, "For now, you will need to be a German adjunct to this panzer commander and Konstanza will need to show documents that she is his wife." She turned to Father Ami. "Spyros, warm up some milk and cut a slice of bread. Try to get some of it down Konstanza. She needs to recover her strength. It will take a few days."

"Franz, come with me," she ordered and led the way to a corner of the kitchen next to the stove. She pushed the large woodbox a few feet aside, revealing an opening in the floor. She brought a ladder from behind a curtain and lowered it into the cavity below the kitchen. "Follow me," she said to Franz, and he followed her down the ladder. She went to a table and lit a kerosene lamp. When Franz had reached the bottom, Frau Meltzer pulled the ladder down into the basement, picked up a grappling hook that was lying nearby and pulled the woodbox back over the opening. As she raised the lamp Franz was astonished to see tables laden with art supplies of all kinds. Brushes, pens, paint pots, ink stands, reams of paper, cardboard, rubber stamps, knives and blades for every type of cutting need, and stacks of paper. A treadle sewing machine stood in one corner. A sink and dark room equipment was half hidden by a curtain in another corner. In the middle of the room stood a rack of movable type, a printing press and a box of engraving plates used for making watermarked document-like passports and currency.

She told Franz to brush back his hair, and then, from an armoire against one wall, she produced a military-type cap which she placed on his head. With a small Leica camera, she took a couple of pictures.

After developing the photographs, Gertrude set them out

to dry and began to assemble the necessary tools to produce identification papers for Franz and Konstanza. Franz was able to help with some of the printing. Gertrude showed him how to set the type and turn the handle of the printing press. But most of the work needed specialized expertise. Franz uttered words of amazement at her skills and she told him that she had been an art major at the Academy of Arts and Letters in Berlin.

When all was ready to her satisfaction, she bundled everything into her huge apron pocket, used the grappling hook to pull the woodbox to one side, put up the ladder and followed Franz up into the kitchen. After replacing the woodbox and ladder, she handed Franz the paperwork she had worked on all night.

"These will do as long as you stay in character and in Germany," she said.

"I don't want to stay in Germany," Franz said. "Or let the Russians get me." He cleared his throat and almost in a whisper he added, "But I want to be with Konstanza."

Chapter 24

Christmas celebrations were strictly curtailed that year. Almost everyone in Danzig was able to get a tree, thanks to the brave efforts of Father Ami. He put runners on his wagon and braved heavy snow to bring a load of trees into the city. He stopped near the train station and sold every tree in a matter of minutes. He was able to save a small spruce for Gertrude, and she hung it with paper chains she had made from discarded paper products and old newspapers. She pulled cotton balls apart and spread them over the tree to represent angel hair or snow. The tree looked festive even without the usual candles.

The city of Danzig was totally dark every night. A war-time blackout had been ordered, and any infraction was severely punished. The usual Christmas market was cancelled, but with the heavy snow there would have been few customers.

After delivering Gertrude's Christmas tree, Father Ami had taken his horses to the stable. He had hoped to reach his parish by nightfall, but wanted to give the horses a rest and some food. He had attached the sled runners to the wagon and started to hitch up the horses when he heard the roar of cannons in the distance. The sound was coming closer and he decided not to chance going in that direction. He was walking back to the print shop when he saw a lone figure pulling a hand cart on sled runners through the snow-covered street.

A familiar voice shouted at him through the wind and the approaching gun fire. "Father Ami, is that you?" The figure, wrapped in a heavy shawl, came closer, and he saw it was the washerwoman from the village near his church.

"Frau Worjek! Yes, it is me," Father Ami said. "Did you walk all the way from the village?"

"Oh, Father," she replied. Her breath was coming in deep gulps. "It is so good to see a familiar face." She put down the handles of the cart and stepped in front of Father Ami as if to make sure of what she was seeing. He lifted his woolen cap in greeting but quickly pulled it down again so his ears wouldn't freeze.

"I have been walking for two days. This sudden snowstorm started just as I came into the city." She stopped to catch her breath, and Father Ami pulled her into a nearby doorway.

"I want to sell the goods in the cart to buy a train ticket to Breslau," she explained. "I have a cousin there. The Russians have entered the village, and I barely stayed ahead of the fighting,"

"Where is your daughter, the one who helped you with the laundry?" the father asked.

"Dead," was her flat reply. "The Russians raped her to death."

Father Ami closed his eyes, uttered a curse and searched in his pockets for some money. "There is a train due later, if it gets through. Here are some Reichsmark. Even if you buy a ticket, you need to be very quick and aggressive to find a space on the train."

"Bless you, Father," Frau Worjek said, tears streaming down her wrinkled cheeks. "There are towels and bed linens in the cart. I was bringing them back to the Occupation Headquarters, but no one came to take them from me. I went inside the villa and they were all dead." She stopped talking, lowered her eyes and shivered. "It was a ghastly sight, Father. I ran out, took the cart home and started to run to the police station. It was then that the Russian tanks came into the streets."

Frau Worjek was trembling so badly now that Father Ami put an arm around her to steady her. "There were only a few old women and some children left in the village. The Russian soldiers climbed down from their tanks and rushed into the houses, began to steal the food and then to rape any female they found. I ran back to the house when I saw what was happening. I was too late" Now she was openly sobbing. "They are worse than the Nazis!" she screamed.

Father Ami stepped out into the snowy street and took up the handles of the cart. "Go get your ticket, and even if you don't get on this train, it will be warm in the station. I brought them a load of wood this morning."

Frau Worjek sobbed, "Thank you, Father," and started to leave. She turned back and asked. "Do you know what happened to Konstanza? I hope she got away."

"Yes," Father Ami answered. "I heard she got away." Before Frau Worjek could ask anything else, he picked up the handles of the cart and headed down the street.

When Father Ami arrived at the print shop with a cart full of towels and linens, Gertrude looked at him askance.

"I bought them from a refugee so she could buy train tickets," he explained. "They are a Christmas present for you, my little treasure." He kissed her fondly on the cheek and carried the contents of the cart upstairs to the linen closet. He called out to Konstanza who came out into the hall. "Help me put these away properly," he said to her.

When they had made order in the cupboard, he said, "I bought these from the washerwoman, the one from our village." Then he told Konstanza what she had said about the men at the occupation headquarters. Her face froze into a neutral mask and she just nodded her head and went back into her room and closed the door. Her loud sobs brought Father Ami into the room. "Oh, Father," Konstanza gulped down the lump in her throat. "I have a terrible confession to make."

Father Ami raised a hand to silence her, "I can listen to your confession, but it is not in my power to give you absolution."

Quickly and in a very low tone, Konstanza told him how she had poisoned the whole garrison that night before the planned roundup of the villagers.

"You saved hundreds of lives from a certain fiery death, Konstanza," he assured her. "These are terrible times and the rules we lived by before no longer apply. The Nazis have trampled morality and decency under their bloody boots. Until they are destroyed, we must do whatever we can to defeat them. There is no difference from what you did to what a soldier does when he shoots the people who are shooting at him."

After he spoke these words, Father Ami walked to the door and left a softly crying Konstanza lying face-down on the bed. In a little while, she got up, straightened her skirt, and went downstairs to help prepare an evening meal. Although her physical strength had returned, her mind was not yet able to make plans for her future.

Franz had nursed Konstanza through the infection that she had contracted after her miscarriage. He had enough medical training to recognize postpartum trauma. With Father Ami's expertise and a pair of tweezers contributed by Gertrude, the men were able to remove the infected uterus lining. The bleeding was profuse, but Father Ami had seen similar cases when he had helped his wife with her midwife duties. He no longer believed in prayer, but a few familiar words slipped from his lips as he gently, but firmly, removed the remaining tissue of the afterbirth.

That was almost two months ago and Konstanza had recovered sufficient strength to move upstairs to the studio apartment where the restaurant owners had lived. It was across the hall from the bedroom where Father Ami used to sleep and Franz now stayed. He worked in the print shop and chopped wood for his rent. Every week he went to the nearby police station to register his and Konstanza's continued sojourn in Danzig.

On the day before Christmas Eve, Konstanza was sitting in her room across from the small fireplace that kept half the room warm. This afternoon, she finally felt the strength coming back into her body, and she became more aware of her surroundings. As she inspected the room for the first time since she began to occupy it, she noticed a bookshelf above the fireplace. She had to stand on a chair to reach the shelf. The two dusty books were heavy, and she had to take them down one at a time.

She laid the books down on the table by the window, got a rag from the kitchen area, and wiped the dust from the ornate covers. Her eyes widened in surprise and then her whole being filled with pleasurable excitement. The two books were the world-renowned *The Culinary Guide* by Auguste Escoffier, copyright 1903 (revised in 1921), and the even more popular *Guide to the Fine Art of Cookery,* containing 2,973 recipes. These were the textbooks used by culinary institutes around the world. She began to read immediately.

When the daylight faded, Konstanza pulled the blackout curtain tightly across the window and turned on the small desk lamp and continued reading. These books were not a substitute for graduating from a prestigious culinary institute, but they contained all the information a person needed to organize a well-run restaurant. Every detail was covered, from the cookware and utensils required, as well as how to arrange an efficient restaurant kitchen. There was a chapter devoted to table setting and another on the plating process. "Presentation" was emphasized and illustrated.

She was so engrossed in the books she had found that when Franz knocked on her door, which was slightly ajar, she let out a startled little scream.

"Frau Meltzer wants to know if you would like to come down for something to eat," he asked, then, seeing the open books on the table before Konstanza, he offered to bring some bread and cheese up to her room. "Would you like a glass of wine or some hot tea?" he asked, while coming into the room to take a closer look at the books.

"Oh Franz, would you be a dear and bring me a slice of buttered bread and some hot tea?" Konstanza asked. "I have found these fabulous books and I just can't tear myself away."

Franz took another look at the open book on the table. The pictures and drawings were all of food and kitchen equipment. The writing was in French. Since most schools taught French as a second language, Franz could say a few words, but reading was beyond him.

Konstanza saw his puzzled frown and told him about her great, good fortune to have found these books. "They contain all the information one needs to open and run a successful restaurant." She smiled her radiant smile, so much like her mother's. "That is my dream—to be a master chef in my own restaurant someday."

Franz went to the door and turned back "I will bring you some bread and tea and a glass of red wine to help restore your stamina."

A few minutes later, Franz returned with two plates of bread, a bottle of red wine, and two glasses on a small tray. He set the tray on the clear side of the table. "Konstanza, please join me for a small repast," Franz pleaded. "Everyone downstairs has finished eating and I hate to eat alone."

Konstanza moved the books to a chair, and asked Franz to lift the tray while she placed a tablecloth on the table. She also produced two linen napkins and set the table for two. From a shelf she took down a candle stick with a half-burned candle. "Do you have a match?" she asked Franz. He produced a matchbook and lit the candle. They sat down opposite each other and Franz poured the wine into the glasses.

"Merry Christmas!" Franz said and raised his glass. Konstanza raised her glass in salute and wished him good health.

"I have not had a merry Christmas for several years now," Konstanza sighed and drank some wine. "Franz, tell me about some of the things your family did for Christmas."

For the next half-hour, Franz talked about the food, the sweets, the little Christmas tree which was decorated with real candles and little else. Besides cooking a goose dinner, his mother knitted a present for each of the family. "We were a happy family," he said, his voice breaking a little as he repeated the phrase. "After all this fighting is over, I plan to go back to Klagenfurt and see if any of my family survived."

They ate the bread and drank another glass of wine. Then Franz said. "I am going to the St. Mary Cathedral tomorrow night for the midnight mass. Would you come with me?"

"I thought you Austrians were all Catholic." Konstanza said. "The services at that Cathedral are protestant now."

"The Oliwa Cathedral is the only Catholic Church the Germans left, but it is too far away. Besides, I have always wanted to see this church. It is the largest brick building in the world and over five hundred years old." Franz's had lowered his voice to express the awe he felt. "Will you come to the service with me?" he asked again.

Konstanza shook her head. "I will stay home and read some more of Auguste Coffier. You can't imagine what a find this was for me." She looked at Franz with her wide green eyes, which startled him each time he looked into them.

There was just enough wine for another glass and they drank it in two gulps. Franz got up and started to gather the plates and glasses onto the tray. He picked it up and then set it down again. Konstanza got to her feet and they stood looking at each other. Franz bent down and kissed Konstanza on the cheek and quickly stepped back, anticipating that she might slap him.

Instead she raised her arms, pulled his head down and kissed him softly on the mouth. Franz tightened his arms around her waist and the kiss became more passionate. When Franz released her, Konstanza gasped for air. Quickly she stepped back and let him pick up the tray.

"I'll be right back," he said. Then he backed out of the room.

Chapter 25

It was impossible to start reading again, so Konstanza just sat quietly trying to think about what had just happened. She liked and trusted Franz. He had been the one who nursed her during that long month of illness. She blushed a little to think of how he had seen all of her already. She was embarrassed, remembering how he had to help her on and off the chamber pot. Could they be lovers after such an experience?

Her reverie was cut short when Franz came back into the room. He sat down across the table from her and they looked into each other's eyes. Franz spoke first. "I love you, Konstanza," he said. "When I say such a thing to a woman, it means I am hers, totally and forever. Actually I have never said such a thing to a woman."

He had taken Konstanza's hand and gently folded his other hand over hers. She could have easily pulled away but she sat quietly with her hand in both of his.

"I am very fond of you, Franz," she said in an even tone. Then she took a deep breath and continued. "Love is a complicated emotion and I don't think I am ready to love a man again. The time may come when I can give myself completely, but for now my soul needs to rest."

Franz tried to hide his disappointment but the light went out of his eyes and his whole body seemed to shrink. "Is it because I am younger than you are?" His voice had risen. "Five years is nothing between people who love each other. My mother was eight years older than my father and they had a good union. Father Ami is much younger than Frau

Meltzer . . ." His voice trailed off and he stood up. "You kissed me as if you really loved me," he said.

"Yes, I liked kissing you," she said. "You are a handsome man with a fine character and a sincerity that I admire. If I love again, it will be someone very much like you." She smiled—a bit ruefully. "I loved someone once. He changed from the person I loved to someone I could only abhor." Her voice became almost inaudible.

Their hands were still entwined as they sat looking at each other in the dim lamp light.

Then Franz said. "Tell me about Walter."

Konstanza took in a sharp breath. "How do you know about him?" she asked.

"When you were feverish you hallucinated, you thought I was Walter. I couldn't make out what you were trying to say to him, but you said his name over and over. It was obvious that you were in love with him. Such passion dies slowly. But I will wait until you are ready to love again," Franz said and released her hand.

"I will tell you about Walter," Konstanza said in a low monotone.

For the next hour she told Franz her long history with Walter. "Our last conversation revealed his true nature and I knew that I could no longer love him. I thought my feelings for him were dead, but I was wrong. Yet little by little, they are fading away. Give me time, Franz. Don't abandon hope—or me."

Franz took her hand again, kissed it and stood up. "Someday, when you return my love, it will be the happiest day of my life."

Konstanza also stood up and said, "Our future is very uncertain. We could be arrested any time. Actually, that is true of everyone living under Nazi rule. They don't need a reason to take people away. They function at the whim of their leader."

Her tone was grim. When Franz had closed the door

behind him, she wiped a tear away from the corner of her eye.

In the early afternoon of Christmas Eve, Father Ami had brought a chicken with the feathers still on it. (No one asked where it had come from.) Gertrude had been soaking a pot of brown beans for two days and they were now cooking on the stove with a small piece of salt pork she had saved for this occasion. Franz had stopped at a green grocery on his way home from registering at the police station. He now proudly handed Gertrude a small bag of beets and two potatoes.

"We are going to have a real feast," Gertrude said to Franz.

"What's this about a feast," Konstanza said from the kitchen doorway.

Gertrude and Franz looked her way and thought a stranger had walked down the stairs.

Konstanza was wearing a pink blouse and a navy blue skirt with shoes to match. Her shiny, black hair was rolled up into two fashionable rolls above her forehead. She had a white apron in her hand and began to unfold it and put it on. She addressed Gertrude. "It would be my pleasure to prepare a dinner for this festive night."

Gertrude, who could cook, but did not relish the chore, said. "It would be my pleasure if you would do us the honor."

With a broad smile she went into the print shop to finish some last-minute orders. Franz went along to help with the typesetting and Father Ami went back out into the cold to feed and bed down his horses. Konstanza started the tedious task of plucking the chicken. While the chicken soaked in hot water, Konstanza gathered the herbs and spices she would need to season the beans and make the beets and potatoes into a tasty side-dish.

During the afternoon each member of the household found an excuse to come through the kitchen to savor the aroma of roast chicken.

Three hours later, the four of them sat down to a delicious dinner. The dessert was a surprise. Konstanza had packed a small box of sugar as well as dried fruits in her suitcase. At the end of the chicken dinner she presented an apple strudel right out of the oven. The fragrance filled the room and made all their mouths water. Franz also mentioned that the strudel brought memories of home into his mouth. Gertrude sighed. Calling Konstanza by the name on her new identity papers, she said. "Frau Richter your talents are wasted being the wife of a colonel. You should be running a restaurant."

Konstanza grinned broadly and handed Franz another piece of strudel she had set aside for him.

Father Ami helped Gertrude clear the table and wash the dishes while Franz got ready to go out. "Are you sure you don't want to come with me?" he asked Konstanza. "St. Mary's Cathedral has a highly regarded organ. Some say it is the best in Europe, if not in the world."

"Thank you for asking," she told Franz, "but it is a cold night and I prefer to stay here and read."

Franz started for the back door of the kitchen which led out into a courtyard. This was the private entrance to the apartment in back of the print shop. Gertrude stopped him.

"It is bitter cold tonight. You need an overcoat and a hat." With these words she handed Franz an old-fashioned great coat with a fur lapel and collar. He put it on. It was a bit large for him, but it was warm and he felt quite debonair in the wide-brimmed felt hat.

As he put his hands into the deep pockets his fingers encountered a hard surface and then curled around the familiar butt of a Luger P08. He glanced up at Gertrude; she gave him a knowing look.

"St. Mary's cathedral is near the waterfront. It must be God's grace that it hasn't been destroyed yet," Father Ami said. "Be careful, Franz. Many dangers are out there, besides bombs. By the way, how are you getting there? It is a long walk from here."

"The streetcars are running until after the midnight mass tonight," Franz answered. "I checked at the police station when I was out this morning."

This time before going out the door Franz stepped in front of Konstanza. "I almost forgot," he said, and kissed her on the cheek. "Merry Christmas, Frau Richter, and thank you for a memorable meal." His dark eyes twinkled as he tipped his hat to her and went out the door.

Before he left the darkness of the courtyard he pulled the gun out of his pocket to examine the weapon to make sure it was in working order. It was loaded and the safety catch was oiled to keep it from making any noise.

The interior of the church was more splendid than he had expected and Franz was dazzled by the opulence of the main altar. Gold leaf abounded on the statues and paintings and reflected the thousands of candles that actually made the cavernous space feel warm. The midnight services were very similar to the ones he had experienced in the village church, and his eyes began to water as he heard the hymns he had heard his mother hum while she worked around the house and the garden.

At the end of the service everyone stood at once and began to move toward the two wide doors. When he heard his name called Franz was surprised, since he was certain he didn't know anyone in the city. When he turned to look where the caller might be, he saw the chief of police from the district where he reported each week.

The man came closer, his bald head shining in the candlelight. "I thought that was you," he said. "Did you enjoy the service? I am always overwhelmed by the beauty of this place."

Franz had no choice but to nod in agreement, and then he tried to lose himself in the crowd. But the police chief was persistent. "It is serendipity that I encountered you this evening. How did you get here?"

"I came on the streetcar," Franz answered "And I need to hurry so I can get a seat on the next one." Franz made a valiant effort to get himself wedged in among the crowd but the police chief put out a hand and grabbed his arm.

"I can give you a ride," he said. "My driver is waiting outside." Then he pulled Franz through a small side door that he hadn't noticed before. A cold gust of wind whipped Franz's coat. A black Mercedes was standing at the curb. A man got out, opened the back door and the police chief pushed Franz into the back seat, getting in quickly beside him.

"I need to inform you that Colonel Richter has been killed in the line of duty."

"Oh no!" Franz exclaimed. "How terrible. Has anyone informed Frau Richter?"

"I was hoping you could do that," the police chief said. "But wait until Tuesday; we don't want to spoil Christmas Day for her."

"That is very thoughtful of you," Franz said. "I am staying in a room near where she is and I can try to tell her as gently as possible."

"There is a problem that you need to be aware of." The police chief looked at Franz and then asked him where he was staying. Franz gave him an address on Langegasse toward the harbor and the driver headed in that direction. The car moved very slowly since the headlights were off because of the blackout.

The police chief continued. "The people at army headquarters needed to notify a relative of the Colonel's death. Since they did not know the whereabouts of his wife they notified his mother in Frankfurt. When they asked her to be so kind as to notify Colonel Richter's wife, they were told that he did not have a wife." The police chief stopped and looked at Franz and then out the front window of the car as he waited for an explanation.

Franz tried to look confused, cleared his throat and felt for the luger in his pocket. Slowly he released the safety catch and felt for the trigger. "Perhaps he didn't tell his mother about his wife." He paused for a full minute, and then added, "She is dark like a Gypsy and the older Frau Richter most likely would not have approved of such a racially-mixed marriage." With a pounding heart Franz waited for the police chief's next words.

"I don't want to speak badly of the dead, but could she be his mistress?" The police chief sounded as if he wanted Franz to answer.

"Sir, I wouldn't know about that. The Colonel introduced the woman as his wife and asked me to take her to Danzig and make sure she gets on a train to Berlin." Franz felt his armpits moisten. He had raised his voice a little to imply he was affronted.

The police chief only nodded. "If there is any suspicion about the woman's identity, Frau Meltzer would have reported it," he said. Then he added, "I have known her since our school days, and she is a loyal Nazi, without any doubt." The men sat in silence until the car stopped at the address Franz had indicated. He got out of the car, put on his hat and watched as the car moved away and down the street. It was a long walk to the print shop and Franz planned to use the time to formulate a plan for Konstanza's and his departure from Danzig. In spite of the biting cold he could feel the sweat running down his sides and under his hatband.

The wind almost blew his hat into the street and Franz had to hold it down with one hand. The hand holding the hat was soon numb, and he had to trade his hands every few minutes to keep from losing his fingers to frostbite. Try as he might, he could only think of when he needed to switch the hand on his hat with the one in his pocket. It took all his strength to keep moving forward into the snow flurries that hit his face like hail.

It took an hour to travel the route he had covered in twenty minutes on the streetcar. The streetcars had stopped running at midnight and the faithful who had used them to get to the cathedral now had to make their way home on foot. As he struggled along against the wind, he saw couples plowing their way along the street, trying to shield their children from the punishing cold. These people had stood for hours during the mass and prayed to their God. Franz thought their God might at least calm the wind until they reached their homes.

Chapter 26

It was two o'clock in the morning when Franz arrived at the back of the print shop and he expected everyone to be asleep. He used the key on the heavy door, hoping no one had put down the iron bar that was used for extra precaution at night. The door swung open with a slight creak, and he closed it quickly and lowered the bar.

He was standing in the small foyer. A sliver of light came from under the door leading to the kitchen. He felt around for the door handle and when he found it he opened the door slowly so as not to wake anyone.

To his surprise, the lone bulb that hung over the kitchen table was on—a Christmas gift from the electric company. Usually the power was turned off each night at nine unless there was a bombing raid, which meant no electricity—possibly for the duration. Kerosene lamps were much more reliable anyway so many households didn't even bother to turn on the electric lights.

Gertrude and Father Ami were playing cards and they didn't look up as Franz appeared in the doorway. "Merry Christmas," Father Ami called out as Franz came into view. Konstanza was sitting at the other end of the kitchen table, her head bent over a book.

Franz came around the table and stroked her smoothed out hair, his fingers brushing the bun at her neck, stopping just short of touching her skin. The room was comfortably warm from the fire in the wood stove, and Franz felt a little dizzy from the sudden change in temperature. He took off his coat and hat, brushed the snow off into the sink, and then took them to the coat closet near the door. The blood was pounding in his head and he went to the sink to get a glass of water. He noticed his hands were shaking.

Gertrude said, "You must be hungry. There are some potatoes left over from dinner and a piece of Swiss cheese. I'm afraid we ate all the apple strudel, although there is a bit of bread to go with the cheese. I hope the bakery is open tomorrow, because even on Christmas people need fresh bread. For two years now, we haven't tasted hard rolls or *lebkuchen* ('gingerbread cookies')."

In the pantry Franz found the potatoes and cheese, put them on a plate, and took it back to the table. "Is there any beer left?" he asked Gertrude, who pointed to a space under the kitchen sink where a small barrel lay concealed behind a pile of dishrags. He ate and drank in silence, watching the card game without much interest. When he had finished he put down his knife and fork and, in a voice that betrayed his nervousness, he said. "I met the police chief at the cathedral. He had important information that I must tell you." Two faces turned toward him with worried frowns. "Colonel Richter has been killed in the line of duty."

There was a little gasp from his audience. He continued: "They tried to notify his widow and when they could not ascertain her whereabouts they contacted his mother and asked her to pass on the information to her daughter-in-law. However, Frau Richter revealed that as far as she knew, Colonel Richter was not married."

Gertrude said, "I had hoped to give Konstanza a little more time to get her strength back and postpone her travels until the weather is warmer." Then she gave a deep sigh, "We need to get her on a train by tomorrow."

"That may not be possible," Father Ami said. "Tomorrow, actually today, is Christmas Day and the trains may not be running. I am going to the stable to check on my girls, and I'll find out about the trains."

"We should all leave. Danzig is getting very dangerous, what with the bombing every night," Gertrude said. "Until now the raids have been primarily on the shipyards and the docks, but it won't be long until they start on the rest of the city."

"Our original plan was to send Konstanza away on a merchant ship." Father Ami explained to Franz. "We have been successful with that route in the past. Now the harbor is in shambles and the only way to leave is overland."

Hearing her name, Konstanza finally looked up from the book in which she had been totally engrossed. She had not heard what Franz had just revealed and looked at the troubled faces around her with an air of confusion.

"Konstanza," Franz said softly. Did you hear what I said about Colonel Richter?" Konstanza shook her head and waited for him to continue. "He has been killed and the regimental commander is looking for his widow to inform her of his death but the colonel was never married."

With great difficulty Konstanza dragged her mind away from the restaurant kitchen being described in minutest detail in the Escoffier book in front of her. She still had not registered Franz's words, but she could tell by his tone and by the looks on the three faces staring at her that it was a matter of grave importance.

Franz repeated the words he had just spoken. Konstanza's eyes widened and turned a deeper shade of green. She looked from Franz to Father Ami and on to Gertrude.

"I will do whatever you think is best, Father Ami," she said in a resigned tone. "Just tell me what you want me to do and when to do it."

"You must leave here as soon as possible," Franz tried to keep his voice low, but urgent. "The authorities will come here to question you and you must be gone by then."

"Konstanza, you get yourself ready to leave. Pack only the bare necessities. I am going to the train depot to see about tickets and the schedule." With these words, Father Ami went to the coat closet and began to prepare himself to assault the storm raging through the city.

Then he addressed Gertrude. "We are going to need papers," he said, and gave her a meaningful look.

"The papers are ready," she said. "I will explain later about how and when to use them." Their eyes met for an instant before he slipped out the back door and walked with determination into the blizzard. He was acutely aware of the irony that the inclement weather was the reason for the twenty-four hour ceasefire, and not the fact that this was a holy night.

Chaos reigned at the train depot. Hundreds of people crowded the platform, jostling to be closest to the track when the train should arrive. There was still a long line at the ticket booth and the two clerks were hard-pressed to provide tickets fast enough to please the purchasers. Father Ami tried to get close enough to the ticket booth to ask about when the train was due, but the crowd was too dense and no one was about to let him pass by.

Eventually he went back out to the platform and asked a man when the train was due. The man glowered at him and shrugged. Just then an ear-splitting whistle from an approaching train echoed through the station. The train didn't even slow down, but sped past the crowd on the platform. Heads, some completely bandaged, could be seen at every window, and men were hanging from the posts between the cars and even from the railings along the roofs.

The crowd on the platform turned ugly. Father Ami could hear the angry shouts about how this was the second train that night that had sped through the station without stopping. When an eastbound train with empty rail cars went by the people on the platform began to wave their fists at it. Then they turned as if on command and went toward the ticket booth with demands for their money back, but the two clerks were gone.

Father Ami hurried to the stable. Fortunately, the sled

runners were already attached. The way they clipped on over the wheels was an invention that he had worked out himself and now he felt a tinge of pride at his prowess. Gaia and Sibyl seemed glad to see him, and he apologized for getting them up and out into the cold at this early hour.

Franz, Konstanza and Gertrude were just putting on coats and boots in preparation to go to the train when the wagon entered the courtyard. Konstanza had packed her suitcase and was wearing the winter coat with the deep inside pockets. Franz pulled the felt hat down to his ears, and shouldered his backpack over the coat that Gertrude had given him to wear to church. He felt for the Luger in the right side pocket and discovered a spare clip of ammunition had been slipped into the other pocket. All three of them came to the kitchen door and stopped when Father Ami called out to them, "The trains are not stopping. They are packed with wounded soldiers."

It took a few moments for this news to sink into their consciousness and then they stepped back into the kitchen. Father Ami dropped the reins and followed them inside.

"I would offer you the horses and wagon." Father Ami said, "but it is much too cold for a long journey right now." They took off their outer clothing, while Gertrude set a pot of water on the stove for tea. Over the noises of the storm they heard a tapping sound coming from the print shop.

"I'll go see who it is." Gertrude said. "Spyros," she turned to Father Ami, "go help Konstanza and Franz underground, quickly. It is best that they not be found here. In case there is an inquiry, we will say that Franz took Frau Richter to the train for Berlin this morning and then planned to return to his regiment." She walked very slowly to the print shop door, then turned around to make sure that all traces of Konstanza and Franz were out of sight.

The police chief was standing at the door, stamping his feet and flailing his arms about himself in an effort to keep warm. "Merry Christmas!" he said as Gertrude peeked around the drawn shade to see who was at the door. "Please let me in, I am freezing out here!"

Erich Schroeder had followed his father into the profession of law enforcement and had grown up next door to Gertrude in a neighborhood where their families had lived for many generations. There was a time when he thought he might marry the girl with the golden hair and the flashing blue eyes. But those eyes saw only Herbert Meltzer and so, instead of Gertrude, Erich had married the police department.

He had managed to keep his position by being outwardly a loyal member of the Nazi party. He flew a Nazi flag outside the police station and never forgot to give the Nazi salute when the Gestapo officers came by to check on his prisoners, who were mostly petty thieves or public drunkards. He left the political arrests to the German occupation forces. Under martial law, anyone could be arrested at the whim of the authorities. Fear and suspicion were palpable in the very air of the city. Thousands of Jews—men, women and children—had vanished overnight.

Without preamble, Erich stepped into the print shop and began to speak to Gertrude. "A warrant has been issued for the arrest of Frau Richter. It is believed she is an imposter." Gertrude's eyes became a darker blue and she gasped as if in surprise.

"Frau Richter left on a train for Berlin this morning and Franz, the young corporal, said he was returning to his regiments as soon as he saw her safely onto the train." Gertrude spoke in a matter-of-fact tone. "Come in, Erich and have a warm drink before you go back out into the cold."

He followed her into the kitchen and stopped at the door when he saw Father Ami. "You remember the drayman who brings us wood in the winter?" she asked as she went to the stove to prepare the tea. "I rented him a room for now. The Russians are advancing on the village where his church is located. It's not safe for him to go back until the victorious German Army drives them back across the Ural River." She smiled widely and added, "Certainly that will be very soon."

Erich drank his tea in three gulps and started for the print shop door. "The Gestapo is planning to search this property before dawn," he said. "If they find anything slightly suspicious they will arrest you." He gave Gertrude and Father Ami a meaningful look before hurrying out of the print shop door.

"Come, let's go to bed." Gertrude took Father Ami by the hand and led him to the bedroom. "It's 4:30 in the morning. Maybe we can get a couple of hours sleep before dawn," Gertrude yawned.

The thorough search of the print shop and the rest of the house was uneventful. The presence of two high-ranking officers prevented the Brownshirt louts, who did the actual searching, from the usual looting that accompanied a Gestapo search.

Chapter 27

After a short conference about what to do next, it was decided that Konstanza and Franz would hide in the underground room until the snow melted. Father Ami and Gertrude joined them during the frequent bombing raids. For most of January, 1945, Danzig was bombed by the Royal British Air Force by day and the American B52s by night. Almost all the German civilians had left the city as the Russians were due to cross the Vistula River momentarily. Twice, the German Army pushed them back a few kilometers, but it was a temporary maneuver to give the bulk of the army time to retreat to a better defensive position across the Oder River, where they were to defend Stettin.

The six weeks the two young people spent in the underground room were busy and productive. They learned how to work the small printing machine, the mimeograph, and the photo developing equipment. Konstanza spent every spare moment reading and re-reading the Escoffier Culinary books. Eventually Franz, who had learned a little French in grade school, began to read them also.

Occasionally they played chess, and Franz found that Konstanza was a formidable opponent. "My father taught me how to play," she told Franz one day. And he could hear the tears in her voice. He waited for her to say more, but she never spoke of him again.

At night they lay in their separate cots and talked about their lives, sometimes until morning, when Gertrude came down with coffee and rolls.

Konstanza found out that the Jews were not the only group that suffered persecution by the Nazi fiends. Anyone who disagreed with their philosophy of Aryan superiority and the abject obedience to their leader was in danger of disappearing into their massive, efficient assembly line of murder.

Franz revealed that after finishing grade school he had been apprenticed to a veterinarian near the city of Klagenfurt. He expected to go to a training school to get his certificate of completion and eventually start his own practice in the mostly rural province of Burgenland in southern Austria. Suddenly all further education was closed to him.

He repeated the story he had told while they were hiding in the cave about how, after the Nazis took over Austria, every Slavic Austrian over the age of ten was sent to work in German factories. The younger children were taught to be totally obedient, as they were considered "subhumans," fit for only menial labor. Men of military age were sent to the Russian Front to fight with the German army,

"Only criminally insane leaders would drag productive farmers off their land, especially during wartime." Konstanza was appalled at such stupidity. "No wonder food was getting scarce in all of Austria and Germany."

In the middle of February, the warm wind, called the Foehn, began to waft across central Europe. The melting snow turned the roads into muddy mires. The trees that were still standing began to show signs of green buds. Much of the city of Danzig was in ruins, but the buildings in the print shop area were only slightly damaged. Those few people of German descent who remained in the city were making plans to depart as soon as possible. Gertrude and Father Ami decided it was safe for Konstanza and Franz to come out of hiding and take on their new identities.

According to their identification papers and officially stamped passports, they were a married couple, Swiss Citizens volunteering with the International Red Cross, based in Basel. Their mission was to inspect prisons and other detention centers in Eastern Europe. They were on their way back to Switzerland when they were trapped by the war.

Father Ami brought the horses and wagon back into the city. He had taken them to a remote farm after the destruction of the stable near the railroad station. The plan was to load up the wagon with food, utensils and blankets. Father Ami would drive the wagon to the Dutch border where the British forces were pushing the German army back into the original borders of Germany. According to the shortwave broadcasts from England, the Germans were slowly retreating from that area and might soon surrender.

From an old map that Gertrude found in a desk drawer, Father Ami plotted a route for their journey. Around the edges of the faded map were descriptions of the terrain. "The forests along the Baltic and North Seas are not dense. There is little underbrush; the trees are spindly and far apart because of the sandy, saline soil. Ancient paths are overgrown with moss but become visible to the discerning eyes of experienced travelers."

On a foggy morning at the end of February, the tarp-covered wagon drawn by Sybil and Gaia joined the stream of refugees making their way out of Danzig. Father Ami sat on the driver's seat, his heart burdened by sadness. The night before, he had tried to persuade Gertrude to come along on the journey towards the Allied lines. She had flatly declined, stating that her place was in Danzig, no matter what.

"Please, *please,* come along," Father Ami had begged her. Putting his right arm around her slim waist he had pulled her close. Cupping her right breast with his left hand he gave her nipple a playful pinch, "Trudie," he whispered into her ear, "I love you and I can't stay away from you for the weeks it will take me to get back—*if* I get back." He had kissed her warm lips, softly at first and then with more passion, hoping that if he aroused her she would consent to come along. But Gertrude had remained cool and reasonable, although he had sensed the quickening of her breathing and felt her heart pounding against his chest.

"I must stay *here*," she had declared, with emphasis on the word *here*. "The Russians can't be worse than the Nazis. They won't bother me. After all, I am Polish and a fellow Slav."

Father Ami had wanted to believe her but expressed doubts about her safety. "The Russians will need the services of a printer, just like the Germans," she had said. "I will make myself useful to them. I am like a chameleon; I change color to blend into my surroundings."

By morning he was reconciled to Gertrude's decision to remain in Danzig. Before he had climbed up into the wagon, where Konstanza and Franz were waiting, he held Gertrude for a moment, and she whispered, "Spyros, come back to me."

"I will be back, no matter how long it takes," he whispered into her ear.

The wagon trundled along the muddy road surrounded by people pulling hand carts loaded with household goods, children and old or crippled relatives. Many people were carrying as much of their belongings as they could on their backs. For two hours the horses kept up a slow, but steady, pace along the crowded road, then Father Ami turned them into the forest. It was the same path he had used to approach the city and the horses knew their way, even in the dense fog that hid the trees.

For several days, Father Ami, Franz and Konstanza took turns driving. They stopped every night to let the horses rest. With the constant roar of bombers overhead, it was impossible to do more than doze for a few minutes at a time. They ate a few bites of bread and cheese, nibbled on a hard-boiled egg, and took a few gulps of the water out of the bucket they had brought along. Ten days went by before they finally splashed their way across a creek with clean water and they were able to replenish the bucket.

The roar of the bombers was constant and the tremendous

explosions shook the ground as they drew nearer to Berlin. They had crossed the Oder River on one of the few bridges left. Father Ami guided the horses north, hoping to avoid the city of Hamburg on the Elbe River, then veering south toward Bremerhaven, and then the border. He kept the wagon far away from the roads, but the sound of motor vehicles could be heard in the distance. Also, the rattling of machine guns was unnerving since they could not tell where it was coming from.

The dense forests of Prussia gave way to the wider-spaced trees of the North Sea area. Eventually they reached the mossy ground mentioned on the map. Pulling the wagon through the soft ground was hard work for the horses, and Konstanza and Franz often walked alongside the wagon to lighten the load.

By their calculations, they were about a week away from the Dutch border when the dappled mare stepped into an unseen hole under the moss. Gaia sank in above her right front knee. In the momentary quiet between bombardments, Franz, who was walking beside the horse, heard the crack of a bone. The mare began to sink onto her side. Franz and Konstanza pushed hard against the side of the wagon and managed to keep it upright as Gaia fell over, her three loose legs off the ground.

Quickly, Father Ami unhitched Sibyl and led her a few feet away, while Franz untangled the reins and harnesses from Gaia. He crouched down and stroked her head. She neighed in fright and pain. Franz slowly pulled the Luger from his pocket. He knew what he had to do and he also knew that he had to do it quickly, before he had time to think about it. He motioned Father Ami to take Konstanza to the other side of the wagon. She went without any resistance but she was trembling. Just then the planes came roaring overhead and the sound of the shot was drowned out in the subsequent explosions.

With the gun in his hand still smoking, Franz sat down on the ground near Gaia's head and began to cry. His whole body was shaking with loud, wracking sobs. Father Ami had walked further into the forest to quiet Sibyl, whose trembling haunches revealed her nervousness. Konstanza sat down next to Franz and carefully took the gun out of his hand. Laying it down on the ground she took both of his hands into hers and waited for him to stop crying. Eventually he looked up into her face. His eyes were blank and his voice was flat.

"I've never killed anything before, not even a chicken." He tightened his grip on Konstanza's hands. "I had to do it," he said, but it sounded more like a question.

"Yes," Konstanza said quietly. "There was no choice. I heard the leg break." She put her arms around Franz in an effort to console him and she could feel something melt inside of her. She could feel the warmth going from her into Franz's still-trembling body. Without letting go of each other they stood up. While they embraced Father Ami got busy centering the harness along the traces. Finally, the young couple turned to face him. There was resignation in Franz's dark eyes and their smiles indicated sadness. Father Ami smiled back.

Chapter 28

The thick morning fog turned to a cold drizzle as Sibyl plodded along the sandy ground near the North Sea. Her flanks sparkled with the wet drops and when she flicked her tail, Father Ami felt the cold spray on his face. Franz walked beside the wagon, his boots making a squishing sound each time he raised his foot. Konstanza was still in the wagon where she had spent the night, while the men had wrapped themselves in blankets and lain under the wagon, hoping to stay dry. The days were getting warmer and the ground no longer froze during the night. Father Ami calculated it would take another two days to reach the German border. Hopefully by then the Germans would have surrendered.

The last few days had been eerily quiet. Franz speculated that the weather must have kept the bombers grounded. Father Ami articulated the hope that the war was over. Konstanza was just grateful for the few hours of silence in which she could actually sleep.

Later that day, as they let Sibyl rest for an hour, Franz brought out his razor and a bar of soap. He hung a small mirror on a nearby tree and began to shave off his two-week beard. He decided to leave a mustache much like Father Ami's. When Konstanza reminded him that he needed to resemble the picture in his passport, he reluctantly shaved it off.

"As you wish, Frau Hoffmann," he said. The name still sounded strange to him. Gertrude had told him that changing a name is easier if it has similar letters. So Franz Hausmann became Franz Hoffmann, and his wife (née Konstanza

Nikiolopolis) became Katarina Hoffmann. They tried not to giggle as they practiced saying the new names.

The cheese and stale bread was running low, and Father Ami hoped they would get to a village or a farmhouse soon. In that part of the world, farmers tended to cluster their houses together in villages and their fields were spread out around them. Each village had a church, a tavern, a baker and, sometimes, a small grocery store/tobacco shop. Some of the larger villages also had a stable, a shoemaker, and even a barber shop. But they were usually a day's travel apart.

Toward sunset they could see rooftops in the distance, and then a church steeple came into sight. With the promise of food and shelter, even Sibyl walked with a lighter step. Father Ami guided the wagon onto a gravel road where they were stopped by a barrier.

As they approached, a man in uniform stepped out of the guardhouse and into the middle of the road. He held up one hand while cradling a rifle in the other. "Halt!" he called out, and two other men came out from the guardhouse. With relief, the three travelers saw that the men wore light brown uniforms and berets instead of helmets. Konstanza recognized the language they spoke as English.

She took out her passport and approached the men in front of her. "We are Swiss, on our way home," she said in broken English, and when they looked suspicious, she tried French. One of the men understood her, and they continued conversing in French. Father Ami and Franz understood French, although neither of them was fluent. It was with great relief that they found out that they were in the Netherlands. They had crossed the border a few yards back. The area had been liberated from the Germans, who were now surrendering by the thousands to the Canadian troops that were occupying the terrain.

One of the Canadians led them to the tent that served as camp headquarters. The major in charge inspected their documents and questioned Father Ami in German. After a lengthy discussion about their plans, the major directed them to a guest house at the edge of the town with a stable nearby.

Konstanza still had the Swiss francs that her grandfather, Kurt von Stahlenberg, had given her seventeen years ago. She now offered to pay the proprietor of the guesthouse for their rooms. The woman who ran the guest house was Dutch, but she also spoke German, and Konstanza asked her about where to get food for their evening meal. "I can provide you with a nice supper," the Dutch woman said in her strangely-accented German. "You can pay me in Swiss francs, of course," she added

While Father Ami went to the stable to bed down Sibyl and put some oats into her feed bag, Konstanza and Franz followed Frau Van Nooten's ample form up a narrow stairway to an immaculate bedroom. Two beds covered with white linens stood on either side of a nightstand.

"We do not have electricity as yet," Frau Van Nooten apologized. "But we do have running water and even an indoor water closet. Those Canadian boys have done a marvelous job of clearing the rubble and they promised we would have our electricity back in a few weeks." She started out of the room then turned around to ask if they had any luggage she could bring up to them. Franz told her he would get the suitcase from the wagon himself, and they followed her back down the stairs to the kitchen.

"First we eat, and then I make hot water for a bath," she announced.

The meal of bread, Edam cheese and some slices of salt herring was sparse, but more than they had eaten in several days. After supper Franz went to the wagon to fetch Konstanza's suitcase and his backpack. Father Ami said he would sleep in the wagon. He wanted to be near Sibyl.

The young couple went back upstairs and unpacked their suitcase. Konstanza carefully hung the light gray Red Cross uniforms on hangers in the wardrobe closet. They looked very authentic, even to the armbands and epaulets, thanks to

Gertrude's skills with a needle. After wrapping themselves in blankets, Konstanza washed out their undergarments in the wash basin and hung them over the chairs and bedsteads. She picked up a clean nightgown and started out the door, handing Frau Van Nooten several Swiss francs for the extra coal to heat the water. It had been several weeks since she had immersed herself into the icy creek of snow runoff. At the time, she had tried to remember the stories her mother had told her about swimming nude in the warm, silky waters of the Aegean Sea.

Franz followed her down the hall to the opaque glass door where she could see little wafts of steam drifting out to the hall. She opened the door and was greeted by a cloud of warm air. Without hesitating she hung her blanket on a hook near the door and stepped into the welcoming water. Franz, to her surprise, followed her example and climbed into the bathtub after her.

Franz smiled amiably. "No need to be bashful at this stage of our lives," he said when he saw Konstanza blush. She lowered her eyes and crossed her arms over her ample breasts, smiling at her own silliness. This man had seen her at her worst—helped her through a miscarriage, bathed her with cold compresses to lower her fever, disposed of her bodily wastes, and even carried her to the toilet when she was too weak to sit up.

~

It was near midnight when Konstanza and Franz returned to their bedroom. While Konstanza put on her nightgown and sat down on the bed to brush her hair, they talked about their plans. Konstanza wanted to get to Basel, Switzerland, and Franz planned to travel to Klagenfurt, Austria, to see if any of his family had come back.

After turning out the kerosene lamp, they embraced, began to kiss with real passion, and then suddenly realized how exhausted they both were. They climbed into one of the narrow beds and promptly fell asleep, their arms wrapped around each other.

Konstanza slept soundly all night. It was nearly eight o'clock when she stretched out luxuriously, and then noticed that Franz was gone. She looked into the wardrobe closet and saw that he had taken out his Red Cross uniform. After washing and twisting her hair into a bun, she dressed in the light gray skirt, white blouse and smartly-fitted jacket. She put the perky hat on her smoothed-out hair and took a quick look in the mirror. She was pleased with the way she looked, only the skirt seemed a bit short after the long, baggy dresses she had been wearing.

It was evident to Konstanza as she entered the kitchen that Father Ami and Franz had been talking about her. They cut off their conversation abruptly and stared at her with a glint of admiration in their eyes. She sat down at the table and started to nibble on the piece of bread Franz offered her.

"There is a convoy of army trucks leaving this afternoon for a place near Munich," Franz said. "They have supplies for the Americans, and then they will take some American supplies to the French troops near Freiburg," he explained and looked at Konstanza expectantly. "You said you wanted to get to Basel, and Freiburg is near the Swiss border."

"Yes," Konstanza said without emotion. "I know where Freiburg is. I went to school there." She tried not to show how the memory of that place disgusted her.

"Since you told me you wanted to get to Basel I inquired about transportation, and there is a train from Freiburg. It is only an hour's ride," Franz said. He hoped Konstanza would be pleased at the news, but she kept looking into space, her eyes focused on the window.

When she turned her head to look at Franz and Father Ami her voice sounded far away. "The people walking outside look so thin—especially the children. They look hungry and tired, old beyond their years."

"Frau Van Nooten tells me the Germans destroyed all

the crops during their occupation, would not let any food supplies into the town, and took all their food with them when they were finally driven out by the Canadian troops," Father Ami explained. "The people all over the Netherlands are starving. The Canadian, British and American soldiers are doing everything they can to get food to them," he sighed, and then he added, "I do not understand what happened to the Germans. When I first came to Germany about forty-five years ago, they seemed so civilized and cultured. During the last twenty years, they have turned into barking, mad dogs."

Konstanza agreed and thought about the conversation with the Canadian major in the headquarters tent. He had spoken to them like rational adults who had certain human rights, no matter how they looked. (And they looked very dirty and disheveled.) He had listened to their story, examined their papers and generally treated them with a courtesy they had not encountered during their entire time in the German Third Reich.

While they sat around the table drinking the last of their lukewarm tea, Father Ami announced that he was leaving that morning to make his way back to Danzig. Although they expected him to return there someday, Konstanza and Franz had hoped he would wait a while, at least until the fighting stopped. Even in this remote town of Arnhem, the sound of cannon fire could still be heard and planes droned overhead constantly.

"Sibyl and I will be all right," he said. "We know how to avoid trouble." He looked at the two young people in front of him with loving eyes. "You two are probably the last of the many youngsters whom Gertrude and I saved from those murdering swine."

Father Ami sighed deeply, stood up and patted Franz's hand, put an arm around Konstanza's shoulder, and kissed her cheek. And without looking back, he walked out the door and out of their lives.

Chapter 29

The sun felt good on their backs as Franz and Konstanza walked through the town to the headquarters tent. Some of the buildings were totally destroyed; others had walls missing, and many were riddled with bullet holes. Here and there a window still had glass in its frames. The Canadian army engineers were working on restoring the water system. Trenches were everywhere, and men with shovels were diligently making more.

The officer who was in charge that morning told them that the convoy was scheduled to leave by two o'clock that afternoon, providing the supplies they were awaiting from Sweden arrived on time.

Back at the guesthouse, Konstanza paid for their rooms, Franz brought down their suitcase, and they made their way to the village square to await the convoy. When the long line of trucks arrived, they stopped to load up the boxes that had arrived with horse-drawn wagons that morning. The markings on the boxes said FARMING TOOLS in Swedish.

A truck near the middle of the line was designated for them, and Franz and Konstanza climbed into the back. There was barely space for them to sit and the large suitcase had to stand up on the narrow bench between them. The driver had told them it would take about twelve hours to get to their first destination somewhere near Munich. "It all depends on the roads, which are covered with rubble or may have land mines near them. We are somewhere near the middle of the convoy, so if we do hit mines it will be the lead trucks that get it," he had explained to them in English. Fortunately they only understood the "twelve hours" part.

The roads had been cleared by the engineering corps with the help of local residents and the trip was uneventful. They stopped every four hours to stretch and the drivers passed out jugs of water to those who had brought cups. The soldiers all had canteens, but some had tin cups among their gear, and they graciously loaned them to Konstanza and Franz.

The night was clear and a half-moon helped to light the way. Patches of snow were clustered around the bare trees that were left standing. During one stop, about eight hours into the journey, they could see burned out tanks in the middle of fields near the road. Then a peculiar odor began to drift into the truck. As they neared their destination, it became stronger and soon Konstanza began to feel sick from the stench. With the help of Franz and a soldier sitting near her, she was able to open the suitcase and take a scarf out to wind around her nose and mouth. Several of the men covered their mouths and noses with their beret-style hats. Others just sat with their teeth clenched to keep from gagging.

It was near dawn when they arrived at the gates of a large enclosure. The trucks were obviously expected, and they drove past the gates, into a wide-open space, and halted in a semi-circle. People dressed in baggy pajama-like clothing were mingling around the trucks as the drivers got out and opened the rear canvas covers to let soldiers out of the back. Konstanza and Franz were told to stay in the truck with their suitcase, and Konstanza was only too happy to comply. Franz, on the other hand, became curious about where they were, and told the soldier helping to unload the truck that he needed to find a latrine.

The first thing Franz saw as he jumped down from the truck was that the men helping to open the Swedish boxes were very thin and frail. The boxes contained heavy shovels, the type used for digging graves. American soldiers with rifles over their shoulders were passing out the shovels to groups of people lined up along a barbed wire fence. Still gagging from the stench, Franz stepped toward a nearby building, thinking to throw up facing away from the people around him. By now it was daylight and he saw a row of uniformed men lying on the ground at his feet. He could see that they had been mowed down by machine gun fire, He stepped back involuntarily and began to vomit where everyone could see him.

An officer (judging by his uniform and epaulets) came over to Franz and handed him a handkerchief. "You get used to it after a while," he said in English, and then, realizing that Franz did not understand him, he tried broken German.

"What is this place?" Franz asked him in very slow German.

"Dachau Concentration Camp," the American said, expecting Franz to understand.

Franz had heard of Dachau. After all, the Nazis had threatened to send him to that place if he did not join the army. He pointed to the dead Germans against the wall and the officer told him they had been German guards. "They tried to surrender, but after my men saw the devastation and depravity of this place they could not control their rage. They shot every uniformed German they saw, and they might have shot all the civilians but I told them that we needed the townspeople to bury the dead." Franz got the gist of the words by the hand gestures the soldier made.

It was full daylight now and Franz looked around and saw what appeared to be hundreds of yards of stacked cordwood about six feet high. He started to walk toward the strange sight and began to gag again. The stacks were thousands of skeletal remains of human bodies. They were all naked and looked like they had been lying there for some time. The soft flesh of their genitals was rotting away. Franz took a few steps toward the human pile, then turned around and fled for the truck. He no longer needed a latrine, his pants were soaked and he didn't even notice. One of the soldiers unloading the boxes of shovels helped him up into the truck and he fell down at Konstanza's feet. He was weeping convulsively, his body shaking. Konstanza tried to talk to him, but he could not talk. He wanted to tell her to stay in the truck but the words wouldn't come. One of the Canadian soldiers tried to stop her from climbing out, but she was too fast for him.

She saw the well-dressed German civilians lined up in rows as the American soldiers pushed shovels into their hands. It was a puzzling sight, but in the next few minutes she saw how they were set to digging trenches around the perimeter of the chain link fence. She walked on a few more feet, thinking to find a latrine. Although she had not eaten for many hours, the stench drove out all thought of food. After a few more feet she saw the stacks of bodies. She gasped for air then her whole body went numb. Her mind went to thoughts of Hedy. Was this how her darling girl wound up?

For a few more minutes, she watched the Germans digging along the wall then she looked again at the mangled, skeletal bodies heaped in long rows between the fence and the long barrack-like building. Men were coming out of the nearby buildings. They looked like walking skeletons, and were staggering as if blinded by the daylight and moved along slowly toward a makeshift soup kitchen the Americans had put up on the far end of the courtyard.

Konstanza stepped backwards until she was up against one of the empty crates that had held the shovels. She sat down heavily and waited for the numbness to leave her body. It slowly dissipated and she was consumed by a blind rage. It engulfed her like a burning flame and if she had had access to a gun she would have shot each of the Germans working along the fence.

For a few minutes she searched their faces. They were mostly women of all ages, a few old men and several younger men who, she guessed, had changed into civilian clothing to escape becoming prisoners of war. They all looked solemn but not outraged or even disturbed by the sight of the corpses they were to bury. Walter's words came back to her. He had felt remorse about burning those villagers alive in their church—but only because they were not Jews.

She climbed back into the truck and found Franz still lying on the floor, but no longer shaking. "Get up," she said to him. "We need to find some food before we continue on to Freiburg." Her voice was dry, unemotional, bereft of all feelings.

The Americans had made a soup out of their C-rations and some potatoes they found in the homes of the residents of the small, picturesque town of Dachau. Some root vegetables were ready to pull up, even though they were not quite ripe. So the soup had turnips, carrots, and a couple of chickens that the soldiers found in a field. It was not nearly enough food for the hundreds of skeletal men standing in line. Konstanza, holding her small tin cup, got into line behind two men who looked less-starved than most of the others. They were speaking in Polish.

"As I told you last night, the food in the kitchen was all poisoned. One of the camp guards warned the cook and me just in time," the older of the two men said.

"I was wondering why we didn't use the camp kitchen this morning," the younger man said.

The younger man turned around and Konstanza could see his face. His blue eyes were wide with disbelief. "After all these years it would be ironic to die of rat poisoning," he chuckled. Then his voice became sober. "Well, the German fiend said we should all be exterminated like vermin."

"They almost got away with it," the older man mumbled and wiped his eyes on his ragged sleeve.

Konstanza's stomach began to churn all over again. She wondered if she would ever overcome the seething rage that coursed through her body. She filled the tin cup she had borrowed and went back to the truck. By now she was accustomed to the stench and she sat on the narrow bench and drank the thin, hot soup. Franz sat stiffly beside her, his eyes staring straight ahead.

The trip to Freiburg took all night. The convoy had to stop

several times and everyone got out to help clear the rubble from the road. Most of the work had to be done by hand, and after the first stop Konstanza noticed her hands were bleeding. She looked at the torn skin and thought of how she should be feeling pain, but she felt nothing. Her body was still numb.

At a roadblock just outside Freiburg they were stopped by a soldier dressed in the blue uniform of the French army. The driver from the lead truck came back to get Konstanza to translate the French into German, which he could barely understand. It was a tedious project, but finally they were clear about where to take the convoy with the supplies the Americans were sending to the French army. The boxes in the trucks were not marked, and Konstanza had no curiosity about their content. She only thought about getting the train to Basel.

Franz carried the suitcase, while Konstanza led the way to the train station. Some of the building had been destroyed by artillery or bombs, but the tracks and the train cars looked to be in good order. Konstanza stopped at the ticket window and asked Franz if he were coming too. He set down the suitcase, put his arms around Konstanza, and kissed her gently on the mouth.

"Do you have all the papers you will need to get to Basel?" he asked. These were the first words he had spoken since they left Dachau. When she nodded, he said. "I am going to see if there is a train to Klagenfurt. I need to find my family." He kissed her again, and when she didn't respond, he let her go. "I will always love you," he said.

Konstanza nodded, her teeth tightly clenched and turned to the clerk behind the counter.

"A one-way, second-class ticket to Basel, Switzerland," she said, handing him the required Swiss francs. He handed her the ticket. When she turned around Franz was gone.

She picked up her suitcase and went to the designated track. The train was almost ready to leave so Konstanza boarded and with the help of a porter, stashed the suitcase under her seat. Three other people were already in the compartment, and Konstanza squeezed in between two heavyset German women who had evidently survived the war without going hungry.

An hour later the train crossed the Rhine River into Switzerland. Konstanza had visited Basel several times while the Mandel family went to Vienna for the summer. Each time she had crossed the Swiss border, she had felt her heart beat a little faster in anticipation of seeing the friendly, beloved faces of Berta and Berti, tasting the incomparable fondue, sleeping under the fluffy feather beds and enjoying the pristine Alpine air. Today she just felt empty and tired.

Chapter 30

When the train pulled into the Basel station, Konstanza waited until the other passengers left the compartment, and then struggled to pull her suitcase out from under the seat. She walked through the cavernous waiting room and out the door to the main street. Then she climbed into the red streetcar that went up and down Bahnhoffstrasse. The Hotel Schweizerhof was the one nearest the train station and Konstanza decided to get off there. She gave the conductor one Swiss franc, and shook her head when he wanted to give her change. He helped her get the suitcase down to the sidewalk, tipped his hat, and jumped back onto the clanging tram.

Konstanza was well aware of how disheveled she looked as she entered the elegant lobby of the Schweizerhof. Since she was wearing the Red Cross armband she hoped the desk clerk would think she had just come from a disaster assignment. *Well,* she thought to herself, *I have just come through an enormous disaster.* For a moment her head reeled as the sight of corpses swam before her eyes. She reached out to the railing beside the ornate doors to steady herself. *How long is this going to go on?* she thought, and fought to clear her head. Half-stumbling as if she had drunk too much wine, she crossed the palm-lined lobby toward the front desk.

When she asked for a single room with an attached bath, the desk clerk looked at her but did not flinch. He told her the price of the room. She unfolded the right amount of Swiss francs for the first night and booked the room for a week. It was then that the clerk looked a little surprised, but he calmly pushed the ledger in front of her. She signed her name. He gave her the key and rang for a bellboy to carry her suitcase to the room. It was only one flight up and Konstanza decided to use the stairs. It felt good to stretch her legs.

The hotel room was small but clean. A window overlooked the inside courtyard surrounded by the other two wings of the hotel. The bathroom was the size of a broom closet, but it had all the amenities she needed. The bed was narrow but festooned with a down feather bed, two pillows and ironed sheets. It was everything Konstanza could ask for and she sat down on the chair in front of the mirror and began to undress. She had been in these clothes for over twenty-four hours, and she could hardly wait to take a bath in the little bathtub.

The food from room service was beautifully served on china, with real silver flatware and crystal goblets filled with ice cold mineral water. Konstanza could not remember what she had ordered or how it tasted. The minute she lay down under the feather bed and closed her eyes she was asleep. She slept all night for the first time in weeks.

The next day Konstanza dressed in a blouse and skirt, and left a note for the maid to send her Red Cross uniform to the cleaners. She had breakfast in the hotel and set out for the Basel branch of the Schweizer Bank.

The clerk who showed her the balance in her account was deferential, and Konstanza was surprised at the figures on the page. She had deposited funds on her few previous visits to Basel, but not enough to account for the fortune in the account now. A few minutes later, as Konstanza sat in the branch manager's office, he showed her the huge deposit made from the estate of Kurt von Stahlenberg after his death. "It appears that you were his only heir," the manager said. He handed her the last will with a murmur of condolences.

Konstanza looked at her grandfather's calligraphic signature at the bottom of the short document. The trustees of his estate were directed to sell all his possessions and, after taking out their fee, to exchange the German marks into Swiss francs and deposit them into the designated account. She thanked the branch manager, asked him to keep the will in his files for safekeeping, withdrew some cash, and walked out of the bank into the spring sunshine.

She slowly walked back to the hotel and up the stairs to her room. Locking the door behind her she sat on the bed for a long time. She thought about all the people she had loved who were no longer alive. She was now a rich woman and she was desolate. What could she do with all that money? She had no desire to buy anything, to travel anywhere. She felt like she was in a dark abyss, so deep that she would never be able to climb out. Deep sorrow washed over her and she felt as if she were drowning in her own tears. The rest of that day until the next morning, Konstanza sat on the narrow bed and wept until there were no more tears.

Finally, she lay down on the bed and fell asleep. She woke up to shafts of sunlight across her face. After bathing, she got dressed in the other skirt and blouse from her suitcase and went to the dining room to have coffee and a roll. The two men at the next table were talking about the Jewish problem. They were Germans who had evidently been in Switzerland during the war and were discussing when it would be safe to return to Germany. They expressed concern that the surviving Jews of Europe would take vengeance against the Germans for what had been done to them and for the murder of their families.

Konstanza had taken the last bite of her crusty role and finished her coffee when she heard the men chuckling over something. She began to listen in earnest.

"Too bad so many of them got away," one man was saying. "But I heard that the Poles know what to do with the ones who try to return to their homes."

"Most of them will soon be going to Palestine, if the British let them in," the other man said. "If they send them all to one place, it will be easier to exterminate them next time."

They both chuckled again.

A blinding, murderous rage began to rise from the pit of her stomach. Konstanza got up quickly, upsetting her coffee cup and knocking over her chair. She fought the urge to pick up the knife on the table and stab the two men. If she possessed a gun she would surely have shot them, and any other Germans in the room. As it was, the two men at the next table barely noticed her exit as she sped out of the dining room.

She had drawn the drapes before she had gone downstairs and her room was in semi-darkness. She sat down heavily on the bed. Her legs felt like gelatin. The fiery pain in her chest was like a knife being stabbed into her heart and twisted back and forth. She tore at her clothes, pounded her fists against her head, then threw herself face down on the bed, attempting to smother her howling screams in the pillows. Eventually, hours later, the outward rage subsided. But for the rest of her life, it roiled just beneath the surface, and it took an inhuman effort to keep it from surfacing when she saw a swastika or heard German.

The rage subsided only to have the sorrow overwhelm her. Yet, there were no more tears left for her to cry, and she began to think about what to do next. She thought of calling Berta at the Chalet but did not trust her voice. So she sat down at the small writing desk and used the hotel stationary to write a note. She explained that she needed to rest after her journey and would call them shortly. Toward evening she asked the clerk at the front desk to mail the note and put a few coins on the counter for the stamps.

Not wanting to go back to the hotel dining room, Konstanza decided to find a place to eat in the neighborhood. She started down a side street and remembered the Blue Parrot restaurant was in that block. The place had not changed. The blue checkered tablecloths covered the dozen tables, and several couples were sitting at the bar.

She hesitated at the door. The last time she had been in this restaurant all the people she loved were there with her. Yes, even Walter, who had come very late. Now they were all dead except Dr. Werner and Renée Heinemann.

Lydia Gottlieb was also gone. Her grandfather's mistress, the dear, sweet Lydia, had to flee for her life from Nazi Vienna. The last Konstanza had heard, Lydia was on the other side of the earth, in Melbourne, Australia. Konstanza had her hand on the big brass door handle, but before she could turn it the tidal wave of sorrow overwhelmed her and she returned to the hotel.

That night, Konstanza slept fitfully and the next day she could not get herself to go down to the hotel dining room. She did not want to see any people, perhaps ever again. For the next two days she stayed in bed, sent for light meals from room service, but barely touched the food. She felt cold all over, even under the thick featherbed. She did not answer the telephone which seemed to ring endlessly at least once each day.

In the late afternoon of the third day a gentle knock on the door brought Konstanza out of a trance-like state. Thinking it might be room service she opened the door to see Renée Heinemann's smiling face. Renée, who had changed very little in the last seven years, held out her arms, and Konstanza fell into her embrace.

~

Renée could imagine some of what Konstanza had endured under the German occupation in Poland. She herself had sheltered a few of the lucky ones who had escaped the reign of terror. The distraught women who had lost husbands, the orphaned children who saw their parents murdered, and men who had been betrayed and beaten half-to-death by their countrymen told tales of unbelievable horror. She knew that not all Germans were evil. After all, she had married a German, but she was not surprised at their jubilation with the Nazi takeover.

For a long time the two women just held each other, and finally, Renée led Konstanza to a chair and sat down opposite her. Renée had seen the blank stares of traumatized people and had learned that patience and kindness eventually healed them enough to lead an almost normal life.

"Berta came to see me and showed me the note you wrote her. She tried to call you but you didn't answer the telephone, so she asked me to check on you." Renée waited a moment to see if Konstanza understood. "Berta told me that she and Berti have a full house for the whole summer. They have even given up their own rooms to accommodate their guests. So you must come and stay with me." Konstanza did not object to this suggestion, so Renée continued.

"Werner is away on a business trip so I will really be glad of the company. The guest room has a bathroom and a separate outside door, so you will have complete privacy." Renée smiled encouragingly and was relieved to see Konstanza nod her agreement.

Chapter 31

Renée and Konstanza arrived at the Heinemann's apartment house just as the sun set behind the snow-covered mountains in the distance. A light in the front window spread a warm, orange glow onto the walkway and over the front porch. Anna, a short, stout woman with straw colored braids wrapped around her head, opened the door. Her blue eyes sparkled as she wiped her hands on her white apron, and then took Konstanza's wrap and motioned to the dining room where she had laid out the supper.

"I am going home now," she said in the strangely-accented German known as Schweizerdeutsch, then slid out the door and was gone.

Carrying Konstanza's suitcase, Renée led the way down the long hallway to the guest bedroom. The door was open and Konstanza let her eyes travel around the room. She saw a huge bed, a chest of drawers, a wardrobe closet, a small writing desk, and, as promised, an adjoining bathroom with all the most modern conveniences. "We had the kitchen and bathrooms remodeled last year," Renée told Konstanza, who again just nodded, her face expressionless.

Renée put the suitcase on the bed. "That was a long tram ride," she said, and pointing to the bathroom, "Perhaps you want to freshen up. Then let's eat and drink something."

When Konstanza just stood in the middle of the room with blank eyes, Renée took her hand and led her to the bed. Sitting down beside Konstanza she put an arm around her and waited. Eventually Konstanza turned to look at Renée.

Her eyes were very dark, like the Loden green suits worn by the natives of Steiermark, Austria.

Again Konstanza nodded, and walked out of the room toward the dining room. Renée sat at the head of the table with Konstanza at her right. She sliced some cheese, buttered a piece of dark rye bread, put some pickled herring and a halved hard-boiled egg on a plate in front of Konstanza. After serving herself the same fare, she poured them each a glass of sherry from a decanter on the sideboard.

"You must eat a few bites," Renée told Konstanza. "Anna will be insulted if you don't at least taste the snack she has prepared." Konstanza nodded and began to eat. When the women had finished, Renée poured another glass of sherry and uncovered a dish of strawberries with powdered sugar. She ate a few of them, but Konstanza just stared at the fruit.

Renée had hoped to have a conversation with Konstanza, but it was obvious that she herself would need to do the talking. She went on to tell Konstanza that Werner had gone to Germany with a delegation from the university where, although he was in his mid-eighties, he still worked in the medical research department. The group was going to the displaced persons camps to work as translators for the Red Cross and other aid organizations. The people in the camps were the survivors of the concentration camps and came from every part of Europe. Werner was especially valuable since he was fluent in Greek, Italian, French and English. He could get by in Polish and in other Slavic languages, if necessary. After thirty years in the Kaiser's navy, he had retired to Switzerland and, as a hobby, he decided to learn Hebrew.

"The Hebrew will come in handy with those Jewish people who speak only Yiddish," Renée said. "It is a language with a German base, but has many Hebrew, Polish, Russian, and even English words." She smiled to herself as she remembered that it was rumored that Werner had a Jewish Grandmother, which was the reason he wound up in a Swiss Medical School instead of a German University. How ironic that this flaw in his background had spared him the devastation of the Nazi era in Germany.

An hour passed, and Konstanza had still not said a word. When Renée asked her a question, she either nodded or shook her head. When more than a yes or no would be required, she lowered her head and waited for Renée to change the subject. After another glass of sherry Renée told Konstanza that she was tired and it was best they both go to bed. Konstanza nodded, got up, and went to her bedroom. Renée's room was two doors away, but she heard Konstanza sobbing for a long time before they both fell asleep.

Renée had experience with traumatized victims of the Nazi terror. Starting in 1934, Werner and Renée provided food and shelter to countless refugees—first from Germany, then from all the other countries that were brutalized by the German occupation. Until 1939, there were mostly families that had the means to pay for Swiss residency, or could buy transportation to other countries.

By 1940, there were many orphaned children who trickled over the Swiss border and found their way to Basel, then to Werner and Renée Heinemann. Many of the refugees, both children and adults, were so traumatized that they could hardly speak, and often woke up screaming from unimaginable nightmares. Renée, Werner, and even Anna would hold their sweat-drenched bodies, murmuring soothing words until they fell asleep again. There were times when dozens of people were huddled in their apartment. Sometimes they stayed for days or even months until the various Zionist and Jewish organizations found a home for them on every continent except Europe.

Berta and Berti had also done their share of rescue work. They turned the Chalet into a virtual orphanage. Dr. Heinemann provided the medical services for the refugees. Many of the children were terribly undernourished, and some had bullet wounds. It seems the Germans, who were actually trying to get rid of all the Jews in the countries they occupied, also shot at Jews who tried to escape. Children were easy targets, as they couldn't run very fast.

In Basel there was no official residence for them. If people wanted to feed and shelter these stateless souls it was their responsibility. The Government of Switzerland had insisted that the Jews of Europe have a large, red "J" printed on their passports and if the Swiss border guards caught them trying to get into their country, they sent them back to their deaths. But if they were able to evade the border guards and were not apprehended until they were in the country they were allowed to stay, but they were strictly on their own.

Renée took Konstanza on long walks along the esplanades along the Rhine River, to the various parks that dotted the city and to the grounds of the university where her mother had worked as a translator. After a week of fresh air and exercise, Konstanza recovered sufficiently to talk a little while they walked.

Konstanza told Renée about Father Ami, Gertrude, Franz, the journey across Germany and loosing Gaia. She mentioned, somewhat offhandedly, that she had hidden some boys in the villa's numerous woodboxes. Renée understood exactly how dangerous this action was and expressed her admiration for Konstanza's courage.

Toward the end of the summer Renée received a letter from Werner. He would be coming home on the Freiburg train the 15th of August (the year being 1945). He mentioned that he was deliriously happy that the war was over. He also wrote that he was acutely aware that the rebuilding of the destroyed cities and the ravaged countryside would be hampered by the fact that the Nazis had driven out or murdered most of the productive, educated, cultured and competent people from the continent. In his capacity as interpreter and medical advisor to the Red Cross he had met some of the remnant of these persecuted people, who would have been very valuable in the reconstruction, but most of them wanted to put Europe behind them as soon as possible. He wisely and accurately predicted that the countries to which they immigrated would greatly benefit by their presence, while Europe would be the poorer without them.

Dr. Heinemann got off the train, carrying a small valise and his medical bag. He was pale and drawn and his eyes were bloodshot. For the first time in his life, he looked his age.

Renée and Konstanza rushed toward the doctor. A smile lit up his wan face, and he held out is arms to embrace them both. He clung to Renée for a long time, while Konstanza took his bags. When he finally released his wife, he patted Konstanza on the cheek. "It is wonderful to see you again," he said, his eyes full of tears. The three of them walked through the station, arm in arm. They took a taxi back to the apartment. It was an extravagance, but this was a day for celebration.

Anna had prepared a sumptuous meal; Dr. Heinemann's favorite dishes covered the table. He politely tasted everything, but ate very little. "I am exhausted," he said as he got up from the table. He thanked Anna for the feast she had prepared, and excused himself to Konstanza. With Renée by his side he stumbled toward their bedroom.

For several more days, Werner Heinemann slept most of the time, ate very sparingly, and spoke only monosyllables. He became a little more animated every day, and Renée spent many hours just sitting by his side, holding his hand. She was delighted when he squeezed her hand or looked into her eyes and smiled. Eventually she got him outside to take walks around the lake, and by the beginning of September, the three of them took long hikes into the hillsides around Basel. The breathtaking scenery of mountains, lakes, rivers and green pastures was restorative, for Konstanza as well as Dr. Heinemann, and Renée made sure they had the best meals for newly-acquired appetites.

After a week at home, Werner Heinemann had begun to have terrible nightmares. He woke up screaming, his nightshirt soaked in sweat. Konstanza was familiar with the nightmares. She still had them, but less often, and she usually woke up before she started to scream. When the loud groans began in the other bedroom, she covered her ears with the pillow, murmured vile curses between her clenched teeth, and prayed that the God she no longer believed existed would grant Werner peace.

It took many more nights of turmoil before Werner began to tell Renée what he had seen when he first arrived at the various concentration camps. Konstanza could barely hear his voice through the bedroom wall, but eventually he would talk louder and louder, while Renée kept telling him to lower his voice. When Konstanza heard him describe the mountains of emaciated bodies she began to tremble uncontrollably. "The enormity of the crimes committed by Germans is almost impossible for the human brain to absorb. What is so frightening is that most European countries, centers of Western culture, were complicit in the systematic murder of innocent people." Werner Heinemann had a momentary relapse. His voice broke and he sobbed, "They murdered all those children!" Werner and Renée wept together all that night and many nights thereafter.

Renée had mixed feelings about letting him talk about what he had seen and experienced. At first, she thought he should try to forget or bury the horrors he had seen and make an effort to go back to the peaceful life she and Werner had enjoyed for almost thirty years. In her heart she knew that forgetting was impossible and burying was temporary. To go on with living as if these horrendous crimes had not been committed would be an atrocity almost as bad as the original one.

One day Renée read an article written by a psychologist in England about living a normal life after horrendous trauma. One of the suggestions was to write down the experience which could free the mind from the obligation of remembering every gruesome detail. Renée advised Werner to try this suggestion. He only nodded, but gave no reply.

Another month went by before Werner decided to take Renée's advice. He began to write down what he wanted to forget. His resolve was strengthened by the news that General Eisenhower and General Montgomery had given orders to the military and civilian photographers to take pictures of the unimaginable sights they encountered as they fought their way through Europe. Newspapers around the world began to run pictures of the horrors that the Allied soldiers (many of them just boys out of high school) encountered when they liberated one semblance of hell after another.

The hundreds of concentration camps bore witness to an inconceivable depth of depravity. A few of the walking skeletons, who had survived the torture of starvation and constant physical abuse, lost their humanity. These brutalized men and some of the women, used shovels, tools, and their bare hands to kill the guards they could catch. Yet, the majority of the Jews were not interested in wreaking vengeance. They just wanted to leave Europe.

Chapter 32

The concentration camps were replaced by DP camps (displaced persons) all over Western Europe. (The Russians, who now occupied all the lands east of Berlin, didn't bother with housing the displaced persons in their jurisdictions. They liberated the concentration camps and told the people they could leave. Many found their way to Western Europe where the Allies and many relief organizations housed, fed, and clothed the remnants of European Jews and other persecuted victims of the Nazi regime.)

Newspapers all over the world printed whole editions filled with the names of survivors, in the hope that someone would see they were still alive. New names were added daily. Millions of people spent hours searching through the names in the hope of finding a loved one, a friend, or just someone from their hometown.

Konstanza, Renée and Werner sat at their kitchen table every night, reading the DP names in every newspaper from all over Europe. A new list would be printed almost daily and they started the process all over again.

They knew that there was only an incredibly small chance that Hedwig Mandel was still alive. After all, over two million children had been murdered—most of them taken to the gas chambers as soon as they arrived in Auschwitz. Why should their Hedy be an exception? Yet, they persisted in reading the names and hoping for more than a year. It was Konstanza who finally called a halt to the fruitless search. She went to the synagogue in Basel and asked the Rabbi to say Kaddish (prayers for the dead) for her Hedy. The Rabbi gave her a candle the size of a coffee mug and told her to light it on the anniversary of Hedy's death. Each night before she went to sleep she looked at the candle, but, with a tiny ray of hope in her heart, she never lit it.

Konstanza often thought about Father Ami and Gertrude, and once in a while she dreamed about Franz. This seemed strange since she hardly gave him a conscious thought.

Life returned to a normal rhythm in the pile of rubble that was post-war Europe. When mail service resumed it was slow and undependable, but most letters eventually reached their destination. With that in mind, Konstanza wrote a letter to Gertrude, addressing it to the print shop. When the postmaster in Basel saw the address in Danzig, he shook his head. "That city does not exist any longer," he said. "Every building was burned to the ground two years ago. It is now called Gdansk and is in Poland."

Konstanza didn't try to hide her dismay at this news. The postmaster continued. "I had a stamp collector friend in that area and he recently sent me a curt note, telling me not to write him ever again. A letter from the West would put him in danger of arrest."

With a troubled feeling about her friends, Konstanza slipped the letters she had intended to mail into her pocket. She then took a walk around the lake before meeting Renée at the tram stop. The two women planned to go shopping and stay in the city for lunch.

It was only recently that Renée felt she could leave Werner alone for a whole day. Werner, who had started writing with some reluctance, was now enjoying the project. After he finished his memories of the concentration camps, he started to write about his adventures as the ship's doctor on the Kaiser's private yacht. He was now totally involved in the story of his last and most interesting voyage—the one on which he met Konstanza's mother and his Renée.

While walking past the elegant shops on the main street,

Renée and Konstanza talked about the future. "Do you still have plans to be a chef?" Renée asked Konstanza. She had been doing some of the cooking on weekends when Anna had her days off. "You are such a natural in the kitchen," Renée went on. "Werner and I would miss you, but you really should think about what you want to do with your life."

When Konstanza didn't answer they walked along silently for a time.

"I have the funds to open a restaurant," Konstanza confided. "I have thought about doing just that." They stopped in front of a store window to look at the new styles. The hemlines had dropped to mid-calf that year, and wearing anything shorter was beginning to look dowdy. They stepped into the dress shop and soon came out wearing their new purchases.

Renée, well into her mid-seventies, had no problem keeping up with Konstanza as they strode up the incline toward the restaurant area. They ate lunch in a small, French bistro just off the Frei. The veal and mushroom crepes were light as air, and they each had two glasses of white wine. The waiter brought a dessert tray with the coffee, and the flaky pastry was irresistible.

Walking to the tram stop they passed the Blue Parrot Restaurant and were surprised to see a for sale sign in the window. Regardless of the memories Konstanza associated with the restaurant, it had remained a favorite place for both the women. They went inside to inquire about the sale.

The owner/chef had died and his widow didn't want to keep the business. She hoped to find a buyer who would retain the loyal employees. "There is a stable clientele," she told Konstanza and Renée. "The same families have been coming here for generations for their Sunday dinners. The foreign students from the university frequent the place because the waiters speak so many languages. Finding a chef to replace my husband will be the main problem." She sighed and started to go back into the kitchen.

"How much are you asking for the establishment?"

Konstanza asked her.

The widow mentioned a huge sum. "Do you own the building or are you renting?" Renée put the next question.

"The price includes the building. There are two apartments upstairs and an attic above that. They are rented, including the attic." The widow informed them. "Considering the rental property as well as a profitable restaurant, I don't think I am asking too much," she added.

Two weeks later, Konstanza was the owner of a valuable piece of property and the head chef in her own restaurant kitchen. The work was much harder than she had expected, but it was a dream come true and she was willing to put in the hours that running a successful restaurant required. Getting up before dawn to go to the markets for ingredients, working out menus, scheduling shifts for employees, studying which wines to acquire, and working out slight changes to the decor—all of it kept Konstanza busy and often too exhausted to think of anything else beyond her business.

She moved into one of the apartments above the restaurant. It faced the back of the building and had a view of the Rhine River in the distance. Konstanza hired Renée to do the interior decorating, and it took her several months to find the right furnishings. Eventually, everything was running smoothly and her routine was under control.

Most nights, Konstanza studied the Escoffier books she brought with her. There were chapters about buying an existing restaurant and how to handle the transition. The suggestion was to change the interior just enough to make it look like an upgrade, but to leave a few reminders of the way it was before. The same advice went for the staff. Upgrade, but retain the best ones. So now there were white table cloths on the tables; goblets replaced the mugs of the Blue Parrot; but the menu was still geared to international taste. She kept on most of the staff, but hired a retired butler as the maître d'. He had just the right attitude that an upscale restaurant needed. Konstanza watched with pride as the elegantly painted sign went up over the door: *Maison d'Auguste*—in honor of her mentor.

The restaurant began to acquire a permanent clientele. Standing reservations filled the registration roster. Families came weekly for Sunday afternoon dinners. Couples and business travelers had favorite tables and menu items. By the summer of 1946, the venture was proclaimed a success and Konstanza had replenished her bank account.

Some of the survivors of the Nazi murder machine had tried to return to their homes, only to find a hostile "welcome" from the new owners. Many of these returnees were murdered when they tried to reclaim their stolen property. There was only one place for these homeless people to go and that was to the DP camps. Their names were placed on a growing list to be published weekly around the world. Konstanza kept reading the lists every week. Her hope of finding Hedy was fading, and finally she felt she should do something to help the unfortunate souls lingering in those dismal camps.

Most of the survivors wanted to leave the cursed continent of Europe as soon as possible. However, there were a few who would opt to become Swiss citizens if they could afford it. The process was expensive and tedious. Just getting permission to live in Switzerland was a lengthy and costly enterprise. Konstanza contacted several potential Swiss immigrants who were willing to go through the process and gave them the funds for the project. One had been apprenticed to a pastry chef and he came to work in the Maison d'Auguste where his desserts were irresistible. Another young woman, who had learned many languages while imprisoned with people from all over Europe, started as a waitress at the restaurant, but soon became an interpreter for the United Nations after classes at Basel University. There were many others who came to Switzerland with Konstanza's generous help and became productive assets to the Swiss economy.

The restaurant was closed on Monday and Tuesday for cleaning and restocking of supplies, chores that Konstanza delegated to her competent staff. On those days she spent her time reading lists from the DP camps and recipe books, and when the weather was not inclement she took walks along the Rhine River or visited Renée and Werner. More and more, she started to think about Franz, but she had no way to contact him.

One clear Monday morning in October, Konstanza decided to visit Renée and Werner. She dressed accordingly, wearing her best suit, a beret to match, and her city shoes. While walking to the tram stop she began to think about Berta and Berti. They had talked on the telephone, but she had not seen them for over a year. Suddenly, Konstanza had an overwhelming urge to see them, drink their delicious hot chocolate, and talk with Berta about recipes Within minutes she had returned to her apartment, changed to clothes and shoes that were more appropriate for the unpaved road at the end of the tram line. It was always breezy on the hike up the hill to the Chalet, so she tied a kerchief over her, still very black, hair. She thought about calling the Chalet, but it was getting late and, besides, she was certain of her welcome. Returning to the street she crossed the tram tracks to reach the platform for the opposite direction.

While waiting at the tram stop she saw a man walking toward her. He looked familiar but he had his hat pulled down so his face was in shadow. He was tall and walked with a familiar loose stride. Her heart leaped into her throat. Yes, it was Franz.

~

Franz was overjoyed to see the woman he had been looking for all over Basel. Not knowing how she might feel, he held out his hand and inanely said the first thing that came to his mind. "How nice to see you again," in a casual tone as if he had just seen her a week ago.

Konstanza started to extend her hand and utter a similarly neutral greeting. Suddenly she gave in to the exquisite thrill that suffused her whole body as she looked into his eyes. Throwing her arms around his neck she whispered into his shoulder, "Oh, Franz, I am so very happy to see you."

Gently, Franz put one arm around her waist and, with his other hand, drew her chin up to his face. When their lips met, it was like an explosion of fireworks in Konstanza's head. Franz kept his lips on hers and held her tightly until she stopped trembling.

The tram came and went and they were still standing on the narrow platform in a tight embrace. Passersby stopped briefly to look at the lovers who were kissing with abandon, oblivious to everything around them.

When they stepped apart to catch their breath, Konstanza became aware of how thin Franz was. His face was gaunt, his fingers were bony, and the jacket hung loosely from his shoulders. A haunted look filled his brown eyes, and when he tipped his hat, she saw how thin his hair had become. She took his arm and led him to a doorway across the street. She had many questions, but she waited for him to speak first.

Franz had trouble keeping the tears from running down his face as he told Konstanza that there was no trace of his family in the area around Klagenfurt. The farm had been confiscated by a German family who had no knowledge of who had owned it before them. The woman and her young sons had signed papers declaring that they bought the property from the Third Reich for two Reichmarks (equivalent to fifty cents).

"Where there was once the quaint town of Klagenfurt, there were only piles of rubble." Franz wiped his eyes with the back of his hand, the one that was not holding tightly to Konstanza's. "There were no landmarks to indicate where anything had been before the war." Franz held back a sob. "I asked the woman who took over my family's farm if I could work for her, help with harvesting the hay and plant a garden. So I worked for her all summer, taught the boys about farming, and helped the local priest to open an orphanage."

He wiped his eyes again and continued. "All that winter I collected food and clothing for hundreds of homeless, orphaned children. In the spring some of the gardens had vegetables ready to harvest and by the end of September the older boys were running the farm and the UNRRA was sending food to the orphanage." He sighed deeply just thinking of the hunger, destruction and the stripping away of all vestiges of humanity that had followed, when criminally insane maniacs had been allowed to take over Europe.

"Konstanza, during all that chaos and misery, you were always on my mind. As soon as I had enough money for train fare, I decided to come to Basel and look for you. It is a big city and I had no idea where to start. Just today I remembered you telling me about the summers in Switzerland. The brother and sister who managed the Chalet outside of Basel. I went to a travel agent and asked about Chalets outside the city—specifically, one run by a brother and sister. He looked though his records and found a place called B & B Chalet. He described the location and the surrounding countryside and it sounded familiar. So I was on my way to see the place, with the faint hope of finding you." Noticing her clothing, he asked. "Do you work there?"

In that moment Konstanza realized that she was dressed like a woman who might work on a farm. Without waiting for her to answer, he continued. "I remembered that you spoke of eating at the Blue Parrot, so I asked about that restaurant. I was told it is gone." He looked at her with a sad smile. "I want to take you to lunch. Is there a restaurant nearby?"

Her eyes sparkling like emeralds, Konstanza gave Franz her most dazzling smile. "Come along, Franz." She said, "I know a great place just around the corner."

Chapter 33

Haifa, Israel, 1959

Oskar Menkes, head of the Haifa division of the Israeli national intelligence agency known as Mossad, and his wife Hedy were hosting a dinner party at a local restaurant. Some of the men and women around the table had lived in the Polish forests for years, after escaping from ghettos or concentration camps. Others had survived the brutality of places like Dachau and Auschwitz, only to find themselves in displaced persons camps waiting to be given permanent homes.

By various routes they had made their way to what was then the British Mandated Palestine and then entered the country illegally. Four of the eight guests had spent time in British prisons for having the audacity to enter the land from which their ancestors had been dispersed throughout Europe by the Romans two thousand years ago.

These young people had been robbed of their childhood and had learned to live clandestine lives. Their experiences helped to make them valuable members of a special branch of Mossad. They had a reputation for being intractable Nazi hunters and ruthless killers when necessary.

The meal was consumed in almost total silence. The people around the table had suffered real hunger for long periods of time. Eating had become a source of pleasure that needed to be savored. Occasionally, one or the other would look out the windows at the view of Haifa Harbor.

Each of them had a memory of how they came to enter that Harbor and what happened when they stepped ashore. Hedy Mandel Menkes had been one of the lucky ones who had papers (forged, of course), which allowed her to disembark from a ship and walk into freedom.

After the coffee was served and a dessert of fruit and cheese was passed around, the conversation turned to the planned Holocaust Memorial (Yad Vashem).

"Many people owe their survival to non-Jews who risked their lives and those of their families to hide Jews from certain death," said one of the higher-ranking officers named Samuel. He had met Hedy just after her escape from the Berlin villa of the Grand Mufti of Jerusalem. For the first time he began to talk about his experiences in the Polish woods. "It was bitter cold and we had no clothes. A younger boy and I crawled out of a pit filled with corpses." He had to stop talking, as he felt the cold and the horror course through his body. His teeth began to chatter.

Another Mossad officer at the other end of the table began to speak. "None of us would have survived if it hadn't been for that woman who lived at the German Headquarters. It was a villa at one end of the village and right at the edge of the forest. That's where we stole some clothes for Samuel and the little guy with him."

Samuel had recovered his nerve and continued his story. "This small gang of boys had escaped from a train and made a camp deep in the woods. They took turns stealing food from the villagers." He sighed and continued. "Poor devils, they didn't have much to eat either."

Another man spoke up. "I was a part of that group and the only good food was at the German Occupation Headquarters. They had this housekeeper who knew how to cook. Too bad the only meat the Germans seemed to like was pork. But eventually we ate that too." Everyone chuckled at this confession.

"I would like to find that woman who fed us and left warm clothes in the latrine. In the winter, she even let us spend whole nights in the kitchen woodbox." Samuel's voice became stronger as he kept talking. "Every week, an old

Greek man came to deliver wood for the stove and fireplaces. She must have been Greek, too, because they spoke Greek with each other."

Hedy began to pay closer attention at this point. "Do you know the name of the village or where it was?" she asked

"It was near Torun. There was a textile mill in the area but it was closed. The workers had all been taken away by the Germans," Samuel said.

"Can you describe the woman who hid you?" Hedy asked the men.

One of the officers who had told of being with the group of boys in the forest spoke up.

"She was tall for a woman. She had dark skin, so she might have been Greek."

Another man cut in. "She kept her hair covered with a scarf, but one day I saw a strand and it was very black."

Samuel spoke again. "She had remarkable green eyes. I was surprised to see such eyes in a person with that coloring."

Hedy's deep blue eyes began to widen at each word she heard. When the officer mentioned the green eyes she clapped one hand over her mouth to stifle a scream. Everyone at the table looked at her. Fighting for composure she lowered her hand and placed it on Samuel's wrist.

"You are describing my nanny, Konstanza. How old do you think this woman was?"

"It is hard to tell. She dressed like my grandmother, in loose smock, her face was always dirty with soot, ashes, or sometimes flour. She moved like a young woman. I watched her help the Greek fellow pile wood. She was strong, like a man," Samuel said. His face became somber as he added, "Those two saved many of the boys. She hid them in the woodbox right under the noses of the Germans. When he came—the Greek—they smuggled them into his wagon and took them to Danzig."

"How do you know this?" Hedy asked.

"I met some of those boys after the war. Quite a few of

them are in the Mossad and in the Israeli Defense Forces. The Greek got them on a ship to Sweden or other neutral ports. Some of the older ones worked on cargo ships until they could get to Palestine." Samuel looked at Hedy and noticed that her usual pale skin was turning pink and her deep blue eyes blazed with excitement. "If this woman was your nanny, perhaps you can help us find her."

At that point Hedy's husband, Oskar, chimed in. "There can't be many Greek-speaking women in that part of Poland," he said. "Or dark-skinned ones with green eyes, like you men describe. How old would Konstanza be now?"

"She would be forty-seven years old, since she was sixteen years older than I am," Hedy offered.

The men started recounting their adventures in the forest, and soon the general conversation drifted to other matters, but Hedy and Samuel continued talking only with each other.

Just before he left, Samuel took Oskar aside. "Sir, with your permission, I want to find this woman who might be Konstanza—for Hedy's sake, and to honor her decency and courage."

Oskar was only pretending to listen as Samuel kept talking.

In his mind's eye, Oskar saw the pale, thin form of Hedy standing in the long line of naked, shivering children. She had been only a few yards from the door to what she thought were "showers" and only minutes away from chocking to death in the gas-filled bunker, along with hundreds of other children. At the last moment, Oskar had thrown a blanket over her and stuffed her under his feet in the black Mercedes. A few hours later she was in the clutches of the Mufti.

When Hedy talked about Konstanza, Oskar always felt a smoldering anger. Why hadn't that woman hidden Hedy, instead of allowing those brutes to take her away?

Each time the anger threatened to come to the surface, he reminded himself that if she had been hidden he would never have met her.

As a Zionist spy, Oskar, known then as Omar, served as personal secretary to the Grand Mufti of Jerusalem. The Mufti had fled Palestine when the British found out he was aligned with the Axis powers. As a good friend of the German leader, he was invited to take up residence in the former Rothschild mansion, a huge villa on the Wannsee, a lake near Berlin.

In order to distract suspicion from his sexual orientation, the Mufti ordered his secretary to procure women for his harem. Preferably blond, blue-eyed young girls with no family. Where better to find such females than at the entrance to the gas chamber?

Hedy had been the third girl Oskar had brought to the villa. The other two girls had not lived long. The first, the daughter of a Rabbi, starved to death for lack of Kosher food. The other had tried to escape and was beaten to death by her jailers. Hedy had taken the advice Konstanza had given her as a parting gift: "Do whatever you have to do to stay alive."

As he had watched Hedy adjust, with wisdom and patience, to the restricted life of the women in an Islamic household, Oskar had fallen in love with her. He and Yusef, his mute valet, had eventually helped her to escape. Yusef, who was not "mute" after all, took Hedy to behind the British lines as they approached Berlin. She was dressed as a boy and was loaded into a truck with other Jewish boys who had survived the Nazi death machine.

Samuel, one of the older boys, realized she was a girl almost from the moment he saw her climb up into the truck and had loved her ever since. When they met again in Haifa, Samuel told Hedy he loved her, but she was still in love with Oskar, whom she thought of as Omar, She told Samuel that she would always love him as a brother—which was appropriate since they had similar coloring and features and were often thought to be siblings. It was Hedy who contrived to get Samuel the job with the Mossad.

Oskar had remained with the Mufti long enough to represent him at the United Nations Conference on Palestine. His real mission was to undermine the Arab leaders who wanted to thwart a Jewish State in the Mideast. He only succeeded in keeping some of them from voting against the resolution to form such a state. But it was sufficient to bring in a majority vote for creating Israel.

After the end of the war Oskar came to Haifa to be near his family and head the Haifa office of the Mossad. He never forgot Hedy and was desperate to find her again. For the next three years he looked for Hedy's name on every list of survivors distributed by the various DP camps throughout Europe. Unbeknownst to Oskar, Hedy had been working as a translator in the same building all that time.

By pure chance they were reunited on a Haifa hillside near the home of his family.

Whenever Oskar remembered that moment when he saw Hedy again, his heart leapt to his throat. She still loved him in spite of thinking he was Omar, working for her enemy. Even now he found it hard to believe that this woman with the golden hair and eyes the color of Egyptian skies was his wife and the mother of his two children. His heart filled with gratitude each time he looked at her.

"So the business is settled." Samuel was saying. "Hedy and I will leave for Poland as soon as possible."

Oskar couldn't remember agreeing to let Samuel take the time off or that Hedy should go with him. But Samuel sounded so official and he knew his mind had been elsewhere for the last few minutes. He decided it would be best to say nothing at the moment. He nodded as if in agreement and said his farewells.

Later that night Oskar asked Hedy if she really wanted to go back to Poland.

"No, I don't ever want to see that place again," she said. "But I feel obligated to help Samuel find the woman who saved him and so many others."

"She didn't save you," Oskar finally said the words he had been thinking for many years. "She could have arranged to hide you. She turned you over to those fiends."

Hedy sighed. "I always knew how you felt about her. I believe she had deep regrets about not hiding me. But she was naive, like so many people at that time. She could not believe the brutality that she saw would affect her or the innocent twelve-year-old girl in her care."

Chapter 34

The Last Chapter

It took several weeks before Samuel and Hedy were actually able to enter Poland. The countries to the east of a divided Germany were behind, as Winston Churchill had named it, an "Iron Curtain" totally dominated by the Russian Communist dictator. The vetting process for any foreigner to gain entry into that virtual prison fortress was lengthy and very costly. Once inside there was always the chance one would not be allowed out. There was a pretense of a rule of law, but in reality the course of everyone's life was at the whim of the dictator. People were imprisoned and even murdered with impunity for no rational reason, just like under the Nazi regime.

Many Jewish survivors who had returned to Poland found their families had disappeared. Samuel and Hedy were very aware of the dangers they faced. They had an advantage since they were blond, fair-skinned, blue-eyed, and spoke fluent Polish. Also they carried official-looking documents identifying them as members of the United Nations Relief and Rehabilitation Administration (UNRRA) based in Geneva, Switzerland.

From Tel Aviv they flew to Paris, and then on to Warsaw, where one half of the airport terminal was still in ruins. During the train ride to Torun they were shocked by the miles upon miles of rubble, piled ten feet high, which lined the roads beside the tracks. In the city they were gratified to see the University of Copernicus had been rebuilt and was functioning. Walking to their hotel, Hedy and Samuel felt a cold chill and a growing rage as they noticed that many of the paving stones on the street were headstones from the Jewish Cemetery.

Their travel permits allowed them to stay two nights in the town they had permission to visit, but they had to change hotels each night. Because only Polish zlotys could be used for any payments and a preset amount of foreign currency was allowed to be exchanged each day, they were forced to spend many valuable hours in long lines at the money exchange offices.

When they finally arrived at the village on the outskirts of Torun, they began to go house to house, asking questions about a Greek woman. After several hours they arrived at the house of the local washerwoman. "Yes," she answered. "A Greek woman worked for the Germans. During their retreat she disappeared. Probably went with them." When asked about the woman's name, the washerwoman said she never knew that. "A Greek guy brought wood to our village. Maybe he knows more about her. I heard them talking Greek to each other one day." She said and turned her back to resume her chores.

Hedy and Samuel decided that finding the woodcutter should be their next move. After changing hotels they went back to the village. When they visited the local priest he told them that the woodcutter was a Greek Orthodox priest and lived near the river in his isolated church, and that he and his wife operated a small print shop somewhere in the town.

Later that day Hedy and Samuel were standing in the town square, speculating on which way to go, when an elderly man, his hatless head covered with thinning white curls and wearing a black apron over a coarse shirt and brown trousers, approached them. "I heard you were looking for a Greek woman," he said, without a formal greeting. "I think it might be the woman I took to the Netherlands back in 1945. We managed to stay ahead of the Russians." He smiled, revealing several missing teeth.

Hedy described Konstanza and the old priest's eyes lit up with pleasure. Hedy took a chance and told him why she and

Samuel were looking for her. Suddenly the old man stepped back and shook his head. A black sedan circled the square and drove away down a side street. From where she stood Hedy could see it was parked just a few yards back from the square.

"They are watching me," he mumbled in Polish, "It is dangerous to be seen talking to Westerners."

"Please," Hedy whispered. "We have come a long way. Just tell me if Konstanza said anything about her plans for after the war."

"She mentioned Basel, Switzerland." The old man stepped back a few more paces and almost ran out of the square.

Since their permits for Poland were expiring, Hedy and Samuel decided to leave for Warsaw the next day. On the way to the train station they noticed a black sedan, similar to the one that had appeared in the village square the day before, was following them.

Getting out of Poland was much more difficult than getting in. When they had arrived in Warsaw from Paris, their backpacks had been casually searched, but now before entering the departure area the search was rigorous. Every item was examined and Samuel was asked about money he was carrying. When he told them he had only a few Zlotys, they ordered him into a booth behind the counter and strip-searched him. When the two stout, red-faced guards didn't find any western currency, they "confiscated" his shaving kit, a shirt, and two pieces of his underwear. They did not bother to search Hedy, who had Swiss francs in the false bottoms of her shoes, but also "confiscated" her nightgown, slippers and toothpaste.

When the El Al plane landed in Munich, Hedy and Samuel drew their first deep breaths since leaving Poland. They took a taxi to the Hauptbahnhof for the four-hour train ride to Basel, Switzerland. Driving through Munich they were dazzled by the bright street lights, the neon signs, the traffic, the well-stocked stores, which were a stark contrast to the bare, dusty shelves in the stores on the streets of Warsaw.

It was near noon when Hedy and Samuel arrived in Basel.

They stopped at a money exchange counter, hoping to exchange the Zlotys for Swiss francs, and were told that no one in Switzerland would take them and they should just throw them away. "Let's keep these for now," Samuel told Hedy. "If we send agents to Poland they will be able to use them."

From the many hotels around the train station they chose a modest, low-priced one which was within easy walking distance to the local tram. Hedy and Samuel had no idea where to start looking for Konstanza but they were trained Mossad agents, and if she was in Basil they were confident they would find her.

However, the first thing they needed to do was find a place to eat. On the train ride to Basel, Hedy had remembered Konstanza telling her about family dinners at a restaurant called the Blue Parrot. "After my parents disappeared, Konstanza began to tell me stories from her life in Basel. She wanted to distract me. There were always tears in her eyes but she never cried."

At the hotel desk Hedy asked about a restaurant called "The Blue Parrot."

"It has been replaced," the clerk told her. "I think it is called Maison d'Auguste. There are several restaurants along that street that are less expensive. Just turn left when you get to the corner." The clerk waved his hand indicating the area.

A telephone booth stood on the corner where they were turning left. "Let me just take a quick look on the telephone book to see if there is a Nikiolopolis listed." Hedy said and stepped into the booth. A glance through the pages revealed no Greek names at all. Coming out of the booth her face showed her disappointment.

Samuel was sympathetic. "Look, Hedy, we are just getting started. Some of our agents have spent many years on a case."

She agreed that, after all, they had only started their search a few months ago. "I am too hungry to think straight," Hedy said. They rounded the corners of Berggasse and the fragrance of onions frying in butter and other flavorful dishes drifted into their nostrils.

Looking to the right and left at the quaint shops and eating establishments, they walked slowly and carefully on the uneven cobble stones. Hedy saw the gilded sign above the sparkling clear, glass doors. They looked inside and were impressed with the white table cloths, the chandeliers, the gilt-framed prints of classic paintings and mirrors on the walls. "That place looks too fancy for my income," Samuel murmured. But Hedy already had her hand on the polished brass handle.

A tall, dark-haired man, wearing a bow-tie and a three-piece suit, opened the door from inside. "Welcome to Maison d'Auguste," he said, bowing slightly, and asked if they wanted a table. They barely understood his strangely-accented Schweizerdeutsch, and replied by nodding their heads and followed him to a table near the kitchen. The nine other tables were all occupied by parties of four to ten people. Waiters were bustling into the room with delectable-looking dishes.

After what seemed a lengthy wait, a girl who looked about nine or ten, brought them two menus, then hurried off toward the door to help departing guests with their coats and hats. Hedy started to study the short menu, but she felt distracted, "Did you notice that girl's eyes are green?" she asked Samuel, who shook his head and continued to read the description of the dishes on the menu, then looked at the prices. He sighed with dismay.

It was two o'clock and the families who came after church every Sunday were getting ready to leave. As they congregated in the aisles between the tables, Konstanza, her graying hair tucked into a pleated toque blanche, a white apron over her black dress, came striding out of the kitchen. She walked past Hedy and Samuel sitting at their unobtrusive little table. Hedy was thinking there was something familiar about this woman, wearing the chef's hat, smiling and shaking hands with the departing guests.

While the waiters began to clear the tables Konstanza took the hand of the young girl with the green eyes and started to walk toward the kitchen. It was then that she saw the couple at the table near the back, looking at the menus. The young woman had a thick, golden braid curled into two buns at the nape of her neck, a round hat perched jauntily to one side of her head, and when she looked up from the menu, Konstanza saw that her eyes were almost as blue as the United Nations pin in the lapel of her dark suit. Konstanza gasped, "Hedy!" and clapped her left hand over her mouth.

Konstanza was engulfed in sheer joy and elation of seeing Hedy alive, but it was mixed with the years of anguish, self-recrimination, and rage at the Germans and their minions. A guttural wail came up from deep within her. Suddenly giddy from the rush of emotions she put out her right hand to steady herself but the tall man from the door was already by her side and the girl with the emerald green eyes put her arm around Konstanza's waist.

For a few seconds Franz, Konstanza and their daughter, Estanza, stood frozen in place. Still clutching the menu, Samuel watched Hedy stand up and slowly approach the three people in front of her. She held out her arms, enfolding the weeping Konstanza, who finally knew that she was forgiven.

Epilogue

Jerusalem, Israel, 1965

Dan Jerusalem Hotel

It had taken years of planning and organizing, but finally Konstanza Nikiolopolis had a reunion with the boys she had hidden in the woodboxes. They brought their wives and children to introduce them to the woman who had saved their lives. The reception room was filled with happy chatter, laughter and gasps of recognition. Many different languages were heard as the guests had come from every part of the globe.

When the Mossad agent guarding the door opened it to admit another guest, a hush began to spread among the crowd. They were surprised to see a Dominican nun stride across the room toward Konstanza, whose green eyes were wide open with surprise. Konstanza held out her hand in greeting, waiting for the nun to introduce herself.

Instead of shaking hands, the nun held out a thick, black wool shawl. Smiling broadly, she said in perfect Hebrew, "It is my greatest pleasure to return this to you."

Konstanza's heart leapt into her throat as she recognized her mother's shawl and remembered the last time she had seen it.

Acknowledgments

Most of the information for this book came directly from survivors who had been saved by brave people with a conscience. The names have been changed, but the stories are real.

Some of the survivors were not able to provide details because they found it difficult to talk about the horror they experienced.

I used William L. Shirer's well-documented book, *The Rise and Fall of the Third Reich,* to fill in the specifics.

NOTES

Part 1

Chapter 28

1. Twenty years later the Greek government finally passed a law that forbade all exports of Greek antiquities.

Chapter 30

1. Stettin has been known as Szczecin, Poland, since 1945.

Part 2

Chapter 1

1. Although Switzerland was not a combatant in the war that raged around Europe, the Swiss people were involved in many ways. They saw what happened to "neutral" Belgium when German troops overran that country and began to brutalize the population. There were at least two factions in Switzerland. One favored the French and one was on the German side of the conflict. Even in Basel, some friendships were stretched thin. Eventually the Red Cross, a Swiss organization that soon reached worldwide, asked the Swiss government to help with caring for wounded soldiers of both sides of the conflict. Since the usual income from the northern tourists was being sorely missed, permission was given to send wounded soldiers to Swiss hospitals to be treated and, eventually, to convalesce in the hotels and resorts around the country.

The four million people of Switzerland welcomed over 68,000 wounded soldiers from the French, German and English army. These men were treated well, and they were housed in homes, hotels, and many of the charming chalets that dotted the alpine meadows.

2. In the summer of 1920, Europe was in an economic depression and many formerly wealthy people were reduced to working for a living, if they could find the scarce jobs available. Men stood around in the streets waiting for day jobs, handouts or soup from the soup kitchens. Germany and Austria, having lost the Great War, were in the worst condition. Along with the dearth of jobs, prices were going up every day. The rampant inflation was very demoralizing. No matter how hard a person worked, it was impossible to keep up with prices. A wheelbarrow of paper money was needed to buy a loaf of bread.

   In Switzerland the economy was more stable. The Swiss franc kept its value due to the stringent rules of the Swiss banking system. For a foreigner to reside in Switzerland they had to have a Swiss bank account.

3. In the village of Distomo at that time, single mothers were not tolerated. If a girl had the misfortune of getting pregnant before her marriage, the wedding followed as quickly as possible. If the father disappeared or the girl refused to name him or marry him, it was in her best interest to leave the area as soon as possible, for she and her child would be shunned by everyone in the village. (For more on the fate of this little Greek village and the terror it would face during World War II, visit http://www.pappaspost.com/haunting-images-from-the-june-1944-nazi-massacre-at-distomo/)

Chapter 3

1. The 1928 Olympic Games would be the first in which women were allowed to compete.
2. Hilde joined HaKoah Vienna swim team, won a medal for Austria in the 1932 Olympics in Los Angeles. She boycotted the 1936 Olympics in Berlin and narrowly escaped to Melbourne, Australia in 1938. Source: 2004 film *Watermarks*.

Chapter 5

1. "Aryan" was defined by the Nazis to mean a non-Jewish Caucasian, especially of Nordic heritage.
2. The area specified as "German soil" would encompass practically all of Europe in the very near future.

Chapter 7

1. In 1928, bloody fights between Fascists and Communists on the streets of German cities were a common occurrence, especially in Berlin.

Chapter 14

1. *Kristallnacht*: During the night of November 9, 1938, until early the next morning, the Nazi hoards that had been ruling Germany for the last five years carried out a well-organized pogrom against the Jews of Germany. Every business owned or thought to be owned by a Jew was destroyed and looted; thousands of Jewish men were rounded up and sent to Dachau Concentration camp. Every Jewish house of worship, from the largest synagogue to the smallest temple, was looted. The books and Torah scrolls were thrown onto huge bonfires, and the buildings burned to the ground. In Stettin the stately, little Greek church of St. Nikolas was mistaken by the overzealous louts as a synagogue.

Chapter 20

1. The Warsaw Ghetto had been liquidated. The German army occupied Rome. Japan had conquered an island near Alaska. German U-boats had sunk a large number of British ships.

Chapter 21

1. In 1920, the League of Nations had divided the Austrian-Hungarian Empire into the states that had existed before the Empire annexed them. A small southern section of, what was to be, the truncated Austria was populated by people who had Slavic ancestors and spoke a Slavic dialect in their homes, but considered themselves loyal Austrians. When given the chance to vote whether they wished to be a part of Austria or to join the newly formed country of Yugoslavia, they voted to remain Austrian. They were mostly farmers who had been on that land for many generations and supplied the region with grain, hay, vegetables, and dairy products.

   When the Germans annexed Austria in 1938, they began to persecute the Slavic-speaking peoples in the region. The use of the Slavic language, even in private, was forbidden, and any infractions were punished by imprisonment in a concentration camp. All schools in the region were closed and these productive farmers were taken off their farms and sent to work camps in Germany. For a short time, the Slavic Austrians were allowed to stay with their families in the crowded quarters of the camps. But after a few months, the women and men were separated and the children who were too young to be useful were sent to care centers, where they spent their days learning to march in formation and be totally obedient to commands.

   The adults and older children went to work in factories.

After the war started, the men were drafted into the army. A few of the very young children (who appeared sufficiently Aryan) were taken away from their mothers and given to German families for adoption.

2. In 1920, the League of Nations had designated the city of Danzig a "Free City-State" with an autonomous government. This thriving city on the Baltic Sea had a mixed population of Germans and Poles, and a Jewish community that went back five hundred years. In 1933, the citizens of Danzig voted for the Nazi Party and greeted the criminally insane leader of the Third Reich and his minions with a jubilant frenzy. At first the Nazis persecuted only the Jews. When almost all of these decent, productive people had been hounded out of the city, the heavy boots of fascism began to stomp on everyone's freedom. Now, no one was safe. Anyone could be imprisoned at the whim of the local *Gauleiter* (or "commander").

If You Enjoyed

They Will Not Be Forgotten, be sure to pick up *To Survive Is Not Enough* available online, in stores, in gift shops and from the author.

CPSIA information can be obtained
at www.ICGtesting.com
Printed in the USA
FFHW011934140219
50533651-55818FF

9 781732 456709